THE BEAST & THE SOVEREIGN

THE SEMINARS OF JACQUES DERRIDA

Edited by Geoffrey Bennington & Peggy Kamuf

The Beast & the Sovereign

VOLUME I

Jacques Derrida

Edited by Michel Lisse, Marie-Louise Mallet,
and Ginette Michaud

Translated by Geoffrey Bennington

The University of Chicago Press ‡ CHICAGO AND LONDON

The University of Chicago Press, Chicago 60637
The University of Chicago Press, Ltd., London
© 2009 by The University of Chicago
All rights reserved. Published 2009.
Paperback edition 2011
Printed in the United States of America

20 19 18 17 16 15 14 13 12 11   2 3 4 5 6

ISBN-13: 978-0-226-14428-3 (cloth)
ISBN-13: 978-0-226-14429-0 (paper)
ISBN-10: 0-226-14428-3 (cloth)
ISBN-10: 0-226-14429-1 (paper)

Originally published as *Séminaire: La bête et le souverain,
Volume 1 (2001–2002)*. © 2008 Éditions Galilée.

This book was published with the support of the
French Ministry of Culture—National Book Center.
Cet ouvrage a été publié avec l'assistance du
Ministère de la culture—Centre National du Livre.

Library of Congress Cataloging-in-Publication Data

Derrida, Jacques.
[Bête et le souverain. English]
The beast and the sovereign / Jacques Derrida; translated by Geoffrey Bennington.
p. cm. — (Seminars of Jacques Derrida; v. 1)
Translation of: Séminaire: La bête et le souverain.
ISBN-13: 978-0-226-14428-3 (cloth : alk. paper)
ISBN-10: 0-226-14428-3 (cloth : alk. paper)
1. Sovereignty. 2. Power (Social sciences)—Philosophy. 3. Responsibility.
4. Capital punishment. 5. Perjury. I. Bennington, Geoffrey. II. Title.
III. Series: Derrida, Jacques. Selections. English. 2009; v. 1.
B2430.D483B4813   2009
194—dc22   2009011389

♾ This paper meets the requirements of
ANSI/NISO Z39.48-1992 (Permanence of Paper).

CONTENTS

When the decision was made to edit and publish Jacques Derrida's teaching lectures, there was little question that they would and should be translated into English. From early in his career, in 1968, and annually thereafter until 2003, Derrida regularly taught at U.S. universities. It was his custom to repeat for his American audience the lectures delivered to his students in France the same year. Teaching first at Johns Hopkins and then at Yale, he read the lectures in French as they had been written. But from 1987, when he began teaching at the University of California, Irvine, Derrida undertook to lecture in English, improvising on-the-spot translations of his French text. Recognizing that the greater part of his audience outside of France depended on translation was easier, however, than providing an *ad libitum* English version of his own elegant, complex, and idiomatic writing. In the circumstance, to his evident joy in teaching was often added a measure of suffering and regret for all that remained behind in the French original. It is to the memory of Derrida the teacher as well as to all his students past and still to come that we offer these English translations of "The Seminars of Jacques Derrida."

The volumes in this series are translations of the original French editions published by Éditions Galilée, Paris, and will in each case follow shortly the publication of the corresponding French volume. The scope of the project, and the basic editorial principles followed in establishing the text, are outlined in the "General Introduction to the French Edition," translated here. Editorial issues and decisions relating more specifically to this volume are addressed in an "Editorial Note." Editors' footnotes and other editorial interventions are, with a few exceptions, translated without modification, except in the case of footnoted citations of quoted material, which refer to extant English translations of the source as necessary. Additional translator's notes have been kept to a minimum. To facilitate scholarly reference, the page numbers of the French edition are printed in the margin on the line at which the new page begins.

Translating Derrida is a notoriously difficult enterprise, and while the translator of each volume assumes full responsibility for the integrity of the translation, as series editors we have also reviewed the translations and sought to ensure a standard of accuracy and consistency across the volumes. Toward this end, in the first phase of work on the series, we have called upon the advice of other experienced translators of Derrida's work into English and wish to thank them here: Pascale-Anne Brault, Michael Naas, Elizabeth Rottenberg, and David Wills.

Geoffrey Bennington
Peggy Kamuf
JANUARY 2009

The complete edition of Jacques Derrida's seminars and lectures will give the reader the chance of an unprecedented contact with the philosopher's teaching voice. This edition will constitute a new part of his oeuvre, to be distinguished from the books and other texts published during his lifetime or revised by him before his death, and with a clearly different status. It is not certain that Jacques Derrida would have published the seminars as they stand: probably he would have reorganized or rewritten them. Taken as a whole, but also in their relation to Derrida's philosophical oeuvre, these lectures and seminars will constitute an incomparable research tool and will, we believe, give a different experience of his thinking, here linked to his teaching, which was always, both in France and abroad, a truly vital resource of his writing.

The corpus we are preparing for publication is vast. From the beginning of his teaching career, Derrida was in the habit of completely writing out almost all his lectures and seminars. This means that we have at our disposal the equivalent of some fourteen thousand printed pages, or forty-three volumes, on the basis of one volume per academic year. This material can be classified according to a variety of criteria. First, according to the place where the teaching took place: the Sorbonne from 1960 to 1964; The École normale supérieure in the rue d'Ulm from 1964 to 1984; the École des hautes études en sciences sociales from 1984 to 2003.[1] Second, according to

10

1. We must add the American places too: from fall 1968 to 1974 at the Johns Hopkins University in Baltimore, then as Visiting Professor in the Humanities from 1975 to 1986 at Yale Unversity, where he gave each year, in the fall or spring semester, a regular seminar. From 1987 to 2003, Derrida taught regularly at the University of California, Irvine, and at the New School for Social Research, the Cardozo Law School, and New York University (1992–2003). This American teaching (which, with a few exceptions, repeated the Parisian seminar) was given at first in French but after 1987 most often

the type of teaching: classes with a very variable number of sessions (from one to fifteen) until 1964; what he always called "seminars" thereafter. Finally—and, no doubt, most relevantly for the editorial work—according to the tools used: we have handwritten sessions from 1960 to 1970; typescripts, with manuscript annotations and corrections, from 1970 to 1988; electronic files and printouts from 1988 to 2003.

Derrida's seminars, which already had their own style and had already attracted a broad and numerous following at the rue d'Ulm (where the choice of subjects and authors, if not the way they were treated, was constrained by the program of the Agrégation),[2] take on their definitive character at the EHESS, where, on Wednesdays from 5:00 PM to 7:00 PM, a dozen times a year, Jacques Derrida, sometimes improvising a little, would read before a large audience the text of his seminar, entirely written out for each session as the year proceeded. (Add to that a few improvised sessions, sometimes around a reading, and a few discussion sessions.) Henceforth free in his choice of subjects, Derrida launched research projects over periods of several years, which link together in explicit, coherent, and gripping fashion. The great question of philosophical nationality and nationalism (1984–88) leads to that of the "Politics of Friendship" (1988–91), and then to the long series of "Questions of Responsibility" (1991–2003), focusing successively on the Secret (1991–92), on Testimony (1992–95), Hostility and Hospitality (1995–97), Perjury and Pardon (1997–99), and the Death Penalty (1999–2001), with the final two years devoted to "The Beast and the Sovereign" (2001–3).

Jacques Derrida was in the habit of drawing on the abundant material of these seminars for the very numerous lectures he gave every year throughout the world, and often, via this route, parts of the seminars were reworked and published. Several of his books also find their point of departure in the work of the seminar: *Of Grammatology* (1967), for example, in large part develops sessions of the 1965–66 seminar on "Nature, Culture, Writing"; the seminar on "Hegel's Family" (1971–72) is picked up in *Glas* (1974). *Politics of Friendship* (1994) is explicitly presented as the expansion of the first session of the 1988–89 seminar, and there are traces in it of other sessions too. But in spite of these partial convergences and correspondences,

---

in English: Derrida would improvise during the session an English version of his text, which he had previously annotated for this purpose.

2. [Translator's note:] The Agrégation is the notoriously competitive qualifying examination taken by prospective higher-level teachers in the secondary and university systems.

the vast majority of the pages written from week to week for the seminar remain unpublished and will provide an incomparable complement to the work already published. Whenever a session was later published by Jacques Derrida, in modified form or not, we will give the reference. We do not consider it appropriate for the edition of the seminars themselves, as original material, to offer a comparative reading of those versions.

As we have already pointed out, the editorial work varies considerably according to the mode of production of the text. For the typewriter period, many handwritten amendments and annotations require a considerable effort of decipherment; the more so for the seminars entirely written in Jacques Derrida's handsome but difficult handwriting, which require laborious transcription. So we shall begin by publishing the seminars of the last twenty years, while beginning preparation of the rest. In all cases, our primary goal is to present the *text* of the seminar, as *written* by Jacques Derrida *with a view* to speech, to reading aloud, and thus with some marks of anticipated orality and some familiar turns of phrase. It is not certain that Jacques Derrida would have published these seminars, although he occasionally expressed his intention of doing so,[3] but if he had taken up these texts for publication, he would probably have reworked them, as he always did, in the direction of a more written text. Obviously we have not taken it upon ourselves to do that work in his place. As we mentioned above, the reader may wish to compare the original version presented here with the few sessions published separately by Jacques Derrida himself.

Geoffrey Bennington
Marc Crépon
Marguerite Derrida
Thomas Dutoit
Peggy Kamuf
Michel Lisse
Marie-Louise Mallet
Ginette Michaud

3. See, for example, the foreword to *Politiques de l'amitié* (Paris: Galilée, 1994), p. 11; trans. George Collins as *Politics of Friendship* (London: Verso Books, 1997), p. vii.

The seminar entitled "The Beast and the Sovereign" was the last seminar given by Jacques Derrida at the École des hautes études en sciences sociales (EHESS), in Paris, from the fall of 2001 to the spring of 2003. Rather than attempt what could only be a reductive summary, we reproduce here the presentation given by Derrida in the École's yearbook:

We pursued the research that in previous years, centering on the problem of the death penalty, had led us to study *sovereignty*, the political and ontotheological history of its concept and its figures. This year we deliberately privileged what intertwined this history with that of a thinking of the living being (the biological and the zoological), and more precisely with the treatment of so-called animal life in all its registers (hunting and domestication, political history of zoological parks and gardens, breeding, industrial and experimental exploitation of the living animal, figures of bestiality and *bêtise*, etc.). The point was not merely to study, from Aristotle to contemporary discussions (Foucault, Agamben), the canonical texts around the interpretation of man as a "political animal." We had above all to explore the "logics" organizing both the submission of the beast (and the living being) to political sovereignty, and an irresistible and overloaded analogy between a beast and a sovereign supposed to share a space of some exteriority with respect to "law" and "right" (outside the law: above the law: origin and foundation of the law).

We studied a great many philosophical, rhetorical, political, and other indices of this overdetermined analogy (La Fontaine's *Fables* and the tradition that precedes and follows them, texts by Machiavelli, Schmitt, etc.). We also attempted a sort of taxonomy of the animal figures of the political, notably from the point of view of sovereignty (always outside the law: above the laws). Alongside the lion, the fox, etc., the "character" of the wolf (in many cultures) and often the "werewolf" (in Europe) interested us a great deal, from Plautus to Hobbes and Rousseau.

On the permanent horizon of our work were general questions about

14

force and right, right and justice, of what is "proper to mankind," and the philosophical interpretation of the limits between what is called man and what is improperly and in the generic singular called the animal. As "bestiality" and *bêtise* are supposedly proper to man in his relation to his kind, and foreign to "the animal," we began from this point of view a problematizing reading of certain texts by Lacan on "bestiality," by Deleuze (*Difference and Repetition*) on *bêtise*, and by Deleuze and Guattari (*A Thousand Plateaus*) on the becoming-animal of man.[4]

This edition reproduces the written text of the seminar read by Jacques Derrida at the sessions that took place at the EHESS. The first volume of this seminar corresponds to the year 2001–2 and comprises thirteen sessions,[5] while the second (2002–3) has ten. The greater part of this seminar is unpublished, with the exception of a few sessions from this first volume, which were presented at various colloquia and were subsequently published, with slight variations.

With the exception of the ninth and the thirteenth, all the sessions of this seminar are completely written out. The ninth is devoted to an improvised commentary on D. H. Lawrence's poem "Snake" (alluded to in Derrida's *Rogues,*[6] published in 2003), and the thirteenth is a concluding session that begins with a return to the opening of the seminar. We thought in both cases that it would be a pity not to add these pieces to the whole, and so we have made a transcription on the basis of some brief notes and, more especially,

---

4. Jacques Derrida, "Questions de responsabilité (IX. La bête et le souverain)," in *Annuaire de l'EHESS 2001–2002* (Paris: Editions de l'EHESS, 2002), pp. 607–8.

5. There are two sets of texts of "The Beast and the Sovereign" seminar deposited at the Institut Mémoires de l'édition contemporaine (IMEC): the first is very lightly and sparsely annotated by Jacques Derrida, who would continue to correct his text while reading it out, which he always did pen in hand. This set comprises all the sessions of the seminar in order, numbered from 1 to 12 (a sequence that is modified here by the insertion of the ninth, improvised, session: see session 9, n. 1, below); this is the set we have used as the reference text for this edition, and to which we shall henceforth refer as "the typescript." The second set comprises the series that Jacques Derrida used for the seminar given in the United States in the spring of 2002 at the University of California, Irvine, and in October 2002 at New York University, at the New School for Social Research, and at Cardozo Law School; with the exception of the first session, this set has the entire series, numbered from 2 to 12.

6. J. Derrida, "La raison du plus fort (y a-t-il des États voyous?)," in *Voyous: Deux essais sur la raison* (Paris: Galilée, 2003), p. 23; trans. Pascale-Anne Brault and Michael Naas, "The Reason of the Strongest (Are There Rogue States?)," in *Rogues: Two Essays on Reason* (Stanford: Stanford University Press, 2005), p. 5.

a recording (made and preserved by Marie-Louise Mallet), even though the reader must of course be aware that these sessions are inevitably less reliable than the others, in that the author could not read and review the transcription. Also, Derrida often left time for discussion with seminar participants. We have signaled such moments in the sessions, but we also decided not to include these discussions, which, although they were recorded (but often in a technically deficient manner, with some voices being inaudible and above all difficult to identify), seemed to us to raise too many questions. In this we have followed what was most usually done at the Cerisy and other major conferences devoted to Derrida's work.

In the typescript of the seminar, the bibliographical indications were, most often, clearly indicated but in abbreviated form: we have completed them and filled in those that were missing. A number of quotations were *16* not copied out in the typescript: they were included as photocopies of pages from books, and we have reinserted them, where necessary resorting to the tape recording of the sessions to be sure of where to begin and end. Elsewhere, we used Jacques Derrida's own books, whenever it was possible to find them in the library of his house at Ris-Orangis. In doubtful cases or where it was impossible to track down the copy he would have used, we have referred to the editions that are generally thought to be the most reliable. We have checked and where necessary corrected the quotations made by Jacques Derrida, rectifying without signaling the fact whatever seemed to be obvious errors of transcription; but we have signaled, when they might be significant, certain modifications to quotations or translations. Finally, to end on this question of references: Jacques Derrida makes numerous references throughout the seminar to his own earlier work, whether published or not: we give references whenever the citation is explicit, even when the work cited belongs to the still unpublished body of the seminars themselves.[7]

As for the more technical aspects of our work, they are relatively slight. This edition is of the entire text of Derrida's 2001–2 seminar as it was composed and laid out by him, notably as to its sometimes very long sentences and paragraphs. Similarly, at a more micrographic level, the punctuation has been preserved; in particular all the brackets, which are Derrida's own.[8] We have, however, on rare occasions made some corrections or minute al-

---

7. [Translator's note:] Unless otherwise indicated, all notes are provided by the editors of the French edition. I have added references to English translations where appropriate.

8. [Translator's note:] Except for translator's glosses.

terations when the proliferation of signs such as brackets, parentheses, and dashes (or else their absence) made it difficult to follow the argument.

We have kept all the signs of the seminar's oral quality, and especially the "pickups" Derrida placed in brackets, even if these were often quite substantially modified in the actual reading out. In the same spirit, we have chosen to leave in parentheses some stage directions, such as "(Board)," "(Read and comment)," "(Reread)," "(Develop)," which give a sense of the rhythm of the seminar, its accents and intonations. In the case of expressions that recur with slight differences in spelling (use of capital letters, quotation marks, italics or roman face, optional elisions, and so on), we did not see fit to attempt any systematic harmonization of these variations, as they do not hinder the legibility of the text. Words placed in angle brackets were added by us to fill certain lacunae in the typescript—most often omitted words.[9] On the typescript, at the end of each session, Derrida was in the habit of noting down in more or less telegraphic style lines of research to be explored. These "off cuts" are sometimes reproduced from one session to the next, sometimes modified and augmented. Given that they did not constitute a sustained text, they have not been included in this edition.

Finally, we thank Gil Anidjar, Joseph Cohen, Jean-Jacques Lavoie, Ursula Sarrazin, and Stéphanie Vanasten, whom we consulted to explain or verify linguistic points concerning the transliteration of Hebrew words, the translation of German expressions, and certain references. We especially and warmly thank Georges Leroux, who carefully revised the transliterations from the Greek. On his suggestion, we decided to follow here the code used by Émile Benveniste in his *Vocabulary of Indo-European Institutions*.[10]

Michel Lisse
Marie-Louise Mallet
Ginette Michaud

9. [Translator's note:] Not all such cases are reproduced in the translation.

10. [Translator's note:] Greek transliterations in the translation follow the ISO 843 standard.

December 12, 2001[1]

Feminine . . . masculine [*La* . . . *le*].

Let me recall the title proposed for this year's seminar: the beast [feminine: *la bête*] and the sovereign [masculine: *le souverain*]. *La, le.*

Naturally I shall try to justify this title as I go along, step by step, perhaps stealthily, like a wolf [*peut-être à pas de loup*]. Those of you who followed the last few years' seminars on the death penalty know that the huge and formidable question of sovereignty was central to them. So this inexhaustible question will provide for a certain continuity between the previous seminars and what still remains untrodden from this new approach, by the turn or at the turning of the seminar to come.

The question of the animal was also, here and elsewhere, one of our permanent concerns. But the beast is not exactly the animal, and it was only after the fact, after having chosen this title, the literal formulation of this title, the [feminine] beast and the [masculine] sovereign, that I understood

1. This session was published, almost in its entirety, in the proceedings of the 2002 Cerisy conference, *La démocratie à venir*, ed. Marie-Louise Mallet (Paris: Galilée, 2004), pp. 433–56. With some variants and additions, it was again given as a lecture at the 2003 Coimbra conference (*La souveraineté: Critique, déconstruction, apories: Autour de la pensée de Jacques Derrida*), and published, first separately in a bilingual edition, under the title *Le souverain Bien / O soberano Bem* (Portuguese translation by Fernanda Bernardo [Viseu: Palimage Editores, 2004]), and then in the proceedings of the conference *Jacques Derrida à Coimbra / Derrida em Coimbra* (ed. Fernanda Bernardo [Viseu, Palimage Editores, 2005], pp. 75–105), under the title "Le souverain Bien, ou Être en mal de souveraineté" [The Sovereign Good, or Being Wanting Sovereignty]. Finally, preceded by a quite long introduction, the Coimbra text was used again (with some further variants and additions) for the last lecture Jacques Derrida gave in France, in 2004 at Strasbourg, published by Joseph Cohen in the journal *Cités*, special issue, *Derrida politique — La déconstruction de la souveraineté (puissance et droit)*, no. 30 (2007): 103–40, under the title: "Le souverain bien—ou l'Europe en mal de souveraineté: La conférence de Strasbourg du 8 juin 2004."

one at least of the lines of force or one of the silent but insistent connotations in what seemed to me to impose the very letter, down to my unconscious, down to the title's unconscious, "La bête et le souverain," namely the sexual difference marked in the grammar of the definite articles, *la, le* (feminine, masculine), as if we were naming in it, ahead of time, a certain couple, a certain coupling, a plot involving alliance or hostility, war or peace, marriage or divorce — not only between two types of living beings (animal and human) but between two sexes which, already in the title, and in a certain language — French — *se font une scène,* are going at each other, are making a scene.

What scene?

"We're shortly going to show it" [*Nous l'allons montrer tout à l'heure:* literally, "We are going to show it in a moment"].[2] (Board)

Stealthy as a wolf. Imagine a seminar that began thus, *stealthy as a wolf:*

"We're shortly going to show it."

What? What are we going to show shortly? Well, "We're shortly going to show it."

Imagine a seminar that began thus, saying almost nothing, with a "'We're shortly going to show it.' 'What? What are we going to show shortly?' Well, 'We're shortly going to show it.'"

Why would one say of such a seminar that it moves *stealthy as a wolf?*

This is, however, what I'm saying. Stealthy as a wolf. I'm saying it with reference to the [French] proverbial expression *à pas de loup*, which in general signifies a sort of introduction, a discreet intrusion or even an unobtrusive effraction, without show, all but secret, clandestine, an entrance that does all it can to go unnoticed and especially not to be stopped, intercepted, or interrupted. To move *à pas de loup* is to walk without making a noise, to arrive without warning, to proceed discreetly, silently, invisibly, almost inaudibly and imperceptibly, as though to surprise a prey, to take it by surprising what is in sight but does not see coming the one that is already seeing it, already getting ready to take it by surprise, to grasp it by surprise. Speech (for we are dealing with silent speech here) — speech proceeding *à pas de loup* would not be proceeding *à pas de colombe*, dove-footed, according to what a great philosophical tradition says of the dove, of the all but unnoticeable procedure or proceeding of truth advancing in history like one thiev-

2. [Translator's note:] In La Fontaine's classical French, "tout à l'heure" means "forthwith," rather than, as in modern French, "later on."

ing or else flying [*comme un voleur ou encore en volant*] (remember,[3] while we're in the columbarium of philosophy, what Kant already said about it in the Introduction to the *Critique of Pure Reason*, about the light dove [*die leichte Taube*][4] which, in its flight, does not feel the resistance of the air and imagines it would be still better in empty space. And especially Zarathustra, in the book that is one of the richest bestiaries in the Western philosophical library. A political bestiary, what is more, rich in animal figures as figures of the political. A dove crosses a song at the very end of the second part of *Also sprach Zarathustra, "Die stillste Stunde,"* "The Hour of Supreme Silence" ([The stillest hour] that's the title of the song). This hour of supreme silence speaks, speaks to me, addresses me, and it is mine, it is *my* hour, it spoke to me yesterday, he says, it murmurs in my ear, it is closest to me, as though in me, like the voice of the other in me, like my voice of the other, and its name, the name of this hour of silence, *my* hour of silence, is the name of a fearsome sovereign mistress [souveraine]: "*Gestern gen Abend sprach zu mir meine stillste Stunde: das ist der Name meiner furchtbaren Herrin*" [Last night my hour of supreme silence (my hour of the greatest silence, of sovereign silence) spoke to me: this is the name of my terrifying sovereign mistress: "*das ist der Name meiner furchtbaren Herrin.*"][5] (Commentary: the hour, my hour, the hour of my sovereign silence speaks to me, and its name, the name of this absolutely silent one, is that of my most fearsome mistress, the one who speaks to me in silence, who commands me in silence, whispering through the silence, who orders me in silence, as silence.) So what is she going to say to him, *to me*, during this song I'm leaving you to read? After saying to him (to me, says Zarathustra), "what is the most unpardonable thing about you [*dein Unverzeihlichstes*] is that you have the power [*Macht*] and you do not want to reign [*du willst nicht herrschen*]," you have the power and you do not want to be sovereign. Zarathustra's reply, again convoking sovereign power and beast: "For all command I lack the lion's voice." At that moment, his most silent voice tells him, as though in a whisper: "(*Da sprach es wieder wie ein Flüstern zu mir): Die stillsten Worte sind es, welche den Sturm bringen. Gedanken, die mit Taubenfüssen kommen, lenken die Welt.*" ["It is the stillest

22

---

3. The parenthesis opened here does not close in the typescript.

4. Immanuel Kant, *Critique of Pure Reason*, A5/B8.

5. Friedrich Nietzsche, *Also sprach Zarathustra*, in *Kritische Gesamtausgabe*, tome 6, vol. 1, ed. Giorgio Colli and Mazzino Montinari (Berlin and New York: Walter de Gruyter, 1968), p. 183. Derrida's own translation. [Translator's note: For the sake of consistency, I have translated these passages with an eye to Derrida's French version, as well as to the original German.]

words that bring the storm. Thoughts that come with dove's footsteps guide the world."]

Read what follows: a still small voice, one might say in a parody of the biblical book of Kings [1 Kings 19:12], the silent voice commands him to command,[6] but to command in silence, to become sovereign, to learn how to command, to give orders (*befehlen*), and to learn to command in silence by learning that it is silence, the silent order that commands and leads the world. With dove's footsteps, on dove's feet.

Now, where were we just now? Not like a dove, we were saying, and above all not on dove's feet, but "stealthy like a wolf," on wolf's feet. Which also means, although quite differently than in the case of dove's feet: silently, discreetly and unobtrusively. What the dove's footsteps and the wolf's footsteps have in common is that one scarcely hears them. But the one announces war, the war chief, the sovereign who orders war, the other silently orders peace. These are two major figures in the great zoopolitics that is preoccupying us here, which will not cease to occupy us and is already occupying us in advance. These two figures *pre*occupy our space. One cannot imagine animals more different, even antagonistic, than the dove and the wolf, the one rather allegorizing peace, from Noah's Ark, which ensures the future the safety of humanity and its animals, the other, the wolf, just as much as the falcon, allegorizing hunting and warfare, prey and predation.

A great number of idiomatic and quasi-proverbial expressions feature the wolf ("howl among wolves," "cry wolf," "have a wolf in one's stomach," "cold enough for a wolf," "between dog and wolf," "a young wolf," "the big bad wolf," etc.).[7] These expressions are idiomatic [in French]. They are not all translatable from one language or culture to another, or even from one territory or geography to another — there are not wolves everywhere, and one does not have the same experience of the wolf in Alaska or in the Alps, in the Middle Ages or today. These idiomatic expressions and these figures of the wolf, these fables or fantasies vary from one place and one historical moment to another; the figures of the wolf thus encounter, and pose for us, thorny frontier questions. Without asking permission, real wolves cross humankind's national and institutional frontiers, and his sovereign nation-states; wolves out in nature [*dans la nature*] as we say, real wolves,

---

6. The typescript has "lui commande de commander de commander" [commands him to command to command], apparently a typing error.

7. [Translator's note:] These are the idioms in French: "hurler avec les loups," "crier au loup," "une faim de loup," "un froid de loup," "entre chien et loup" [the twilight hour], "un jeune loup" ["a young Turk"], "le grand méchant loup."

are the same on this side or the other side of the Pyrenees or the Alps;[8] but the figures of the wolf belong to cultures, nations, languages, myths, fables, fantasies, histories.

If I chose the expression that names the wolf's "step" in the *pas de loup*, it was no doubt because the wolf itself is there named *in absentia*, as it were; the wolf is named where you don't yet see or hear it coming; it is still absent, save for its name. It is looming, an object of apprehension; it is named, referred to, even called by its name; one imagines it or projects toward it an image, a trope, a figure, a myth, a fable, a fantasy, but always by reference to someone who, advancing *à pas de loup*, is not there, not yet there, someone who is not yet present or represented; you can't even see its tail; as another proverb says: "When you speak of the wolf, you see its tail," meaning that someone, a human this time, shows up just when you are talking about him or her. Here you don't yet see or hear anything of what is advancing *à pas de loup*, when at the beginning of a seminar I might say: "We're shortly going to show it."

For one of the reasons — they are many, too many, I won't get through enumerating them, and I will in fact be devoting the whole seminar to them — one of the many reasons why I chose, in this bunch of proverbs, the one which forms the syntagm *pas de loup*, is precisely that the absence of the wolf is also expressed in it in the silent operation of the *pas*, the word *pas* which implies, but without any noise, the savage intrusion of the adverb of negation (*pas, pas de loup, il n'y a pas de loup* [there is no wolf], *il n'y a pas le loup* ["the wolf is not here," perhaps even "there is no such thing as the wolf"]) — the clandestine intrusion, then, of the *adverb* of negation (*pas*) in the *noun,* in *le pas de loup.* An adverb haunts a noun. The adverb *pas* has slipped in silently, stealthy as a wolf, *à pas de loup*, into the noun *pas* [step].

Which is to say that where things are looming *à pas de loup*, the wolf is not there yet, no real wolf, no so-called natural wolf, no literal wolf. There is no wolf yet when things are looming *à pas de loup*. There is only a word, a spoken word, a fable, a fable-wolf, a fabulous animal, or even a fantasy (*fantasma* in the sense of a revenant, in Greek; or fantasy in the enigmatic sense of psychoanalysis, in the sense, for example, that a totem corresponds to a fantasy); there is only another "wolf" that figures something else — something or somebody else, the other that the fabulous figure of the wolf, like

---

8. [Translator's note:] French readers would perceive the allusion to Pascal's remark about truths on one side of the Pyrenees being errors on the other. See *Pensées,* 60 (in Blaise Pascal, *Oeuvres complètes,* ed. L. Lafuma [Paris: Éditions du Seuil, 1963]); (Brunschvicg ed., p. 294; see n. 12 below).

a metonymic substitute or supplement, would come both to announce and conceal, to manifest and mask.

And do not forget that in French we also call *loup* the black velvet mask that used to be worn, that women especially, "ladies" more often than men, used to wear at one time, in certain milieux, and especially at masked balls. The so-called *loup* allowed them to see sovereignly without being seen, to identify without allowing themselves to be identified. This woman in the *loup* would be the feminine figure of what I once called a "visor effect," the upper part of the armor played on by the father or spectral king in *Hamlet*, who sees without being seen when he puts down his visor.[9] This time, in the case of the *loup*, the mask nicknamed *loup*, the visor effect would play especially, or at least most often, on the feminine side.

Why this *loup*, why *loup*-woman rather than the *loup*-man, in this masked unobtrusiveness, whereas in the proverb "When you speak of the wolf, you see its tail," we seem to be taken more toward the masculine side of sexual difference?

In both cases, in any case, of sexual difference, *pas de loup* signifies the absence, the literal non-presentation of the wolf itself in response to its name, and so an evocation that is only figural, tropic, fabulous, phantasmic, connotative: there is no wolf, there is *pas de loup*. And the absence of this wolf, ungraspable in person other than according to the words of a fable—this absence bespeaks at the same time power, resource, force, cunning, ruse of war, stratagem or strategy, operation of mastery. The wolf is all the stronger, the meaning of its power is all the more terrorizing, armed, threatening, virtually predatory for the fact that in these appellations, these turns of phrase, these sayings, the wolf does not yet appear in person but only in the theatrical *persona* of a mask, a simulacrum or a piece of language, i.e. a fable or a fantasy. The strength of the wolf is all the stronger, sovereign even, is all the more all-conquering [*a raison de tout*] for the fact that the wolf is not there, that there is not the wolf itself, were it not for a *pas de loup*, except for a *pas de loup*, save a *pas de loup*, only a *pas de loup*.

I would say that this force of the *insensible* wolf (*insensible* because one neither sees nor hears it coming, because it is invisible and inaudible, and therefore nonsensible, but also insensible because it is all the crueler for this, impassive, indifferent to the suffering of its virtual victims)—that the force of this insensible beast seems then to overcome [*avoir raison de*] everything because through that other untranslatable idiomatic expression (*avoir raison*

9. See Jacques Derrida, *Spectres de Marx* (Paris: Galilée, 1993), especially pp. 26–27; trans. Peggy Kamuf as *Spectres of Marx* (London: Routledge, 1994), pp. 5–6.

de, to overcome, to win out over, to be the strongest), the question of reason comes up, the question of zoological reason, political reason, rationality in general: What is reason? What is a reason? A good or a bad reason? And you can see that already when I move from the question "What is reason?" to the question "What is a reason?" a good or a bad reason, the sense of the word "reason" has changed. And it changes again when I move from "to be right" [*avoir raison*] (and so to have a good reason to bring forward in a debate or a combat, a good reason against a bad reason, a just reason against an unjust reason), the word "reason" changes again, then, when I move from *avoir raison* in a reasonable or rational discussion, to *avoir raison de* [to overcome] in a power relation [*rapport de force*], a war of conquest, hunting, or even a fight to the death.

"We're shortly going to show it," I was saying.

Imagine a seminar, I was also saying, that began thus, *à pas de loup*:

"'We're shortly going to show it.' What? Well, 'We're shortly going to show it.'"

Now, it's high time, you had already recognized the quotation.

It is the second line of a fable by La Fontaine that puts on stage one of those wolves we'll be talking about a lot: here, then, the wolf from the fable *The Wolf and the Lamb*. Here are its first two lines; the fable begins with the moral, this time, before the story, before the narrative moment which is thus, somewhat unusually, deferred.

> The reason of the strongest is always the best;
> As we shall shortly show.[10]

Let me point you at once to a fine chapter that my colleague and friend Louis Marin devoted to this fable by La Fontaine, in his book entitled *La*

27

---

10. Jean de La Fontaine, "Le loup et l'agneau" ["The Wolf and the Lamb"], Livre premier, fable X, in *Fables*, ed. Marc Fumaroli (Paris: Le livre de poche, 1985), p. 51. [Translator's note: This famous fable, known to every French schoolchild, has of course been variously translated into English, giving, for example, "Might is right: the verdict goes to the strong. / To prove the point won't take me very long" (Michie); "The strongest argue best and always win. / Read on: you'll find the proof thereof herein" (Schapiro). In their translation of Derrida's *Voyous* (Paris: Galilée, 2003) [*Rogues: Two Essays on Reason* (Stanford: Stanford Unversity Press, 2005)], in which these two lines appear as an epigraph, Pascale-Anne Brault and Michael Naas use the translation by Norman B. Spector: "The strong are always best at proving they're right. / Witness the case we're now going to cite." Given Derrida's attention to the letter of the opening lines, I have preferred to offer a more literal and prosaic rendition here.]

parole mangée, et autres essais théologico-politiques.[11] This chapter of Marin's book is, moreover, entitled "La raison du plus fort est toujours la meilleure" [The reason of the strongest is always the best] and it is preceded by a brief chapter entitled "L'animal-fable" [the fable-animal]. Although the path we're going down is not exactly the same, we'll often be crossing this analysis of Marin's, which I therefore strongly recommend that you read. One of the many interesting things about Marin's approach is that it proposes a historical articulation between several exactly contemporary texts: this fable of La Fontaine's, then the Port-Royal *General Grammar* and *Art of Thinking*, and finally a famous *Pensée* of Pascal's on the relation between justice and force, a *Pensée* to which Marin often returned, and the logic of which is very important to us here. I'm referring to what Pascal places under the title "Reason of effects," and I'll read the whole fragment, even though we'll have to come back to it in more detail later, because interpreting it requires whole treasure-houses of attention and vigilance (298 in Brunschvicg's classification, 103 in Lafuma's):

> *Justice, force.* It is just that what is just be followed; it is necessary that what is strongest be followed. Justice without force is impotent; force without justice is tyrannical. Justice without force is contradicted, because there are always bad people; force without justice stands accused. So justice and force must be put together; and to do so make what is just, strong and what is strong, just.
>
> Justice is subject to dispute; force is easy to recognize and indisputable. And so one could not give force to justice, because force contradicted justice and said that it was unjust, and said that it was force that was just. And thus not being able to make what is just, strong; one made what is strong, just.[12]

28 Apart from Marin's, I refer you, among the texts that are one way or another devoted to this fragment, to my little book *Force de loi*[13] and the remarkable chapter that Geoffrey Bennington devotes to Paul de Man in *Legislations: The Politics of Deconstruction.*[14]

---

11. Louis Marin, *La parole mangée, et autres essais théologico-politiques* (Paris: Méridiens/Klincksieck, 1986).

12. Blaise Pascal, *Pensées et opuscules,* ed. Léon Brunschvicg (Paris: Hachette, 1946), no. 298, p. 470.

13. Jacques Derrida, *Force de loi* (Paris: Galilée, 1994); trans. Mary Quaintance, in *Acts of Religion,* ed. G. Anidjar (London: Routledge, 2002), pp. 230–98.

14. Geoffrey Bennington, "Aberrations: de Man (and) the Machine," in *Legislations: The Politics of Deconstruction* (London: Verso Books, 1994), pp. 137–51.

Many wolves will, then, be crossing the stage of this seminar. We are going to show in a moment that one cannot be interested in the relations of beast and sovereign, and all the questions of the animal and the political, of the politics of the animal, of man and beast in the context of the state, the *polis*, the city, the republic, the social body, the law in general, war and peace, terror and terrorism, national or international terrorism, etc., without recognizing some privilege to the figure of the "wolf"; and not only in the direction of a certain Hobbes and that fantastic, phantasmic, insistent, recurrent altercation between man and wolf, between the two of them, the wolf *for* man, man *for* the wolf, man *as* wolf *for* man, man as humankind, this time, beyond sexual difference, man and woman (*homo homini lupus*, this dative making clear that it is also a way for man, within his human space, to give himself, to represent or recount to himself this wolf story, to hunt the wolf by making it come, tracking it (in French this wolf hunt is called *louveterie*) [it is just as much a way for man, within his human space, to give himself, to represent or recount to himself this wolf story, to hunt the wolf] in a fantasy, a narrative, a mytheme, a fable, a trope, a rhetorical turn, where man tells himself the story of politics, the story of the origin of society, the story of the social contract, etc.: *for* man, man is a wolf).

When I say wolf, you mustn't forget the she-wolf. What counts here is no longer the sexual difference between the wolf as real animal and the mask [*loup*] worn by the woman. Here we are not dealing with this double wolf, this "twin" word, masculine in both cases, the natural wolf, the real wolf and its mask *le loup*, its simulacrum, but indeed with the she-wolf, often a symbol of sexuality or even of sexual debauchery or fecundity, of the she-wolf mother of other twins, for example the she-wolf that, at the foundation of Rome, suckled turn by turn, each in turn or both at once, the twins Remus and Romulus. And while we're on twins[15] and myths of originary foundation, it is frequent among North American Indians — for we have also been in America for a moment — for two twins to fight over their mother's breast; and among the Ojibwa, in certain variants of the story, the hero Manabozho (who most of the time gets on well with his brother) either remains inconsolable at his death or else kills him himself; and his brother, dead or killed by him, is a Wolf: the Wolf. His brother is the wolf, his next of kin is the wolf. For this man, the twin brother is a wolf: a friendly wolf, a friendly brother whose death leaves him inconsolable, beyond all possible

29

15. [Translator's note:] In all three occurrences in this sentence, Derrida supplies the English word "twins" as well as the French word "jumeaux."

work of mourning; or else an enemy wolf, an enemy brother, a twin he will have killed, and whom he will not have mourned here either. Those close to me, brothers, friendly or enemy brothers are wolves who are my kind and my brothers.

And then, given that the pack of mythical wolves is without number, remember Wotan among the German gods (Wotan or Odin in the North). Wotan is a warrior god, a god of warlike fury (cf. *wüten* in modern German: to be in a fury, to ravage through warfare), and Wotan decides as Sovereign King, as war chief. Sovereignty is his very essence. When he sits on the throne, he is flanked by two wolves, who are like the insignia of his majesty, living coats of arms, the living heraldry of his sovereignty, two wolves to whom he gives everything anyone hands him to eat, for he himself does not eat, he only drinks, especially mead. What is more, Odin Wotan also had the gift of being able to change himself at will into a wild animal, into a bird, fish, or serpent.

We will keep trying to think through this becoming-beast, this becoming-animal of a sovereign who is above all a war chief, and is determined as sovereign or as animal faced with the enemy. He is instituted as sovereign by the possibility of the enemy, by that hostility in which Schmitt claimed to recognize, along with the possibility of the political, the very possibility of the sovereign, of sovereign decision and exception. In the legend of Thor, son of Odin (or Wotan) and of Iord, the Earth, we can also find a terrible wolf story. The giant wolf Fenrir plays an important part on the day of the twilight of the gods. Just to say a word about a long and complicated story (that I am leaving you to piece together for yourselves), I recall that the gods, threatened by this sinister and voracious, yes voracious, wolf, lay for him a highly ingenious trap that the wolf discovers, and to which he agrees to subject himself on one condition; once the condition is met, he ends up closing his jaws around the wrist of the god Tyr, who was to place him in the trap, according to the contract. After which the god Tyr, who had accepted a mutilated hand in order to respect the contract and redeem the disloyal trial proposed to the wolf, becomes the jurist god, the god of justice and oaths, fixing the code and the rules of what was called the *Thing* (*Ding,* read Heidegger), the Thing, the Cause, that is, the place of assemblies, debates, common deliberations, conflicts and litigations and decisions of justice. The god of the Thing, of the Cause, of justice, of oaths had his hand devoured, cut off at the wrist by the wolf, in the wolf's mouth.

And then, but the list would be too long, think of Akela, the sovereign chief of the wolves and the father of the wolf cubs who protect and raise Mowgli.

Now, about this she-wolf or all these wolf-men, about the foundation of the town or the city, the origin of the political, the originary social contract and sovereignty, let me quickly recall a well-known fact. That is, that Rousseau will oppose a certain fantastics or phantasmatics of the wolf-man or Plautus's *homo homini lupus* in his comedy *Asinaria*: "Lupus est homo homini, non homo, quom qualis sit non novit" ("When one does not know him, man is not a man but a wolf for man"),[16] a phrase the proverbial nucleus of which was taken up, reinterpreted, reinvested, and mediated by so many others: Rabelais, Montaigne, Bacon, especially Hobbes. And it is, as you know, against the *homo homini lupus* of Hobbes or equally against Grotius that Rousseau thinks and writes the *Social Contract*. As for the man — wolf for man in Plautus and especially Montaigne and Hobbes — we will come back to him only at the end of next week's session, after a certain detour the necessity of which must be put to the test in the meantime.

Back to Rousseau. As early as chapter 2 of the *Social Contract* ("On the First Societies"), on the threshold, then, of the immediately following chapter, which seems to be responding to La Fontaine in that it is entitled "Of the Right of the Stronger" — as early as chapter 2, then, Rousseau opposes Grotius and Hobbes as theorists of the political, of the foundation of the political, who reduce citizen to beast, and the originary community of men to an animal community. An animal community the chief of which would be, all in all, a kind of wolf, like the wolf-tyrant, the tyrant turned wolf in Plato's *Republic* (book 8, to which we shall return later, along with everything I would call the *lycology* of Platonic politics, politics as discourse about the wolf, *lukos*) in any case, to come back to Rousseau, a sovereign who would be simply stronger and thereby capable of devouring those he commands, namely *cattle*. Rousseau had, however, written somewhere, I don't remember where, "I was living like a real werewolf" (we shall return at length to the werewolf, which is something else). Here in the *Social Contract* (chapter 2), Rousseau is, then, opposing a certain animalization of the origins of the political in Grotius and Hobbes, when he writes:

> It is doubtful, then, according to Grotius, whether the human race belongs to a hundred or so men, or if that hundred or so men belong to the human race: and throughout his book he seems to lean toward the former opinion: this is also Hobbes's feeling. So, here we have the human race

16. Plautus, *Asinaria*, line 495.

divided into herds of cattle, each one with its chief who keeps it in order to devour it.[17] [reread]

32   [Notice the "in order to devour it": don't forget this word "devour": he, the chief, does not keep the beast *by devouring* it, while devouring the beast (and we are already in the space of *Totem and Taboo* and the scenes of devouring cruelty that are unleashed in it, put down, repressed in it and therefore displaced in it into symptoms; and the devouring wolf is not far away, the big bad wolf, the wolf's mouth, the big teeth of Little Red Riding Hood's Grandmother-Wolf ("Grandmother, what big teeth you have"), as well as the devouring wolf in the Rig Veda, etc., or Kronos appearing with the face of Anubis devouring time itself)—notice, then, the "in order to devour it" in Rousseau's text ("So, here we have the human race divided into herds of cattle, each one with its chief who keeps it in order to devour it"): he, the chief, does not keep the beast *by devouring* it, he does not first keep the cattle and then, subsequently, devour said cattle, no, he keeps the cattle *with a view to devouring it*, he only keeps the cattle *in order to* devour it, *so as to* devour it savagely and gluttonously, tearing at it with his teeth, violently, he keeps it for himself the way one keeps for oneself (in what is a larder) but with a view to keeping even more completely for oneself by devouring, i.e. by putting to death and destroying, as one annihilates what one wants to keep for oneself—and Rousseau does say "cattle," i.e. an animality not domesticated (which would be something else again), but already defined and dominated by man *in view of* man, an animality that is already destined, in its reproduction organized by man, to become either an enslaved instrument of work or else animal nourishment (horse, ox, lamb, sheep, etc.: animals, let us note, that can become the victims or the prey of the wolf).

Rousseau continues, and we are still in the order of *analogy* ("analogy" is Rousseau's word, as you'll see), we are in the order of the figure, of the "like" of metaphor or comparison, or even fable:]

> *As* a shepherd is of a nature superior to that of his herd, the shepherds of men, who are their chiefs, are also of a nature superior to that of their peoples.
33 > This is, according to Philon, how Caligula reasoned, correctly concluding from this *analogy* [my emphasis] that kings were gods, or that peoples were beasts.
>   The reasoning of this Caligula . . .[18]

17. Jean-Jacques Rousseau, *Du contrat social* (Paris: Classiques Garnier, 1954), p. 237. [Translator's note: My translation.]
18. *Du contrat social,* p. 237. Derrida's emphasis.

[And this is indeed the reasoning of a sovereign, the reason given by a sovereign, let us not forget that: Rousseau is certainly marking the fact that this discourse, this "reasoning," was signed, and signed not by a philosopher or a political scientist but by a chief, an emperor, and therefore by a sovereign himself situated by analogy and in the "animal" analogy that he thus accredits, an analogy from which man has in the end disappeared, between god and beast: "kings were gods, peoples were beasts." The sovereign says, the emperor Caligula proclaims, he edicts, speaking thus of sovereignty from sovereignty, from the place of the sovereign, he says: there are gods and there are beasts, there is, there is only, the theo-zoological, and in the theo-anthropo-zoological, man is caught, evanescent, disappearing, at the very most a simple mediation, a hyphen between the sovereign and the beast, between God and cattle. Taking up the thread of the quotation again:]

> The reasoning of this Caligula comes down to the same thing as in Hobbes and Grotius. Aristotle, before any of them, had also said that men are not naturally equal, but that some were born for slavery and others for domination.
>
> Aristotle was right [*avait raison:* reason again! This time in the syntagm "avoir raison" the point is not to *avoir raison de* but just to *avoir raison*, to be just or right]; but he took the effect for the cause. Any man born into slavery is born for slavery, nothing is more certain. Slaves lose everything in their irons, even the desire to be free of them; they love their enslavement as Odysseus's companions loved their brutishness. So if there are slaves by nature, this is because there have been slaves against nature. Force made the first slaves.[19]

Rousseau's thesis is thus both that "the reason of the strongest" is *in fact* the best, that it has prevailed and prevails in fact (the stronger has reason of the weaker, the wolf of the lamb), but that if *in fact* the reason of the stronger wins out, *by right* the reason of the strongest is not the best, ought not to be, ought not to have been the best, ought not to have been right, and everything will turn around the semantic pivot of the word "reason" in the fable: when the fable says "the reason of the strongest is always the best," is it reason itself, the good reason, the most just reason, true reason, or the reason given, alleged by the stronger (Caligula or the sovereign or the wolf in the fable) which is the best? And "best" can still mean two radically hetero-

34

---

19. Ibid., p. 237. This last sentence of Rousseau ends thus: "Force made the first slaves, their cowardice perpetuated their slavery."

geneous things: either the reason that prevails in fact or else, on the contrary, the reason that ought to prevail by right and according to justice.

If I'm already quoting Rousseau at some length and insistently, while asking you to read what precedes and follows in the *Social Contract*, this is, precisely, for several reasons.

1. The first is that we have just seen, in the warp of a few sentences, a crossing of most of the lines of force of our future problematic, beginning with this insistent "analogy," this multiple and overdetermined analogy that, as we shall see, through so many figures, now brings man close to the animal, inscribing them both in a relation of proportion, and now brings man and animal close in order to oppose them: heterogeneity, disproportion between the authentic *homo politicus* and the apparently political animal, the sovereign and the strongest animal, etc. Of course, the word "analogy" designates for us the place of a question rather than that of an answer. However one understands the word, an analogy is always a reason, a *logos*, a reasoning, or even a calculus that moves back up toward a relation of production, or resemblance, or comparability in which identity and difference coexist.

Here, whenever we speak of the beast and the sovereign, we shall have in view an analogy between two current representations (current and therefore problematical, suspect, to be interrogated) between this type of animality or living being that is called the "beast" or that is represented as bestiality, on the one hand, and on the other a sovereignty that is most often represented as human or divine, in truth anthropo-theological. But cultivating this analogy, clearing or plowing its territory, does not mean either accrediting it or simply traveling in it in only one direction, for example by reducing sovereignty (political or social or individual — and these are already different and terribly problematical dimensions), as it is most often situated in the human order, [reducing it, then] to prefigurations said to be zoological, biological, animal or bestial (four concepts — the zoological, the biological, the animal, the bestial — that we shall also, prudently, have to tell apart).

We should never be content to say, in spite of temptations, something like: the social, the political, and in them the value or exercise of sovereignty are merely disguised manifestations of animal force, or conflicts of pure force, the truth of which is given to us by zoology, that is to say at bottom bestiality or barbarity or inhuman cruelty. It would and will be possible to quote a thousand and one statements that rely on this schema, a whole archive or a worldwide library. We could also invert the sense of the analogy and recognize, on the contrary, not that political man is still animal but that the animal is already political, and exhibit, as is easy to do, in many examples of what are called animal societies, the appearance of refined, complicated organizations, with hierarchical structures, attributes of authority and power, phenomena of symbolic credit, so many things that are so often attributed to and so naïvely reserved for so-called human *culture*, in opposition to *nature*. For example—to cite only this sign, which has interested me for a long time and touches on what so many philosophers and anthropologists hold to be proper to man and human law—the interdiction of incest. Among all that modern primatology has taught us, and among all the features that—forgive me for recalling this—I have been emphasizing wherever (i.e. just about everywhere) I have been interested in the great question of the animal and what is proper to man, as everything I nicknamed *carnophallogocentrism* (among the most recent and the most recapitulatory texts I permit myself, for simple reasons of economy in order to gain time in this seminar, to refer to: *Of Spirit*, "Eating Well" in *Points* . . . , "The animal that therefore I am," in *L'animal autobiographique*, and *For What Tomorrow* . . . , read, and follow up the references given in all the texts in *L'animal autobiographique*),[20] for some time now I have been emphasizing the fragility and porosity of this limit between nature and culture, and the fact that there is also avoidance of incest in some societies of so-called great apes— the limit between avoidance and interdiction will always be difficult to recognize—just as there is also, in human societies, some inevitability about incest, if one looks closely, in the very place where incest appears forbidden. The only rule that for the moment I believe we should give ourselves in this seminar is no more to rely on commonly accredited oppositional limits between what is called nature and culture, nature/law, *physis*/*nomos*, God, man, and animal or concerning what is "proper to man" [no more to rely on commonly accredited oppositional limits] than to muddle everything and

36

20. *De l'esprit: Heidegger et la question* (Paris: Galilée, 1987); trans. Geoffrey Bennington and Rachel Bowlby as *Of Spirit: Heidegger and the Question* (Chicago: University of Chicago Press, 1989); "Il faut bien manger, ou le calcul du sujet," in *Points de suspension* (Paris: Galilée, 1992), pp. 269–301; trans. Peter Connor and Avital Ronell as "'Eating Well,' or the Calculation of the Subject," in *Points* . . . : *Interviews 1974–1994* (Stanford: Stanford University Press, 1995), pp. 255–87; "L'animal que donc je suis (à suivre), in M-L Mallet, ed., *L'animal autobiographique: Autour de Jacques Derrida* (Paris: Galilée, 1999), pp. 251–301. Subsequently published in Jacques Derrida, *L'animal que donc je suis*, ed. M-L. Mallet (Paris: Galilée, 2006), pp. 15–77; trans. David Wills as *The Animal That Therefore I Am* (New York: Fordham University Press, 2008), pp. 1–51 Jacques Derrida and Elizabeth Roudinesco, "Violences contre les animaux," in *De quoi demain: Dialogue* (Paris: Fayard/Galilée, 2001), pp. 105–27; trans. Jeff Fort as *For What Tomorrow* . . . (Stanford: Stanford University Press, 2004), pp. 62–76.

rush, by analogism, toward resemblances and identities. Every time one puts an oppositional limit in question, far from concluding that there is identity, we must on the contrary multiply attention to differences, refine the analysis in a restructured field. To take only this example, very close to our seminar, it will not be enough to take into account this hardly contest-able fact that there are *animal societies*, animal organizations that are refined and complicated in the organization of family relations and social relations in general, in the distribution of work and wealth, in architecture, in the inheritance of things acquired, of goods or non-innate abilities, in the con-duct of war and peace, in the hierarchy of powers, in the institution of an absolute chief (by consensus or force, if one can distinguish them), of an absolute chief who has the right of life and death over the others, with the possibility of revolts, reconciliations, pardons granted, etc. — it will not suf-fice to take into account these scarcely contestable facts to conclude from them that there is *politics* and especially *sovereignty* in communities of non-human living beings. "Social animal" does not necessarily mean political animal; every *law* is not necessarily ethical, juridical, or political. So it is the concept of *law*, and with it that of contract, authority, credit, and therefore many, many others that will be at the heart of our reflections. Is the law that reigns (in a way that is moreover differentiated and heterogeneous) in all the so-called animal societies a law of the same nature as what we under-stand by law in human right and human politics? And is the complex, al-though relatively short, history of the concept of sovereignty in the West (a concept that is itself an institution that we shall try to study as well as we can) the history of a law, or is it not, the structure of which is or is not, also to be found in the laws that organize the hierarchized relations of authority, hegemony, force, power, power of life and death in so-called animal socie-ties? The question is all the more obscure and necessary for the fact that the minimal feature that must be recognized in the position of sovereignty, at this scarcely even preliminary stage, is, as we insisted these last few years with respect to Schmitt,[21] a certain power to *give*, to *make*, but also to *suspend* the law; it is the exceptional right to place oneself above right, the right to non-right,[22] if I can say this, which both runs the risk of carrying the human sovereign above the human, toward divine omnipotence (which will more-over most often have grounded the principle of sovereignty in its sacred and

21. See among others the unpublished seminar "Politics of Friendship" (1988–89), and *Politics of Friendship*.

22. [Translator's note:] "Droit" in French can correspond to both "law" (in the gen-eral sense: "le droit civil" is civil law), and "right."

theological origin) and, because of this arbitrary suspension or rupture of right, runs the risk of making the sovereign look like the most brutal beast who respects nothing, scorns the law, immediately situates himself above the law, at a distance from the law. For the current representation, to which we are referring for a start, sovereign and beast seem to have in common their being-outside-the-law. It is as though both of them were situated by definition at a distance from or above the laws, in nonrespect for the absolute law, the absolute law that they make or that they are but that they do not have to respect. Being-outside-the-law can, no doubt, on the one hand (and this is the figure of sovereignty), take the form of being-above-the-laws, and therefore take the form of the Law itself, of the origin of laws, the guarantor of laws, as though the Law, with a capital L, the condition of the law, were before, above, and therefore outside the law, external or even heterogeneous to the law; but being-outside-the-law can also, on the other hand (and this is the figure of what is most often understood by animality or bestiality), [being-outside-the-law can also] situate the place where the law does not appear, or is not respected, or gets violated. These modes of being-outside-the-law (be it the mode of what is called the beast, be it that of the criminal, even of that grand criminal we were talking about last year and of whom Benjamin said that he fascinates the crowd, even when he is condemned and executed, because, along with the law, he defies the sovereignty of the state as monopoly of violence; be it the being-outside-the-law of the sovereign himself) — these different modes of being-outside-the-law can seem to be heterogeneous among themselves, or even apparently heterogeneous to the law, but the fact remains, sharing this common being-outside-the-law, beast, criminal, and sovereign have a troubling resemblance: they call on each other and recall each other, from one to the other; there is between sovereign, criminal, and beast a sort of obscure and fascinating complicity, or even a worrying mutual attraction, a worrying familiarity, an *unheimlich,* uncanny[23] reciprocal haunting. Both of them, all three of them, the animal, the criminal, and the sovereign, are outside the law, at a distance from or above the laws: criminal, beast, and sovereign strangely resemble each other while seeming to be situated at the antipodes, at each other's antipodes. It happens, moreover — brief reappearance of the wolf — that the nickname "wolf" is given to a head of state as Father of the Nation. Mustapha Kemal who had given himself the name Atatürk (Father of the Turks) was called the "gray wolf" by his partisans, in memory of the mythical ancestor Genghis Khan, the "blue wolf."

39

23. [Translator's note:] "Uncanny" is in English in the text.

I believe that this troubling resemblance, this worrying superposition of these two beings-outside-the-law or "without laws" or "above the laws" that beast and sovereign both are when viewed from a certain angle—I believe that this resemblance explains and engenders a sort of hypnotic fascination or irresistible hallucination, which makes us see, project, perceive, as in a X-ray, the face of the beast under the features of the sovereign; or conversely, if you prefer, it is as though, through the maw of the untamable beast, a figure of the sovereign were to appear. As in those games where one figure has to be identified through another. In the vertigo of this *unheimlich,* uncanny[24] hallucination, one would be as though prey to a haunting, or rather the spectacle of a spectrality: haunting of the sovereign by the beast and the beast by the sovereign, the one inhabiting or housing the other, the one becoming the intimate host of the other, the animal becoming the *hôte* (host and guest),[25] the hostage too, of a sovereign of whom we also know that he can be very stupid [*très bête*] without that at all affecting the all-powerfulness ensured by his function or, if you like, by one of the "king's two bodies."[26] In the metamorphic covering-over of the two figures, the beast and the sovereign, one therefore has a presentiment that a profound and essential ontological copula is at work on this couple: it is like a coupling, an ontological, onto-zoo-anthropo-theologico-political copulation: the beast becomes the sovereign who becomes the beast; there is the beast *and* [*et*] the sovereign (conjunction), but also the beast *is* [*est*] the sovereign, the sovereign *is* [*est*] the beast.[27]

Whence—and this will be one of the major foci of our reflection, its most current political focus—whence the accusation so often made today in the rhetoric of politicians against sovereign states that do not respect international law or right, and which are called "rogue states" [*États voyous*], i.e. delinquent states, criminal states, states that behave like brigands, like highway robbers or like vulgar rapscallions who just do as they feel, do not respect international right, stay in the margins of international civility, violate property, frontiers, rules and good international manners, including the laws of war (terrorism being one of the classic forms of this delinquency, according to the rhetoric of heads of sovereign states who for their part

24. [Translator's note:] "Uncanny" is in English in the text.

25. [Translator's note:] "Host" and "guest" are in English in the text, to specify the ambiguity of the French word "hôte."

26. See Ernst Kantorowicz, *The King's Two Bodies: A Study in Mediaeval Political Theology* (Princeton: Princeton University Press, 1957).

27. [Translator's note:] Derrida spells out the copula *est* (e-s-t), which is a homophone of the conjunction *et*.

claim to respect international right). Now *État voyou* is a translation of the English *rogue,* rogue state (in German, *Schurke* which can also mean "rascal," bounder, cheat, crook, rabble, blackguard, criminal, is the word also used to translate *rogue*). "Rogue state" in English seems to be the first name (*voyou* and *Schurke* are merely translations, I think), for the accusation was first formulated in English, by the United States. Now we shall see, when we go in this direction and study the uses, the pragmatics, and the semantics of the word *rogue*, very frequent in Shakespeare, what it also tells us about animality or bestiality. The "rogue," be it to do with elephant, tiger, lion, or hippopotamus (and more generally carnivorous animals), [the "rogue"] is the individual who does not even respect the law of the animal community, of the pack, the horde, of its kind. By its savage or indocile behavior, it stays or goes away from the society to which it belongs. As you know, the states that are accused of being and behaving as rogue states often turn the accusation back against the prosecutor and claim in their turn that the true rogue states are the sovereign, powerful, and hegemonic nation-states that begin by not respecting the law or international right to which they claim to be referring, and have long practiced state terrorism, which is merely another form of international terrorism. The first accused accuser in this debate is the United States of America. The United States is accused of practicing a state terrorism and regularly violating the decisions of the UN or the agencies of international right that they are so quick to accuse the others, the so-called rogue states, of violating. We shall return at length to this problematic zone. There is even a book by Noam Chomsky entitled *Rogue States: The Rule of Force in World Affairs,*[28] a book the principal aim of which, supported by a great number of facts and evidence from the geopolitical history of the last decades, is to support an accusation made against the United States. The United States, which is so ready to accuse other states of being rogue states, is in fact allegedly the most rogue of all, the one that most often violates international right, even as it enjoins other states (often by force, when it suits it) to respect the international right that it does not itself respect whenever it suits it not to. Its use of the expression "rogue state" would be the most hypocritical rhetorical stratagem, the most pernicious or perverse or cynical armed trick of its permanent resort to the greater force, the most inhuman brutality. To take, provisionally, only one example from the overwhelming case made by Chomsky in *Rogue States*, and selecting within it the bestiary lexicon that is important to us here, I shall invoke

41

28. Noam Chomsky, *Rogue States: The Rule of Force in World Affairs* (Cambridge, MA: South End Press, 2000).

only from the beginning of the book the example of the long and complex history of the relations between the USA and Saddam Hussein's Iraq. Certainly, Chomsky has no indulgence for Saddam Hussein or for Iraq, which he describes, relying on a number of well-known facts, as a "leading criminal state" (p. 24, read all the pages around this). But if Saddam's Iraq indeed comes in at the top of the list of criminal states, if, as US diplomacy has been reminding us regularly for ten years, Saddam is guilty of using weapons of mass destruction against his neighbors and his own people, Chomsky has no difficulty recalling that for a very long time Saddam was well treated by the USA, as an ally and a client. This treatment only came to an end, leading to a terrible biological war whose Iraqi victims are counted by the thousands (malnutrition, illness, five thousand children dying every month according to UNICEF quoted by Chomsky, etc.)—this treatment of Saddam as respected ally and client only came to an end, then, when Saddam stopped following the political and militaro-economic strategy of the USA (and one could say the same about the Taliban). Only at that moment did Iraq, ceasing to be an ally, an accomplice, or a docile client, become a *rogue state* and only then did one begin to speak of Saddam Hussein, the leader of a rogue state, as a beast, "the beast of Baghdad."[29] I make this remark to announce the fact that we will no doubt be talking a lot, later in this seminar, about what has become known as "September 11."

That, said too briefly and in pure anticipation, is the obscure place toward which we are directed by the word, itself obscure, "analogy," analogy between the political sovereign and the beast. This word *analogy* is not only obscure, like a word whose concept or theorem, whose theoretical tenor, is invisible or inaccessible: it is obscure and dark and black, this word *analogy*, like the reality of a frightening cloud that announces and carries within it the threat of thunder, of lightning, of tempest and hurricane; it is dark because it is heavy with all the (actual and virtual) violences and nameless historical ravages, disasters we won't (already don't) have a name for, when the names of right (national or international), war, civil war or international war, terrorism (national or international) lose their most elementary credit.

2. The second reason why I quote these first chapters of the *Social Contract* is that we already see cited in them philosophers and philosophemes, political philosophies, that ought to occupy us as a first priority: for example, as you heard, Aristotle, Grotius, and Hobbes. Rousseau here inscribes all three of them rather quickly into the same tradition, neglecting the massive fact that it was in order to break with Aristotle, and with the consequences

29. Ibid., p. 28. [Translator's note: Derrida quotes Chomsky here in English.]

that Aristotle draws from his famous but still just as enigmatic definition of man as political creature or animal (*politikon zōon*), that Hobbes wrote his *Leviathan* and his *De Cive*, and developed a theory of sovereignty that will interest us later. Naturally we shall have to read or reread these texts.

3. The third reason why I refer to these first chapters of the *Social Contract* is that in the lines I have just quoted, Rousseau adds a footnote to the word "brutishness" [*abrutissement*] ("they love their enslavement as Odysseus's companions loved their brutishness"). The note refers to Plutarch. It says, "See a little treatise by Plutarch, entitled: *That Beasts Have Reason*." You will find this fascinating text by Plutarch [*Bruta Animalia ratione uti*], translated [into French] by Amyot, in the collection published and prefaced by Élisabeth de Fontenay, *Trois traités pour les animaux*.[30] The treatise to which Rousseau refers is found there under the title "That brute beasts use reason." The word "brute" will often be very important to us, where it seems to connote not only animality but a certain bestiality of the animal. I cannot recommend too strongly that you read these texts, which could detain us for a long time. In "That brute beasts use reason," the first words of a philosophical discussion with several voices already or again convoke the figure of the wolf, the analogy and the quasi-metamorphosis that organizes the passage between man and wolf (but also lion). The discussion begins, then, with this metamorphic analogy: "I think I've understood what you're saying, Circe, and I'll bear it in mind. But please could you tell me whether there are any Greeks among the people you've turned into wolves and lions?"[31]

44

Read what follows and notice too that in praising a certain virtue of the animal, one of the participants in the discussion, Gryllus, places, precisely, this animal virtue above or at a distance from the law. Let me read this ethical and political praise of the animal, whose moral and social, even political, virtue goes above or before the law—a bit *like* (a "like" that carries the whole charge of the question of an analogy), a bit "like" the sovereign:

> You can see, however, that when animals fight with one another or with you humans, they do not employ tricks and stratagems: they rely in their battles on blatant bare bravery backed up by real prowess. *They don't need a law to be passed* [my emphasis] to summon them to battle, and they don't fight because they're afraid of being court-martialled for desertion: they see

30. Plutarque, *Trois traités pour les animaux*, ed. Élisabeth de Fontenay (Paris: P.O.L., 1992); "On the Use of Reason by 'Irrational' Animals," in Plutarch, *Essays*, trans. Robin Waterfield (London: Penguin Books, 1992), pp. 383–99.

31. Ibid., p. 125 [p. 383].

the fight through to the bitter end and refuse to give in because they instinctively loathe defeat. [Read what follows; and, further on:]

[. . .] You don't find animals begging or pleading for mercy or admitting defeat [error of Plutarch's: comment]. Cowardice never led a lion to become enslaved to another lion, or a horse to another horse, as it does human beings, who readily welcome the condition which is named after cowardice. Suppose humans trap or trick animals into captivity: if the animals are mature, they choose to reject food, reject thirst and choose to bring about and embrace death rather than accept enslavement.[32] [Comment.]

If we wanted to place this note in the *Social Contract* referring to Plutarch's plea for animal reason into a network, a Rousseauist network, we should have to study closely, in *Émile* (book 2) a very long quotation (more than three pages) from the opening of the first of Plutarch's *Three Treatises* . . . ("If It Is Permissible to Eat Flesh" [*De esu carnium*]). Before quoting Plutarch, the one who speaks to Émile, the imaginary pupil, warns him against eating meat. Children are naturally vegetarian, and it is important "not to turn them [. . .] into meat eaters." Both for their health and for their character. For, the master says:

> It is certain that great meat eaters are in general more cruel and ferocious than other men: this observation is for all places and times. The barbarity of the English is well known. [. . .] All savages are cruel; and their customs do not lead them to be so: this cruelty comes from their food [comment: cruelty and without,[33] cruelty and death sentence]. They go to war as they go to the hunt, and treat men *like* bears [my emphasis: always this "like" of the anthropo-zoological analogy]. In England even butchers are not allowed to bear witness, and no more are surgeons. Great criminals harden themselves for murder by drinking blood.[34]

(Rousseau adds a note here, because of a scruple, because his translator pointed out to him, and translators are always the most vigilant and formidable readers, that in fact English butchers and surgeons did have the right to bear witness and that only butchers, and not surgeons, were refused the right to sit as jurors in criminal trials.) Read what follows, and the very long quotations from Plutarch's plea or indictment, one of the most eloquent in

---

32. Ibid., pp. 129–30 [p. 387, very slightly modified].

33. "Cruauté et sans" in the typescript: perhaps a typing error for "cruauté et sang" [cruelty and blood].

34. Jean-Jacques Rousseau, *Émile* (Paris: Garnier-Flammarion, 1966), pp. 196–97. [Translator's note: My translation.]

history in the trial of carnivorous culture and its "cruel delights" ("You do not eat these carnivorous animals, you imitate them; you hunger only for the innocent and gentle beasts who do no harm to anyone, who are attached to you, who serve you, and that you *devour* [my emphasis] as a reward for their services.")

You have no doubt already noticed the recurrence of the lexicon of de-vourment ("devour," "devouring"): the beast is on this account devouring, and man devours the beast. Devourment and voracity. *Devoro, vorax, vora-tor*. It's about mouth, teeth, tongue, and the violent rush to bite, engulf, swallow the other, to take the other into oneself too, to kill it or mourn it. Might sovereignty be devouring? Might its force, its power, its greatest force, its absolute potency be, in essence and always in the last instance, a power of devourment (mouth, teeth, tongue, violent rush to bite, engulf, swallow the other, to take the other into oneself too, to kill it or mourn it)? But what goes via interiorizing devourment, i.e. via orality, via the mouth, the maw, teeth, throat, glottis, and tongue — which are also the sites of cry and speech, of language — that very thing can also inhabit that other site of the visage or the face, i.e. the ears, the auricular attributes, the visible and therefore audiovisual forms of what allows one not only to speak but also to hear and listen. "Grandmother, what big ears you have," she says to the wolf. The place of *devourment* is also the place of what carries the voice, the *topos* of the *porte-voix* [megaphone, literally "voice-carrier"], in a word, the place of *vociferation*. Devourment, vociferation, there, in the figure of the figure,[35] in the face, smack in the mouth, but also in the figure as trope, there's the figure of figure, vociferating devourment or devouring vocifera-tion. The one, vociferation, exteriorizes what is eaten, devoured, or interior-ized: the other, conversely or simultaneously, i.e. devourment, interiorizes what is exteriorized or proffered. And on this subject of devouring, proffer-ing, eating, speaking, and therefore listening, of obeying in receiving within through the ears, on the subject of the beast and the sovereign, I leave you to muse on the ass's ears of King Midas that Apollo inflicted on him because he had preferred his rival in a musical competition. The ass is thought, un-fairly, to be the most stupid of beasts [*la plus bête des bêtes*]. Midas hid these ass's ears under his crown, and when his hairdresser denounced him and divulged his secret to the earth, the rushes, Ovid tells us, murmured in the wind, "King Midas has ass's ears!" And then in *Tristan and Yseult*, another king, another animal's ears, the horse's ears of King Mark.

35. [Translator's note:] "Figure" in French means both "figure" and "face."

The reason of the strongest is always the best
As we shall shortly show.

In a sense, no seminar should begin that way. And yet every seminar does
begin that way, anticipating and deferring in some manner the monstration
or demonstration. Every seminar begins with some fabulous "As we shall
shortly show."
    What is a fable?

We could, to begin, ask ourselves (yes, "ask ourselves," but what are we
doing when we ask ourselves? When one asks *something* of oneself? When
one poses oneself a question, when one interrogates oneself on this or
that subject or, which is something different, when one asks *for* oneself?
When one asks oneself for oneself as if that were possible or as if it were
an other)—we could, to begin, before even beginning, ask ourselves what
relation there can be between a seminar and a fable, between a seminar and
the mode of fiction, simulacrum, fictive speech, "once upon a time" and
"as if" narration that we call a fable. Especially if said fable stages some
fabulous beast, the lamb, the wolf, the great aquatic monsters created by
God in Genesis (1:21), or the four beasts in Daniel's dream or vision (which
I leave you to read, starting at Daniel 7:2: and "These great beasts, which
are four, *are* four kings, *which* shall arise out of the earth" (7:17), i.e. four
bestial figures of historico-political sovereignty); or again, and especially,
all the beasts from John's *Revelation,* which clearly present themselves as
political or polemological figures, the reading of which would merit more
than one seminar on its own; or again Behemoth or Leviathan, the name of
that apocalyptic marine monster, that political dragon renamed by God in
almost his last address to Job (40:15),[36] which I invite you to reread: "Behold
now behemoth, which I made with thee; he eateth grass as an ox. Lo now,
his strength *is* in his loins . . . ," and, just a little further on, just afterward
in the Book of Job:

> [1]Canst thou draw out leviathan with an hook? or his tongue with a cord
> *which* thou lettest down? [2]Canst thou put an hook into his nose? or bore
> his jaw through with a thorn? [. . .] or his head with fish spears? [8]Lay thine
> hand upon him, remember the battle, do no more. [9]Behold, the hope of
> him is in vain: shall not *one* be cast down even at the sight of him? [10]None

36. [Translator's note:] I have normalized all biblical references to correspond to the
chapter and verse numbers of the King James version.

is so fierce that dare stir him up: who then is able to stand before me? [. . .] [12]I will not conceal his parts. (Job 41:1–12)

Read what follows, but remember this "I will not conceal his parts." Read too Isaiah (27:1): "In that day the LORD with his sore and great and strong sword shall punish leviathan the piercing serpent, even leviathan that crooked serpent; and he shall slay the dragon that *is* in the sea."

Or else read Psalms (74:13, 14), and you will find that it is always addressed to a God capable of destroying, putting to death, the hideous, powerful, and repugnant beast, the Leviathan:

> [13]Thou didst divide the sea by thy strength: thou brakest the heads of the dragons in the waters. [14]Thou brakest the heads of leviathan in pieces, *and* gavest him *to be* meat to the people inhabiting the wilderness.

49

Just where the animal realm is so often opposed to the human realm as the realm of the nonpolitical to the realm of the political, and just where it has seemed possible to define man as a political animal or living being, a living being that is, on top of that, a "political" being, there too the essence of the political and, in particular of the state and sovereignty has often been represented in the formless form of animal monstrosity, in the figure without figure of a mythological, fabulous, and non-natural monstrosity, an artificial monstrosity of the animal.

Among all the questions that we shall have to unfold in all directions, among all the things that we shall have to ask ourselves, there would, then, be this figuration of man as "political animal" or "political living being" (*zōon politikon*, according to Aristotle's so well-known and so enigmatic formula (*Politics* 1.1253a3). It is obvious, says Aristotle, that the *polis* forms part of the things of nature (*tōn physei*) and that man is by nature a political being (*kai oti anthropos physei politikon zōon*); from which he concludes, after having strongly insisted (contrary to what is sometimes understood or read) in the same text, in the same pages, and again just before this, on living and life as, ζῆν (*zēn*), and not as βίος (*bios*), on the εὖ ζῆν (*eu zēn*), living well (we shall have to come back to this too) — he concludes, then, that a being without a city, ἄπολις (*apolis*), an apolitical being, is, by nature and not by chance (*dia physin kai ou dia tuchēn*), either much worse (*phaulos*) or much better than man, superior to man (*kreittōn ē anthrōpos*)[37] — which clearly marks the fact that politicity, the being-political of the living being called man, is an intermediate between those two other living beings that are beast

50

---

37. For the whole passage, see Aristotle, *Politics,* 1252b 27–1253a 4.

and god, which, each in its own way, would be "apolitical") — so, to return to our point, among all the questions that we shall have to unfold, among all the things we shall have to ask ourselves, there would, then, be this figuration of man as "political animal" or "political being," but also a double and contradictory figuration (and figuration is always the beginning of a fabulation or an affabulation), the double and contradictory figuration of political man as *on the one hand* superior, in his very sovereignty, to the beast that he masters, enslaves, dominates, domesticates, or kills, so that his sovereignty consists in raising himself above the animal and appropriating it, having its life at his disposal, but *on the other hand* (contradictorily) a figuration of the political man, and especially of the sovereign state *as animality*, or even as bestiality (we shall also distinguish between these two values), either a normal bestiality or a monstrous bestiality itself mythological or fabulous. Political man as superior to animality and political man as animality.

Whence the most abstract and general form of what we shall have to ask ourselves: Why is political sovereignty, the sovereign or the state or the people, figured sometimes as what rises, through the law of reason, above the beast, above the natural life of the animal, and sometimes (or simultaneously) as the manifestation of bestiality or human animality, i.e. human naturality? I leave these questions as they are for the moment. But the principle of a reply (I shall call it prosthetic or prostatic or prosthstatic, i.e. following the technical or prosthetic logic of a supplement that supplements nature by adding to it an artificial organ, here the state) seems to come to us from what is no doubt the most arresting example (the one that is most present to our memory, and we shall return to it) of this figuration of the political, of the state and sovereignty in the allegory or the fable of the monstrous animal, and precisely the dragon called Leviathan in the Book of Job: I am referring to Hobbes's book *Leviathan* (1651).[38] Right from its Introduction, and in an opposition to Aristotle that we shall have to specify later, Hobbes's *Leviathan* inscribes human art in the logic of an imitation of divine art. Nature is the art of God when he creates and governs the world, i.e. when, by an art of life, a genius of life, he produces the living and thus commands the living. Well, man, who is the most eminent living creation of God, the art of man that is the most excellent replica of the art of God, the art of this living being, man, imitates the art of God but, being unable to *create, fabricates* and, being unable to engender a natural animal, fabricates an artificial animal. Art goes so far as to imitate this excellent life-form that

51

---

38. [Derrida quotes from] *Leviathan,* Authoritative Text, Backgrounds, Interpretations, ed. Richard E. Flathman and David Johnston (New York: Norton, 1997), p. 9.

is man, and I quote: "*Art* goes yet further, imitating that Rationall and most excellent work of Nature, *Man*. For by art is created that great LEVIATHAN" (the frontispiece of the book represents this gigantic and monstrous man who dominates the city, and Hobbes cites in Latin, in this frontispiece, a passage of Job (41:33), "Upon earth there is not his like," words followed in the text by "He beholdeth all high *things*: he *is* a king over all the children of pride.")[39]

Once again, I leave you to read or reread, I invite and urge you to do so, these two or three pages, which describe, in God's words, the monster Leviathan. Let me pick up again my quotation from Hobbes's Introduction to *Leviathan:* "*Art* goes yet further, imitating that Rationall and most excellent work of Nature, *Man*. For by art is created that great LEVIATHAN, called a COMMON-WEALTH or STATE, (in latine CIVITAS) which is but an Artificiall Man; though of greater stature and strength than the Naturall, for whose protection and defence it was intended" (p. 9). [So Leviathan is the state and political man himself, the artificial man, the man of art and institution, man producer and product of his own art, which imitates the art of God. Art is here, like the institution itself, like artificiality, like the technical supplement, a sort of animal and monstrous naturality. And Hobbes will analyze, describe in detail, "not conceal his parts," as it says in Job, detail the members of the monstrous body of this animal, this Leviathan, produced as political man by man. And he begins with sovereignty, which is both absolute and indivisible (we shall return to this—and Hobbes no doubt had read Bodin, the first great theorist of political sovereignty); but this absolute sovereignty is, as we shall also see, anything but natural; it is the product of a mechanical artificiality, a product of man, an artifact; and this is why its animality is that of a monster as prosthetic and artificial animal, like something made in the laboratory; and by the same token, I would say, leaving the genre of commentary for that of interpretation, i.e. following the consequence of what Hobbes says beyond his own explicit intention: if sovereignty, as artificial animal, as prosthetic monstrosity, as Leviathan, is a human artifact, if it is not natural, it is deconstructible, it is historical; and as historical, subject to infinite transformation, it is at once precarious, mortal, and perfectible. Let me return to my quotation and continue it:]

52

39. [Translator's note:] I here quote the King James version: "Children of pride" corresponds in the French translation used by Derrida (Le Livre de Job, trans. Pierre Alferi and Jean-Pierre Prévost, in *La Bible*, nouvelle traduction [Paris: Bayard, 2001]) simply to "fauves" ("wild beasts"); another French translation, by Louis Segond, has "les plus fiers animaux" ("the proudest animals"). The Vulgate has "filios superbiae."

Art goes yet further, imitating that Rationall and most excellent work of Nature, *Man*. For by art is created that great LEVIATHAN, called a COMMON-WEALTH or STATE, (in latine CIVITAS) which is but an Artificiall Man; though of greater stature and strength than the Naturall, for whose protection and defence it was intended; and in which, the *Soveraignty* is an Artificiall *Soul*, as giving life and motion to the whole body; The *Magistrates*, and other *Officers* of Judicature and Execution, artificiall *Joynts*; *Reward* and *Punishment* (by which fastned to the seate of the Soveraignty, every joint and member is moved to perform his duty) are the *Nerves*.

53 Let me interrupt the quotation for a moment to emphasize two points. On the one hand, sovereignty is the artificial soul: the soul, i.e. the principle of life, life, vitality, vivacity of this Leviathan, and so also of the state, of this state monster created and dominated by the art of man, artificial animal monster which is none other than artificial man, says Hobbes, and which lives as a republic, state, commonwealth, *civitas* only through this sovereignty. This sovereignty is like an iron lung, an artificial respiration, an "Artificiall *Soul*." So the state is a sort of robot, an animal monster, which, in the figure of man, or of man in the figure of the animal monster, is stronger, etc., than natural man. Like a gigantic prosthesis designed to amplify, by objectifying it outside natural man, to amplify the power of the living, the living man that it protects, that it serves, but like a dead machine, or even a machine of death, a machine which is only the mask of the living, like a machine of death can serve the living. But this state and prosthetic machine, let's say prosthstatic, this *prosthstate* must also extend, mime, imitate, even reproduce down to the details the living creature that produces it. Which means that, paradoxically, this political discourse of Hobbes's is vitalist, organicist, finalist, *and* mechanicist. Right down to the detail, the *analogistic* description of the *Leviathan* follows in the body of the state, the Republic, the *Civitas*, the *Commonwealth*, the whole structure of the human body. For example, the nerves are the *penal law*, the reward and punishment by which, says Hobbes, sovereignty, fastening to its service each articulation and each member, puts them in motion in order to fulfill their duty. So it is when talking about penal law that Hobbes, in this physiology of the political, names a sovereignty that is, therefore, the nerve or nervous system of the body politic, which both ensures its articulation and sets it into motion. Wealth and riches are the state's strength, the *salus populi*, or safety, is the state's *business*, the *counselors* are its *memory*, *concord* is its *health, sedition* is its *illness*, and finally, a point to which we shall return often, *civil war* is its *death*. Civil war is the death of the Leviathan, the death of the state, and that

54 at bottom is the subject of our seminar: What is a war, today, how can we

tell the difference between a civil war and a war in general? What is the difference between civil war as "war of partisans" (a notion of Schmitt's, who sees in Hobbes "truly a powerful and systematic political thinker")[40] and a war between states? What is the difference between war and terrorism? Between national terrorism and international terrorism? This systematics of Hobbes is inconceivable without this prosthstatics (at once zoologistic, biologistic, and techno-mechanist) of sovereignty, of sovereignty as animal machine, living machine, and death machine. This prosthstatic sovereignty, which Hobbes recalls in [chapter 9 of] the *De Cive,* is indivisible[41]—this is a decisive point that will be very important to us—presupposes the right of man over the beasts. This right of man over the beasts is demonstrated in chapter 8 [of the *De Cive*], "Of the right of Masters over slaves," just before chapter 9, "Of the right of parents over children and on the Patrimonial Kingdom," during which sovereignty, domination, or sovereign power is said to be *indivisible* (a feature to which we shall return constantly); and Hobbes demonstrates that this sovereignty, within the family, belongs to the father who is, I quote, "a little king in his house" ["un petit roi dans sa maison"],[42] and not to the mother, although by natural generation, in the state of nature, in which, following Hobbes, "it cannot be known who is a *child's father*" (an old and tenacious prejudice), it is the mother, the only certain generatrix, who controls the child; when one leaves the state of nature through the civil contract, it is the father who, in a "civill government," has at his disposal authority and power. And so just before treating "Of the right of parents over children and on the Patrimonial Kingdom" (and therefore   55
the absolute right of the father in civil society), at the end of chapter 8, entitled "Of the right of Masters over slaves," Hobbes posits the right of man over the beasts. So we have here a configuration that is both systematic and hierarchical: at the summit is the sovereign (master, king, husband, father: ipse-

40. Carl Schmitt, *La notion de politique* [*Der Begriff des Politischen,* 1928], trans. Marie-Louise Steinhauser (Paris: Champs-Flammarion, 1992), p. 109; trans. George Schwab as *The Concept of the Political* (Chicago: University of Chicago Press, 1996; expanded edition [but still slightly abridged] 2007), p. 65.

41. Thomas Hobbes, *Le citoyen, ou Les fondements de la politique* [*De Cive*], trans. Samuel Sorbière [1649] (Paris: Garnier-Flammarion, 1982), sec. 2, chap. 9, p. 186; *On the Citizen,* ed. and trans. Richard Tuck and Michael Silverthorne (Cambridge: Cambridge University Press, 1998), p. 108.

42. [Translator's note:] This quotation from Sorbière's 1649 translation does not seem to correspond exactly to the text of the *De Cive.* See however, *On the Citizen,* ed. and trans. Tuck and Silverthorne, p. 102: "For to be a *King* is simply to have *Dominion* over many *persons,* and thus a *kingdom* is a *large family,* and a *family* is a *little kingdom.*"

ity itself [comment]), and below, subjected to his service, the slave, the beast, the woman, the child. The word "subjection," the gesture of "subduing" is at the center of the last paragraph of chapter 8, on the right of the master over the slaves, which I'll read to conclude for today:

> Right over non-rational animals is acquired in the same way as over the *persons* of men, that is, by natural strength and powers. In the natural state, because of the war of all against all, any one may legitimately subdue or even kill Men, whenever that seems to be to his advantage; much more will this be the case against animals. That is, one may at discretion reduce to one's service any animals that can be tamed or made useful, and wage continual war against the rest as harmful, and hunt them down and kill them. Thus *Dominion* over animals has its origin in the *right of nature* not in *Divine positive right.* For if no such right had existed before the publication of holy scripture, no one could rightly have slaughtered animals for food except someone to whom the divine will had been revealed in the holy scriptures; and the condition of mankind would surely have been very hard, since the beasts could devour them in all innocence, while they could not devour the beasts. Since therefore it is by natural right that an animal kills a man, it will be by the same right that a man slaughters an animal.[43]

Conclusion: the beast *and* [*et*] the sovereign (couple, coupling, copula), the beast *is* [*est*] the sovereign, man is the beast for man, *homo homini lupus*, Peter and the wolf, Peter accompanies his grandfather on the wolf hunt, Peter, the grandfather and the wolf, the father is the wolf.

56   In "The Question of Lay Analysis" (*Die Frage der Laienanalyse*, 1926), Freud pretends to be in dialogue, as you know, with an impartial person, and he reminds him that every time a ravenous animal ("like the wolf," says Freud) enters the scene in a story, "we shall recognize as a disguise of the father."[44] And Freud explains that we cannot account for these fables and myths without returning to infantile sexuality. In the series of the devouring father, we will also find, he says, Cronus, who swallows up his children after having emasculated his father Uranus and before being himself emasculated by his son Zeus, saved by his mother's cunning.

    But, on the subject of these zooanthropological *analogies*, or even these

43. *On the Citizen,* pp. 105–6.

44. Sigmund Freud, "The Question of Lay Analysis," in *The Standard Edition of the Complete Psychological Works of Sigmund Freud*, 24 vols. (London: Hogarth Press, 1953–74), 20:183–258 (p. 211).

zooanthropotheological tropes of the unconscious — for Freud says in *Das Unbehagen in der Kultur* (1929–30) that, thanks to technology and mastery over nature, man has become a "prosthetic God"[45] — Freud, in the same work (at the opening of chapter 7), asks himself the question why, despite the analogies between the state institutions of animal societies and human state institutions, the analogies encounter a limit. The animals are related to us, they are even our brothers, says one French translation,[46] they are our kin, and there are even animal states, but we humans would not be happy in them, says Freud in sum. Why? The hypothesis he leaves hanging is that these states are arrested in their history. They have no history and no future; and the reason for this arrest, this stabilization, this stasis (and in this sense animal states seems more stable and therefore more statelike than human states), the reason for their relatively a-historical stasis is a relative equilibrium between the environment and their drives. Whereas for man (this is the hypothesis that Freud leaves hanging), it is possible that an excess or relaunching of libido might have provoked a new rebellion on the part of the destructive drive, a new unleashing of the death drive and of cruelty, and therefore a relaunching (be it finite or infinite) of history. That is the question that Freud leaves open for us. (Read Freud, *Civilization and Its Discontents,* p. 123.)

57

> Why do our relatives, the animals, not exhibit any such cultural struggle? We do not know. Very probably some of them — the bees, the ants, the termites — strove for thousands of years before they arrived at the State institutions, the distribution of functions and the restrictions on the individual, for which we admire them to-day. It is a mark of our present condition that we know from our own feelings that we should not think ourselves happy in any of these animal States or in any of the roles assigned in them to the individual. In the case of other animal species it may be that a temporary balance has been reached between the influences of their environment and the mutually contending instincts within them, and that thus a cessation of development has come about. It may be that in primitive man a fresh access of libido kindled a renewed burst of activity on the part of the destructive instinct. There are a great many questions here to which as yet there is no answer.[47]

45. Sigmund Freud, "Civilization and Its Discontents," in *The Standard Edition*, 21: 64–145 (p. 92).

46. *Le malaise dans la civilisation*, trans. Ch. et J. Ogier (Paris: Presses universitaires de France, 1971), p. 79 ("nos frères les animaux"). [Translator's note: *The Standard Edition* has "our relatives, the animals" (21:123).]

47. *The Standard Edition*, 21:123.

December 19, 2001[1]

The [feminine] beast and the [masculine] sovereign, *la . . . le.*
What and who? Who or what? Go figure [*Allez savoir*].
Go figure what who, that's what who our question will be made of today.

The beast *and* [*et*] the sovereign, the beast *is* [*est*] the sovereign, that's how our couple seems first to show up, a couple, a duo or even a duel, but also an alliance, almost a hymen, whose boisterous tête-à-tête we already began to interrogate last week. Tête-à-tête or face-to-face, haunted by virtual sexual differences, between, *on the one hand*, the simple conjunction (and [*et*]), which seems to pose, oppose, or juxtapose them as two species of living beings radically heterogeneous to each other, the one infrahuman, the other human or even superhuman, and, *on the other hand*, the copula (is [*est*]), which seems to couple them in a sort of ontologico-sexual attraction, a mutual fascination, a communitarian attachment, or even a narcissistic resemblance, the one recognizing in the other a sort of double, the one becoming the other, being the other (the "is" then having the value of a process, a becoming, an identificatory metamorphosis), the beast being the sovereign, the sovereign being the beast, the one and the other being each engaged, in truth changed or even exchanged, in a becoming-beast of the sovereign or in a becoming-sovereign of the beast, the passage from the one to the other, the analogy, the resemblance, the alliance, the hymen depending on the fact that they both share that very singular position of being outlaws, above or at a distance from the law, the beast ignorant of right and the sovereign having the right to suspend right, to place himself above the law that he is, that he makes, that he institutes, as to which he decides, sovereignly. The sovereign is not an angel, but, one might say, he who plays the sovereign plays

1. This session was published, with some cuts, in *La démocratie à venir* (see session 1 above, n. 1), pp. 456–76.

the beast.[2] The sovereign makes himself the beast, has himself the beast, sometimes in the most troubling sense of a zoophilia or even a bestiality the historical symptoms of which we would need to inventory, detect, or even interpret. That's our first impetus, the nerve of our *et/est* analogy. Our *eh eh*,[3] undecided or even undecidable. Because every decision (by its essence a decision is exceptional and sovereign) must escape the order of the possible, of what is already possible and programmable for the supposed subject of the decision, because every decision worthy of the name must be this exceptional scandal of a passive decision or decision of the other, the difference between the deciding decision and the undecided decision itself becomes undecidable, and then the supposed decision, the exceptionally sovereign decision looks, like two peas in a pod, just like an indecision, an unwilling, a nonliberty, a nonintention, an unconsciousness and an irrationality, etc.; and then the supposed sovereign subject begins, by an invincible attraction, to look like the beast he is supposed to subject to himself (and we already know, having often—last time too—verified it, that in place of the beast one can put, in the same hierarchy, the slave, the woman, the child).

I'm now going to offer for your reflection a French expression that is heavily equivocal, also undecidable and no doubt untranslatable, to wit [*à savoir*] "faire savoir"[4] (Board).

What does "faire savoir" [make to know] mean?

What is meant in "make to know" by this coupling of two such charged verbs, "make" and "know"? What is one making known when one says *faire savoir*?

Let us leave this question suspended. No doubt we shall return to it shortly or *tout à l'heure*. Right on time [*toute à l'heure*], it will come back at its own time. Remember Zarathustra talking about "his hour" of his "my hour," the stillest (*die stillste Stunde*), about his own sovereign hour which

61

2. [Translator's note:] French readers would immediately recognize the reference to Pascal's *Pensée* that reads, "*L'homme n'est ni ange ni bête, et le malheur veut que qui veut faire l'ange fait la bête*" [Man is neither angel not beast, and the misery of it is that whoever tries to act the angel acts the beast]. (No. 678 in the Lafuma classification.)

3. [Translator's note:] The standard interjection "eh" (which can correspond to English "Eh," "Uh," "Um," "Er," "Heh," among others) is homophonous with both "et" and "est."

4. [Translator's note:] Literally "to make to know" or "to have [someone] know," "to make known": but "faire" also means simply "to do," and "savoir" is also a noun meaning "knowledge" or, especially in the expression "savoir-faire," "know-how."

addressed him to tell him, almost in silence, murmuring, the story of what comes at its own time "on dove's feet."

> The reason of the strongest is always the best,
> As we shall shortly show.

These are the first words, and the moral, as they say, of a fable, *The Wolf and the Lamb,* which is to occupy us for some time. Starting next week. In a sense the "Nous l'allons montrer tout à l'heure" can be translated by a "We're going to make known," "We will not delay in making known"; and the difference between *monstration* and *demonstration,* between the intuitive image of the story, which is an audiovisual scene, and the discursive reasoning of the moral, is here suspended, as on television: we are going to make it known to you, by showing images and an audiovisual story, in an immediately sensory way, as though it were live, we are going to demonstrate what we want to show, namely that "The reason of the strongest is always the best."

In principle, in the noblest tradition of the university institution, a seminar is not a kind of fable. It does not belong to the genre of the fable. It can, of course, on occasion, present itself as a discourse of knowledge *on the subject of* that law of genre that is called the fable; it can no doubt give itself out as a learned, historical, critical, theoretical, philosophical discourse, a discourse of knowledge *on* the fable, on the subject of the fabulous in general.

But in principle, and according to its statutory vocation, according to its law and the contract it presupposes, the discourse of teaching ought not to be fabular. It gives something to be known, it dispenses knowledge, and knowledge must be without fable. And you must make known without fable. Similarly, in the prevalent or hegemonic tradition of the political, a political discourse, and above all a political action, should in no case come under the category of the fabular, of that type of simulacrum called fabular, that type of speech known as the fable, be it the fable in general, or the fable as determinate literary genre in the European West. For, as its Latin name indicates, a fable is always and before all else speech—*for, fari,* is to speak, to say, to celebrate, to sing, to predict, and *fabula* is first of all something said, a familiar piece of speech, a conversation, and then a mythical narrative, without historical knowledge, a legend, sometimes a theatrical play, in any case a fiction that claims to teach us something, a fiction supposed to give something to be known, a fiction supposed to *make known [faire savoir],* *make so as to know,* in a double sense: (1) in the sense of bringing some knowledge to the awareness of the other, to inform the other, share with the other, <make> the other know, and (2) in the sense of "making like" knowledge ["*faire*" *savoir*], i.e. giving the impression of knowing, giving the effect of knowledge, resembling knowing where there isn't necessarily any knowing: in the latter case of *faire savoir*, *giving the effect* of knowing, the knowing is a pretend knowing, a false knowing, a simulacrum of knowing, a mask of knowing, something like that *loup* over a person's face that we were talking about last time. But there must be a technique, there must be a rhetoric, an art of the simulacrum, a *savoir-faire* to *faire savoir* where it is not a matter of knowing, where there is no knowing worthy of the name.

One of our questions could then be announced as follows, within a classical seminar discourse, i.e. a theoretical, philosophical, constative discourse, a discourse of knowledge, or even a reflection within political philosophy: What would happen if, for example, political discourse, or even the political action welded to it and indissociable from it, were constituted or even instituted by something fabular, by that sort of narrative simulacrum, the convention of some historical *as if*, by that fictive modality of "storytelling" that is called fabulous or fabular, which supposes giving to be known where one does not know, fraudulently affecting or showing off the making-known, and which administers, right in the work of the *hors-d'oeuvre* of some narrative, a moral lesson, a "moral"? A hypothesis according to which political, and even politicians', logic and rhetoric would be always, through and through, the putting to work of a fable, a strategy to give meaning and credit to a fable, an affabulation—and therefore to a story indissociable from a moral, the putting of living beings, animals or humans, on stage, a supposedly instructive, informative, pedagogical, edifying, story, fictive, put up, artificial, even invented from whole cloth, but destined to educate, to teach, to *make known*, to share a knowledge, to bring to knowledge.

The fabular dimensions of this political logic and rhetoric would not be limited to discursive operations, to spoken words, as they say, to the sayings and writings of political decision-makers, heads of state, sovereigns and the great and good, citizens or the media; in other words, these affabulations would not be limited to the sayings, writings, or even images of everything that concerns politics in the public space. The fabular dimension would also, beyond the sayings, writings, and images, determine the political actions, military operations, the sound of arms, the din of explosions and killings, puttings-to-death of military and civilians, so-called acts of war or of terrorism, or civil or international war, the war of partisans, etc., with or without condemnation to death according to the law.

What is fabulous in the fable does not only depend on its linguistic nature,

63

on the fact that the fable is made up of words. The fabulous also engages act, gesture, action, if only the operation that consists in producing narrative, in organizing, disposing discourse in such a way as to recount, to put living beings on stage, to accredit the interpretation of a narrative, to *faire savoir*, to make knowledge, to make performatively, to operate knowledge (a bit like the way Augustine spoke of making the truth, *veritatem faciare*). Well, given this, the fabulous deployment of information, of the teletechnologies of information and of the media today, is perhaps only spreading the empire of the fable. What has been happening on big and small television channels, for a long time now, but in particular in time of war, for example over the last few months, attests to this becoming-fabulous of political action and discourse, be it described as military or civil, warlike or terroristic. A certain effectivity, a certain efficacy, including the irreversible actuality of death, are not excluded from this affabulation. Death and suffering, which are not fabular, are yet carried off and inscribed in the affabulatory score.

64   We could take countless examples of this. I'll do no more than recall a few of them. One wonders what would have been the sense and efficacy of an operation of so-called "international terrorism" (we shall no doubt have the opportunity to return to this notion, which for the moment I shall do no more than cite) [one wonders what would have been the sense and efficacy of an operation of so-called "international terrorism"] if the image of the airplanes gutting the Twin Towers, if the image of <what> I would call, between two languages, the *collapsus* of the World Trade Center towers, had not been, *as* an image, precisely, recorded, not only archived and filmed but indefinitely reproducible and compulsively reproduced, immediately, throughout the USA, but also, all but instantaneously, via CNN for example, from New York to Paris, from London to Berlin, Moscow, Tokyo, Islamabad, Cairo, even Shanghai, where I happened to be at that moment. This technical reproducibility is an integral part of the event itself, from its origin on. As are the making-known [*faire-savoir*] and the know-how [*savoir-faire*] of the making-known that are immediately at work, put to work in organized fashion on both sides of the front, by the supposed aggressor no less than by the supposed victim who have an equal interest in knowing how to make this making-known as efficient, powerful, reproducible, and widely broadcast as possible. In other words, the technical reproducibility of the archive does not come along after the fact to accompany it, but conditions its very putting-to-work, its efficacy, its scope and its very meaning, if there is a meaning. Even if the interminable looped repetition of these disaster-movie images could serve, in a sort of jubilatory grief, both the work of mourning and the deadening of a trauma which depended less

on the announced numbers of "innocent victims" and the suffering provoked by a terrible aggression in the past, than on the experience of the
vulnerability of the invulnerable, on anxiety about what was to come, about
the risk of attacks to come, which threaten to be still worse, still more terrible (similar attacks, or the use of nuclear, biochemical, or bacteriological
weapons, etc.). Without the deployment and the logic of image-effects, of
this making-known, this supposed making-known, without this "news,"   65
the blow struck would have been, if not nothing, at least massively reduced
(let's say reduced to what is made of the news of a famine or a typhoon
scarcely reported or felt when they come from a county far from Europe
or America, or reduced to the number of traffic accidents in all the holi-
day weekends in a year, or those dead from AIDS in Africa, or the effects
of the embargo on Iraq, so many human catastrophes which are anything
but natural and inevitable accidents like an earthquake—and even there,
hurricanes or earthquakes, qua catastrophes said to be natural and inevitable, do not produce the same effects, as we know so well, according to the
wealth and level of development of the country concerned. Which reminds
us of this obvious fact: the effect and repercussion of these cataclysms are
also conditioned, in their breadth and their impact, by a politico-economical
situation, and therefore by the power of the media, a signifying power,
then, both ethological and ethical, the *ethos* of ethology here making the
link between the organization of the natural habitat and ethics, therefore
so-called human responsibility in the fields of economics, ecology, morality,
law, and politics). The putting to work of the image, as we well know, is
not, then, limited to archiving, in the sense of a preserving recording, but
it makes archiving an active interpretation, one that is selective, productive
qua reproductive, productive of a "making-known" narrative as much as
reproductive of images: know-how of making-known which works just as
well for the *collapsus* of the Twin Towers as for the name, and much less
the image, of the Pentagon, as much for the apparitions (I think that's the
best word) of Osama bin Laden on screens the world over, initially relayed
by the channel Al Jazeera, whose role in this process would be worth more
than one seminar.

Among the innumerable indices of this power of high-tech[5] archiving
which conditions the political efficacy of the event, rather, earlier [*plutôt,
plus tôt*], than it records it so as to preserve it, which produces, co-produces
the event that it is supposed merely to reproduce and archive, I am thinking, for example (there would be so many other examples), of what I saw

5. [Translator's note:] The words "high tech" are in English in the text.

66   on television when I was in New York two weeks or so after September
      11. On the one hand, even beyond the censorship or half-imposed half-
      spontaneous control over the main radio and TV channels (so beyond
      hetero- or autocensorship, in a distinction to which it is harder and harder
      to give credit), at the very moment when, given that the logic of the mar-
      ket is part of the logic of war, capitalist control of the news consisted quite
      simply in the American administration's *buying* (as was clearly its right in
      the logic of a globalized world), buying all the images taken and broad-
      cast by a satellite able to see and make seen every inch of Afghanistan, and
      therefore to *make known* to the whole world what was happening on the
      ground, and in particular the victims among the civilian population, the
      real effects of the bombing—at that very moment, at the apparently op-
      posite extreme of this control of *making-known* by purchasing power, by the
      political *savoir-faire* of the market, at the apparently opposite extreme, at
      the pole of archiving and public broadcasting of the archive, of panoptical
      and panauditory transparency, one could have access to an extraordinary
      recording. And what was it? Well, during the attack on the Twin Towers
      and their collapse, an anonymous private individual, a very well-equipped
      amateur radio enthusiast in San Francisco, woken by a phone call at 6:00
      a.m. on September 11 (given the time difference between East and West
      coasts), had immediately fired up a sophisticated system, as they say, that
      he had set up and that allowed him clandestinely to intercept and record,
      from San Francisco, all the messages exchanged around the Twin Tow-
      ers, by the New York police and fire department (NYPD, FDNY), cries
      of victims and all, on the other side of the country. This man testified on
      camera and placed his recordings at the disposal of the TV channels (he
      probably sold them, he no doubt sold his know-how-to-make-known), so
      that to all those mute images, all those photographic and cinematographic
      images taken in public by who knows how many cameras and broadcast
      continually for days and days (with the order never to show a body—it is
      true that most of the bodies had disappeared, with only the "disappeared"
67   remaining), [to all these images taken in public by who knows how many
      cameras and broadcast continually for days and days] one could henceforth
      add a soundtrack, sound images of nonpublic discourse, which could have
      remained secret among the police, the firemen, and so on. In this way it was
      possible to have the impression, illusory or not, of having at one's disposal
      the total archive, both public and nonpublic, of the totality of the event,
      <of> all making-known in an exhaustive making-known (with the obvious
      exception of the death experienced within the towers by those who disap-
      peared without even leaving a body). This disappearance of the bodies, this

death in general, with or without bodies, will have become, in the undecidability of making-known that is occupying us here, an essential structure of the trauma (for New York, America, the world) bearing the impossible mourning as much of the past, the pastness of the blow struck, as of what remains to come, and which, from bad to worse, installs the virtuality of the worst threat at the heart of everything we can currently know, know how to do and to make known. In all cases it has to do with knowing how to cause fear, knowing how to terrorize by making known. And this terror, on both sides of the front, is undeniably effective, real, concrete, even if this concrete effectivity overflows the presence of the present toward a past or future of the trauma, which is never saturated with presence. So that all this knowledge, this know-how, this making-known, might well go via fable, simulacrum, fantasy, or virtuality, might well go via the unreal and fabular inconsistency of media or capital (for on both sides the violence also moves indissociably via media and capital, in ways that are simultaneously fabular, unreal, virtual, dependent on belief, on faith and credit—no capital without an accredited fable—and yet terribly effective and efficacious in their effects), this know-how-to-make-known, this making makes knowing, and so touches nonetheless effectively, affectively, and concretely both bodies and souls. And that is the essence without essence of terror, the becoming-terrorism of terror, both antistate terror and state terror, be it actual or virtual.

We really are dealing here with that fear, that terror or panic that Hobbes in *Leviathan* said was the political passion par excellence, the mainspring of politics. If we were to do a history of Terror or Terrorism, so-called national and international terrorisms (the modern name "terrorism" coming initially, as you know, from the Terror of the French Revolution, of a Revolution that was also at the origin of all the universal declarations of human rights), if we were to proceed to a conceptual genealogy of terrorism, to wit, of know-how (always technically equipped, sometimes poorly, sometimes highly), of this know-how that organizes the panic of supposedly civil populations in order to exert the pressure of public opinion on public, governmental, or military policy, we should have to reconstitute all the political theories that have made fear or panic (and so terror or terrorism as knowing-how to make fear reign) an essential and structural mainspring of subjectity, of subjection, of being-subject, of submission or political subjection. And there we should find, as close as can be to sovereignty—which is, as it were, its correlate—fear: fear as it is defined by the Leviathan, for example. Leviathan is the name of an animal-machine designed to cause fear or of a prosthetic and state *organon*, a state as prosthesis, the organ of a state prosthesis, what I nickname a *prosthstatics*, which runs on fear and reigns by fear. For example, in chapter 27 of *Leviathan*,[6] fear is defined <as> the "onely thing" (p. 150) that, in the humanity of man, motivates obedience to the law, noninfraction of the law, and keeping the laws. The correlate on the side of the passions, the essential affect of the law, is fear. And as there is no law without sovereignty, we shall have to say that sovereignty calls for, presupposes, provokes fear, as its condition of possibility but also as its main effect. Sovereignty causes fear, and fear makes the sovereign. The chapter that recognizes in fear a fundamental political passion is entitled *Of Crimes, Excuses and Extenuations*. Reading or rereading it, you will see that the condition for there to be crime, in the strict sense of the term, and so for there to be infraction of the law and infraction punishable by law, is that there be a sovereign, a sovereign power. "The Civill Law ceasing, Crimes cease," says Hobbes, or again: "when the Soveraign Power ceaseth, Crime also ceaseth: for where there is no such Power, there is no protection to be had from the Law; and therefore every one may protect himself by his own power" (p. 147). So: as long as there is not yet instituted sovereignty (sovereignty, for Hobbes, is always an institution, and therefore a non-natural prosthesis), everyone has the right to preserve his own body and does not have to give up this self-protection. He can then kill, without crime and without being incriminated, out of legitimate self-defense (and one should not even call this "legitimate" or "legal," as there is no law yet); he can kill to *protect* himself without it being a crime, since there is not yet sovereignty and thereby law. Sovereignty is "ordained," says Hobbes, there is "Institution of Soveraign Power" to ensure the bodily security of the subjects. Once this sovereignty is instituted, once it has been delegated, by contract, by convention, to ensure the *protection* of the citizens, then there can be crime if someone ensures his own protection without going via the state to which he has entrusted it by contract. I will not go here into the detail of this long chapter, which you will read for yourselves. I'll retain only this: if I kill a man who threatens to kill me as soon as he can, when, as Hobbes says, I have "time, and means to demand protection, from the Soveraign Power" (p. 150), then I commit a crime. Just as if, when exposed to offense, I fear

6. Thomas Hobbes, *Leviathan,* ed. Flathman and Johnston, Second Part, "Of Common-Wealth," chap. 27: "Of Crimes, Excuses, and Extenuations," pp. 146–55. Jacques Derrida recalls here in parentheses the plan of *Leviathan:* "(Second Part: 'Of Common-Wealth' [First Part: 'Of Man'; Third Part: 'Of a Christian Common-Wealth'; Fourth Part: 'Of the Kingdome of Darknesse' [chapter 46, 'Of Darknesse from Vain Philosophy, and Fabulous Traditions'])."

contempt, and then exert terror (Hobbes's word: "Terrour") by "private re-   70
venge," this terror I exert is a crime. So that everything comes down to fear:
I can commit a crime and exert terror by fear, but it is the same fear that
makes me obey the law. Fear is "sometimes cause of Crime, as when the
danger is neither present, nor corporeall" (p. 150). This is an important precision: Hobbes privileges "Bodily Fear" and the "present" of the body, but
there is in all fear something that refers, essentially, to non-body and nonpresent, if only the future of a threat: what causes fear is never fully present
nor fully corporeal, in the sense that the purely corporeal is supposed to be
saturated with presence. Fear always exceeds corporeal presence, and this is
why it is also the passion correlative to the law; fear is thus both the origin of
the law and of the transgression of the law, the origin of both law and crime.
And if you take fear to the limit of the threat either exerted or felt, i.e. terror, then you have to conclude that terror is both what motivates respect for
laws and the transgression of laws. If you translate "law" by "sovereignty"
and "state," you have to conclude that terror is equally opposed to the state
as a challenge as it is exerted by the state as the essential manifestation of
its sovereignty. Whence Hobbes's measured statements—I mean measured
into more and less, more or less. There is, at bottom, only fear, fear has no
opposite, it is coextensive with the whole field of the passions, and here with
political passion. The political subject is primarily subjected to fear, and it
is fear that is sometimes *the most propitious*, sometimes *the least propitious*,
but one cannot not count on it and with it. And fear is primarily fear for
the body, for the body proper, for one's own proper body, i.e. for life. Life
lives in fear. Life is essentially fearful, fear is the passion of life, etc. "Of all
Passions, that which enclineth men least to break the Lawes, is Fear." (Note
the strange logico-grammatical turn of this definition. Hobbes does not say   71
that fear drives one to obey the laws, more than any other passion; he says
that among the passions that incline men to crime, felony, transgression of
the law—with the implication that they all do, fear included because he will
say at the end of this paragraph that one can commit crime through fear—
among all the passions that incline humans to crime, felony, transgression
of the law, fear as passion, as affect, is the one that does so *least*. And then
he will take things the other way around, and examine the other side of the
same assertion, from the side not of the transgression but the keeping of
the laws; if fear is a passion that is *less* inclined, *less* propitious to the infraction of the laws, then it is the most propitious, and even the only one that
is propitious, to their being kept—with the exception, the rare exception
only of some "generous natures" who can assert the laws without fear, who
can preserve the laws or not break them other than by the negative reactiv-

ity of fear.) "Nay (excepting some generous natures,) it is the onely thing (when there is appearance of profit, or pleasure by breaking the Lawes,) that makes men keep them. And yet in many cases a Crime may be committed through Feare" (p. 150).

What is becoming clearer here is that the fear that pushes one to respect the laws and therefore to respect a sovereignty destined, by convention, to ensure the protection of the citizens—that this fear is here defined as a human thing, as proper to mankind. Hobbes twice specifies this humanity, this properly human quality ("Of all Passions, that which enclineth *men* least to break the Lawes, is Fear. Nay [. . .] it is the onely thing (when there is appearance of profit, or pleasure by breaking the Lawes,) that makes *men* keep them"). This humanity, this proper to man here signifies that sovereignty, laws, law and therefore the state are nothing natural and are posited by contract and convention. They are prostheses. If there is a prosthetic structure to the Leviathan as political animal or monster, this is because of its conventional, thetic, contractual structure. The opposition between *physis* and *nomos* (nature and law), as opposition between *physis* and *thesis* (nature and convention, or nature and positing), is here fully and decisively functional. It follows that law, sovereignty, the institution of the state are historical and always provisional, let's say deconstructible, essentially fragile or finite or mortal, even if sovereignty is *posited as immortal*. It is posited as immortal and indivisible precisely because it is mortal and divisible, contract or convention being destined to ensure for it what it does not have, or is not, naturally. So that if sovereignty is, as Hobbes says, the "Soule of the Common-wealth,"[7] this soul is an artificial, institutional, prosthetic and mortal soul: it lasts only as long as law, sovereignty, and the state are able to *protect* fearful subjects against what is causing them fear. The word *protection* here bears the whole burden of the political, i.e. the insurance contract made between scared or terrorized subjects to delegate to the state or the sovereign the charge of protecting them when they cannot protect themselves. They must then obey what protects them. For the fear that pushes them to obey the laws, obedience to the laws, their condition as subject to the law only lasts the time that the sovereign can ensure their protection. This insurance policy [*police d'assurance*] which basically entrusts to sovereignty the very police [*police*], the protection of security, comes down to moving from one fear to another. One institutes sovereignty because one is fearful (for one's life, for one's own body) and therefore because one needs to be protected, and then one obeys the law one has instituted through fear

7. Chap. 21, "Of the Liberty of Subjects," p. 121.

of being punished if one breaks the law. Between protecting and obliging to obey there is an essential link. "I protect you" means, for the state, I oblige you, you are my subject, I subject you. Being the subject of one's fear and being the subject of the law or the state, being obliged to obey the state as one obeys one's fear, are at bottom the same thing. If you like, in the two senses of the word "oblige." I oblige you by forcing you to obey, by constraining you, because I oblige you by doing you the service of protecting you. I oblige you by forcing you to obey in the same movement by which, obliging you by doing you the service of protecting you, I oblige you to have gratitude, I oblige you to recognition [*reconnaissance:* recognition and gratitude]: to recognize the state and the law, and to recognize them for obliging you (in both senses of the word: constraining and doing a service by protecting, obliging to recognize). It is in this sense that Schmitt, in a passage that I shall read in a moment, will say that "*Protego ergo obligo* is the *cogito ergo sum* of the state." In the paragraph of *Leviathan* that I am going to read, I emphasize the lexicon of *protection*, where this lexicon and its logic explain the paradox of the mortal immortality of sovereignty. Sovereignty—the soul, and therefore the life of the state, the artificial respiration of the state—is posited, instituted, promised, contracted, *artificially, as immortal* only because it is *naturally mortal*. It is prosthetic and artificial technique that immortalizes it or in any case guarantees it an indefinite survival: (read and comment)

73

> The Obligation of Subjects to the Soveraign, is understood to last as long, and no longer, than the power lasteth, by which he is able to *protect* them. For the right men have by Nature to protect themselves, when none else can protect them, can by no Covenant be relinquished. The Soveraignty is the Soule of the Common-wealth; which once departed from the Body, the members doe no more receive their motion from it. The end of Obedience is *Protection*; which, wheresoever a man seeth it, either in his own, or in anothers sword, nature applyeth his obedience to it, and his endeavour to maintaine it. And though Soveraignty, in the intention of them that make it, be immortall; yet is it in its own nature, not only subject to violent death, by forreign war; but also through the ignorance and passions of men, it hath in it, from the very institution, many seeds of a naturall mortality, by Intestine Discord. (p. 121)

As it is for Schmitt, here a good disciple of a Hobbes he often quotes and in whom he sees a decisionist theorist of sovereignty, evil is civil war. This is what Schmitt says about the great law of protection, which he analyzes in utterly historical fashion, i.e. both as historical in the sense of being produced by pact, contract, alliance, institution, and as a historical theory, i.e.

74

produced, as political philosophy, on the basis of historical experiences such as those that dictated to Hobbes his political theory:

> Furthermore, it would be a mistake to believe that a nation could eliminate the distinction of friend and enemy by declaring its friendship for the entire world or by voluntarily disarming itself. The world will not thereby become depoliticized, and it will not be transplanted into a condition of pure morality, pure justice, or pure economics. If a people is afraid of the trials and risks implied by existing in the sphere of politics, then another people will appear which will assume these trials by protecting it against foreign enemies and thereby taking over political rule. The protector then decides who the enemy is by virtue of the eternal relation of protection and obedience.

[Schmitt's Note]

> On this principle rests the feudal order and the relation of lord and vassal, leader and led, patron and clients. This relation is clearly and explicitly seen here. No form of order, no reasonable legitimacy or legality can exist without protection and obedience. The *protego ergo obligo* is the *cogito ergo sum* of the state. A political theory which does not systematically become aware of this sentence remains an inadequate fragment. Hobbes designated this (at the end of his English edition of 1651, p. 396) as the true purpose of his *Leviathan,* to instill in man once again "the mutual relation between Protection and Obedience"; human nature as well as divine right demands its inviolable observation.
>
> Hobbes himself had experienced this truth in the terrible time of civil war, because then all legitimate and normative illusions with which men like to deceive themselves regarding political realities in periods of untroubled security vanish. [. . .] The fundamental correctness of the protection-obedience axiom comes to the fore even more clearly in foreign policy and interstate relations: the simplest expression of this axiom is found in the protectorate under international law, the federal state, the confederation of states dominated by one of them, and the various kinds of treaties offering protection and guarantees.[8]

A little further on, Schmitt explains, as he often does, what he calls the anthropological bases of political theories, namely that the only theories of politics worthy of the name are based on a pessimistic anthropology, on a vision of man as bad, corrupt, dangerous, fearful, or violent. On the basis of this criterion (a pessimistic anthropology of man as a dangerous animal), Schmitt grants the quality of political theorist worthy of the name to Ma-

8. Carl Schmitt, *The Concept of the Political*, pp. 51–53.

chiavelli, Bossuet, de Maistre, Donoso Cortés, Hegel, Marx, Taine—and above all Hobbes. All of them are thinkers of evil, whatever form that evil may take, and one has no difficulty recognizing the features generally attributed to the beast (brutality, poorly controlled instincts, the irrationality of the living being, etc.: these are Schmitt's terms). And this is when Schmitt evokes the fables that put on stage animals whose behavior can be given a political interpretation. I quote: (read)

> The problematic or unproblematic conception of man is decisive for the presupposition of every further political consideration, the answer to the question whether man is a dangerous being or not, a risky or a harmless creature.
>
> [Schmitt's Note]
>
> The numerous modifications and variations of this anthropological distinction of good and evil are not reviewed here in detail. Evil may appear as corruption, weakness, cowardice, stupidity, or also as brutality, sensuality, vitality, irrationality, and so on. Goodness may appear in corresponding variations as reasonableness, perfectibility, the capacity of being manipulated, of being taught, peaceful, and so forth. Striking in this context is the political signification of animal fables. Almost all can be applied to a real political situation: the problem of aggression in the fable of the wolf and the lamb; the question of guilt for the plague in La Fontaine's fable, a guilt which of course falls upon the donkey; justice between states in the fables of animal assemblies; disarmament in Churchill's election speech of October 1928, which depicts how every animal believes that its teeth, claws, horns are only instruments for maintaining peace; the large fish which devour the small ones. Etc. This curious analogy can be explained by the direct connection of political anthropology with what the political philosophers of the seventeenth century (Hobbes, Spinoza, Pufendorf) called the state of nature. In it, states exist among themselves in a condition of animal danger, and their acting subjects are evil for precisely the same reasons as animals who are stirred by their drives (hunger, greediness, fear, jealousy).[9]

76

Human nature, political anthropology, conventionalist theory of sovereignty, and therefore of the state, thesis, prosthesis, *prosthstatic*—all of that presupposes, recalls or entails at least *three assertions* that we shall have ceaselessly to take into account.

On the one hand, this conventionalist (and not naturalistic) theory makes prosthstatic sovereignty proper to man. And this artificial prosthesis of the

---

9. Ibid., pp. 58–59.

sovereign state is always a protection. The prosthesis protects. Protection is its essential purpose, the essential function of the state.

On the other hand, this protectionist prosthstatic posits the absolute indivisibility of sovereignty (indivisibility is an analytic part of the concept of sovereignty: divisible or sharable sovereignty is not sovereignty).

Third, finally, the convention, the *thesis*, the prosthesis, the contract at the origin of sovereignty excludes God just as much—and this will be the important point for us here—as it excludes the beast.

In order to recognize the logic of these three theses, which are, at bottom, posited on the originary thesis or prosthesis, you can read, among other things, chapter 18 of *Leviathan,* entitled "Of the RIGHTS of Soveraignes by Institution." Hobbes begins by positing that a state is "instituted" ("A Common-wealth is said to be Instituted") when a multitude of men, as it were, become One in their representation, when the One emerges to represent the many. To this end, the multitude comes to an agreement and a convention, a *Covenant* (a word that is also used, as you'll remember later, to translate the Alliance between God and the Jewish people—and "covenant" is both a noun meaning contract, convention, alliance, commitment, and a verb: "to covenant," meaning to commit oneself, to sign a convention, to be party to a contract or an alliance): they "Agree and Covenant," says Hobbes: "*A Common-wealth is said to be* Instituted*, when a* Multitude *of men do Agree and* Covenant*, every one with every one, that to whatsoever* Man*, or Assembly of Men, shall be given by the major part, the* Right *to* Present *the Person of them all, (that is to say, to be their* Representative) [. . .]" (p. 121). According to this *Covenant*, according to this convention designed to *protect* them from each other in peace—*protect* is the most frequent word in these pages, along with *convention*—they "authorize" themselves to authorize *all* (I repeat: all) the actions and *all* (I repeat: all) the judgments of the man or assembly of men that the majority of this multitude has given the right to represent them. Even those who *voted against* are obliged, they oblige themselves to be obliged to obey unconditionally. And it is during the exposition of everything that is entailed by this unconditional obedience to the convention (I leave you to follow this at the beginning of chapter 18) that Hobbes encounters and rejects the objection that one can place a convention or a commitment above the one that institutes the state. For example, a commitment with respect to God. Some people might claim that they are disobeying the human sovereign because they are obeying God, whose sovereignty trumps that of statesmen. As you can imagine, this point is a delicate one for those who, like me, often speak of an onto-theologico-political structure of sovereignty (to be deconstructed). For Hobbes's response (like Bodin's, for that matter) seems, I say *seems*, to want to untie so-called modern state sovereignty, as established by convention or institution, from divine sovereignty. But things get complicated, in Bodin as well as in Hobbes, and we shall have more than one sign of this: in any case in Hobbes, as that's where we are, it gets complicated by the fact that this humanity, this anthropological essence of prosthstatics is produced, from the opening pages of *Leviathan,* on the divine model. The artificial man, as Hobbes says, the artificial soul, the "Artificial Animal" that the Leviathan is, imitates the natural art of God: "*NATURE (the Art whereby God hath made and governes the World) is by the* Art *of man, as in many other things, so in this also imitated, that it can make an Artificial Animal*" (p. 9). These are the opening words of *Leviathan,* we already read them, and the consequences can be seen constantly and everywhere. And this human *mimesis* produces automats, machines that mimic the natural life created by God. The life of these automats, of these machines, is compared to that of clocks and watches. Why could we not say, Hobbes asks immediately afterward, that all the automata (machines or engines that move by virtue of springs and wheels, like a watch) have an artificial life? In this way, a philosophy and even a theology of *mimesis* grounds in the last analysis the most humanist and anthropologist discourse of sovereignty. So that, however difficult it remains, we must ceaselessly understand how the so-called modern humanist or anthropologist insistence on the specificity of the state or of so-called modern political sovereignty gets its irreducible originality, i.e. its artificial, conventional, if you will techno-prosthstatic nature, only by grounding itself in a profound ontotheology, or even in a religion. If you read at least chapter 8 of the first book of Bodin's *Six Books of the Republic* (1583; *Leviathan* dates from 1651), a chapter entitled "On Sovereignty" (and which begins by defining sovereignty, "absolute and perpetual power of the state" in more than one language—*majestas, majestatem* in Latin, *akran exousian, kurian arkh[ē], kurion politeuma* in Greek, *segnioria* in Italian, *tismar shabat* in Hebrew),[10] you will see that although he posits that "sovereignty

79

10. Jean Bodin, *Les Six Livres de la République* (Paris: Le Livre de Poche, 1993), book l, chap. 8, pp. 111–37. In this edition, the Greek expressions contain a number of errors. Jacques Derrida had noticed only some of them (corrected in pencil on his printout), and consequently his transliteration was not completely correct. Having verified the text in the edition of the "Corpus des oeuvres philosophiques en langue française" (in *Les Six Livres de la République: Livre premier,* ed. Catherine Frémont, Marie-Dominique Couzinet, and Henri Rochais [Paris: Fayard, 1986], p. 179), we confirm that the exact text should read: "que les Latins appellent *majestatem,* les Grecs ἄκραν ἐξουσίαν, et κυρίαν ἀρχ[ήν], et κυρίον πολίτευμα [. . .]: les Hebreux l'appellent תׁומֶך שֶרֶט." We give

is not limited, neither in power, nor in charge, nor to a certain time," and although, infinite though it be, it remains human, its *model* is divine, and the sovereign remains the *image* of God. "Model" and "image" are Bodin's words, in the conclusion of this chapter: "For if justice is the end of law, law the work of the prince, the prince the *image* of God; then by this reasoning, the law of the prince must be *modeled* on the law of God."[11] Elsewhere, in the same chapter, Bodin has remarked that "he is absolutely sovereign who recognizes nothing, after God, that is greater than himself," and again that the sovereign Prince "is answerable only to God."[12] These are also what Bodin calls, as will Hobbes, the "marks of sovereignty" and the end of the first of the *Six Books of the Republic* declares that he who usurps the marks of sovereignty must be punished by death.[13] The expression "marks of sovereignty" is common to Bodin and Hobbes, and on this subject I refer you to a fine article that Étienne Balibar published last year in a special issue of *Les Temps Modernes* devoted to sovereignty,[14] in which he recalls that the expression "marks of sovereignty" comes "no doubt" from "a whole theological and juridical history," and in passing he contests the appropriation of Bodin by Schmitt, who sees in him the first decisionist theorist of sovereignty, the first theorist of the exception that authorizes the sovereign to suspend right, that gives him the right to suspend right and place himself above the law that he embodies. I cannot get into this debate here. Balibar thinks that

80

---

the Greek transliteration on the basis of this edition. The expressions transliterated by *akran exousian, kurian arch'* and *kurion politeuma* can be translated, respectively, as "supreme power," "sovereign power," and "sovereign government," according to Georges Leroux. For the Hebrew, Derrida here gives the transliteration *tismar shabat;* further on, in the eighth session, he writes *Tismar schabet.* According to Jean-Jacques Lavoie, the retranscription of these words also involves errors, and the text cited is difficult to read because the last letter is cut off. The Hebrew expression corresponding to the Greek text is the following: *twmk shbt* (pronounced *tomek shevet*). The expression literally signifies "holding a scepter," and is rare, appearing only in Amos 1:5 and 1:8. [Translator's note: A selection from Bodin's book is available as *On Sovereignty*, ed. and trans. Julian H. Franklin (Cambridge: Cambridge University Press, 1992). The opening of book 1, chapter 8, is there translated as follows: "Sovereignty is the absolute and perpetual power of a commonwealth, which the Latins call *maiestas;* the Greeks *akra exousia, kurion arche,* and *kurion politeuma;* and the Italians *segnioria* [. . .] while the Hebrews call it *tomech shévet*—that is, the highest power of command."]

11. *On Sovereignty,* p. 45.

12. Ibid., p. 4.

13. Ibid., p. 87.

14. Étienne Balibar, "Prolégomènes à la souveraineté: la frontière, l'État, le peuple," *Les Temps Modernes,* "La souveraineté," no. 610, September–November 2000, pp. 47–75.

Bodin's whole doctrine belies this "[Schmittian] primacy of the exception." And in support of his thesis, Balibar affirms that Schmitt's interpretation amounts to "distorting the sense of Bodin's construction, which considers the state of exception precisely as an exception, the status and treatment of which depend on the constituted norm."[15]

No doubt. But does Schmitt say anything different? The exception is the exception, it must remain the exception, it is not the norm even if it appears as exception only with respect to the norm. Schmitt has not said that the exception is normal, which would be absurd, any more than sovereignty is normal, even if he has said that the exception is more interesting and decisive than the norm . . . But let's leave that there—it refers us again to the paradoxes of a philosophy or a theory of the exception (and of the sovereign decision). A *theory* of the exception, especially a juridical or political theory of the exception, is impossible qua *philosophical theory*, even if the *thought* of exception is necessary. This is perhaps the site of a difference between, on the one hand, the theoretical, science, philosophy, even the concept, and, on the other hand, what one can call, for want of a better term, thought. But it goes without saying that at the very place at which he attempts to think the exception, Schmitt, for his part, would not accept the distinction I have just proposed and would claim to remain within the order of political philosophy, of theory, and even of the concept, of conceptual generality or universality. That one cannot make the exception into a general norm, a rule, a law, or a theorem is indeed the question. But precisely, sovereignty, like the exception, like the decision, *makes the law in excepting itself from the law*, by suspending the norm and the right that it imposes, by its own force, at the very moment that it marks that suspense in the act of positing law or right. The positing or establishing of law or right are exceptional and are in themselves neither legal nor properly juridical.

Hobbes, less than a century after Bodin, would also like to save the human autonomy of the institution of state sovereignty, while basing himself on the model of divine art. He will reject the objection of a convention above the human convention, for example a convention with God. And what I would like to emphasize is that this exclusion of any convention with God will be, as it were, symmetrical with another exclusion, that of a convention with the beast. This symmetry of the two living beings that are not man, i.e. the beast and the sovereign God, both excluded from the contract, convention or covenant—this symmetry is all the more thought-provoking for the fact that one of the two poles, God, is also the model of sovereignty,

81

15. Ibid., p. 58.

but of a sovereignty, an absolute power, that would here be outside all contract and institution. God is beyond the sovereign but as the sovereign's
sovereign. Which is as much as to say that this theological model of the
Leviathan, work of human art or artifice imitating the art of God, this theological model of the political, excludes from the political everything that is
82   not proper to man, God as much as the beast, God *like* the beast. If God is
the model of sovereignty, saying "God *like* the beast" puts us again on the
same track, sniffing out everything that might attract the one to the other,
via this *like*, the sovereign and the animal, the hypersovereign that God is,
and the beast. God *e(s)t* [is/and] with or without "s," and so *with or without
being,* the beast. The beast *e(s)t* God, with or without being (one). The beast
is God *without being (one),* a God without being, according to the equivocal
syntagma I ventured a very long time ago, I no longer know where.[16]

    Let's look first at the rather awkward exclusion of the convention with
God. Hobbes strongly condemns—in a rather symptomatic, scathing tone,
I think—those who invoke such a convention with God. He does so in
chapter 18 of the *Leviathan*. This is the moment when he recalls that some
people, in order to disobey their human sovereign, and therefore the convention that commits them with respect to the sovereign, have claimed to
refer to another convention, to a "new Covenant," made this time not with
humans but with God—the moment when he recalls, basically, that some
people posit a law above the laws, a justice above right, and a sovereign
above the sovereign; and here Hobbes energetically replies: No; it is just
as "unjust" to claim that as it is to disobey the sovereign. For there is no
convention, no covenant with God. As this is difficult to say and have accepted in this form, Hobbes has to complicate things a little by distinguishing the *mediate* from the *immediate.* He basically specifies that there is no
immediate convenant with God, but only "by mediation of some body that
representeth God's person, which none doth but Gods Lieutenant," who
has sovereignty under God. "But," he adds, "this pretence of Covenant with
God, is so evident a lye, even in the pretenders own consciences, that is not
onely an act of an unjust, but also a vile, and unmanly disposition."[17]

83   This passage is rich, complex, and abyssal. It merits a highly stratified

16. See Jacques Derrida, "Comment ne pas parler: Dénégations," in *Psyché: Inventions de l'autre,* 2 vols. (Paris: Galilée, 2003), 2:150, note 1; trans. Ken Frieden as "How
to Avoid Speaking: Denials," in Jacques Derrida, *Psyche: Inventions of the Other,* 2 vols.,
ed. Peggy Kamuf and Elizabeth Rottenberg (Stanford: Stanford Unversity Press, 2008),
2:147 and note 3.

17. Hobbes, *Leviathan,* chap. 18, p. 97.

analysis. Clearly, Hobbes is very angry, very aggressive, cannot find words hard enough to describe those who in his eyes are guilty of vile lies: they are liars who know that they are lying, they are unjust, cowardly, vile, and unwholesome. Of what are they guilty in their very lie? Before coming back to this, we have to imagine that in order to be effectively and affectively so motivated, so dogged, so violent and passionate, Hobbes must have had in view risks close at hand, enemies even in the politics of his country, where he was subject and actor, as you know. What is always remarkable with the great philosophers of politics, with all philosophers when they deal with politics, is that, more than ever, their philosophemes are also, in a very marked way, those of citizens and politicians of their own time, implicated and exposed in the national political field of their time. Of course this is true of all philosophers in general when they talk about politics, from Plato to Kant, Hegel, or Heidegger. But in another way, with a stricter style of commitment, that of statutory players in politics, as it were, office-holders, politicians, it is more true still, true in another sense, of philosophers who were essentially thinkers *of the political* on the verge of modernity, of people like Machiavelli, Hobbes, and in another way Bodin, Montaigne, or Schmitt. All these people were involved, as players, in the affairs of their countries or cities; they were, in some capacity or other, at one moment or another, in politics. And we need to be attentive, especially where it is difficult to do so, to separate out the threads that tie them to the political web of their time and their nation even as they remain for us, beyond that initial web, guiding threads for a vaster problematic that, while always remaining historical and periodized, epochal, nonetheless still adapts to broader historical sequences, sometimes up to our own time. For example, why and how is it that what Bodin and Hobbes say about sovereignty, which is so essentially and internally marked by the political turbulences of their time and countries, retains nonetheless such a strong and durable conceptual relevance for the fundamental problems, the basic problems of sovereignty still today, even where the basis of sovereignty and the rigor of a logic of nation-state sovereignty are traversing a zone which is more than critical?

84

Back to Hobbes's anger. Where is the guilt of the "unjust," the "cowards," those who lie and know that they are lying when they claim to have a covenant with God himself, immediately? They are guilty of at least three things.

1. First, of lying to men. What they claim is not true and they cannot testify to it or bring human proof of it, by definition. Or at least *immediately* perceptible proof or signs of an *immediate* convention with God. Whence Hobbes's concession, we'll be coming back to it, as to a possible mediation

and a possible human "lieutenant" of God. What Hobbes refuses is the "immediate" alliance or covenant with God. So the lie is in the allegation of immediacy.

2. These cowardly unjust liars are guilty of placing a law above the laws, of authorizing themselves to disobey right and political law in the name of a transcendent law and a superhuman and metapolitical duty. They are disobedient citizens, and this can go as far as treason. They are above all people who have no respect for right, and especially for the political, in the sense of the right and politics of the human City. Today they would be conscientious objectors, partisans of civil disobedience,[18] etc., who place a law above the laws or above the constitution of the country. Or again, today, in a way that is at least *analogous*, those people who place the rights of man above the rights of the citizen or nation-state politics. They are, basically, agents of depoliticization (in Schmitt's sense), people who threaten politics as grounded in territory, nation-state, the nation-state figure of sovereignty, etc.

3. These terrible people who claim to have an immediate convention or covenant with God are like Jews, and this resemblance is accredited by the word "covenant," the term most often used to translate into English the alliance of Iahve with the nation of Israel, a "covenant" that precisely makes them into a "chosen people" receiving its law, its orders, its mission, its right and its duties, only from divine transcendence, beyond all politics or all human politico-juridical institution. Whether or not there be here on Hobbes's part a reference to the "covenant" of the "chosen people," there is little doubt that the awkward insistence on the difference between mediacy and immediacy, especially the allusion to the mediator, the one who intercedes as the (human) lieutenant of God, the one who, standing in for [*tenant lieu de*] God, representing God on earth among men, God made man, as it were, articulating a human politics, a human sovereignty, a human state in accord with God but without an immediate convention with God—there is little doubt, then, that this concept of standing in, of *lieu-tenance*, of the substitute representative of God in the earthly city of human politics and state, is there to justify or in any case leave open the possibility of a Christian foundation of politics, but a mediate, mediated foundation, not breaching, threatening, or reducing the human specificity and autonomy of the political, and therefore the human face of sovereignty and of the convention that founds it. I must insist on this point, for what is at stake is decisive. It is about nothing less than the foundation—theological or not, religious or not, Christian or

18. [Translator's note:] "Civil disobedience" is in English in the text.

not—of the concept of political sovereignty, in any case of one of the most powerful, prevalent, accredited, legitimated concepts of properly human, political and supposedly modern sovereignty.

Many expert commentators on Hobbes, or on Bodin, believe it necessary to insist on the modernity of their concept of sovereignty, insofar as it is supposed to be, precisely, emancipated from theology and religion and would supposedly have finally landed on purely human soil, as a political and not a theological concept, as a non-theologico-political concept. But things seem much more complex to me, as do the logic and rhetoric of these theorists of the political. Even though it is indeed scarcely to be contested that Hobbes, for example, does all he can to anthropologize and humanize the origin and foundation of state sovereignty (for example, by reaffirming literally and explicitly that the convention that institutes the sovereign is a convention among men and not with God), the fact remains that this anthropologization, modernization, this secularization, if you will, remains essentially attached by the skein of a double umbilical cord.

On the one hand, there is this *imitation* we were talking about just now, which, from the opening of the *Leviathan*, describes and analyzes the human institution of the state (artificial man, artificial soul, Leviathan, etc.) as copies of the work of God.

On the other hand, <there is> this logic (Christian or not) of *lieutenance* (I[19] say "Christian or not" out of prudence or respect for the implicit that must remain implicit, but the allusion to *some body*, in two words, *that represents God*, seems indeed to refer to some one who is also a body, an incarnation of God on earth, to a son of man as son of God, or to some one who, in the Bible, will have represented God. I refer you, to make this difficult point more specific, to the gripping chapter 16 of *Leviathan,* on the concept of person and personification, a chapter that puts forward three examples of the personal "representation" of a "personated" God, all three of whom speak therefore *for* God, *in the place* of God, *in the name of* God: Moses, Jesus Christ, and the Holy Spirit. In any case, this logic, be it Jewish, literally Christian or not, of the *lieu-tenance* of God, of the lieutenant as sovereign after God, clearly marks the fact that the *proper place* of the sovereign, the appropriate *topos* of the *topolitics* of this human sovereignty, is indeed that of an authority that is subject, subjected, submitted to, and underlying divine sovereignty. Be it Moses, Christ, the monarch king as Christian king or an assembly of men elected and instituted as sovereigns, their place always

86

---

19. The parenthesis opened here does not close in the typescript.

stands for the place of God [*tient lieu de Dieu*]. The (human) sovereign takes place as place-taking [*lieu-tenant*], he takes place, the place standing in for the absolute sovereign: God. The absoluteness of the human sovereign, his required and declared immortality, remains essentially divine, whatever the substitution, representation or *lieutenance* which institutes it statutorily in this place.

87   If this is really so, if my reading is not unfair, in other words if this humanistic or anthropologistic modernity of the institution of sovereignty and the state retains a profound and fundamental theological and religious basis, if the apparent exclusion of all convention with God does not contravene, to the contrary, this theologico-politics, then we could try, without any further transition, by a sudden movement, the better to attempt to understand further the architecture, the essential architectonic of this so-called modern, humanistic, and secular construction, we could try to move all in one go to the place of another exclusion. An exclusion that would not be the entirely apparent exclusion of a covenant or convention with God. What exclusion? Well, precisely, the exclusion (entirely symmetrical in its apparent asymmetry), of a convention with the beast. Earlier in *Leviathan,*[20] the two exclusions (that of the contract with God and that of the contract with "brute beasts") are, as it were, juxtaposed and consecutive, contiguous, even superimposed. This superimposition (one paragraph above the other, one immediately after the other) lays open their proximity to a stereoscopic vision, that of the relief that is properly, as is true of any relief, what remains to our seminar.[21] What remains on the table in this seminar is what remains to be thought of this metonymic contiguity between the beast and God, the beast, the sovereign and God, the human and political figure of the sovereign being right there, *between* the beast and God, the beast and God becoming in all senses of this word the *subjects* of the sovereign, the sovereign subject of the sovereign, the one who commands the human sovereign, and the subject subjected to the sovereign. These three figures replace each other, substitute for each other, standing in for each other, the one keeping watch as lieutenant or stand-in [*suppléant*] for the other along

88   this metonymic chain. Double exclusion, then, of the convention with God and the convention with the beast, but this time—and this is the point I

20. Hobbes, *Leviathan,* chap. 16, "Of the first and second Naturall Lawes, and of Contracts."

21. [Translator's note:] Playing on the French word "relief," which means relief in the sense of a relief map (whence the reference to "stereoscopic vision"), but also "remains" in the sense of leftovers.

think it important to note—the exclusion, the justification of the exclusion of the covenant with God as with the Beast invokes language, a question of language and more especially of response. If one cannot make a convention with the beast, any more than with God, it is for a reason of language. The beast does not understand our language, and God cannot respond to us, that is, cannot *make known* to us, and so we could not know in return if our convention is or is not *accepted* by him. In both cases, there could not be an exchange, shared speech, question and response, proposition and response, as any contract, convention, or covenant seems to demand. I shall say in a moment why it is important to me to insist not only on language as exchange but on this dimension and this moment of *response* or *responsibility*. Before I do that, I quote these two paragraphs from chapter 16. The second concerns the exclusion of the covenant with God, but if it is not redundant with respect to the one I have already quoted, this is precisely because of the argument he puts forward this time, that of the *acceptance* of the contract in a *response*. Here is the quotation:

> To make covenant with God, is impossible, but by Mediation of such as God speaketh to [argument of the lieutenant again, then], either by Revelation supernaturall, or by his Lieutenants that govern under him, and in his Name: For otherwise we know not whether our Covenants be accepted or not. (p. 77)

Just before, in the preceding paragraph, Hobbes had posited (and I mean *posited*, for there is something profoundly thetical and dogmatic in this gesture) that a covenant with beasts, brute beasts, is impossible. He used the same terms and the same syntax as for God at the beginning of the following paragraph ("To make covenant with God, is impossible") and here for the beast: "To make Covenant with bruit beasts is impossible." And in the argument about language, that beasts do not understand, we find again the word "accept": brute beasts could not *accept* or make known to us, any more than God could, that they *accept* a convention or enter into that mutual acceptance that a convention is. Here:

89

> To make Covenant with bruit Beasts, is impossible; because not understanding our speech, they understand not, nor *accept* of any translation of Right; nor can translate any Right to another: and without *mutuall acceptation*, there is no Covenant. (Ibid., my emphasis)

I shall not hasten to say brutally, as I in fact think, that all that is brutally false, that it is false to say that beasts in general (supposing any such thing to exist) or so-called brute beasts (what does "brute" mean?) do not understand our language, do not respond or do not enter into any convention. I shall not hasten to recall the often refined understanding that many of said beasts have of our language; nor even to recall that even if they probably don't make literal, discursive conventions with men, in our languages and with a notary public present, *on the one hand*, there are nevertheless all sorts of conventions, i.e. agreements or disagreements acquired by learning and experience (and so not innate or natural), between what one calls animals and what one calls humans (and I am not just thinking of all the relations that are organized in domestication, training (in horse riding, for example), and then taming, and then organization of territory, marking of frontiers and interdictions—we shall speak at length, later, of the political history of menageries and zoos, but there is, beyond these forms of violence, which, moreover, have their human equivalents, I mean all sorts of human zoos and menageries of which we shall speak too);[22] *and on the other hand,* conversely, no one can claim (and certainly not Hobbes) that the human conventions at the origin of states always or even most often take the form of literal, discursive and written contracts, with mutual and rational consent of the subjects concerned. As always, to stick to the schema of my recurrent and deconstructive objections to this whole traditional discourse on "the animal" (as though any such thing could exist in the general singular), one must not be content to mark the fact that what is attributed as "proper to man" also belongs to other living beings if you look more closely, but also, conversely, that what is attributed as proper to man does not belong to him in all purity and all rigor; and that one must therefore restructure the whole problematic.

So I shall not hasten to recall or announce all that today. I shall insist only on the motif of the "response" which one finds at work in the double exclusion from convention—in the case of God as well as in that of the beast. From Descartes to Lacan inclusive, from Kant to Hegel to Heidegger inclusive, thus passing through Hobbes, the most powerful, impassive, and dogmatic prejudice about the animal did not consist in saying that it does not communicate, that it does not signify, and that it has no sign at its disposal, but that it does not respond. I have tried elsewhere, in published and unpublished texts, to show in detail how this distinction between reaction and response remains dogmatic and thereby problematic.[23] In all those I have just named. I will not

90

---

22. [Translator's note:] The syntax of this parenthesis appears to be incomplete in the French text.

23. See, among other places, J. Derrida, *L'animal que donc je suis,* pp. 54, 79–80, 115–19, 125, 154; trans. Wills, pp. 32, 52–53, 81–84, 89, 112.

go back over that here. I simply remark that Hobbes is Cartesian from that point of view, that his discourse on the beast belongs to that tradition. Later, we shall read a chapter from *De Cive* in which, criticizing Aristotle, Hobbes says more about the beasts and the reasons why, in his view, animal societies do not merit the name of "civil societies."[24] And, above all, and this is more interesting for us at this point, the double exclusion we are talking about, in associating in nonconvention beast and God, but also in nonresponse, gives us to think that the sovereign's sovereign, God himself, like the beast, does not respond, that in any case we cannot be assured of his acceptance, we cannot count on his response. And that is indeed the most profound definition of absolute sovereignty, of the absolute of sovereignty, of that absoluteness that absolves it, unbinds it from all duty of reciprocity. The sovereign does not respond, he is the one who does not have to, who always has the right not to, respond [*répondre*], in particular not to be responsible for [*répondre de*] his acts. He is above the law [*le droit*] and has the right [*le droit*] to suspend the law, he does not have to respond before a representative chamber or before judges, he grants pardon or not after the law has passed. The sovereign has the right not to respond, he has the right to the silence of that dissymmetry. He has the right to a certain irresponsibility. Whence our obscure but I believe lucid affect, whence the double sentiment that assails us faced with the absolute sovereign: like God, the sovereign is above the law and above humanity, above everything, and he looks a bit stupid [*bête*], he looks like the beast, and even like the death he carries within him, like that death that Lévinas says is not nothingness, nonbeing, but nonresponse. The sovereign *like* a God, *like* a beast, or *like* death, those are the remains of a "like" that are still on our table. If sovereignty were (but I don't believe it) proper to man, it would be so much *like* this expropriating ecstasy of irresponsibility, like this place of nonresponse that is commonly and dogmatically called bestiality, divinity, or death.

At this point, and to conclude today by recalling what we have not ceased to follow, stealthy as wolves, the trace of the wolf that we shall be seeing again in January when we read La Fontaine's *The Wolf and the Lamb* after September 11, I shall be content to reconnoiter very rapidly a sort of strange genealogy of the wolf (*lukos*), a genelycological filiation, a strange genelycology, the path of a track that, from one cave to another, leads to the alliance (from north, south, east or west) between all these claimants to sovereignty who thus assemble and so resemble each other: the wolf, man, God. The one *for* the other.

I believe that we shall be better placed now to hear not only the *homo homini lupus* but better to understand the passage of God in this landscape. On the track of this common genelycology, the sovereign, the wolf, man, God, the wolf-man, God-man, God-wolf, God-the-father-the-wolf or grandmother-wolf, etc., I shall leave, as markers for next year, three quotations to be put on the stand, retracking the thread of the story of *homo homini lupus*, a syntagma that has never ceased being transferred or onto which one has never ceased transferring, with God always on the path of this transference. Three quotations only for the moment.

1. Hobbes, first, at the beginning of the *De Cive*'s Dedicatory Epistle to the Right Honorable Earl of Devonshire. After having invoked (in a demonstration I hope to read with you) the saying of Cato, who, in the name of the Roman Empire, condemned those monarchs who, he said, "are to be classed as predatory animals," Hobbes then wonders about the Roman people itself in its very imperialism: "But what sort of animal was the Roman People? By the agency of citizens who took the names *Africanus, Asiaticus, Macedonicus, Achaicus* and so on from the nations they had robbed, that people plundered nearly all the world," so that Pontius Telesinus in his combat against Sylla decided that Rome had to be demolished because, he said, "there would never be an end to *Wolves* preying upon the liberty of Italy, unless the forest in which they took refuge (one is tempted to add: like in a cave in Afghanistan) was cut down." Hobbes continues: "There are two maxims which are surely both true: *Man is a God to man,* and *Man is a wolf to Man.*"[25]

2. From Hobbes we move back in time to Montaigne (*Essays*, book 3, chapter 5, "On some verses of Virgil"). Here, it is in the course of a meditation on marriage, I would even say on the contract, the covenant, the alliance of marriage, that we see the *homo homini lupus* go past. And the fact that the occasion, the very theme here, is a certain folly of marriage is far from secondary, contingent, or accidental. We would need to follow this long paragraph as closely as possible, to the letter and the comma. Where does Montaigne situate the "good marriage," if there is such a thing, "if there be any such," as he says himself? On what side? He situates it not on the side of love but on the side of friendship. I quote: "A good marriage, if there be any such, rejects the company and conditions of love, and tries to represent those of friendship." Admire the prudence of the formulations. Everything here is in the conditional and under the sign of a tendency or a task which is assured of nothing: a good marriage, if there be any such . . . tries to represent the

25. Hobbes, *De Cive,* p. 3; *On the Citizen,* ed. Tuck and Silverthorne, p. 3.

conditions of friendship. It is not certain that it succeeds, or even that there is any marriage, but if there is, this will only be by merely *representing* the conditions of friendship, not even *being in friendship, being* mistress or female friend, but representing the conditions of friendship. And Montaigne adds: "No woman who savors it [this social life representing friendship] [quotation from Catullus here][26] would wish to stand as beloved mistress and friend to her husband. If she is lodged in his affection as a wife, she is much more honorably and securely lodged there."[27] Now at this moment in the writing there passes a first animal. A first animal crosses the text, an animal both wild and/or domestic. A bird. A "sound marriage," a precious and rare thing that we cannot do without and that we constantly decry, is like a cage from which one would like to escape when one is inside, and in which one would like to be enclosed when one is outside (and this is one of the examples of what thus lets itself be tamed—trained, broken, domesticated—here an example of that domestication we were talking about just now, domestication in the proper sense of the term, one of those conventions, both human and animal, that bend a living being to the law of the household or the family, to the *oikos* and the *domus*, to domestic economy). Conjugality, then, explains Montaigne, is like a cage from which one would like to escape when one is inside, and in which one would like to be enclosed when one is outside. He says: "It happens, as with cages, that the birds outside despair of getting in, and those inside despair of getting out." Then he quotes Socrates, who says that, in any case, whether one takes a wife or not [and you see that the question, the decision (to marry or not) is proper to man and not to woman: the question is that of knowing whether to *take a wife* or not]—Socrates who, to this question of marriage as a question of "taking a wife," replies, and this is again the double bind[28] of a bird with respect to the cage, who wants both to get in and to get out, whatever you do, you will regret it: "Whichever one does," he says, "one will repent." Which means that the man (*vir, aner*), the husband or the father, virtual head of family, the patriarch, the domestic sovereign, feels like a bird trapped in advance by the *double bind* of domestication: whether he enter or leave the house-cage, not only will he regret it, but he will be accused, he will accuse himself, of a capital fault, rather than an accident: all that will remain is to repent: "Whichever one does," he says, "one will repent." Now immediately afterward, with no further transition,

94

26. Jacques Derrida skips the quotation from Catullus that is in Montaigne's text.

27. Montaigne, "Sur des vers de Virgile," in *Essais* (Paris: Gallimard, 1950), book 3, chap. 5, p. 952. [Translator's note: My translations of Montaigne.]

28. [Translator's note:] Here and elsewhere, "double bind" is in English in the text.

as though it were simply the extension of this saying of Socrates and the appearance of the bird trapped by the cage, by the *double bind* of the domestic cage (and, in spite of appearances, the cage itself, the apparatus called "cage" is not the trap, the trap is not the cage: the trap is the double bind, this double link, this double obligation, this double injunction: enter/leave, inside/outside) [so, immediately afterward, as I was saying, with no further transition, as though he were simply adding a commentary to Socrates' saying and to the appearance of the bird trapped by the cage, by the *double bind* of the domestic cage], Montaigne lets the wolf in, into the house, as it were, if not into the menagerie or the sheepfold.[29] But the wolf in the company of man and God. And you will admire the *either/or* [*ou . . . ou*] that follows the *homo homini*: "either 'God' or 'lupus'" (*either/or, be it this, be it that*: an "or" than is undecidably either the "or" of an equivalence or else the "or" of alternative, *vel* or *aut*). And it is not insignificant that the word "contract" [*convention*] appears in the same sentence: "It [marriage] is a convention to which fits perfectly the saying 'Homo homini, either "deus," or "lupus."'"

95 And since, in Montaigne's *homo homini lupus,* the question is marriage, love or friendship, and therefore sexual differences, this is perhaps the right or appropriate moment to recall, in this genelycology, some wolves from Plato. Not merely the tyrant-wolf or wolf-tyrant from the *Republic* (8.566a), where, if you look it up, you will see the alternative between "be either slain by his enemies or become a tyrant and be transformed from a man into a wolf" (*ē tyrannein kai lykō ex anthrōpou genesthai*). But also, even more relevantly for us, the wolf and the lamb of the *Phaedrus* (241c–d), where the question of love and friendship is adapted to the desire to eat the other, to a "you really have to eat the other."[30] Read everything that precedes this passage as well: "These things, dear boy [my little one, *ō pai*], you must bear in mind, and you must know that the fondness of the lover (*tēn erstou philia*) is not a matter of goodwill, but of appetite which he wishes to satisfy: 'Just as the wolf loves

---

29. [Translator's note:] On the annotated printout of this seminar he used in the USA, Derrida has a marginal note: "*Le loup dans la bergerie*: to set the fox to mind the geese."

30. [Translator's note:] An allusion to Derrida's interview with Jean-Luc Nancy, "Il faut bien manger, ou le calcul du sujet," in *Points de suspension* (Paris: Galilée, 1992), trans. Peter Connor and Avital Ronell as "'Eating Well,' or the Calculation of the Subject," in *Points . . . : Interviews 1974–1994* (Stanford: Stanford University Press, 1995), pp. 255–87. "Il faut bien manger" means literally both "It is necessary to eat well" and "It really is necessary to eat," or "You really do have to eat."

the lamb, so the lover adores his beloved' [*ōs lykoi arnas agaposin, ōs paida philousin erastai*]."

3. Finally, the "common saying," referring to the at least supposed origin of this saying, i.e. Plautus, who was born in Sarsina, in northern Umbria—basically in a colony of Rome—and who learned Latin and came to the capital very young. I will content myself with reading and translating the two lines from the comedy *Asinaria* (we'll come back to all this next time), two lines that propose, or dare I say *prosopose,* the figure of the wolf, the face of the wolf, the mask of the wolf, onto what is most unknown in man. The wolf is, for man, man himself, but for as long as one does not know him, inasmuch as one does not know him [*tant qu'on ne le connaît pas, en tant qu'on ne le connaît pas*]. The wolf is man *tant que* and *en tant que*, during the time and to the extent that he remains unknown and therefore *does not make himself known*. The wolf is man for man to the extent that [*(en) tant que*] he exceeds all knowledge and making-known: "*Lupus est homo homini, non homo, quom qualis sit non novit.*" Literally: "Wolf [the wolf] is man for man, and not a man, when [like or as] one does not know which he is."[31] In other words, wherever man does not make known to man who or which he is, he becomes a wolf. Who or which [*qui ou quel*] (*qualis*) can also mean who or what [*qui ou quoi*].

Just as Montaigne's sentence was inscribed in a marriage-contract scene, here we must not neglect the fact that this sentence from Plautus is placed in the mouth of a merchant (*mercator*) and that we are dealing with a capitalistic market scene, a scene of lending or credit [*de créance ou de crédit*]. The merchant does not want to give credit, entrust or lend money to, someone he does not know, and who could, then, behave like a wolf. Who—or what—is the wolf? And is not the substitution of wolf for man, the substitution, for man, of the wolfman for man, the substitution of *what* for *who*?

Go figure [*Allez savoir*]. That's what the *mercator* is implying. He wants to know and he asks "go figure," because "*Lupus est homo homini, non homo, quom qualis sit non novit,*" which can be translated, as in the [French] translation I have to hand (Alfred Ernout) as "When one does not know him, man is not a man, but a wolf for man," but perhaps too, in a less convincing but grammatically possible way: "Wolf [the wolf] is a man for man, which is not a man, when one does not know him."

This grammar, the same and different, shakes up the decidable authority of the "who" and the "what" and the order of substitution. The beast—is it

96

31. Plautus, *Asinaria*, line 495.

"who" or "what"? When there is substitution, there can always be *qui pro quo*, a *who* for a *who* but also a *who* for a *what* or a *what* for a *who*.

Go figure. Will we be able to show it in a moment? Or make it known next year? In any case, we shall return to all this by different paths, of which at least one will pass via the fable, i.e. orality, an oral speech about a possible devourment, as in *The Wolf and the Lamb* by La Fontaine, which, you see, comes on the scene quite late.

There, it is quite late.

Happy New Year.

January 16, 2002

The [feminine] beast and the [masculine] sovereign. *La . . . le.*

She and he. The she-wolf and the wolf. Beware of the wolf [*gare au loup*]!

"[. . .] and I lived like a real werewolf [*loup-garou*]": that's a confession by Rousseau, at the end of the first book of his *Confessions.*[1] There are others, confessional phrases that present him, Jean-Jacques, as a wolf, as a wolf in his own eyes, as a wolf in the eyes of others, in other contexts, with other rhetorics and meanings.

But here, Rousseau describes himself as a werewolf, he represents himself, presents himself as a werewolf, that is, a wolf-man, and he does so — one might find this surprising — because of an immoderate, compulsive, raging taste for reading, for bookish culture, and for buying books. The question remains of the difference between reading and not reading, neglecting the book or not, neglecting (*neglego, neglegere*) to read. Neglect — is that not always a way of not reading or not electing [*élire*] or gathering (*legere*), the "not" (*ne, nec, neg*) carrying the whole burden of the question on negation, denegation, repression, suppression, forgetting, amnesia, etc., in a context of *legere*, reading, putting together or gathering? Rousseau stops stealing, as he approaches the age of sixteen, in order to devote himself to reading and what he calls his "love of imaginary objects." And this love of reading (*legere*), the love of the book, paradoxically, this love of imaginary objects, far from turning him toward culture and cultivated society, makes him savage, mute, silent, asocial; "savage" is his word: "my humor became taciturn, savage; my head was beginning to spoil, and I lived like a real werewolf."

98

---

1. Jean-Jacques Rousseau, *Les confessions,* vol. 1 of *Oeuvres complètes,* 5 vols., ed. Bernard Gagnebin and Marcel Raymond (Paris: Gallimard, 1959–95), p. 40. [Translator's note:] Unless otherwise indicated, translations from Rousseau are my own.

(I felt the desire to consult an English translation of this passage.[2] And, marvelously for us, "loup-garou" [werewolf] is translated as "outlaw." A little like *rogue*, isn't it: *voyou*, unsociable, outside the law. "I lived like an outlaw . . ." for "je vivais en vrai loup-garou." So the werewolf, the "true" werewolf, is indeed the one who, like the beast or the sovereign, places himself or finds himself placed "outside the law," *outlaw* [Eng.], above or at a distance from the normal regime of law and right.)

So: let's not forget, let's not neglect the wolves, from one year to the next.

Never forget the he- and the she-wolves: Does that mean do not hunt them? Or not suppress them? Or not repress them? Or not neglect them? And if to forget, suppress, repress, neglect, with or without negation, disavowal or denial, is in a certain way to chase (away), is chasing to expel, exclude, flee, neglect, or else, on the contrary, to follow, pursue, persecute, track down, run after?

So we still need to know how to deal with the wolf. And to know what kind of chase we're dealing with, in what we have called our genealogy of the wolf, our book of wolves, our genelycology. A genelycology that must inscribe in its tree, its genealogical tree, what is called the lycanthrope, the wolf-man, man made wolf or wolf made man.

When one associates the wolf with the tree, there immediately arises the dream of Freud's Wolf Man,[3] the *Wolf Mann* who recounts how he saw, in a dream, sitting in a tree, a big walnut tree, six or seven white wolves who, let's not forget, also resembled other animals, foxes, he said — and there are foxes waiting for us today — or sheepdogs, because they had big tails *like* (*like*, always the analogy!) foxes, and ears pricked *like* (*like!*) dogs. So there is a whole menagerie, a whole zoological crowd that does more than swarm, that is meaningfully organized in the Wolf Man's dream. Other animals will come up in the analysis, for example, the wasp and the butterfly. And the Wolf Man immediately admits his fear of being devoured by the wolf: it is this terror, this terrorism of wolves, that wakes him up by making him cry out. He refers himself, to account for his associations, to a book, precisely, a book that Freud does not neglect in his interpretation, namely the illustration of a fable or a narrative, "Little Red Riding Hood." To explain the figure of six or seven wolves, Freud has him be more specific with refer-

2. Jean-Jacques Rousseau, *The Confessions*, trans. J. M. Cohen (London: Penguin Classics, 1953), p. 47.

3. Sigmund Freud, "From the History of an Infantile Neurosis," in *The Standard Edition*, 17:7–122.

ence to another book not to be neglected, another fairy tale, "The Wolf and the Seven Little Kids." Freud sees in the wolf, without hesitation, as you know, a substitute for the castrating father, the more so in that the father often said in jest to the Wolf Man as a child, "I'm going to eat you." Later in the analysis, the mother becomes just as much a wolf, if not a she-wolf, as the father. All the ancestors of the Wolf Man are, then, present in the genealogical tree, in the feminine and in the masculine, in the positions of beast and sovereign, beast and master, the more so in that in the interval we encounter a master-wolf, Wolf being the name of the child's Latin master at school. We shall also be coming back to this question of the schoolmaster today. But I leave you to reread the *Wolf Man,* which I abandon here, for in this genelycological tree, in this library of wolves, what we shall in the end be interested in today is not so much the "Wolf Man" as the wolf-man, the lycanthrope, the becoming-man of the wolf and the becoming-wolf of the man. For example, the werewolf.

It is this metaphor or rather this analogical metamorphosis, this fantastical production, that is important to us in the political entrance we are seeking, in the political access or approach to what can play the role of a mediating schema between the beast and the sovereign. In the political or zooanthropological field. The zooanthropological, rather than the biopolitical, is our problematic horizon.

The [feminine] beast and the [masculine] sovereign. *La . . . le.*

In previous sessions, we paid some attention to a double oscillation. A double vacillation too seemed to give its rhythm to something like the pendulum of this title, of the simple statement or rather the oral saying of this text. In French, in the French tongue, and I insist on the tongue and the genders it imposes on us. La *bête et* le *souverain. La . . . le.* And as for orality, between mouth and maw, we have already seen its double carry [*portée*], the double tongue, the carry of the tongue that speaks, carry as the carry of the voice that *vociferates* (to voci-ferate is to *carry* the *voice*) and the other carry, the other devouring one, the *voracious carry* of the maw and the teeth that lacerate and cut to pieces. Vociferation and devourment, we were saying, but let us not hasten to attribute speech to the mouth of man supposed to speak and voracity or even the vociferation of the cry to the animal's maw. It is precisely this simple and dogmatic opposition, the abuses of this oversimplification that we have in our sights here.

We had, then, started to give some weight to an oscillation, a vacillation come in a not quite fortuitous way to affect the pendulum of the title thus pronounced, in the French tongue: *La* bête et *le* souverain. *La . . . le.* This oscillating or vacillating rhythm is imprinted on each of its words, the articles (*la, le*), the nouns or substantives (*bête, souverain*), the verb, the copula or the conjunction (*et, e[s]t*). And as I have just noted, the suspension of this pendulum is double.

On the one hand, first oscillation, the sexual difference marked at least by French grammar (*la . . . le*), which seemed by chance (as we illustrated with more than one fact and more than one text) to confirm that the beast was often the living thing to be subjected, dominated, domesticated, mastered, like, by a not insignificant analogy, the woman, the slave, or the child. Remember the Hobbes texts we read on this subject, on the subject of the right over beasts, in the *De Cive.* And the sexual difference that seemed also to confirm (as we illustrated with more than one fact and more than one text) that the sovereign appeared most often in the masculine figure of the king, the master, the chief, the *paterfamilias,* or the husband — of the *ipseity* of the *ipse*, concerning which a few years ago, reading Benveniste, we had emphasized that, in its very etymology,[4] it implies the exercise of power by someone it suffices to designate as *himself, ipse.* The sovereign, in the broadest sense of the term, is he who has the right and the strength to be and be recognized as *himself, the same, properly the same as himself.* Benveniste, to whom I refer you, goes on to wonder about the filiation of *poti,* Sanskrit *patyate,* Latin *potior* (to have power over something, to have at one's disposal, to possess, *potsedere*): "The notion of 'power' [. . .] is then constituted and it receives its verbal form from the predicative expression *pote est* contracted into *potest* which engenders the conjugation *possum, potest,* 'I am capable, I can.'"[5] Now, and I insist on this point, for we will not cease to measure its consequences, Benveniste had inscribed the value of ipseity, the *ipse*, the "oneself," the "him(one)self" in the same filiation, as though power were first of all recognized in the one who could be designated or who could be the first to designate himself as *the same, a himself, a oneself.* We commented a few years back on these lines of Benveniste, who is surprised that a word meaning "master" (as he had shown a page earlier: *potis*, in Sanskrit *patih* (master and husband), in Greek *posis* (husband), in composition *despotēs*) should become so enfeebled (Benveniste's word and evaluation, but I do not believe one can speak here of enfeeblement, of loss of power — to the contrary) as to signify "himself." On the other hand, Benveniste un-

101

102

---

4. Émile Benveniste, article "Hospitalité," in *Le vocabulaire des institutions européennes,* 2 vols. (Paris: Éditions de Minuit, 1969), 1:88–91.

5. Ibid., p. 91.

derstands better that a word signifying "himself" could have taken on the proper sense <of> "master." In spoken Latin, Plautus, as Benveniste recalls (and let us not forget, let us never forget the wolves in our genelycology, let us not forget that, be this a coincidence or not, Plautus is the author of *Asinaria* concerning which I recalled last time, during our wolf-hunt, that it contained the first occurrence of *Lupus est homo homini, non homo, quom qualis sit non novit*) — Plautus, then, uses the word *ipsissimus* (the *absolutely himself*) to designate the master, the boss, the most important personage, in short the first, the *princeps* or the prince. In short, the sovereign. In Russian, *sam* (himself) names the lord. Among the Pythagoreans, the master Pythagoras was designated as *autos, autos epha*: he said it himself, i.e. the master said. "In Danish *han sjølv, 'er selbst,'* has the same meaning." The master (and what is said of the master is easily transferable to the first of all, the prince, the sovereign), the master is he who is said to be, and who can say "himself" to be, the (self-)same, "myself."

The concept of sovereignty will always imply the possibility of this positionality, this thesis, this self-thesis, this autoposition of him who posits or posits himself as *ipse, the (self-)same, oneself.* And that will be just as much the case for all the "firsts," for the sovereign as princely person, the monarch or the emperor or the dictator, as for the people in a democracy, or even for the citizen-subject in the exercise of his sovereign liberty (for example, when he votes or places his secret ballot in the box, sovereignly). In sum, wherever there is a decision worthy of the name, in the classical sense of the term. Dictatorship (and in a minimal and strict sense sovereignty is always a moment of dictatorship, even if one does not live in a so-called dictatorial regime) is always the essence of sovereignty, where it is linked to the power to say in the form of dictation, prescription, order or *diktat*. From the Roman *dictatura,* where the *dictator* is the supreme and extraordinary magistrate, sometimes the first magistrate, and so the master of certain cities, to modern forms of dictatorship such as *Führer* or *Duce* or the Little Father of the People or some other "papadoc,"[6] but also in the figure of the dictatorship of the proletariat, in dictatorship in general as power that exercises itself unconditionally in the form of the *Diktat*, of the ultimate saying or the performative verdict that gives orders and has no account to render other than to itself (*ipse*), and not to any superior agency, especially not a parliament — well, that dictatorship, that dictatorial agency, is at work everywhere, wherever there is sovereignty.

6. [Translator's note:] Derrida is here referring to François "Papa Doc" Duvalier (1904–71), the notorious dictatorial president of Haiti from 1957 until his death.

Benveniste continues, defining without using the word *sovereignty* itself, precisely as authority of the *ipse*, of the same, of the properly oneself—and this is why I am insisting on it here and will often use the value and word *ipseity* in this sense, with all its implications [Benveniste continues then, and every word counts]:

> For an adjective that means "oneself" to become amplified to the sense of "master," one condition is necessary: a closed circle of people, subordinated to a central personage who takes on the personality and complete identity of the group to the point of summing it up himself; by himself, he embodies it.
>
> This is exactly what happens in the compound *dem-pot(i)-* [skr.], "master of the house." The role of the personage thus named is not to exercise command, but to take on a representation that gives him authority over the family group, with which he is identified.[7]

104 Apart from sexual difference, the article, *la, le, la bête, le souverain,* clearly marks that we are dealing with common nouns, substantives, and not adjectives or attributes. The distinction is the more critical in that it recalls two obvious things, linked to the idiomatic use of the French language. It is never said of the beast that it is *bête* [stupid] or *bestial.* The adjective, epithet, attribute *bête,* or "bestial" are never appropriate for animal or beast. *Bêtise* is proper to man (or even to the sovereign qua man). Later we shall look closely at a text of Deleuze from *Difference and Repetition,* on this subject (*bêtise* as proper to man).

We shall look at this text of Deleuze, as well as the fine, great book that Avital Ronell has just devoted to *bêtise,* i.e. *Stupidity.*[8] For Deleuze, naturally you should also read the very rich chapter in *Mille plateaux*[9] entitled "1730—Becoming-Intense, Becoming-Animal, Becoming-Imperceptible..." You will find there not only references to the wolf-man, the Wolf Man that the wolves look at, the werewolf (pp. 303 and 323 [249 and 264]) and the phenomenon of wolf-children (p. 335 [273]), the becoming-whale of Ahab in *Moby Dick* (p. 374 [306]). You will also find, among a thousand plateaus

7. Benveniste, "Hospitalité," p. 91.

8. Avital Ronell, *Stupidity* (Urbana: University of Illinois Press, 2002).

9. Gilles Deleuze and Félix Guattari, *Mille plateaux* (Paris: Minuit, 1980), chap. 10; trans. Brian Massumi as *A Thousand Plateaus* (Minneapolis: University of Minnesota Press, 1987). [Translator's note:] I have benefited from consulting Massumi's translation, but have retranslated the passages from *Mille plateaux* in the interests of literality and consistency with Derrida's commentary.

and a thousand other things, the question of taxonomy that will interest us here, the question of the classification of animal figures. In passing, Deleuze makes fun of psychoanalysis when it talks about animals, makes fun as he often does, sometimes a little hastily, and not only does he make fun of it but he says, which is even funnier, that the animals themselves make fun of it. This is on pages 294–95 [240–41] of *Mille plateaux:*

> We would even have to distinguish three sorts of animals: individuated animals, familiar and familial, sentimental, Oedipal animals, part of our little story, "my" cat, "my" dog; they invite us to regress, they draw us into narcissistic contemplation, and psychoanalysis understands only these animals, the better to discover underneath the image of a Daddy, a Mommy, a little brother (when psychoanalysis talks about animals, the animals learn to laugh); *all the people who love cats and dogs are idiots* [*des cons*]. And then there would be a second sort, animals with character or attribute, animals of genus, classification, or state, the way the great divine myths treat them, to extract from them series or structures, archetypes or models (Jung is more profound than Freud, though). Finally, there would be more demoniacal animals, with packs and affects, and who produce multiplicity, becoming, population, fairy tale . . . Or else, once more, is it not all animals that can be treated these three ways? There will always be the possibility that any animal, louse, cheetah, or elephant, be treated as a familiar animal, my little animal. And, at the other extreme, any animal can also be treated after the manner of pack and swarming, which suits us sorcerers better. Even the cat, even the dog . . . And if the shepherd or the leader of the pack, the devil have his favorite animal in the pack, this is certainly not in the same way as just now. Yes, any animal is or can be a pack, but with varying degrees of vocation for it, which makes it more or less easy to discover the multiplicity, the tenor in multiplicity, that it contains actually or virtually in each case. Banks, bands, flocks, populations are not inferior social forms, they are affects and potentials, involutions, which catch up all animals in a becoming that is no less powerful than that of man with animal.

105

And of course the question that will traverse this whole seminar, whether it be itself present and pressing, itself, explicitly, in person, or indirectly, will always be that of the "proper to man." And, moreover, bestiality, characterized *either* as perversion or sexual deviancy, zoophilia that pushes people to make love with beasts or to make love to beasts, *or* as cruelty—this bestiality, this double bestiality (zoophilic or cruel) would also be proper to man. And later we shall look closely at a text of Lacan's on this subject (bestial cruelty as proper to man).

106   *On the other hand,* second oscillation, between conjunction and copula, the *et* which can just as well, in two letters, *e, t,* juxtapose, compare, or even oppose beast and sovereign, but which can just as well, in three letters, *e, s, t,* couple in a thousand different ways the being-beast and the being-sovereign, couple them across a copula, *is,* which describes an affinity through an analogy of proportion, attraction or reciprocal fascination. Or even, as we shall come to confirm today, a predisposition to grafting, composition of mixtures, figures participating in both at once, beast and (sovereign) man, beast and man coupling in the sovereign. For the prosthesis, as graft, is not only what gives rise to the figure of the sovereign state as Leviathan, i.e. says Hobbes, an artificial animal, an animal-machine, what last time I was calling prosthstatics. Prosthesis as graft: that can be a composition or mix of the human beast. This will be one of paths for exploring the analogy and common destiny of beast and sovereign. For example, we shall come to this in a moment, let us never forget the wolves and the werewolf. Not the Wolf Man, but the wolf-man, as werewolf. The beast is the sovereign who is the beast, both sharing (we paid some attention to this) a being outside-the-law, above or at a distance from the laws.

One of the many nodal tensions that we shall have, if not to unknot, at least to reconnoiter in as strict and tight a way as possible, is that if sovereignty is, indeed, defined as the proper of man (in the sense of artifice, law, conventionality, contract, as we had recognized them in Bodin and Hobbes, and even if a theological grounding—we also took this complication into account—continued deep down to legitimate this humanity, this anthropological and supposedly secular dimension of sovereignty), [if sovereignty is, indeed, defined as the proper of man] it is nonetheless also in the name of man, the humanity of man, the dignity of man, therefore a certain proper of man, that a certain modernity has begun to question, to undermine, to put into crisis nation-state sovereignty. Every time one refers to the universal-
107   ity of human rights (beyond the rights of man and citizen), every time one invokes the recent concept (1945) of crime against humanity or genocide, in order to implement an international right or even an international penal tribunal, or even humanitarian actions the initiative for which is taken by NGOs (nongovernmental organizations), every time one militates for the *universal* abolition of the death penalty, etc., then one is calling into question the principle and the authority of the sovereignty of the nation-state, and doing so in the name of man, the right of man, the proper of man. It is in the name of a certain proper of man, which sometimes remains, so I believe, completely to be thought, merely *promised* to a thought which does not yet think what it thinks it thinks and that the *doxa* accredits with

a firmness matched only by its naïveté, it is in the name of a certain supposed proper of man, of the humanity of man, that one limits, delimits, and
circumscribes, even beats back, combats, and denounces the sovereignty
of the nation-state. I'm careful to say the sovereignty of the state and the
nation-state, for the humanity of man or of the human person invoked by
human rights or the concept of crime against humanity, by international
right or the international penal agencies — all these agencies might well be
invoking another sovereignty, the sovereignty of man himself, of the very
being of man himself (*ipse, ipsissimus*) above and beyond and before state or
nation-state sovereignty.

It is, moreover, let it be said in passing, this invocation of the human, the
humanitarian, or even of human rights — above the state — that Schmitt
holds to be de-politicizing, to be responsible for the modern neutralization
of the political or for depoliticization (*Entpolitisierung*). In truth, and this is
why I say "invocation" of the human or the humanitarian above the interest
of the state, Schmitt believes he can always discern in this humanistic and
humanitarian discourse a ruse of war, a strategic ruse put to work by a state
struggling for hegemony, the ruse of a wolf, a werewolf, if not of a fox (let us
never forget the wolves and the foxes). Depoliticization, the move beyond
state sovereignty would on this view be a piece of hypocrisy in the service   *108*
of a sovereignty, of a determinate nation-state hegemony. Schmitt, in the
1930s, is not yet speaking of "globalization [*mondialisation*: worldwidiza-
tion]," but this is clearly what he has in view in his critique of the premises
of a new international right, a Society of nations, etc. The world of globalization would then be a stratagem, a false concept or a concept forged in order to pass off some particular interest as a worldwide or universal interest,
pass off the interest of one nation-state or a restricted group of nation-states
as the world, as the universal interest of humanity in general, as the interest
of the proper of man in general. After having asserted that "humanity as
such [*Die Menschheit als solche*] cannot wage war because it has no enemy,
at least on this planet [comment on this last detail]. The concept of humanity excludes the concept of the enemy, because the enemy does not cease
to be human being — and hence there is no specific differentiation in that
concept"[10] — after having asserted this, i.e. that the concept of humanity
cannot be a political concept or the basis for a politics, Schmitt goes on to try
to show that *in fact*, wherever this concept is put forward in the pursuit of
war (and there would be so many examples today), it is a lying rhetoric, an
ideological disguise tending to mask and smuggle in nation-state interests,

10. Carl Schmitt, *The Concept of the Political* (see session 1 above, n. 40), p. 54.

and therefore those of a determinate sovereignty. Humanity is only a word, then, a name in the name of which particular and momentary interests of particular states are being served:

> That wars are waged in the name of humanity [*im Namen der Menschheit,* Schmitt continues] is not a contradiction [*Widerlegung*] of this simple truth; quite the contrary, it has an especially intensive political meaning [a more intense political meaning, an intensification of the political meaning, *einen besonders intensiven politischen Sinn:* in other words, today, all the combats in the name of the rights of man, supposedly above nation-state sovereignties, would not be a true depoliticization but a marked intensification of the state-political in the service of determinate interests]. When a state fights its political enemy in the name of humanity, it is not war for the sake of humanity, but a war wherein a particular state [a determinate state, *ein bestimmter Staat*] seeks to usurp a universal concept [*einen universalen Begriff zu okkupieren sucht*] against its military opponent. At the expense of its opponent, it tries to identify itself with humanity in the same way as one can misuse peace, justice, progress, and civilization in order to claim these as one's own and to deny the same to the enemy.
>
> The "concept of humanity" is an especially useful ideological instrument of imperialist expansion [*"Menschheit"* — in quotes — *ist ein besonders brauchbares ideologisches Instrument imperialistischer Expansionen*], and in its ethical-humanitarian form [*und in ihrer ethisch-humanitären Form*] it is a specific vehicle of economic imperialism. Here one is reminded of a somewhat modified expression of Proudhon's: whoever invokes humanity wants to cheat. To confiscate the word humanity, to invoke and monopolize such a term [*solche erhabenen Namen:* such a sublime term; the "sublime" goes missing in the English translation (tr.)] probably has certain incalculable effects [*nur den schrecklichen Anspruch manifestieren:* literally, "can only be the sign of the terrifying demand"], such as denying the enemy the quality of being human [*die Qualität des Menschen*] and declaring him to be an outlaw of humanity [*hors la loi* and *hors l'humanité* appear in French in Schmitt's text]; and a war can thereby be driven to the most extreme inhumanity [*zur äussersten Unmenschlichkeit*]. But besides this highly political utilization of the nonpolitical term humanity [*Aber abgesehen, von dieser hochpolitischen Verwertbarkeit des unpolitischen Namens der Menschheit,* I repeat and retranslate: with the exception of the highly political instrumentalization, utilization of the apolitical or nonpolitical name humanity], there are no wars of humanity as such. Humanity is not a political concept [*Menschheit ist kein politischer Begriff*], and no political entity nor society and no status [*Status:* status and state?] corresponds to it. The eighteenth-century humanitarian concept of humanity [*der humanitäre Menschheitbegriff*] was a polemical denial [one ought to say a polemical denegation, *eine polemische*

109

110

Verneinung] of the then existing aristocratic-feudal system and the privileges accompanying it.[11]

Read what follows, on this supposed natural and universal right that is in fact an "ideal social construction" (*soziale Idealkonstuktion*) . . .

What must be noticed in this Schmittian logic — whether or not we subscribe to it — what we must note from our point of view here is first of all this series of gestures (at least three), whereby:

1. Schmitt announces or denounces the nonpolitical nature of the concept of humanity or the humanitarian, of humanitarianism (Universal Declaration of Human Rights beyond the state, etc.).
2. Schmitt announces or denounces, under this apparent nonpoliticality, a self-interested hyperpoliticity, a disguised intensification of political interests of an imperialist and especially economical form.
3. (and this is what will matter most to us), Schmitt announces and denounces what is terrifying (*schrecklich*) and even terrorizing in this pretension, in this hyperstrategic, hyperpolitical hypocrisy, in this cunning intensification of the political. What is terrifying, according to him, what is to be feared or dreaded, what is *schrecklich*, scary, what inspires terror, because it acts through fear and terror, is that this humanitarian pretension, when it goes off to war, treats its enemies as "hors la loi [outside the law]" and "hors l'humanité [outside humanity]" (in French in Schmitt's text), i.e. like beasts: in the name of the human, of human rights and humanitarianism, other men are then treated like beasts, and consequently one becomes oneself inhuman, cruel, and bestial. One becomes stupid [*bête*], bestial and cruel, fearsome, doing everything to inspire fear, one begins to take on the features of the most fearsome werewolf (let's not forget the wolves), because one is claiming to be human and worthy of the dignity [*digne de la dignité*] of man. Nothing, on this view, would be less human than this imperialism which, acting in the name of human rights and the humanity of man, excludes men and humanity and imposes on men inhuman treatments. Treats them like beasts.

One sees here at work, itself in an equivocal — one could even say hypocritical — way, a Schmittian discourse which plays on two registers. *On the one hand*, Schmitt does not hesitate to take on a concept of the political that must be dissociated from every other dimension, not only economic but ethical: the political presupposes the enemy, the possibility of war, the evil

111

11. Ibid., pp. 54–55.

nature of man (remember, the only great theorists of the political are for him theorists who are pessimistic about mankind), and in the tradition of Hobbes, this theory of politics implies the evil tendencies of a man who is essentially afraid and who asks the state to protect him (remember: *protego ergo obligo*); but *on the other hand*, as if there were a good fear and a bad fear, just as he is admitting that fear or terror are the normal and essential mainsprings of politics, of a politics that cannot be reduced to ethics and does not obey ethics, [*on the other hand*, then,] Schmitt does not hesitate to denounce as fearsome or terrible (*schrecklich*) humanitarian gestures that claim to go beyond sovereignty in the name of man and treat enemies as outlaws outside humanity, therefore as non-men, like beasts. Werewolves against werewolves. What is fearsome is not only treating men as beasts, but the hypocrisy of an imperialism that gives itself the alibi of universal humanitarianism (therefore beyond the sovereignty of a nation-state) in order *in fact* to protect or extend the powers of a particular nation-state. Two things are *schrecklich:* on the one hand, treating men as non-men, and on the other, the hypocrisy of the humanistic or humanitarian allegation or alibi. The moral and juridical evaluation (which is in the end very humanistic, more humanistic than it admits, whence Schmitt's hypocrisy too), the evaluation, the moral axiomatics, that surreptitiously underlies all of Schmitt's equivocal discourse on the political—this moral and juridical position is indeed ruled by an imperative: even in warfare and in the violence of the relation to the enemy, European right must be respected, beginning with the law of war; the absolute enemy must be treated without hatred, political hostility is not hatred as a psychological passion, war must be *declared* from state to state, sincerely declared, the rights of war must be loyally respected, and must oppose armies and not terrorist partisans attacking civilian populations, etc. At bottom, when a hypocritical imperialism combats its enemies in the name of human rights and treats its enemies like beasts, like non-men, or like outlaws, like werewolves, it is waging not a war but what would today be called a state terrorism that does not speak its name. It is itself behaving like a werewolf. We shall see later whether and to what extent Schmitt is still Machiavellian, as he often seems to claim, or whether he is not betraying a certain Machiavelli. (It will again be a question, let's not forget, of wolves and a few other beasts.)

So I recommend that you read, then, at least the whole of chapter 6 of the *Concept of the Political*, on the *Entpolitisierung* (the depoliticization), on the "dishonest fiction" (*unehrliche Fiktion*) of a universal peace without states, on universality as total depoliticization and renunciation of the state. It goes without saying that, while taking this argumentation of Schmitt's seriously,

112

but without subscribing to it through and through, what I am seeking, elsewhere but in particular in this seminar, is a prudent deconstruction of this logic and of the dominant, classical concept of nation-state sovereignty (which is Schmitt's reference), without ending up with a depoliticization, a neutralization of the political (*Entpolitisierung*), but with another politicization, a repoliticization that does not fall into the same ruts of "dishonest fiction"—while what an "honest fiction" can be, and on which concept of fiction one is relying, remains to be found out. For here we find again the basically humanistic moralism and the surreptitious evaluations of Schmitt: as just now, for a fright that is good here but to be condemned there, we have here a reference to a dishonest and dishonorable fiction (*unehrliche Fiktion*) that it is difficult to see in the name of what Schmitt can in this way disqualify, discredit, or denounce with horror or contempt—it is difficult to see, in the name of what he can condemn, cunning, hypocrisy, and denial when they becomes arms of war, a war that does not speak its name. Schmitt's implicit but unavowed axiomatic is that a war should speak its name, and that one must always say and sign one's name, that an imperialism should present itself as such, that war should be declared, that states and sovereigns should be sincere and that honor (*Ehre*, glory, good reputation founded on loyalty, as opposed to an *unehrliche Fiktion*, the lie of a disloyal fiction), that this honor remains a secure value: having said that, at the very moment when Schmitt is denouncing dishonest fiction and hypocritical ruse, he is aiming to show that imperialist states with a human or humanitarian face are still in the order of the political, are still doing politics in the service of their state interests, and as that confirms Schmitt's thesis, well, it's fair enough [*de bonne guerre*], etc. [It goes without saying, I was saying,] that all the while taking into account a certain, limited, relevance of this argumentation of Schmitt's, to which I never subscribe unconditionally, in particular for reasons I have just given and others that I have given elsewhere, in *Politics of Friendship*,[12] what I am looking for would be, then, a *slow and differentiated* deconstruction of this logic and the dominant, classic concept of nation-state sovereignty (which is a reference for Schmitt), without ending up with a de-politicization, but an other politicization, a re-politicization that does not fall into the same ruts of the "dishonest fiction," without ending up, then, in a de-politicization but another politicization, a re-politicization and therefore another concept of the political. It is all too

113

12. Jacques Derrida, *Politiques de l'amitié* (Paris: Galilée, 1994), p. 102, note 1 and passim; trans. George Collins as *Politics of Friendship* (London: Verso Books, 1997), pp. 107–8.

obvious that this is more than difficult, and that's why we are working, why we are working at it and allowing ourselves to be worked on by it.

When I say "slow and differentiated deconstruction," what do I mean by that? First, that the rhythm of this deconstruction cannot be that of a seminar or a discourse ex cathedra. This rhythm is first of all the rhythm of what is happening in the world. This deconstruction is what is happening, as I often say, and what is happening today in the world — through crises, wars, phenomena of so-called national and international terrorism, massacres that are declared or not, the transformation of the global market and of international law — what is happening is so many events that are affecting the classical concept of sovereignty and making trouble for it. In this seminar, we are only beginning to reflect on, and take into account, as consequentially as we can, *what is happening*. On the other hand, as we are already realizing — and this is why I say "slow" but especially "differentiated," it cannot be a matter, under the pretext of deconstruction, of purely and simply, frontally, opposing sovereignty. There is not SOVEREIGNTY or THE sovereign. There is not THE beast and THE sovereign. There are different and sometimes antagonistic forms of sovereignty, and it is always in the name of one that one attacks another: for example (we were alluding to this earlier), it is in the name of a sovereignty of man, or even of the personal subject, of his autonomy (for autonomy and liberty are also sovereignty, and one cannot without warning and without threatening by the same token all liberty, purely and simply attack the motifs or the rallying cries of independence, autonomy, and even nation-state sovereignty, in the name of which some weak peoples are struggling against the colonial and imperial hegemony of more powerful states).[13]

In a certain sense, there is no contrary of sovereignty, even if there are things other than sovereignty. Even in politics (and the question remains of knowing if the concept of sovereignty is political through and through) — even in politics, the choice is not between sovereignty and nonsovereignty, but among several forms of partings, partitions, divisions, conditions that come along to broach a sovereignty that is always supposed to be indivisible and unconditional. Whence the difficulty, awkwardness, aporia even, and the slowness, the always unequal development of such a deconstruction. This is less than ever the equivalent of a destruction. But recognizing that sovereignty is divisible, that it divides and partitions, even where there is any sovereignty left, is already to begin to deconstruct a pure concept of sovereignty that presupposes indivisibility. A divisible sover-

---

13. [Translator's note:] This sentence is possibly incomplete in the French text.

eignty is no longer a sovereignty, a sovereignty worthy of the name, i.e. pure and unconditional.

Whether or not one agrees with these propositions of Schmitt's, one can understand why, even though they come from a right-wing Catholic who was more than compromised a few years later with Nazism and anti-Semitism, they should have seduced, and still today retain their power of seduction on the Left for all those who are ready at least to share this vigilance with respect to "humanistic" and "humanitarian" ruses and allegations, which constitute the rhetorical weapon but also the weapon pure and simple, and sometimes a hugely murderous weapon, of new political or economical imperialisms. This argument of Schmitt's, and this is all I want to retain from it for now, is that there is no politics, no politicity of the political without affirmation of sovereignty, that the privileged if not unique form of that sovereignty is the state, state sovereignty, and that such a political sovereignty in the form of the state presupposes the determination of an enemy; and this determination of the enemy can in no case take place, by definition, in the name of humanity. The concept of this sovereignty which never goes without an enemy, which needs the enemy to be what it is, is not necessarily linked or limited to such or such a state structure (monarchical, oligarchical, democratic, or republican). Even when the sovereign is the people or the nation, this does not damage the law, structure, or vocation of sovereignty, as Schmitt defines it (the positing of an enemy without humanist or humanitarian invocation; the right to exception; the right to suspend right; the right to be outside the law).

This is why Schmitt will have quoted, before the passage I just read, an eloquent declaration in this respect by the Committee for Public Safety, in 1793. This declaration, quoted by Schmitt, is first quoted by Ernst Friesenhahn <in> *Der politische Eid* (The Political Oath). (I recall this title to reinscribe this statement in a logic of the oath that makes of the affirmation of sovereignty a performative, a commitment, an act of sworn faith, of war declared against a sworn enemy: sovereignty is a *posited law*, a thesis or a prosthesis, and not a natural given, it is the sworn institution—a faith sworn, and therefore structurally fictional, figural, invented, conventional, as Hobbes clearly shows, moreover—the institution of a law that was never found in nature; but precisely the question then returns of the link between this right, the force of law and force *tout court*, the disposition of force *tout court*, of a force that makes right, of a reason of the strongest which is or is not the best; but I emphasize this reference to oath and fidelity to sworn faith to announce a detour that we shall need to make in a moment, toward Machiavelli's *Prince* and his wolf—that we must not forget). Now this Dec-

116

laration of the Committee on Public Safety, twice quoted by Friesenhahn
and by Schmitt, says:

> Since the French people manifested its will [so, by this manifestation of a
> will, the French people posited itself *as the French people* and as its own sov-
> ereign], everything that is opposed to it is outside the sovereign; everything
> that is outside the sovereign is an enemy.... Between the people and its
> enemies there is nothing left in common but the sword.[14]

Which is what is called sworn faith, and sworn enemy.

Pack [*meute*] of wolves. For a first reconnaissance of these territories, you
remember, we had begun to *ameuter* (to whip up, literally to raise, to put in
motion, *motus*), to whip up, if not to hunt, not dogs but wolves. Never forget the wolves, all the wolves. Many wolves will have crossed the room. You
have understood that all of that was, among other things, a way of preparing us, of advancing us, stealthy as wolves, toward this fable of La Fontaine,
The Wolf and the Lamb, which begins, as we ourselves began, with

> The reason of the strongest is always the best
> As we shall shortly show.

117   We began thus, saying also that no seminar should begin that way, like a
fable, nor should it recommend or command that one begin that way, by
"we shall shortly show."

Show — what? Well, that "the reason of the strongest is always the best."
A violently tautological proposition, then, pragmatically tautological (in La
Fontaine and here too, as though this still remained, as a seminar, a fable
or an affabulation) since I am here using, by force of law, taking into account my accredited position as a professor authorized to speak ex cathedra
for hours, weeks, and years (accredited by a convention or by a fiction the
honesty of which remains to be proved, by you or by me, and even then an
always revisable and renewable consensus gives force of law to the force of
law), a violently tautological proposition, then, pragmatically tautological,
for if "we shall shortly show," what are we going to show, with La Fontaine? Well, that the reason of the strongest is always the best. As the reason
of the strongest is always the best, I authorize myself by the reason of the
strongest (that I am here, by situation, by hetero- and autoposition) to defer
the moment at which I shall show or demonstrate that the reason of the

---

14. [Translator's note:] This passage is omitted from the English translation of
Schmitt's book: I have translated from the text as given by Derrida.

strongest is always the best; but in fact, I've already shown it, already shown it in fact by the very fact of deferring, authorizing myself to defer, I've already demonstrated this prevalence of fact over right. My demonstration is performative *avant la lettre,* as it were, and pragmatic before being juridical and rational and philosophical. I show by the very movement, by doing it, as I go along, by producing the event of which I speak and that I announce I shall speak of, I demonstrate that force wins out over right and determines right, and I do so without waiting. Because it is already demonstrated at the moment I announce that you'll have to wait a little. A violently tautological proposition, then, since I am here using, taking account of, my accredited position as a professor authorized to speak, ex cathedra, of the reason of the strongest, I am using my power, which consists in beginning this way not that way, beginning by having you wait, by deferring, warning you not to forget the wolf, or the werewolf or the outlaw, making you wait for the moment when I'll show you what I promise I will show and demonstrate. The reason of the strongest is at work right here, at the very moment at which I claim to interrogate it, or even to place it in question or even merely to defer the demonstration. The demonstration has already taken place, in the very promise and in the *différance*, the act of deferring the demonstration. Unless one proves the stronger and belies what I say, but in making me a liar, in contradicting me, you will merely displace the site of the greatest force, and the reason of the strongest will (still and) always be the best.

118

As if I were myself, let's never forget it, a wolf, or even the werewolf. That could be, we're coming to it and we're going to show it in a moment, a quotation, more than a quotation, from Rousseau, who, several times, compared himself to a werewolf. Let's never forget the he-wolf and the she-wolf, we were saying. One always forgets a wolf along the way. For example, in the last session, even as I was pointing out that *homo homini lupus* was to be found, literally, long before Montaigne and Hobbes, in Plautus, I neglected or pretended to neglect, I had omitted if not forgotten, a wolf in Machiavelli (another great positive hero, for Schmitt, of the theory of the political), a Machiavelli that Hobbes must have read and a Machiavelli whose *Prince*, precisely, also names the wolf loud and clear. But if I pretended to forget this wolf, to suppress or repress it, to chase it away like another one I'll come to in a moment (Machiavelli will tell us how to beat back, chase away, or hunt this wolf), it was intentionally, for reasons I'm going to show you in a moment, with the intention of drawing your attention today to composite figures, fabulous grafts of man-beasts or human animals, mixes — that we haven't yet talked about. Now, of course Leviathan is a marine monster, a monstrous animal which, like the whale in *Moby-Dick*, belongs to the aquatic element in which it intends to reign, but the Leviathan is not a composite of man and beast. If there is something prosthstatic in it, this is not by reason of a composition, of a synthesis, of a composite essence of man and beast, like those we are getting ready to encounter. The Leviathan, a monstrous animal, is not monstrous after the fashion of Khimaira, the chimera, a monster from Lycia, born of Typhon and Echidna, with three heads, lion, goat, dragon spitting flames, killed by Bellerophon, and which, having descended to a common noun, has given its name to all sorts of fabulations, fantasies, mythical productions, or hallucinations (even in Descartes) which are precisely the element of what is of interest to us here, the element of fabulation in which the analogies between beast and sovereign find their resources and their schemata. I'm using the word *schema* by analogy, but primarily to signal toward analogy, precisely, i.e. toward the mediating element or the mixed. Just as Kant said that the schema of the imagination was the mediation between intuition and the concept of the understanding, participating in both at once, so we are dealing here with schematic and imaginative and fantastic and fabulous and chimerical and synthetic figures that mediate between two orders and participate in two organizations of the living creature, what is still called the animal and what is still called man, or again what is called beast and what is called sovereign. But if it is indeed this fantastic and synthetic and prosthetic composition that matters to us here, today it is neither on the side of the Leviathan nor on the side of the Chimera that we shall search for or encounter our monsters, but on the side of another logic of composition, graft, mixture, and biosynthetic alloy.

(On the horizon of this encounter is a double question, which I leave open: in the first place, why, in the great corpus of animal figures that people the fable of the political, do we find this or that animal and not others? We can make the most open and liberal list, from the wolf to the fox, from the lion to the lamb, from the serpent to the eagle, to ants or frogs, but we'll have to concede that not all the animals of earth and sky are represented, do not seem to be as prone, as equally appropriate, to political figuration. Why? Is it because of the regions of the world, with their specific fauna, because of the geographical and ethological areas in which this fabulous discourse on the political was born and developed its history: the Middle East, Greece, the Mediterranean, Europe? Perhaps. Is it because of the proper nature, the form, and the psychology *supposed* (I stress "supposed") by fiction, anthropomorphized in advance to pertain to such animals (the supposed cunning of the fox, the tranquil strength of the lion, the voracious violence of the wolf, who can also turn protective, paternal, and maternal)? Perhaps. In any case the necessity for a typology and a taxonomy is already

THIRD SESSION ‡ 81

looming, in this rhetoric that runs the risk of looking, if not like the order of Noah's Ark (which certainly did not house all the animals on earth), at least like the order of menageries, zoological parks, or circuses, which I mean to talk to you about quite soon and at some length).[15] That is the first question of this couple of questions I am leaving open. The second, which is linked to it, would be the following: in the obvious though surprising abundance of animal figures that invade discourses on the political, the reflections of political philosophy, how to give due consideration on the one hand to this profound necessity that we are precisely in the process of interrogating and trying to interpret in this seminar, but also, on the other hand, to the compulsion (let's call it psychic and libidinal) that seems to push the philosophers of the political, all of those who are passionately interested in holding a discourse on power, on political power, and who would supposedly represent for their part a certain type of man or woman (usually a man, at least until now), the irresistible compulsion which seems either to push them or to attract them toward zoomorphic visions or hallucinations, push or attract them toward a field where there is a greater chance of fantastic animal *apparitions* (I say "apparitions" in the sense of phenomena, but also of visionary epiphanies, be they chimerical or not)? How to give due consideration to this element of inventive and passionate hallucination, which is interested, compulsive, which is itself possible only if an intrinsic necessity, which we are analyzing here, indeed increases the chances of fantastic and fabulous apparitions in the field of power and therefore of political sovereignty? How to give due consideration to that element and distinguish it from the other element, that of a rhetorical codification, a law of genre which has long meant that one uses metaphors and metonymies or even codified allegories, in any case animal fables attributing cunning to the fox, strength to the lion, voracious and violent and cruel savagery to the wolf (or some wolves at least). But there too, in the element of codified rhetoric and the law of genre, there really must be involved what at the beginning would belong to a nature or an essential structure of the field of the political as such, of political power and political sovereignty: it would properly belong to it to produce in particularly fertile and irresistible fashion such a proliferation of fantastic beasts and zoopoetic visions. So I'll leave this double question open and suspended above our whole seminar. Let's not forget it. And let's not forget the wolves. I insist on the forgetting as much as on the wolves and the genelycology because what we should not

15. One would have expected this parenthesis to close at the end of this long paragraph, on p. 82.

stint on here [*faire l'économie de*] is the economy of forgetting as repression, and some logic of the political unconscious which busies itself around all these proliferating productions and all these chasings after, panting after so many animal monsters, fantastic beasts, chimeras, and centaurs that the point, in chasing them, is to cause them to flee, to forget them, repress them, of course, but also (and it is not simply the contrary), on the contrary, to capture them, domesticate them, humanize them, anthropomorphize them, tame them, cultivate them, park them, which is possible only by animalizing man and letting so many symptoms show up on the surface of political and politological discourse. All of which follows in the wake that we had situated the last times in looking again at *Totem and Taboo*.

The forgotten wolf in Machiavelli, then. *The Prince*[16] (dedicated to Lorenzo de Medicis—who could have been a prince but did not care to become one—*The Prince*, then, dedicated to a virtual prince, as La Fontaine's *Fables* would be dedicated and thus submitted to Monseigneur le Dauphin, *The Prince,* which was published in 1532, five years after Machiavelli's death but written almost a century and a half before the *Leviathan* (1651), *The Prince*, which you will read or reread, includes a chapter 18, entitled "In What Mode Faith Should Be Kept by Princes"[17] (or, in the old French translation by a certain Guiraudet undertaken on the pressing demand or the advice of General Bonaparte, "Whether Princes Should Be Faithful to Their Commitments" [*Si les princes doivent être fidèles à leurs engagements*] [repeat both titles]), on a question that could not be more current (not only the respect of armistices, of cease-fires, of peace treaties, but also, and basically the way it always was, since this is the very structure of any contract and any oath, the respect of sovereigns' commitments before an institution or a qualified and authorized third party: for example, the respect or not of UN resolutions by the USA or Israel, everything that concerns UN resolutions but also the commitments made by the UN with respect to so-called international terrorism (a concept judged to be problematic by the UN itself, we talked about it) and the consequences that it drew from the current situation, with

16. This sentence is unfinished in the typescript.

17. [Translator's note:] Niccolò Machiavelli, *The Prince,* trans. Harvey C. Mansfield, Jr. (Chicago: University of Chicago Press, 1985). I have occasionally modified the translation for the sake of consistency with the versions Derrida is using. Derrida refers to the French version by Périès which translates the title of chapter 18 as "Comment les princes doivent tenir leur parole [How Princes Must (or Ought to) Keep Their Word]."

the authorization given to the USA to ensure its legitimate defense by any means judged appropriate by the USA alone).

Now in this chapter on the faith to be kept by princes, on the question of knowing "in what mode faith should be kept by princes," or "whether princes should be faithful to their commitments," this same question of the fidelity of the prince to his given word or sworn faith appears to be inseparable from the question of what is "proper to man." And this double question, which appears in truth to be but one, is treated in a way that is interesting for us. You'll see the wolf go by, but also more composite animals. The question of the proper of man is indeed placed at the center of a debate about the force of law, between force and law. In this chapter, which passes for one of the most Machiavellian in Machiavelli, he begins by admitting a fact (I stress the word *fact*): in fact, *de facto*, one judges praiseworthy the fidelity of a prince to his commitments. It is praiseworthy, one must agree. After what looks like a concession (yes, it's good, it's praiseworthy, it's a recognized fact that, in principle, by rights, a prince ought to keep his word), Machiavelli comes back to the fact, which in fact he has never left. It is a fact that everyone regards the fidelity of the prince to his given word as laudable, but, in fact, few princes are faithful, few princes respect their commitments, and most of them use cunning: they almost all use cunning with their commitments. For they are constrained, in fact, to do so. We saw, he says, we have been in a position to see that the strongest princes, those who won out, beat those who, on the contrary, took as a rule the respect of their oath (this is why I announced a while ago that I would talk about the oath). 123

Machiavelli's rhetoric is remarkable, as is his logic. For after having noted this *fact* (the nonrespect of the oath that wins in fact, perjury that wins *de facto*, cunning that in reality beats fidelity), he concludes from this fact, always in the constative and realistic regime, that political reason must *take account* and *render account* of this fact. Political reason must count and calculate with the fact that, in fact, there are two ways to fight. Following paragraph, then: "There are two kinds of combat: one with laws, the other with force" (p. 69). The old Giraudet translation [as is the case in the English one by Mansfield] accentuates this constative regime, which is the regime of theoretical knowledge, of the factual description of what one must know, of the knowledge-of-what-one-needs-to-know: "You should then know [Machiavelli is addressing Lorenzo de Medicis as much as the reader] that there are two ways of combating, one with laws, the other with force."

So sometimes with right, justice, fidelity, respect for the laws, contracts, commitments, conventions, institutions, with sworn faith, and <sometimes>[18] with betrayal of commitments, lies, perjury, lack of respect for promises, plain brutal use of force ("the reason of the strongest").

124   From there, from this attested fact that one can *combat* in two ways, with laws or with force (and Machiavelli starts from a situation of *war* and not peaceful management of the city; he does not speak of the ordinary exercise of power by the prince but of a situation of war, which seems to him to be more revealing, exemplary, more paradigmatic of the essence of the vocation of the prince, namely response or riposte to the enemy, dealing with the other city as enemy city), Machiavelli draws strange conclusions, which we must analyze closely. Combat with laws (and so according to fidelity to one's commitments, as a sincere prince respectful of the laws) is, he says, proper to man. These are his words ("proper to man"), a Kantian argument in its principle, as it were: not to lie, to have the duty not to lie or perjure, is proper to man and his dignity. When one lies, when one betrays, which one can always do, in fact one is not speaking as a man, not as a man worthy of human dignity [*digne de la dignité humaine*]; in fact, one is not speaking, one is not addressing the other as a man, as another man. One is not speaking to one's fellow man [*son semblable*] (hold on to this value of *semblable* which will occupy us a great deal later). But what comes next in Machiavelli, who is not here speaking from an ethical point of view but from a political point of view, and who is measuring the possibility of the political, the law of the political against the test of *war*—what comes next in Machiavelli's discourse is, as we might expect, less Kantian. The second way to combat, he says (combat with force) is that of beasts. No longer man but the beast. Force and not law, the reason of the strongest, is what is proper to the beast. After this second moment, Machiavelli notes in a third moment of the argumentation that, in fact, the first way to combat (with the law) is insufficient, and remains, in fact, impotent. So one must, in fact, resort to the other. Thus the prince must combat with both weapons, both law and force. He must then behave *both* as man *and* as beast. "Therefore it is *necessary* for a prince to know how to use *as appropriate the beast and the man*" (p. 69; translation modified; Derrida's emphasis). This "it is necessary," specified by the
125   "as appropriate" (according to the circumstances, fitting in an appropriate manner his response to the urgency of a situation or a singular injunction, etc., to a polemology, a war or a singular machology, a singular conjuncture of combat), this "it is necessary" makes one move from the constative or descriptive regime to the prescriptive regime. When action by the law (fidelity

18. The typescript has "the other."

to one's oath, etc.) is impotent, does not work, is weak, too weak, then *it is necessary* to behave as a beast. The human prince must behave *as though he were a beast*. Machiavelli does not say that the prince is man and beast at the same time, that he has a double nature, but he is not far from saying so and from putting this double nature under the authority of an "it is necessary." If the prince is not man and beast at the same time, if in his very essence he does not unite these two essential attributes, he must nonetheless behave *as if* it were the case—and Machiavelli recognizes in this "as if" what I would here call two imports [*portées*], a pedagogical import and a rhetorical import. The pedagogical import is itself double and touches doubly on this quasi-double nature of the prince, who must act as if he were at once man and beast. Pedagogy *in the first place* because that is, Machiavelli tells us, what the writers of antiquity teach and have taught us. And this teaching will have taken an *allegorical* form (that is Machiavelli's word). It is by allegory or "animal" fabulation, the better to be heard, that these ancient writers called in animal figures. But this time it is not a question of this or that animal but of a man-horse mix, the centaur Chiron (*Kentauros*, the noun; the Greek adjective *kantoris* meant worthy of a centaur, i.e. brutal, coarse, bestial). The *Kentauros* was a hybrid being, born of Kentauros and Thessalian mares: a huge history to which I refer you. One could devote more than one seminar to it. There is a book by Dumézil on the problem of centaurs (1929).[19]

To remain with the minimum that matters to us here, I recall that centaurs (often represented, in their double—human and animal—nature by the articulation of a human front (human trunk and face) and an equine rear, in a horizontal order, then, not vertical, front and rear and not top and bottom) also present another ambiguity, besides that of the human and the (equine) animal. For they are both savages, savage beasts (*ther*), barbarian, terribly natural and, on the other hand, civilizing heroes, masters, pedagogues, initiators into the most diverse domains, skillful with their hands (the name Chiron allegedly comes from *cheir*, hand, whence surgery, and centaurs have not only human trunk and face but also human arms and hands), initiators, then, in the art of hunting, and hence cynegetics, music, medicine, etc. On the one hand, they represent the most asocial savagery, and Apollodorus will say of them that they are "savage, without social or-

126

19. Georges Dumézil, *Le problème des Centaures: Étude de mythologie comparée indo-européenne*, Annales du Musée Guimet (Paris: Librairie orientaliste Paul Geuthner, 1929).

ganization, of unpredictable behavior,"[20] in particular because of their un-
bridled sexuality, which makes them attack women and wine. Sexuality is
most often held to be bestial in itself; sexual desire is the beast in man, the
most boisterous and most avid, the most voracious beast. But—and this is
the case of the centaur Chiron, mentioned by Machiavelli, centaurs are also
virtuous pedagogues. Chiron teaches medicine to Aesculapius. Achilles, as
also evoked by Machiavelli, receives a princely education in the world of the
centaurs, and Chiron teaches him to subdue boars and bears with his bare
hands; he also teaches him music and medicine. Homer says of Chiron that
he is "the most just among centaurs,"[21] a model of ethics. If this genelycological thing interests you, reread the story of the Argonauts and the Golden
Fleece, where you'll find an abundant population of wolves and the centaur
Chiron. Among the seven sons of Aeolus, one, Athamas, king of Boetia,
went mad, because that is what the gods decided, because the gods made
him go mad and delirious to punish him for having planned to kill some
of his children, children of a first marriage. Banished, wandering, Athamas
can only settle where the wild wolves offer him hospitality, in Thessaly. He
does not meet these wolves at just any moment, and the hospitality they offer him is not just any hospitality. He stumbles upon them as they are sharing some lambs they have just killed. On the basis of this lycophilanthropic
hospitality, Athamas founds a city, after marrying Themisto. He is still held
by men to be a wolf, because he had planned to kill his children. But he
returns to the city of men after a detour via the city of wolves, resocialized
after and thanks to the scene of sacrificial sharing. Herodotus's version says
that the city of wolves, the *polis* of wolves, always dissolves rapidly, that the
social bond immediately comes undone, but that the dissolution of the social
bond between the wolves coincides in this case with the hospitality offered
to Athamas, namely a young man more wolf than they, who consequently,
by sitting at their table, takes a place from which they are expropriated. As
though (I'm taking a risk and improvising this interpretation) hospitality
led to the end of the social bond for the hospitable city, which, by giving up
on itself, as it were, by dissolving itself, abdicates into the hands of the guest

20. Derrida here picks up a brief passage from Alain Schnapp's article on centaurs
in the *Dictionnaire des mythologies et des religions des sociétés traditionnelles et du monde
antique*, ed. Yves Bonnefoy (Paris: Flammarion, 1981), 1:146; trans. as "Centaurs," in
Mythologies, comp. Yves Bonnefoy, trans. under the direction of Wendy Doniger (Chicago: University of Chicago Press, 1991), 1:451. The author refers without further detail
to Apollodorus, thinking no doubt of the passage in *The Library*, 2.5.4ff.
21. Schnapp, ibid.; Homer, *Iliad*, book 10, line 832.

who becomes sovereign. This is also the move from beast to what is proper to man. For at that moment Athamas becomes a man again, stops being a wolf by eating the wolves' leftovers. His humanity is returned to him, his life as a lone wolf comes to an end thanks to the wolves' sacrifice. If now you follow the thread of another descendant of Aeolus, another of his sons, Cretheus, king of Iolcos in Thessaly, you will encounter the centaur Chiron. Cretheus's son Aeson, grandson of Aeolus, chased out by a usurper, Pelias, wants to put his newborn son into safety. The son is Jason, who receives his name, Jason, from the centaur Chiron, to whom his father entrusted him to allow him to escape from Pelias, and to have him educated and brought up. And that's where we find the Chiron mentioned by Machiavelli.

If we return to Machiavelli's text, we see that it invokes the teaching of the ancients about these hybrid creatures, centaurs, and especially about something the ancients teach us, namely that the centaurs themselves, and especially Chiron, were teachers. The ancients teach us allegorically that the centaurs taught and what the centaurs taught. A double teaching, then, an allegorical teaching about a teaching dispensed by double beings (humans and animals); and we are going to see that the content of this teaching about teaching by double masters is that it is necessary to be double, necessary to know how to be double, to know how to divide or multiply oneself: animal and man, half man half beast. Let me quote first:

> Therefore it is necessary for a prince to know how to use as appropriate the beast and the man. This was taught to us allegorically by ancient writers, who wrote that Achilles and many other ancient heroes were entrusted to the centaur Chiron to be fed and raised.
>
> By this indeed, and by this half-man half-beast teacher, they meant that a prince must have as it were two natures, and that each needs support from the other. (p. 69, translation modified)

So what the ancients meant to teach us, by recounting this story about teaching, is that one of the greats, a hero, Achilles for example, was raised by a being with a man's head and a horse's body, half-man half-beast, and that what this hybrid taught him is to be, in his image, qua prince, both beast and man, half beast, half man. In this double nature, the beast needs the support of the man, by the face and hands and heart of man (the front of the centaur), and the man needs the support of the body, the rest of the body and the legs of the horse, which allow him to walk and stand upright. But this is not exactly the path followed by Machiavelli, once he has said of the prince that he must have a double nature, half man, half beast. He is going to pursue and appropriate for himself the allegory by having other

128

129 animals enter this political arena. Not overinsisting on the human part of this centaur prince, of this sovereign pupil and disciple of a centaur, on the human part of this prince who must be both man and beast, he prefers to emphasize the need for this animal part to be *itself* hybrid, composite, a mix or graft of two animals, the lion and the fox. Not only one beast but two in one. The prince as beast, the beast that the prince — or this half prince — also is, the princely beast must itself be double: both lion and fox. So at one and the same time man, fox, and lion, a prince divided or multiplied by three. But as for the beast here, Machiavelli insists more on the cunning of the fox, which clearly interests him more, than on the strength of the lion, a strength that he does not even name, whereas he names and renames cunning; cunning, i.e. knowing and know-how as knowing-how-to-trick, knowing-how-to-lie, knowing-how-to-perjure or knowing-how-to-dissimulate, the knowing-how-not-to-make-known of the fox. I quote:

> Thus, since a prince is compelled of necessity to know well how to use the beast, he should pick the fox and the lion: for if he is only lion, he will not defend himself from snares; if he is only fox, he will not defend himself from wolves; so he needs to be a fox to recognize snares and a lion to frighten the wolves. Those who stay simply with the lion are very unskillful. (p. 69, translation modified)

There are at least three things that we need to retain from this passage, from this zooanthropolitical theater, from this multiplicity of animal protagonists.

1. First, the enemy here, the sworn enemy, is always a wolf. The beast that has to be hunted down, chased away, repressed, combated, is the wolf. The point is to "defend oneself against the wolves." But even more interestingly and pointedly, and this I emphasize, it is important to *frighten* the wolves (". . . if he is only fox, he will not *defend* himself from wolves; so he needs to be a fox to recognize snares and a lion to *frighten* the wolves"). If the lion on its own does not suffice to frighten the wolves, one must
130 nonetheless, thanks to the know-how of the fox, frighten the wolves, terrorize the terrorists, as Pasqua used to say in his day,[22] i.e. make oneself feared as potentially more formidable, more terrifying, more cruel, more outlaw than the wolves, symbols of savage violence.

Without multiplying excessively the contemporary and all too obvious

---

22. This was a famous expression of Charles Pasqua, minister of the interior in Jacques Chirac's government (1986–88), used to justify turning against the terrorist enemy the same weapons used by that enemy.

illustrations of these discourses, let me just recall what Chomsky notes in his book *Rogue States*,[23] which I have already mentioned, namely that the Stratcom (US Strategic Command), in order to respond to the threats of what is called "international terrorism" on the part of rogue states—and I recall that "rogue" [in English] can also designate animals that do not even respect the usages of animal society and depart from the group—the Stratcom recommends, then, frightening, scaring the enemy, not only with the threat of nuclear war, which must always be left in place, even beyond bio-terrorism, but especially by giving the enemy the image of an adversary (the USA, then) who always might do just anything, like a beast, who can go off the rails and lose his cool, who might stop behaving rationally, like a reasonable man, when his vital interests are in play. One must not seem to be too "rational," says the directive, in determining what is most precious to the enemy. In other words, one must show oneself to be blind, make it known that one can be blind and stupid [*bête*] in the choice of targets, just so as to be frightening and have the enemy believe that one is acting at random, that one goes crazy when vital interests are affected. One must pretend to be capable of going crazy, mad, irrational and therefore animal. It "hurts," says one of the recommendations of the Stratcom, to depict ourselves as fully rational and cool. It is "beneficial," to the contrary, for our strategy to have certain elements appear to be "out of control."

2. For Machiavelli, in the passage we have just read, cunning does not suffice, one also needs force, and therefore extra animality: "if he [the prince] is only fox, he will not defend himself from wolves." Which means that, being stronger, the lion is also more *bête*, more of a beast than the fox, who is more intelligent, more cunning, but weaker, and so more human than the lion. There is a hierarchy here: man, fox, lion, going from the more human, the more rational and intelligent, to the more animal, even the more bestial, if not to the more *bête*. Precisely because he knows how to be cunning, how to lie, how to commit perjury, because he has the sense and culture of the snare, the fox is closer to the truth of man and man's fidelity, which he understands and knows how to invert. The fox can be cunning and unfaithful; he knows how to betray, whereas the lion does not even understand the opposition of faithful and unfaithful, veracity and lying. The fox is more human than the lion.

3. The privilege of the fox is therefore clear in this princely alliance of the lion and the fox against the wolves. The force of the fox, the sovereign

131

23. Noam Chomsky, *Rogue States: The Rule of Force in World Affairs* (Cambridge, MA: South End Press, 2000), pp. 6–7.

power of the prince, cunning *like* a fox, is that his force is more than force, his power exceeds force qua physical force (as represented by the lion), thus as force of nature (*physis*). The prince, qua fox-man, is stronger than nature or biology, and even than zoology, or than what one thinks is natural under these words, stronger than physical strength: the fox is not *bête* or is no longer simply or absolutely a beast. His force of law consists in exceeding the physical manifestation of force, i.e. his weight, size, amount of energy, everything that can constitute a weapon or even a defensive or offensive army, an invulnerable armored army with no weakness. No, the force of the prince qua man become fox is, beyond natural force or simple life force, beyond even his visible phenomenon and what can, through the image of natural force, strike with awe and fear, intimidate, as the simple spectacle of a lion can strike the imagination before the lion strikes, the force of the prince cunning like a fox, his force beyond force, is science or consciousness, knowledge, know-how, cunning know-how, know-how without making-known [*le savoir-faire sans faire-savoir*] what one knows how to do, knowing how to make his very weakness into a strength, finding a resource just where phenomenal nature did not give him one. The fox, the fox-prince is already (like the slaves and the sick in Nietzsche) one who inverts the originary order of things and makes of his weakness a supplementary force. But this privilege or this dissymmetry does not merely depend on the fox's proper resource, namely knowledge of snares, cunning, skill, etc., which the lion seems to lack. Rather, to the second power, as it were, or abyssally, the fox signifies also the cunning of cunning, the cunning that consists in knowing how to dissimulate, pretend, lie, perjure, and thereby pretend to be what one is not, for example, an animal or, indeed, a non-fox when one is a fox. The fox's cunning allows him to do what the lion cannot do, i.e. to dissimulate his fox-being and pretend to be what he is not. To lie. The fox is the animal that knows how to lie. What in the eyes of some people (for example, Lacan) is supposedly, like cruelty, proper to man, what the animal supposedly cannot do: lie or efface its tracks. (I have explained elsewhere,[24] in unpublished texts, but we will perhaps talk again about it, my reservations about this. For some people, including Lacan, then, animal cunning cannot cross a certain threshold of dissimulation, namely the power to lie and efface one's tracks: in this classical logic, the fox, qua prince, would no longer be an animal but already or still a man, and the power of the prince would be that of a man become fox again but qua man, remaining

---

24. Jacques Derrida, *L'animal que donc je suis*, pp. 55–56 and 82 [pp. 33, 54–55]. See too below, p. 111, n. 19.

human.) This ability to pretend, this power of the simulacrum, is what the prince must acquire in order to take on the qualities of both fox and lion. The metamorphosis itself is a piece of human cunning, a ruse of the fox-man that must pretend not to be a ruse. That is the essence of lie, fable, or simulacrum, namely to present itself as truth or veracity, to swear that one is faithful, which will always be the condition of infidelity. The prince must be a fox not only in order to be cunning like the fox, but in order to pretend to be what he is not and not be what he is. Thus to pretend not to be a fox, when in truth he is a fox. It is on condition that he be a fox or that he become a fox or like a fox that the prince will be able to be both man and beast, lion and fox. Only a fox can metamorphose himself this way, and start to resemble a lion. A lion cannot do this. The fox must be fox enough to play the lion and to "disguise this foxy nature." I'll read a few lines and you will see that Machiavelli has an example in mind, that he is slyly praising a fox-prince of his own day:

> A prudent prince, therefore, cannot observe his promise when such observance would be harmful to him, and the reasons that made him promise no longer exist: this is the advice to give. It would not be good advice of course if all men were good; but because they are wicked and would certainly not keep their word with you, why should you keep yours with them? And moreover, can a prince ever want for legitimate reasons to color his failure to keep his word?
>
> On this matter one can give an infinity of modern examples, and invoke a great number of peace treaties and agreements of all sorts that have become vain and useless through the infidelity of the princes who concluded them. And one can show that those who were best able to act like foxes prospered the most.
>
> But for this to work, it is absolutely necessary to know well how to disguise this foxy nature, and to possess perfectly the art of simulation and dissimulation. Men are so blind, so carried away by the needs of the moment, that a deceiver will always find someone who will let himself be deceived.
>
> [. . .]
> In our own day we have seen a prince it is not well to name never preach anything but peace and good faith, but who, had he always respected them, would no doubt not have retained his states and his reputation. (pp. 69–71)

Where have the wolves gone? Let's not forget the wolves, but this time, as I said, I'm talking about wolves that are a little bit chimera or centaur, wolves of synthetic composition, for example, the lycanthropes that in French are called *loups-garous* [werewolves], about which we opened our session by quoting Rousseau's *Confessions*. Rousseau's werewolves have been as it were *forgotten*, precisely, in a book I warmly recommend you to read, because you will find in it many precious things, reflections and references on sovereignty and on the questions that interest us: I am referring to Giorgio Agamben's *Homo Sacer,* subtitled *Sovereign Power and Bare Life*.[25] We shall be speaking of it again, but for now, to conclude for today, I want to emphasize that in the six or seven pages entitled "The Ban and the Wolf," which you ought to read because they give pride of place to the werewolf (*wargus*, *werewolf*, Lat. *Garulphus*), there are at least two instances of wolves being forgotten: that of Plautus and a few other precedents, since the *homo homini lupus* is here, as by everyone, alas, attributed by Agamben to Hobbes, and then Rousseau's wolf or wolves. These forgettings of wolves, and of wolves that have as it were a priority, are the more interesting and even amusing in that, as is regularly the case with this author, his most irrepressible gesture consists regularly in recognizing priorities that have supposedly been overlooked, ignored, neglected, not known or recognized, for want of knowledge, for want of reading or lucidity or force of thought—priorities, then, *first times*, inaugural initiatives, instituting events that have supposedly been denied or neglected, and so, in truth, priorities that are primacies, principalities, principal signatures, signed by the Princes of Beginning, priorities that everyone, except the author of course, has supposedly missed, so that each time the author of *Homo Sacer* is, apparently, the first to say who *will have been* first.

135   I point this out with a smile only to recall that this is the very definition, vocation, or essential claim of sovereignty. He who posits himself as sovereign or intends to take power as sovereign always says or implies: even if I am not the first to do or say so, I am the first or only one to know and recognize who *will have been* the first. And I would add: the sovereign, if there is such a thing, is the one who manages to get people to believe, at least for a while, that he is the first to know who came first, when there is every chance that it is almost always false, even if, in certain cases, no one ever suspects so. The first then, the *premier*, as its name indicates, is the prince: man, fox, and lion, at least when things are going well for him. For example, on page 21, in a chapter entitled precisely "The Paradox of Sovereignty," one can read, believe it or not, and I quote:

> Hegel was the first to truly understand [of course, it remains to understand what the author implies by this "truly,"[26] because if someone were to show

25. Giorgio Agamben, *Homo Sacer: Sovereign Power and Bare Life,* trans. Daniel Heller-Roazen (Stanford: Stanford University Press, 1998).

26. [Translator's note:] The French translation used by Derrida has "jusqu'au bout" here.

that Hegel were not the first to understand this or that, the author could always pretend to concede the point and say: yes, I agree, others understood this or that before Hegel, but not "truly," the end being defined, determined and interpreted by the author, i.e. by the first to discover that Hegel was the first to understand "truly," so that the real first one is not, is never Hegel or anyone else in truth, but is "çui qu'a dit" [the one who said so] as people say, the one who, finally arriving for the first time at the end, knows what "at the end" means, at the end, right at the end, in this case what Hegel will have understood when, I quote Agamben:] Hegel was the first to truly understand the presuppositional structure thanks to which language is at once inside and outside itself.[27]

There follows a highly interesting paragraph, which I leave you to read, especially on the subject of a language that is sovereign, "in a state of permanent exception, declaring that there is nothing outside language, that it is always beyond itself," so that "To speak is, in this sense, always to 'speak the law,' *jus dicere.*" All of which seems so true and convincing to me that not only was Hegel, who says it in his own way, not the first to say it, but one would have difficulty finding (and not only in the history of philosophy and not only in reflection on language) anyone who had not said it or implemented it or implied it, the "truly" remaining to be determined and being determined only by the latest arrival, who presents himself as the first to know who will have been the first to think something *truly.*

136

Ten pages later, we find another first that the author of *Homo sacer* is the first to identify as the first: this time it's Pindar, I quote, "first great thinker of sovereignty":

> While in Hesiod the *nomos* is still the power that divides violence from law and, with it, the world of beasts from the world of men, and while in Solon the "connection" of *Bia* and *Dikè* contains neither ambiguity nor irony [how can one be sure, I ask you, that a text by Solon or indeed by anyone contains no irony? One can never prove an absence of irony, by definition, that's even where the fox princes find their invincible resource], in Pindar — and this is the knot that makes him, in a certain sense, the first great thinker of sovereignty.[28]

This "in a certain sense" plays the same role as the "truly" did just now with Hegel. This "certain sense" is the sense determined by Giorgio Agamben, i.e. by the first to identify in Pindar the "first great thinker of sovereignty." Same thing with "great": on the basis of what size is one "great," a "great"? On the basis of what criterion, except the size measured by the measure of

27. Agamben, *Homo Sacer,* p. 21.
28. Ibid., p. 31.

the author of these lines, does one determine that a thinker of sovereignty
is great enough to be a great thinker, the first great thinker of sovereignty?
Of the following paragraph, especially concerning, I quote, a "sovereign *no-mos,*" which is "the principle that, joining law and violence, threatens them
with indistinction,"[29] I want to say that every time the word *nomos* appears
in Greek, whether or not it is associated, as in a fragment of Pindar, with
the word *basileus*, it says just that, which is here attributed to Pindar as "first
great thinker of sovereignty," attributed to Pindar by him who lays down
the law by saying that Pindar was the first who, "in a certain sense . . . ,"
etc. Not only was Pindar certainly not the first, but in order to be the self-
proclaimed or so-called first, he really needed to speak Greek, and whoever
speaks Greek and uses the words *nomos* or *basileus* will have said or implied
that, and will not have completely neglected to do so.

On page 120, again, further on, in the chapter entitled "The Politicization of Life" (which I invite you to read closely), another first, a third first,
comes along: "Karl Löwith was the first to define the fundamental character of the politics of totalitarian states as a 'politicization of life.'" There
follows a long quotation which I leave you to read, after which Agamben
makes an objection to Löwith, who, on a certain point, follows "Schmitt's
footsteps" too closely, so that in demonstrating that all this began much earlier, in fact always already, one no longer knows who was the first to define
what, except the very signatory of this discourse.

On page 151, another first, the fourth first in this book alone, is added to
the list. "Lévinas proves himself the first . . ." This is in an astonishing passage which, before naming Lévinas and speaking in the name of the author
of *Homo Sacer*, claims to uncover for the first time, I quote, the "proper
significance" of "the relation between Martin Heidegger and Nazism,"
"situated in the perspective of modern biopolitics," which, I quote further,
"both [Heidegger's] accusers and his defenders fail to do." There too one
smiles, not only because there is so much evidence to the contrary, but especially because the concept of negligence is among the most highly charged,
multiple in its different logics, necessarily obscure and dogmatic when it is
wielded as an accusation, unclear by definition in its uses. One is always a
priori negligent, more or less negligent, and so always too negligent, in particular in the accusation of negligence. What is it to neglect? Starting when
does one neglect? Where does one do what one does, says what one says, in
neglected or negligent fashion? Questions that by definition have no rigorously determined reply. Same question as for irony. "Neglect" is, moreover,

29. Ibid.

an abyssal word that one should not use in a neglected or negligent way or that one should not neglect to analyze interminably, as we began to do but must inevitably neglect to do absolutely adequately in this seminar. Having thrown out this accusation around the "proper significance" of "the relation between Martin Heidegger and Nazism [. . .] situated in the perspective of modern biopolitics (and this is the very thing that both Heidegger's accusers and his defenders fail to do)," the author of *Homo Sacer* writes: "In a text of 1934 that may well *even today still constitute the most valuable contribution* [my emphasis] to an understanding of National Socialism, Lévinas proves himself the first to underline . . ."

After which, having, however, pointed out that "the name Heidegger appears nowhere" in this text by Lévinas, Agamben alludes to a note added in 1991 (so long after, sixty years after, and in the second edition of the *Cahiers de l'Herne,* in which this text from 1934 had first been reprinted)[30] and which, still without naming Heidegger, can indeed be read as an unequivocal allusion to Heidegger (in 1991, then); Agamben writes, in 1995: "But the note added [. . .] in 199[0] [. . .] leaves no doubt as to the thesis that [my emphasis here] *an attentive reader would nonetheless have had to read between the lines,* [etc.]."[31]

So in 1995 we are told that Lévinas was the first, in 1934, to say something or do something that he scarcely even made clear in 199[0], but that an attentive reader—thus one more attentive than Lévinas himself in 1934—*ought* to have, as Agamben is, then, the first to notice and point out in 1995, ought to, I quote, "nonetheless have had to read between the lines."

If there are "firsts," I would be tempted to think on the contrary that they never present themselves as such. Faced with this distribution of school prizes, prizes for excellence and runners-up, a ceremony <at which> the priest always begins and ends, in princely and sovereign manner, by putting himself first, that is by occupying the place of priest or master who never neglects the dubious pleasure to be had by sermonizing and handing out lessons, one might still want to recall, on the subject of Lévinas, what, whether he was first to do so or not, what he said and thought about *anarchy*, precisely, about ethical protest, not to mention taste, politeness, and even politics, about protestation against the gesture that consists in coming

139

---

30. [Translator's note:] The English version of Agamben's text (p. 152) refers to an earlier republication, trans. Séan Hand as "Reflections on the Philosophy of Hitlerism," *Critical Inquiry* 17 (1990): 63–71.

31. Agamben, *Homo Sacer,* p. 152.

first, in occupying the first place among the first, *en arkhē*, to prefer the first place or not to say "after you." "After you," as Lévinas says I no longer know where, is the beginning of ethics. Not to serve oneself first, as we all know, is the ABC of good manners, in society, in the salons, and even when eating at the common table in an inn.

Rousseau says so too, in passing, in another literal and forgotten reference to the werewolf, in the sixth book of the *Confessions,* on which I conclude. Whereas in the first book, Rousseau had said, as I recalled this forgotten reference, "and I lived like a real werewolf," here he writes:

> With my well-known timidity you imagine that I did not so quickly get to know brilliant women and their entourage: but in the end, following the same route, lodging in the same inns, and on pain of passing for a werewolf forced to present myself at the same table, we were bound to get to know each other.[32]

So as not to be unsociable, again, and outside-the-law, so as not to pass for a werewolf, he approaches these women and sits down at the table. I recommend that you read more closely all these texts. In other parts of the *Confessions,* which I owe to the helpfulness of Olivia Custer not to have forgotten and to have located, and which I shall mention at the beginning next time, Rousseau again uses the figures of the wolf and the werewolf to evoke other wars or other trials of which he is the witness, the victim or the accused. It is always a matter of the law and of placing the other outside the law. The law (*nomos*) is always determined from the place of some wolf.

I shall call it *lyconomy*.

No genelycology or anthropolycology without lyconomy.

140

32. Rousseau, *Les confessions*, pp. 248–49.

January 23, 2002

<I would not want to start without expressing> my sadness and paying tribute to the memory of my friend Jean-Toussaint Desanti. He died a few days ago and was, as you know, a great witness to and actor in our times, a lucid and vigilant philosopher, and, I say this with many others, a faithful friend.[1]

> This very cruelty implies humanity. It is directed at a fellow [*un semblable*], even in a being of another species.

This is how Lacan interprets the *homo homini lupus*, when he quotes it in *Écrits*.[2] Before coming back to it as closely as possible in a moment, I shall place the words as an epigraph today.

The [feminine] beast and the [masculine] sovereign: between the two, between the two genders or species of living beings, between the two *genres*, in the sense of sexual gender[3] or between the two genera in the sense of generalities under which one inscribes animal species, the animal species and the human species, or again the animal species and, as they say, the "human race [*genre humain*]," we had already recognized and formalized a large number of possibilities and typical combinations, recurrent and regular forms of problems.

---

1. This passage was reconstituted on the basis of the recording of the session.

2. Jacques Lacan, *Écrits* (Paris: Seuil, 1966), p. 147 ; trans. Bruce Fink as *Écrits: The First Complete Edition in English* (New York: Norton, 2006), p. 120. [Translator's note: Unless otherwise indicated, page references to Lacan are to the French edition, usually followed by page numbers of this English translation in brackets. I have benefited from consulting Fink's translation, but have preferred to retranslate all passages from Lacan in the interests of literality and consistency with Derrida's commentary.]

3. [Translator's note:] Derrida supplies the English word "gender" in parentheses after "genre sexuel."

142   Because I prefer not to use up time on return and recapitulation, I shall merely recall *on the one hand* that, moving between the two *genres* (the [feminine] beast and the [masculine] sovereign), we saw — apart from all those wolves and princes — a procession of Leviathans, chimeras, centaurs, lion-men, and fox-men, and, *on the other hand*, we saw that the enigma of the place of man, of what is proper to man, kept coming back insistently: precisely between the two. We saw why, in an at least apparent contradiction, if the sovereign, the law, the state, prosthstatics were often posited (with or without an explicit theological grounding, with or without religion) as what was proper to man, it is nonetheless in the name of what is proper to man and the right of man, the dignity of man, that a certain modernity supposedly threw sovereignty into crisis. This paradoxical question of what is proper to man also ran through everything we said and quoted (a great number of genelycological texts on the lycanthrope, especially in the figure of the werewolf). In passing, I announced that I would return, as to what is proper to man, to these two features that are said paradoxically to be proper to man and not to the beast, namely *bêtise* [stupidity] (I announced, and I will be good as my word, that we would read a text by Deleuze on this subject for guidance) and *bestiality*, bestial cruelty (and I announced, and I will be good as my word in just a moment, that we would read a text by Lacan on this subject for guidance).

    Before getting to that, I would like to emphasize the way in which the werewolf, the "outlaw" as the English translation of Rousseau's *Confessions* has it (you remember), the outlaw, the wolf-man as werewolf is identified not only as asocial, outside-the-political-law (we illustrated this at length, especially with texts of Rousseau's) but outside-the-theological-and-religious law, as a miscreant, basically as an atheist.

    The werewolf or the outlaw is, then, "without faith or law" [*sans foi ni loi*].

    One "without faith or law." This is <what> comes out in other usages of Rousseau's (a Rousseau who is decidedly obsessed by this figure, by wolves: that's his thing, wolves, *ça le regarde* [that's his thing: literally "that looks at him"], the wolves look at him, like the Wolf Man, and I've already counted in Rousseau six or seven appearances of the wolf or the werewolf, like the

143 Wolf Man who feels he is being looked at by six or seven wolves on the walnut-tree or his genelycological tree. The wolves, *ça le regarde*).

    At least twice more, the same *Confessions* present the wolf, or the werewolf, as someone who basically does not recognize the sovereignty of God, neither religious law nor the church, especially the Christian church, and so is "without faith or law." Rousseau speaks of it as though it were an accusation made by a prosecutor in an indictment or an inquisition: confess, you are a wolf or a werewolf, "without faith or law." But sometimes he is the one doing the accusing (in which case he is the Just Man accusing justly and trying to get the others to confess, confessing them, in sum, instead of confessing anything himself), sometimes it is he who is accused, and then the accusation is unjust. He is wrongly presumed guilty. He does not confess.

Here, very rapidly, are these two examples.

1. The *first*, in book 9 of the *Confessions,* is remarkable to the extent that all the combatants in what is basically a war of religion, and a war of religion that is not far from turning into a *civil* war of religion — all the protagonists in this war, all the belligerents, are compared to "wolves fiercely trying to tear each other to pieces," rather than to Christians or philosophers. In other words, to be a Christian or a philosopher is to cease being a beast and a wolf. And in this war among fierce wolves, Rousseau, for his part, is himself the only non-wolf. In the passage I am going to read, I shall emphasize the words "Christian" and "philosophers," of course, and "religious civil war," but above all, by way of transition to what is to come, the words "cruel" and "faith" (in "good faith"). And the word "craziness" because it is here a question of going crazy or driving crazy.

Beyond this object of morality and conjugal honesty, which belongs radically to the whole social order, I gave myself another more secret one of concord and public peace, a greater object and one perhaps more important in itself, at least at the time we were in. The storm provoked by the *Encyclopedia*, far from abating, was then at its height. The two parties, unleashed against each other with the greatest fury, rather resembled enraged wolves, fiercely trying to tear each other to pieces, than *Christians* and *philosophers* who wish mutually to enlighten each other, to convince each other and bring each other back to the way of truth. Perhaps the only thing lacking to one side or the other for it to degenerate into civil war were vigorous leaders with credit, and God knows what would have been produced by a *religious civil war*, in which the *cruelest* intolerance would be basically the same on both sides. As a born enemy of any partisan spirit, I had frankly told some hard truths to both sides, to which they had not listened. I got the idea of another expedient that in my simplicity seemed to me admirable: that of softening their reciprocal hatred by destroying their prejudices, and showing each party the merit and virtue of the other, worthy of public esteem and the respect of all mortals. This not very sensible project, which assumed good *faith* among men, and by which I fell into the failing for

144

i

which I had reproached Abbé de St. Pierre, had the success it was bound to have: it did not bring the two parties any closer together, and united them only to condemn me. Until experience made me aware of my *craziness*, I gave myself over to it, I dare say, with a zeal worthy of the motive that had inspired it in me, and I sketched out the characters of Wolmar and Julie in a transport that made me hopeful of making them both lovable and, what is more, each through the other.[4]

2. *In the second place*, conversely, whereas here he made an accusation and said that he was innocent, whereas he has just claimed to denounce the wolves, to arbitrate among the wolves in the name of the justice he represents, in the name of the man and the non-wolf that he is—at the very beginning of book 12, to the contrary, he explains how he was himself, so unjustly, accused of being a wolf, and even a werewolf, still in a religious battlefield, in a quasi–civil war of religion, in the war that was being waged *against him*, in a war of religion declared against him, the Antichrist and the werewolf. This is after the publication of *Émile*. The imprecation, war, and religious persecution waged against him is also a political police operation, a censorship, especially French but virtually European and international: against Rousseau the werewolf. The lexicon of *cruelty* reappears in it. As for the word "lycanthropy," which appears in this passage, a note in the Pléiade edition makes it clearer by referring to the Dictionary of the Académie [française] of the time, 1762: "*Lycanthropy*: mental illness in which the patient imagines he has turned into a wolf." But the editor adds: "But here it would rather be the mental state of a man who is full of hatred, *cruel* [my emphasis, J.D.], enraged like a wolf."[5]

> These two decrees were the signal of the cry of malediction that arose against me throughout Europe with a fury that is unprecedented. All the gazettes, all the newspapers, all the brochures sounded the most terrible tocsin! Especially the French, such a gentle, polite, generous people, so proud of their propriety and concern for the wretched, suddenly forgetting their favorite virtues, distinguished themselves by the number and violence of the outrages they showered on me as often as they could. I was an impious man, an atheist, a crazy person, I was enraged, a ferocious beast, a wolf. The continuator of the *Journal de Trévoux* went so far as to my supposed lycanthropy that he clearly showed up his own. In short, you would have said that people in Paris were afraid of police involvement if, when publishing

4. Rousseau, *Confessions*, vol. 1 of *Oeuvres complètes*, ed. Gagnebin and Raymond, pp. 435–36.
5. Ibid., p. 591, and p. 1566, n. 1.

something on any subject at all, they failed to push in some insult against me. Vainly seeking the cause of this unanimous animosity, I was ready to believe that the whole world had gone mad.[6]

<And later:>

After that the people, openly stirred up by the ministers, made light of the King's rescripts, of the orders of the Council of State, and abandoned all restraint. I was preached against from the pulpit, called the antichrist, and pursued across the countryside like a werewolf. My Armenian dress gave me away to the populace: I cruelly felt the drawback it represented, but taking it off in these circumstances seemed cowardice to me. I could not resolve to do it, and walked calmly abroad with my kaftan and fur bonnet surrounded by the cries of the rabble and sometimes its stones. Several times as I walked past a house, I heard the inhabitants saying: bring me my gun so I can shoot him.[7]

146

Cruelty, then, criminality, being outside the (religious or civil) law, being without faith or law, that's what characterizes, not the wolf itself, but the werewolf, the wolf-man, the lycanthrope, the mad or sick man. This cruelty of the "without faith or law" would then be proper to man, that bestiality that is attributed to man and causes him to be compared to a beast, and apparently also proper to man in that he presupposes the law, even when he opposes it, whereas the beast itself, even if it can be violent and ignore the law, cannot, in this classical logic, be held to be bestial. Like *bêtise*, bestiality, bestial cruelty would thus be proper to man. That is the question, and that is also the deep axiomatics the path and statements of which I announced we would follow and problematize in Lacan.

The stakes are sizable. No less than the question of knowing how a psychoanalytic discourse, especially when it alleges a "return" to Freud (some of whose strategies in this field, in the lyconomy, genelycanthropy, or genelycopolitics of this field, we have already mentioned), how such a psychoanalytic discourse (such and such a psychoanalytic discourse and not another, for just as there is not *the* beast and *the* sovereign, just as there is not *one* sovereignty, there is not *one* psychoanalysis but a multiplicity of discourses that take into account the possibility of another so-called logic of the unconscious, a multiplicity that is heterogeneous, conflictual, historical, i.e. perfectible and open to a still undecided future) [a question of wondering, then, how such and such a psychoanalytic-type discourse and not another],

6. Ibid., p. 591.
7. Ibid., pp. 627–28.

147 such and such a discourse the force and relative representativity of which are remarkable, can help us think, but can also fail to help us think or even forbid us to think in this domain. My hypothesis is that Lacan's discourse plays this double role.

Before broadening and gradually diversifying our references to the Lacanian corpus, I shall take as my starting point a noteworthy article in the *Écrits* entitled "Functions of Psychoanalysis in Criminology" (1950),[8] which I invite you to read in its entirety.

Lacan begins by recalling something that is very classical and traditional, however novel it may look under his pen. What? Lacan begins by declaring that what is proper to man, the origin of man, the place where humanity begins, is the Law, the relation to the Law (with a capital L). In other words, what separates Man from Beast is the Law, the experience of the Law, the Superego, and therefore the possibility of transgressing it in Crime. Basically, as opposed to the Beast, Man can obey or not obey the Law. Only he has that liberty. Only he, then, can become criminal. The beast can kill and do what seems to us bad or wicked but will never be held to be criminal, never be incriminated, one cannot have a beast appear before the law (even though that has happened, and we need to remember that fact, but let's leave it for now). Lacan is here on the side of a certain common sense, according to which the beast, ignorant of the Law, is not free, neither responsible nor culpable, cannot transgress a Law it does not know, cannot be held to be criminal. A beast never commits a crime and is never in infraction of the law. Which means that Crime, as transgression of the Law, would be proper to man. With Law and Crime, man begins. I quote:

> One imagines that having received in psychology such an input from the social, Freud the doctor should have been tempted to give something back, and that with *Totem and Taboo* in 1912, he should have wished to demonstrate in the primordial crime the origin of the universal Law. However subject to methodological criticism this work may be, the important thing is that it recognized that with Law and Crime begins man, after the cli-
148 nician had shown that their meanings supported everything down to the form of the individual not only in his value for the other, but in his erection for himself.
> Thus the conception of the superego saw the light of day.[9]

8. Jacques Lacan, "Introduction théorique aux fonctions de la psychanalyse en criminologie," in *Écrits*, pp. 125–49 ["A Theoretical Introduction to the Functions of Psychoanalysis in Criminology," pp. 102–22].

9. Ibid., p. 130 [p. 106].

Naturally, Lacan having recognized that Law and Crime are what is proper to man, the beginning of man, the emergence of a superego being recognized by the same token (the beast is a beast not only in that it cannot say "me" [*moi*] or "I," as Descartes and so many others have thought and as Kant literally wrote in the very opening lines of his *Anthropology from a Pragmatic Point of View)*, but above all, as Lacan is at bottom claiming here, what the beast lacks is not only an "ego" [*moi*] but a "superego."[10] And if Lacan juxtaposes and places into an essential contiguity Law and Crime, by capitalizing their names ("with Law and Crime begins man"), this is because Crime is not only committed against the law and in transgression of the law, but because the Law can also be the origin of crime, the Law can be criminal, the superego can be criminal. And it is this structural possibility that we must not forget, as to what is proper to man, and this is what we are going to follow in Lacan's wake. In any case, Lacan says quite clearly at the bottom of the same page that the superego, which is the guardian of the law, on the side of the law, can also be a delinquent, that there can be felony and crime of the superego itself:

> The signification of self-punishment covers all these ills and these gestures. Will it then be necessary to extend it to all criminals, to the extent that, according to the formula in which the icy humor of the legislator is expressed, given that no-one is supposed to be ignorant of the law, everyone can foresee its incidence and therefore be held to be seeking out its blows?
>
> This ironic remark ought, by obliging us to define what psychoanalysis recognizes as crimes or felonies issuing from the *superego*, to permit us to formulate a critique of the scope of this notion in anthropology.[11]

149

What consequences can we draw from this? What consequences does Lacan himself begin by drawing from it for the interpretation of the *homo homini lupus*? For the moment I am limiting myself to this question of the *homo homini lupus,* i.e. the werewolf, the man who behaves like a wolf for man, and leaving to one side the enormous dossier of Lacan and others' interpretation of the Wolf Man, about which there would be so much to say, but about which I have more or less explained myself elsewhere.[12]

10. This is how the sentence appears in the typescript. Perhaps it should read as follows: "Naturally, given that Lacan has thus recognized that Law and Crime are proper to man, the beginning of man, there is recognized ['est reconnue' rather than the 'et reconnue' of the typescript] by the same token the emergence of a superego . . ."

11. Ibid. [p. 107].

12. See Jacques Derrida, "Fors," in N. Abraham and M. Torok, *Cryptonymie: Le verbier de l'homme aux loups* (Paris: Aubier-Flammarion, 1976), pp. 7–73; trans. Barbara Johnson as "Fors," *Georgia Review* 31, no. 1 (1977): 64–116.

"The form of the adage *homo homini lupus* misleads as to its meaning," declares Lacan, still in the article "Functions of Psychoanalysis in Criminology,"[13] in the course of a fifth section in which <he> undertakes to oppose (and one can only follow him in this) the hypothesis that there are such things as "criminal instincts." He wants to demonstrate that psychoanalysis, precisely, even if it comprises a "theory of instincts" or rather of drives (*Triebe*), rejects this assigning of innate (and therefore genetically predetermined) instincts toward criminality. What Lacan immediately implies with this distinction between acquired and innate is that the animal (as he says everywhere else, as we shall see) is confined to this fixity of the innate, innate wiring or programming, whereas man, in his relation to the law (and therefore to crime), is not so confined. Always the question of liberty and the machine. The question, then, is indeed the old question of the innate and the acquired. Not that, for Lacan, there can be no fixed and animal instinct in man: of course there is an animality in man, but crime, cruelty, and ferocity do not come from instinct, they transcend animality, they assume not merely a "liberty" and a "responsibility," and therefore a "peccability" (words that Lacan is careful not to pronounce here, but with respect to which we shall see later that the corresponding and indissociable concepts, especially those of response and responsibility, play a decisive role), these statements also assume that clarity has been achieved with respect to a word that Lacan not only puts forward twice, but that here literally designates the major criterion: namely the word "fellow" [*semblable*].

What is supposed to distinguish man, as "wolf for man," from the animal, what is supposed to distinguish the wolf-man or the werewolf from the animal, and thus from the wolf itself, what is supposed to distinguish human cruelty or ferocity from all animal violence — animal violence to which one cannot consequently give the attribute of cruelty (only man is cruel, the animal can harm, but it cannot do evil for evil and so be cruel) — what is supposed to distinguish cruel humanity from non-cruel (and therefore innocent) animality is that the cruel man attacks his *fellow*, which the animal supposedly does not. So it is this notion of "fellow" which will carry the whole burden of the demonstration (which is, moreover, as classical and traditional as can be, in my view) by which Lacan intends to correct the error he supposes has been made in the interpretation of *homo homini lupus* ("the form of the adage," he says and I recall, "misleads as to its meaning"), an error that supposedly would consist in believing that man is a wolf, and thus an animal for man, which Lacan is about to contest. I'll now quote and

13. Ibid., p. 147 [p. 120].

comment on these two paragraphs, emphasizing as I go the words "fellow" and "cruelty":

> For if instinct indeed signifies the uncontestable animality of man, one cannot see why it would be less docile for being embodied in a rational being. The form of the adage *homo homini lupus* misleads as to its meaning, and Balthazar Gracián, in one of the chapters of his *Criticón*, forges a fable in which he shows what the moralistic tradition means when it indicates that the ferocity of man with respect to his fellow goes beyond anything that animals can do, and that faced with the threat that this ferocity poses to the whole of nature, even the carnivores recoil in horror.
>
> But this very *cruelty* implies humanity. It is a *fellow* that it is targeting, even in a being of another species. No experience has gone deeper than that of analysis in probing, in lived experience, the equivalence signaled to us by the pathetic call of Love: it is thyself that thou strikest, and the glacial deduction of Spirit: it is in the fight to the death for pure prestige that man gets himself recognized by man.[14]

151

What can one reply to this type of discourse? Apparently it makes sense [*tombe sous le sens*], as they say, which implies also that not only is it full of good sense (and continues to hold animality to be innocent, even when it does harm, and man to be guilty, peccable, precisely because he is capable of good and of perfecting himself, amending himself, capable of confessing and repenting, etc.), but that it is inscribed in an ethics of sense, an ethics that tends to save sense, as sense of the human and of human responsibility.

On the other hand, it is difficult not to subscribe to the critique of a theory of the "criminal instincts" of certain individuals, a theory which is not only contestable qua theory but is one that can induce, as we know, all sorts of political, juridical, policing, pedagogical, and even eugenicist and bioethical strategies. What are we supposed to do with individuals presumed to be hereditarily predisposed to crime and cruelty, genetically predisposed, and so potential recidivists? There's no point in trotting out current examples of serial killers,[15] sexual psychopaths, even pedophiles, etc. So one can only subscribe to the vigilance called for by Lacan with respect to a fixist geneticism, and what is at stake here is nothing less than the place of psychoanalysis, a certain psychoanalysis in society, in law, and above all in penal law.

But once we have approved Lacan's argumentation, within the limits of a certain conjuncture and a certain ethico-political motivation, things as I

14. Ibid., Derrida's emphasis.
15. [Translator's note:] "Serial killers" is in English in the text.

see them cannot and should not stop there; and it is the whole Lacanian and even psychoanalytical axiomatic that would need to be recast.

I shall for the moment limit myself to bringing out three points from this particular passage. But they are three points that will constantly, when we read other texts of Lacan's, tie in with an immense discursive woof or warp that seems to me to be problematic through and through.

1. First, the distinction between the innate and the acquired, and thus between instinct and everything that goes with "culture," "law," "institution," "freedom," etc., has always been fragile, <and> is more fragile than ever today, exactly like the presupposition of an animality deprived of language, history, culture, technique, relation to death *as such,* and the transmission of acquired knowledge. I am one of those—it is true that there are not many of us—who have always smiled at this machine of presuppositions to be deconstructed. But it happens moreover that the most positive science today (see the recently published book on the origins of man (Coppens???))[16] shows that some animals (not that hypostatic fiction labeled The Animal, of course, but some among those that are classified as animals) have a history and techniques, and thus a culture in the most rigorous sense of the term, i.e. precisely, the transmission and accumulation of knowledge and acquired capacities. And where there is transgenerational transmission, there is law, and therefore crime and peccability.

2. Saying that cruelty is essentially human because it consists in causing suffering to one's fellow comes down to giving an exorbitant credit to this value of the fellow. Even more so if we say that when one is cruel to another species, it is still one's fellow that one is targeting. Even when one is cruel with respect to this or that animal, Lacan is basically suggesting, it is a man one is targeting—a fertile hypothesis and one no doubt to be taken seriously, but which does not prove that all cruelty with respect to one's non-fellow [*dissemblable*] is immediately rendered innocent because what it is targeting in truth and at bottom is still the fellow, man targeted through the animal. How does one recognize a fellow? Is the "fellow" only what has human form, or is it anything that is alive? And if it is the human form of life, what will be the criteria for identifying it without implying a whole determinate culture, for example European, Greco-Abrahamic culture, and in particular Christian culture, which installs the value of "neighbor" or "brother" in the universality of the world, as totality of all creatures? And I point out that Lacan ends this article with a reference, in spite of every-

16. Question marks in the typescript. The allusion is to *Aux origines de l'humanité*, ed. Yves Coppens and Pascal Picq (Paris: Fayard, 2002).

thing, and in spite of the detail I'll give in a moment, a quite reassuring or reassured reference, I'd say, a little overconfident, to what he calls "eternal fraternity." In *Politics of Friendship* I tried to "deconstruct" the bases of this fraternalism, and I cannot go over this again here.[17]

These are the last words of Lacan's article, and in them, let us not forget, a certain concept of the subject is at stake: "if we can provide a more justly rigorous truth, let us not forget that we owe it to the following privileged function: that of the recourse of the subject to the subject, which inscribes our duties in the order of eternal fraternity: its rule is also the rule of every action allowed us."[18]

Now obviously, and this is the detail I promised, when Lacan talks of this "eternal fraternity," we must not hear in it merely the sort of edifying, irenic, pacifistic, and democratic praise which often denotes and connotes so many appeals to fraternity. Especially to an "eternal fraternity"—which I said a moment ago ran the risk of being overconfident. But Lacan, as he recalls earlier in the same article, does not forget the murderous violence that will have presided over the establishment of the law, namely the murder of the father, thanks to which (thanks to the murder, thanks to the father, thanks to the murder of the father) the guilty and shameful sons come to contract, through a sort of at least tacit oath or sworn faith, the equality of the brothers. The trace of this founding criminality or this primitive crime, the memory of which is kept by the (animal) totem and the taboo—this murderous trace remains ineffaceable in any egalitarian, communitarian, and compassional fraternity, in this primitive contract that makes of any compassional community a *cofraternity*. 154

There remains the immense risk of what is still a fraternalism of the "fellow." This risk is double (and also affects Lévinas's discourse, let it be said in passing): *on the one hand*, this fraternalism frees us from all ethical obligation, all duty not to be criminal and cruel, precisely, with respect to any living being that is not my fellow or is not recognized as my fellow, because it is other and other than man. In this logic, one is never cruel toward what is called an animal, or a nonhuman living creature. One is already exculpated of any crime toward any nonhuman living being. And specifying, *on the other hand*, as Lacan does: "It is a fellow that it [this cruelty] is targeting, even in a being of another species," does not change or fix anything. It is always my fellow that I am targeting in a being of another species. So the fact remains that I cannot be suspected of cruelty with respect to an animal

---

17. See Derrida, *Politiques de l'amitié*, pp. 253–99 [*Politics of Friendship*, pp. 227–70].
18. Lacan, *Écrits*, p. 149 [p. 122].

that I cause to suffer the worst violence, I am never cruel toward the animal *as such*. Even if I can be accused of being criminal with respect to an animal qua human, insofar as I am targeting, through it or its figure, my neighbor or my fellow. Even if it were a foreigner as my fellow. If I am judged, or if I judge myself, to be cruel by killing a beast or millions of beasts, as happens every day, directly or not, it is only insofar as I am supposed to have killed, by "targeting," consciously or unconsciously, my fellows, humans, figures of the human via these beasts—this "via" able to mobilize all sorts of unconscious logics or rhetorics. It is always man, my fellow, the same as I, myself in sum, that I am making suffer, that I kill, in a culpable, criminal, cruel, and incriminable manner.

But does one only have duties toward man and the other man as human? And, above all, what are we to reply to all those who do not recognize their fellow in certain humans? This question is not an abstract one, as you know. The worst, the cruelest, the most human violence has been unleashed against living beings, beasts or humans, and humans in particular, who precisely were not accorded the dignity of being fellows (and this is not only a question of profound racism, of social class, etc., but sometimes of the singular individual as such). A principle of ethics or more radically of justice, in the most difficult sense, which I have attempted to oppose to right, to distinguish from right, is perhaps the obligation that engages my responsibility with respect to the most dissimilar [*le plus dissemblable*, the least "fellow"-like], the entirely other, precisely, the monstrously other, the unrecognizable other. The "unrecognizable" [*méconnaissable*], I shall say in a somewhat elliptical way, is the beginning of ethics, of the Law, and not of the human. So long as there is recognizability and fellow, ethics is dormant. It is sleeping a dogmatic slumber. So long as it remains human, among men, ethics remains dogmatic, narcissistic, and not yet thinking. Not even thinking the human that it talks so much about.

The "unrecognizable" is the awakening. It is what awakens, the very experience of being awake.

The "unrecognizable," and therefore the non-fellow [*le dissemblable*]. If one trusts and binds oneself to a Law that refers us only to the similar, the fellow, and defines criminal or cruel transgression only in what it is targeting as fellow, that means, correlatively, that one has obligations only to the fellow, be it the foreigner as fellow and "my neighbor," which, step by step, as we know, in fact intensifies our obligations toward the most similar and the nearest [*du plus semblable et du plus proche*]. More obligation toward men than toward animals, more obligation toward men who are close and similar than toward the less close and less similar (in the order of probabilities and supposed or fantasized resemblances or similarities: family, nation, race, culture, religion). One will say that this is a *fact* (but can a fact ground and justify an ethics?): it is a fact that I feel, in this order, more obligations toward those who closely share my life, my people, my family, the French, the Europeans, those who speak my language or share my culture, etc. But this fact will never have founded a right, an ethics, or a politics.

3. Finally, if we rely on Lacan's axiomatics or good sense, once there is cruelty only toward the fellow, well, not only can one cause hurt without doing evil [*faire* du *mal* sans faire le mal] and without being cruel not only toward humans not recognized as true humans and true brothers (I leave the choice of examples up to you, and this is not only about racism), but also toward any living being foreign to the human race. The obvious consequence is that not only would one not be cruel (or criminal, criminalizable, or culpable) when one caused suffering to people not recognized and legitimized as such (which happens every day somewhere in the world), but one would have the right to inflict the worst suffering on "animals" without ever being suspected of the least cruelty. There would be no cruelty in industrial abattoirs, in the most horrific stockbreeding establishments, in bullfights, in dissections, experimentations, breaking and training, etc., in circuses, menageries, and zoos (of which more soon). I need not belabor the point.

Here, *two corollaries* that are also *two* virtual *complications* of this schema.

A. *First complication*. One might object to my objection (so this is an objection I'm making to myself and that I will try my best to integrate and take into account) that what I am doing is simply an almost limitless broadening of the notion of "fellow" and that in talking about the dissimilar, the non-fellow, I am surreptitiously extending the similar, the fellow, to all forms of life, to all species. All animals qua living beings are my fellows. I accept this counterproposition, but not without twice further upping the ante by pointing out:

1. *In the first place, the first upping of the ante*: that this broadening would already, of itself, be markedly, significantly, and obviously in breach with everything that everyone has in mind, and Lacan in particular, when they talk about the fellow: fellow means for them, as is undeniably obvious, not "living being in general" but "living being with a human face." There is here an uncrossable *qualitative* limit; I mean a qualitative and essential limit. To put this limit to the test of the worst experimentations, it is enough to imagine (I leave you to do so) a thousand situations in which one would have to decide which life goes first — before the other. According to the humanist logic the presupposition of which we are trying to think through, saving a human

156

157

embryo a few weeks old, destined after birth to live a short life—one day, for example—and a life of mental and physical handicap—saving such a life without the slightest future ought to come before the lives of millions, or an infinite number of living animals in full health and with a full future. Who will say that this choice really is possible or easy? Whatever reply one really gives to this question, whatever decision one takes (and these are not abstract and artificial examples, as one could show, decisions such as this are taken every day), what is certain is that in the humanist logic deployed by Lacan, the putting to death of the newborn, abandoning the newborn to its death, the failure to assist a person in danger that that represents, will be judged to be criminal and cruel, whereas the killing of billions of beasts would not be. The frontier is here qualitative and essential; numbers and time do not count. There is no "crime against animality" nor crime of genocide against nonhuman living beings.

2. *In the second place, the second upping of the ante:* it is not enough to say that this unconditional ethical obligation, if there is one, binds me to the life of any living being in general. It also binds me twice over to something nonliving, namely to the present nonlife or the nonpresent life of those who are not living, present living beings, living beings in the present, contemporaries—i.e. dead living beings and living beings not yet born, nonpresent-living-beings or living beings that are not present. One must therefore inscribe death in the concept of life. And you can imagine all the consequences this would have. Moreover, it is not certain that even in the originary history or fiction of the murder of the primal father according to which the brother-sons subject themselves to the law because, says Freud, the shame of their crime compels them to do so, it is not certain that this shame does not signify, always already, in its possibility, the bond of obligation or debt with respect to the dead.

B. *Second complication.* There are indeed "animal rights": some national legislations proscribe some acts of violence, some forms of torture or violence toward animals; and there are, as you know, all sorts of likable associations in the world that would like to do more, to publish universal declarations of the rights of animals analogous to the declaration of the rights of man. But, to put it briefly, the texts of existing laws only forbid certain forms of cruelty or torture, but they do not forbid the killing of animals in general, be it for the production of meat for food, or for experimentation and dissection. The struggle against certain forms of hunting and against bullfighting is under way and has little chance of getting very far for the moment. Killing an animal, at any rate, is not held to be cruel in itself. As for the declarations of the rights of animals called for by some people, beyond the fact that they never go so far as to condemn all putting to death, they most often follow, very naïvely, an existing right, the rights of man adapted by analogy to animals. Now these rights of man are in a relation of solidarity and indissociably, systematically dependent on a philosophy of the subject of a Cartesian or Kantian type, which is the very philosophy in the name of which the animal is reduced to the status of a machine without reason and without person-hood. This is a major failure of logic, the principle of which I merely point out, there being no need to say anymore about it here. I prefer, since it is a matter of the determination of man as person and personal subject, to look more closely at what is implied here by this concept of subject, including, as to the animal, what becomes of it after the transformation or subversion that Lacan imprints on the concept of the subject. You will recall that it was by what he called a "recourse [. . .] to the subject" that Lacan concluded the article we were reading. Let me read that sentence again:

> if we can provide a more justly rigorous truth, let us not forget that we owe it to the following privileged function: that of the recourse of the subject to the subject, which inscribes our duties in the order of eternal fraternity: its rule is also the rule of every action allowed us.

Would it suffice for an ethics to remind the subject (as Lévinas will have attempted) of its being-subject, its being-host or hostage, and thus its being-subject to the other, the Wholly Other or to any other [*au Tout-Autre ou à tout autre*]?[19]

I do not believe so. This does not suffice to break the Cartesian tradition of the animal-machine with neither language nor response.[20] This is not

159

---

19. The rest of this session repeats a then unpublished portion of the lecture given to the 1997 Cerisy conference, "L'animal autobiographique." It appeared subsequently, without major modifications, under the title "Et si l'animal répondait?" in the *Cahiers de L'Herne*, no. 83: *Derrida*, ed. Marie-Louise Mallet and Ginette Michaud (Paris: Édi-tions de L'Herne, 2004), pp. 117–29. It was also reprinted in the posthumous book by Jacques Derrida, *L'animal que donc je suis*, ed. Marie-Louise Mallet (Paris: Galilée, 2006), pp. 163–91; trans. David Wills as "And Say the Animal Responded," in *Zoontolo-gies: The Question of the Animal*, ed. Cary Wolfe (Minneapolis: University of Minnesota Press, 2003), pp. 121–46, and reprinted in Jacques Derrida, *The Animal that Therefore I Am*, ed. Marie-Louise Mallet (New York: Fordham University Press, 2008). [Transla-tor's note: In the interests of consistency of style and tone I have retranslated the text here.]

20. [Derrida's note:] Here we would need, as I have tried elsewhere, in a rereading of Descartes, to unfold what I shall here call the *question of the response*. And to define the hegemonic permanence of this "Cartesianism" that dominates the discourse and prac-tice of human and humanist modernity—as to the animal. What the programmed ma-

sufficient, even in a logic or an ethics of the unconscious which, without giving up on the concept of the subject, would lay claim to some "subversion of the subject."

With this Lacanian title, "Subversion of the Subject," we are, then, moving from one ethical denial to another. In "Subversion of the Subject and *160* Dialectic of Desire in the Freudian Unconscious" (1960),[21] a certain passage names "the animal" or "an animal"—in the singular and without further specification. It marks perhaps both a step beyond and a step backward from Freud as to the relation between man, the unconscious, and what I call the *animot*.[22] This remarkable page first gives the impression, and the hope, that things are going to change, especially as to the concept of communication or information that is assigned to what is called the animal, the animal in general. This "animal" is supposedly only capable, so one thinks, of a coded message or a narrowly signaling signification, under strict constraint: fixed in its programming. Lacan begins to take on the "platitude" of "modern information theory." It is true that he is speaking here of the human subject and not the animal, but he writes this, which indeed names the sovereign as absolute Master but which seems to announce, and even allow one to hope for, a different note:

> The Other, as prior site of the pure subject of the signifier, holds the master-position in it, even before coming to existence—to say it with and against Hegel—as absolute Master. For what is omitted in the platitude of modern information theory, is that one cannot even speak of a code unless it be

---

chine, like the animal, supposedly cannot do, is not to emit signs but, says the *Discourse on Method* (part 5), to "respond." Like animals, machines that had "the organs and the external shape of a monkey [. . .] could not use words or other signs by composing them as we do to declare our thoughts to others. For we may well conceive of a machine so constructed that it proffers words, and even words relating to bodily actions that cause some change in its organs; so that if touched in a particular place, it might ask what one wishes to say to it, or in another, it might cry out that one is hurting it, and other similar things; but not that it could arrange them diversely to *respond* [my emphasis—J.D.] to the meaning of everything said in its presence, as the dullest of men can do." [Translator's note: my translation of Descartes.]

21. Lacan, *Écrits*, pp. 793–827 (pp. 807ff.) [pp. 683ff.].

22. [Derrida's note:] Translator-to-come's note on the word "*animot*." Quote for example pages 298–99 of "L'animal que donc je suis," on what motivates or justifies the choice of this word "*animot*," more untranslatable than ever. [Editors' note: See *L'animal autobiographique*, pp. 298–99, and *L'animal que donc je suis*, pp. 73–77.] [Translator's note: The editors of the French edition suggest that the opening of the note ("Note du traducteur à venir") should perhaps read "Note au traducteur . . ." ("note to the translator . . .").]

already the code of the Other, whereas it's a quite different matter when it comes to the message, since it is on this basis that the subject is constituted, so that it is from the Other that the subject receives even the message that he emits.[23]

We shall return, after a detour, to this page of "Subversion of the Subject . . ." It *posits* (and I mean *posits,* it emits in the form of a thesis or presupposes without bringing in the slightest proof) that the animal is characterized by its inability to *pretend to pretend* and to *efface its traces,* so that it could not be a "subject," i.e. a "subject of the signifier."

The detour I'll sketch out now will permit us to go back through earlier *161* texts of Lacan's, where, it seems to me, they *simultaneously* announced a theoretical mutation and a stagnant confirmation of the legacy, its presupposition and its dogmas.

What allowed one still to hope for a decisive displacement of the traditional problematic was what, for example, in "The Mirror-Stage as Formative of the Function of the I," as early as 1936, took into account a specular function in the sexualization of the animal. This was quite rare for the time. And that was even the case if, and it is a massive limitation, this passage via the mirror immobilizes the animal forever, according to Lacan, in the snares of the imaginary, depriving it thus of all access to the symbolic, i.e. to the Law itself (which we have just been talking about) and to everything that is supposed to make up what is proper to man. The animal will never be, like man, a "prey of language." "One must posit," we read later, in "The Direction of the Treatment," "that, as a fact of an animal prey to language, the desire of man is the desire of the Other."[24] (This figure of the prey characterizes symptomatically and recurrently Lacan's "animal" obsession at the very moment he is so keen to dissociate the anthropological from the zoological: man is an animal but he speaks, and he is less a beast of prey than a beast that is prey to speech.) There is desire, and therefore unconscious, only of man, never of the animal, unless it be as an effect of the human unconscious, as though by some contagious transfer or some mute interiorization (which would still have to be accounted for), the animal, domesticated or tamed, translated into itself the human unconscious. Careful to distinguish, as we have just seen, the unconscious drive from instinct and the "genetic," in which he encloses the animal, Lacan maintains in "Position of the Un-

23. "Subversion of the Subject and Dialectic of Desire in the Freudian Unconscious," in *Écrits,* p. 807 [p. 683].

24. "The Direction of the Treatment and the Principles of Its Power," in *Écrits,* p. 628 [p. 525].

conscious" that the animal cannot have its own unconscious, properly its own, as it were, and if the logic of this expression were not ridiculous. But it would be ridiculous primarily for Lacan himself, perhaps, since he writes: "At the time of propedeutics, one can illustrate the effect of the enunciation by asking the pupil if he can imagine the unconscious in an animal, unless it be some effect of language: of human language."[25]

162

Each word in this sentence would merit a critical examination. The thesis is clear: the animal has neither the unconscious nor language, it does not have the other, it has no relation to the other as such, except by an effect of the human order, by contagion, appropriation, domestication.

No doubt taking into account the sexualizing specularity of the animal is a remarkable advance, even if it captures the *animot* in the mirror, and even if it holds the female pigeon or the desert locust in captivity in the imaginary. Referring at this point to the effects of a *Gestalt* attested to by a "biological experimentation" which does not fit with the language of "psychic causality," Lacan praises this theory for nonetheless recognizing that the "maturation of the gonad in the female pigeon" presupposes "the sight of a congeneric" and therefore another pigeon, whatever its sex. And that is true to the point that simple reflection in a mirror suffices. A visual image also suffices for the desert locust to pass from solitude to gregariousness. Lacan speaks, in a way that I think significant, of passage from the "solitary" form to the "gregarious" form, and not to the social and still less political form, of course, as though the difference between the *gregarious* and the *social* were the difference between animal and man.[26] This motif and this word "gregarious," and even "gregarism," reappear in force around ten years later, around animality, in "Remarks on Psychic Causality" (1946),[27] a text at the end of which, moreover, Lacan claims that one cannot get beyond Descartes. The analysis of the specular effect in the pigeon is more developed but goes in the same direction: the ovulation of the female pigeon, according to then recent work by Harrison (1939),[28] happens on mere *sight* of a form that suggests a congeneric pigeon, a reflecting sight, basically, even in the absence of a real male. It really has to do with specular vision,

163

25. "Position of the Unconscious," in *Écrits*, p. 834 [p. 707].

26. "The Mirror-Stage as Formative of the Function of the *I*," in *Écrits*, p. 93 [p. 77].

27. "Remarks on Psychic Causality," in *Écrits*, especially pp. 190–91 [pp. 155–56].

28. See *Proceedings of the Royal Society*, series B (Biological Sciences), vol. 126, no. 845 (February 1939).

of image or visual image, and not with identification by odor or cry. Even if the courtship play is physically prevented by a glass plate, and even if the couple is made up of two females, ovulation occurs. It happens after twelve days when the couple is heterosexual, as it were, and after a period that can be as long as two months for two females. A mirror is enough to make it happen.[29]

One of the interesting things about this interpretation, is that, like Descartes basically, and according to this tried-and-true biblico-Promethean tradition to which I keep returning, it puts in relation the fixity of animal determinism, in the order of information or communication, with a certain originary perfection of the animal. Conversely, if "human knowledge" is "more autonomous than that of the animal from the force-field of desire,"[30] and if "the human order is distinguished from nature,"[31] this is, paradoxically, because of an imperfection, an originary defect of man, who, basically, received speech and technology only in place of something lacking. This is what Lacan places at the center of his "Mirror-Stage . . . ," namely "the datum of a true *specific prematurity of birth* in humans."[32] The defect linked to this prematurity supposedly corresponds to "the objective notion of the anatomical incompleteness of the pyramidal system," what embryologists call "fetalization," the link of which to a certain "intraorganic mirror"[33] is recalled by Lacan. An autotelic specularity of the inside is linked to a defect, a prematurity, an incompleteness of the little human.

We must register with the greatest prudence what we have just rather hastily called a limited but incontestable advance, still on the threshold of "Subversion of the Subject . . ." For not only can the animal, held in the imaginary, not accede to the symbolic, the unconscious, and language (and therefore to the egological function of the autodeictic "I"), but the description of its semiotic power remained determined, in the "Rome Discourse"

164

29. "Remarks on Psychic Causality," pp. 154–56. See also pp. 342, 345–46, 452 [pp. 284, 286–87, 377].

30. "The Mirror-Stage . . . ," p. 96 [p. 77].

31. "Variations on the Standard Treatment," in *Écrits,* p. 354 [p. 294]: "For it is appropriate to meditate the fact that it is not only by a symbolic assumption that speech constitutes the being of the subject, but that, via the law of alliance, by which the human order is distinguished from nature, speech determines, from before birth, not only the status of the subject, but the coming into the world of its biological being."

32. "The Mirror-Stage . . . ," p. 96 [p. 78].

33. Ibid., p. 97 [p. 78].

(1953),[34] in the most dogmatically traditional manner, fixed in Cartesian fixism, in the presupposition of a code that allows only *reactions* to stimuli and
not *responses* to questions. I say "semiotic system" and not language, for it
is language that Lacan also refuses to the animal, allowing it only what he
calls a "code," the "fixity of a coding" or a "system of signaling." Other ways
of naming what—in a cognitivist problematic of the animal, which often
repeats, while appearing to oppose, the most tired truisms of metaphysics—is called the "hardwired response" or "hardwired behavior."[35]

165   Lacan is so much more precise and firm in taking up on his own account
the old, modernized *topos* of the bees that he seems, as it were, to have an
uneasy conscience about it. I sense a muted worry under the authority of
this new, but so, so old discourse on bees. Lacan claims to base himself on
what he calmly calls the "animal realm" in order to criticize the current
notion of sign language, in opposition to "human languages." When bees
apparently "respond" to a "message," they are not *responding,* they are *react-*

34. "Function and Field of Speech and Language in Psychoanalysis," in *Écrits*,
pp. 237–322 [pp. 197–268].

35. [Derrida's note:] See Joëlle Proust, *Comment l'esprit vient aux bêtes: Essai sur la
représentation* (Paris: Gallimard, 1997), p. 150. The same author does everything to
make the word "response," in the case of the animal, mean nothing other than a programmed *reaction,* deprived of all responsibility or even of all "intentional" respon-
sivity—this word "intentional" being used with an imprudence, a confidence, not to
say a phenomenological crudeness, that makes one smile. About the syrphid, an insect
"programmed to seek out females by automatically applying a pursuit trajectory according to a certain algorithm to intercept the object pursued," Joëlle Proust cites Ruth
Millikan, and comments as follows: "What is interesting in this type of response is that
it is *inflexibly* produced by certain precise characteristics of the stimulus (here, its size
and speed). The insect cannot respond to other characteristics, nor can it dismiss targets
that show characteristics incompatible with the expected function. It cannot abandon
its flight when it 'perceives' that it is not following a female. This insect appears to have
no means of evaluating how correct its own perceptions are. It therefore seems *unduly
generous* to attribute to it an *intentional* capacity *properly so called.* It *responds to signs, but
these signs are not characteristics of an independent object; they are characteristics of
proximal stimulations. As Millikan says, it follows a 'proximal rule.' However, the pre-
wired response has as its aim the fecundation of a female syrphid, i.e. an object existing
in the world" (pp. 228–29). I emphasize the words that, more than others, would call for
a vigilant reading. The critical or deconstructive reading that we are calling for would
seek less to give back to the animal or to such and such an insect the powers here being
denied it (even though that sometimes seems possible) <than> to wonder if the same
type of analysis could not claim just as much relevance in the case of man, for example
in the "wiring" of his sexual and reproductive behavior. Etc.

ing: they are merely obeying the fixity of a program, whereas the human subject responds to the other, to the question of the other. This is a literally Cartesian discourse. Later, as we shall see, Lacan expressly opposes *reaction* to *response* as animal realm to human realm, just as he opposes nature to convention:

> We are going to show the inadequacy of the notion of sign language via the very manifestation that best illustrates it in the animal realm, and that looks as though, if it had not recently been the object of an authentic discovery, one would have had to invent it with this purpose in mind.
>
> Everyone now admits that the bee, returned to the hive from its nectar-gathering, transmits to its companions by two sorts of dance the indication of the existence of nectar, close or far. The second dance is the more remarkable, because the plane in which it describes the figure eight which has given it the name "wagging dance," and the frequency of the circuits completed in a given time, exactly designate on the one hand the direction determined in relation to solar inclination (whereby bees can navigate in all weather, thanks to the sensitivity to polarized light), and on the other the distance, up to several kilometers, at which the nectar is to be found. And the other bees respond to this message by heading immediately for the place thus designated.
>
> Ten years or so of patient observation sufficed for Karl von Frisch to decode this type of message, for it is indeed a code, or system of signalization that only its generic character forbids us from qualifying as conventional.
>
> Is it a language for all that? We can say that it is distinguished from a language precisely by the *fixed* [my emphasis] correlation of its signs with the reality that they signify. For in a language the signs take their value from their relationship among themselves, in the lexical division of the semantemes as much as in the positional or even flexional use of the morphemes, in contrast with the *fixity* [my emphasis again] of the coding here put in play. And the diversity of human languages takes its full value in this light.
>
> What is more, if the message of the type here described determines the action of the *socius*, it is never retransmitted by it. And this means that it remains *fixed* [still my emphasis] to its function of relay for the action, from which no subject detaches it as symbol of communication itself.[36]

Even if one subscribed provisionally to this logic (to which, moreover, I have no objection, though I would like simply to reinscribe it quite differently, beyond any simple human/animal opposition), it is difficult to reserve, as

166

---

36. "Function and Field of Speech . . . ," pp. 297–98 [pp. 245–46].

Lacan does explicitly, differentiality of signs to human language and not to the animal code. What he attributes to signs, which "in a language" (understand: in the human order) "take their value from their relationships among themselves," etc., and not only from the "fixed correlation of these signs to reality," can and must be granted to any code, animal or human.

As for the absence of response from the animal-machine, as for the trenchant distinction between *reaction* and *response*, there is nothing fortuitous about the fact that the most Cartesian passage is to be found in what follows this discourse on the bee, on its system of information that cannot introduce it into the "field of speech and language." What is at stake is indeed the constitution of the subject as human subject, when it passes the limit of information to accede to speech:

> For the function of language here is not to inform but to evoke.
>
> What I am seeking in speech is the response of the other. What constitutes me as a subject, is my question. In order to have myself recognized by the other, I proffer what was, only in view of what will be. To find him, I call him by a name that he must assume or refuse in order to respond to me.
>
> [. . .] If now I face the other in order to interrogate him, no cybernetic apparatus, however rich you imagine it to be, can make a *reaction of what is response*. Its definition, as second term in the stimulus-response circuit, is only a metaphor sustained by the subjectivity imputed to the animal in order to elide it later in the physical schema to which it is reduced. This is what we have called putting the rabbit into the hat to pull it out later. *But a reaction is not a response.*
>
> If I press an electric button and there is light, there is response only for *my* desire.[37]

Once more, it is not a question here of erasing all the difference between what we call *reaction* and what we commonly call *response*. The point is not to confuse what happens when one presses a computer key and what happens when one asks a question of one's interlocutor; and still less to endow what Lacan calls "the animal" with what he calls a "subjectivity" or an "unconscious" that would allow one, for example, to put said animal in an analytic situation (even though analogous scenarios are not necessarily excluded with *certain* animals in *certain* contexts—and if we had time we could imagine hypotheses to refine this analogy). My reservation bears only on the purity, rigor, and indivisibility of the frontier that separates, already among "us humans,"

---

37. [Derrida's note:] Ibid., pp. 299–300 [p. 247]. My emphasis, except for "*my* desire."

reaction from response: and consequently the purity, rigor, especially the indivisibility of the concept of responsibility — and consequently of the concept of sovereignty, which depends on it. The general disquiet that I am formulating thus is aggravated in at least three ways:

1. when we really do have to take into account a logic of the unconscious that ought to forbid any immediate certainty as to the consciousness of freedom that all responsibility presupposes;

2. especially when, and particularly in Lacan, this logic of the unconscious is grounded on a logic of repetition that, in my view, will always inscribe a destiny of iterability, and therefore some reactional automaticity in every response, however originary, free, decisive and a-reactional it might appear;

3. when (in Lacan in particular) the materiality of speech, the body of language, is recognized. Lacan recalls this <on> the following page: "Speech is indeed a gift of language, and language is not immaterial. It is a subtle body, but it is a body." And yet in the meantime he will have grounded all "responsibility" and, first of all, all psychoanalytic responsibility, and thereby all psychoanalytic ethics, on the distinction that I find so problematical between *reaction* and *response*. He even founds on this distinction — and this is what I really wanted to show — his concept of *subject*:

> From that point on, there appears the decisive function of my own response that is not only, as they say, to be received by the subject as approbation or rejection of his discourse, but truly to recognize or abolish the subject qua subject. This is the *responsibility* of the analyst each time he intervenes by speaking.[38]

Why do the stakes seem so much higher here? By problematizing, as I am doing, the purity and indivisibility of a line between reaction and response, and especially the possibility of tracing this line between mankind *in general* and the animal *in general*, one runs the risk, as people notice and won't fail to complain to me about, of throwing doubt on all responsibility, all ethics, all decision, etc. To which I would respond, as it really is a matter of responding, schematically, on the level of principle, with the following three points:

1. *On the one hand*, having doubts about responsibility, decision, one's own being-ethical, can be, or so it seems to me, and ought perhaps to remain, the indefeasible essence of ethics, of decision, and of responsibility. Any knowledge, certainty, and firm theoretical assurance on this subject

169

38. Ibid., p. 300 [pp. 247–48]. Lacan's emphasis.

would suffice to confirm, precisely, the very thing that one is trying to deny, namely a reactionality in the response. I'm saying "deny" [*dénier*, in the psychoanalytic sense], and that's why I always place denial at the heart of all these discourses on the animal.

2. *On the other hand*, without erasing the difference, a nonoppositional and infinitely differentiated, qualitative, intensive difference, between reaction and response, the point is, on the contrary, to take it into account in the whole differentiated field of experience and of a world of life. And to do so without distributing this differentiated and multiple difference, in such a massive and homogenizing way, between the human subject on the one hand and the nonsubject that is the animal in general on the other, this latter coming to be, in another sense, the nonsubject subjected to the human subject.

3. *Finally*, the point would be to elaborate another "logic" of decision, response, event—as I also try to deploy it elsewhere and which seems to me less incompatible with what Lacan himself, in "Subversion of the Subject . . . ," says of the code as "code of the Other." Meaning that Other from whom "the subject receives even the message he emits."[39] This axiom ought to complicate any simple distinction between *responsibility* and *reaction*, with all its consequences. And so the point would be to reinscribe this *différance* of reaction and response and thereby this historicity of ethical, juridical, or political responsibility, into another thinking of life, living beings, into another relation of the living to their ipseity, and thereby to their supposed sovereignty, their *autos*, their own autokinesis and reactional automaticity, to death, to technique, or to the machinic.

After this detour, if we come then to the later text entitled "Subversion of the Subject and Dialectic of Desire in the Freudian Unconscious," we will, it is true, follow the same logic in it, and the same oppositions—especially the opposition of imaginary and symbolic, of the specular capture of which the animal is capable and the symbolic order of the signifier to which it does not have access. At this juncture of the imaginary and the symbolic, the whole question of the relation to self in general is played out, the position of the self, the ego and sovereign ipseity of course, but also the position of the theoretician or the institution in the history of which said theoretician articulates and signs his discourse on that juncture: here Lacan's discourse and its signature. (We cannot do this here, within these limits, but we should have to place in its proper perspective, a few years after the war, with its ideological stakes, the whole essentially anthropological aim of the

170

39. "Subversion of the Subject . . . ," p. 807 [p. 683].

period, even as it claimed to go beyond any *positive* anthropology or any metaphysico-humanistic anthropocentrism. And, above all, in an entirely legitimate way, beyond biologism, behaviorist physicalism, geneticism, etc. For Heidegger as for Lacan and so many others, the point at that time was to lay out a new *fundamental* anthropology and to reply *to* and *for* the question "What is man?" This moment has not at all been left behind, it is even putting forward new forms of the same dangers.)

In "Subversion of the Subject . . . ," the refinement of the analysis bears on other conceptual distinctions. They seem equally problematic to me as those we have just been analyzing and, moreover, remain indissociable from them.

We are dealing apparently with a parenthesis ("Let us observe in a parenthesis . . ."), but a parenthesis that to my eyes is capital. For it bears on the dimension of testimony in general. Who testifies about what and whom? Who proves, who looks, who observes whom and what? What about knowledge, certainty, and truth? "Let us observe in parentheses," says Lacan, "that this Other distinguished as place of Speech, imposes itself no less as witness of Truth. Without the dimension that it constitutes, trickery in speech would not be distinguishable from mere feint, which, in combat or sexual display, is however very different."[40]

The figure of the animal, then, has just emerged in this difference between *feint* and *trickery*. Recall what we were saying about Machiavelli, about the prince and the fox, and about the fox that feigns not being the fox that it is or even that it is imitating. I am not a fox, the prince can say, basically, the prince who is not really a fox but who is acting like a fox, who knows how to feign being a fox all the while feigning not to feign and therefore not to be the fox that he basically is in what he says or does. Lacan would say that only a prince or a man is capable of this, not a fox. A clean distinction between what Lacan says the animal is able to do, i.e. strategic feint (following, chasing, or persecuting, be it warlike, predatory, or seductive), and what it is unable to do and testify to, namely the trickery of speech in the order of the signifier and of Truth. The trickery of speech, as we shall see, is of course the lie (and the animal cannot really lie, according to common sense, according to Lacan and many others, even if, as we know, it knows how to feign); but, more precisely, trickery is lying insofar as it comprises, in promising the truth, the supplementary possibility of speaking the truth in order to mislead the other, to make the other believe something other than the truth (you know the Jewish joke told by Freud and often

40. Ibid., p. 807 [p. 683].

171

cited by Lacan: "Why tell me you are going to X, so that I'll believe you're going to Y, when you're going to X?"). According to Lacan, it is this lie, this trickery, this second-degree feint that the animal is unable to do, whereas the "subject of the signifier," in the human order, supposedly has the power to do so and, moreover, supposedly comes into being as a subject, institutes and comes to itself as sovereign subject *by virtue of this power*: a reflexive second-degree power, a *conscious* power of trickery through feigning to feign. One of the interesting things about this analysis is that Lacan really does concede a lot, this time—more in any case than anyone in philosophy and more than he himself had done in earlier writings—to this ability to feign on the part of what he always calls "the animal," "an animal," on the part of what he terms here its "dancity," with an "a."[41] "Dancity" is the ability to feign in dance, lure, display, in the choreography of hunting or seduction, in the display shown before making love or to defend oneself when making war, and so in all the forms of the "I am" or "I am followed" that we are tracking here. But whatever he concedes to the animal in this way, Lacan holds it in the imaginary or the presymbolic (as we noted in his "Mirror-Stage" period and in the example of the pigeon or the desert locust). He holds "the animal" prisoner in the specularity of the imaginary; or rather he holds that the animal holds itself in this captivity and speaks with reference to it of "imaginary capture." Above all, he holds the animal down to the first degree of feigning (feigning without feigning feigning) or, what comes to the same thing here, to the first degree of the trace: ability to trace, track, track down [*dépister*], but not to throw the tracking off track [*dé-pister le dé-pistage*] and to *efface* its track.

For a "But" will indeed fold this paragraph in two ("But an animal does not feign feigning"). An accounting separates out the columns of what must be conceded to the animal (feint and trace, the inscription of the trace) and what must be denied it (trickery, lying, the feint of the feint, and the effacement of the trace). But—what the articulation of this "But" perhaps leaves out of sight, discreetly in the shade, among all the features listed, is perhaps the reference to life, to the "vital." And it is indeed the question of life that is occupying us in this seminar, before all and after all, between the beast and the sovereign. Everything conceded to the animal is done so under the heading of "vital situations," whereas—one would be tempted to conclude—the animal, be it hunter or game, is deemed be incapable of an authentic rela-

41. [Translator's note:] Lacan's neologism "dansité" is a homophone of "densité," density.

tion to death, of a testimony to a mortality essential to the heart of Truth or its Speech. The animal is a living being that is only living, an "immortal" living being, as it were. As in Heidegger (to whom Lacan is here closer than ever, in particular, as we shall see, as to what links the *logos* to the possibility of "tricking" and "making mistakes" [*"tromper" et "se tromper"*]), the animal does not die.[42] Moreover, for this same reason the animal supposedly knows nothing of mourning, sepulcher, and corpse—which Lacan says is a "signifier":

> Let us observe in parentheses that this Other distinguished as place of Speech, imposes itself no less as witness of Truth. Without the dimension that it constitutes, trickery in Speech would not be distinguishable from mere feint, which, in combat or sexual display, is however very different. Deploying itself in imaginary capture, the feint is part of the play of approaching and breaking away that constitutes the originary dance, in which these two *vital* situations find their scansion, and the partners who follow it—what we shall venture to write as their dancity. The animal, moreover, shows itself capable of this when it is tracked: it is able to *throw off track*[43] by feigning a departure in one direction. This can go so far as to *suggest* among game animals the nobility of honoring the aspect of display that is part of the hunt.

42. [Derrida's note:] Allow me to refer here to *Apories* (Paris: Galilée, 1996), especially around pages 70 and 132 [trans. Thomas Dutoit as *Aporias* (Stanford University Press, 1993), pp. 36 and 76].

43. [Derrida's note:] Lacan explains in an important note to the "Seminar on the Purloined Letter" (*Écrits,* p. 22) the original use he makes here of the word "dépister": not to track, sniff out, trail but, on the contrary, as it were, to cover the trail by erasing one's tracks, *dé-pister*. In this note he invokes both Freud's famous text on "The Antithetical Sense of Primal Words," Benveniste's "magisterial correction" of it, and a piece of information from [the etymological dictionary of] Bloch and Wartburg, who date from 1875 the second usage of the word *dépister*. The question of the antithetical meaning of certain words "remains entire," says Lacan, "if one bring out in its rigor the agency of the signifier." Indeed, I would be tempted to say, upping the ante, especially if, as is the case here, we put to the test the axioms of a logic of the signifier in its double relation to the distinction between the animal order (imaginary capture) and the human order (access to the symbolic and the signifier), on the one hand, and a different interpretative putting to work of undecidability, on the other. The supposedly established difference between *pister* and *dépister*, or rather between *dépister* (to trace or follow a trail) and *dépister* (to erase a trail or voluntarily lead the follower astray), gathers and guarantees the whole distinction between human and animal according to Lacan. This distinction only has to tremble for the whole axiomatic to be ruined, in its very principle. This is what we are going to have to clarify.

174 [This, of course, is merely an anthropomorphic and figural suggestion, the "rabbit in the hat," for what is going to be made clear immediately, by the "But" that follows, is that honor and nobility, linked to the given Word as they are to the symbolic, are precisely what the animal cannot do; an animal doesn't give its word, and one doesn't give one's word to an animal, except by projection or anthropomorphic transference. One doesn't lie to an animal either, especially not by feigning to hide something one is showing it. Is this not self-evidence itself? And even the whole organization of this discourse? This at any rate is what we are looking at here.]

> *But an animal does not feign feigning.* It does not make tracks the trickery of which would consist in their being taken to be false when they are true, i.e. tracks that would present the right path. *Any more than it effaces its tracks, which would already be for it to make itself subject of the signifier.*[44]

Being a subject of the signifier, of which the animal is here deemed incapable: what does this mean? Let us first note in passing that this confirms the old (Adamo-Promethean) theme of the profound innocence of the animal, which, incapable of the "signifier," incapable of lie and trickery, incapable of crime and cruelty, of feigned feint, is here allied, in just as traditional a fashion, to the theme of a violence that knows nothing of cruelty: the innocence, then, of a living being that is a stranger to evil, prior to the difference between good and evil.

But being subject of the signifier means also, and again, two indissociable things that couple in the subjectity of the subject. The subject of the signi-
175 fier is subjected to the signifier. Lacan constantly insists on the "dominance" "of the signifier over the subject,"[45] as on the "symbolic order which is, for the subject, constitutive."[46] The "subject" does not have mastery over it. Nor

44. [Derrida's note:] "Subversion of the Subject . . . ," in *Écrits,* p. 807 [p. 683], (my emphasis, of course). Elsewhere I shall study a text that, obeying the same logic ("the sexual instinct [. . .] crystallized on a relation that is [. . .] imaginary"), especially about the stickleback and the "copulation dance with the female," addresses the question of death, of the *being already dead,* and not only the being-mortal of the individual as "type" of the species: not horses, but the horse. See *Les écrits techniques de Freud* (Paris: Seuil, 1975), pp. 140–41 [trans. John Forrester as *The Seminar of Jacques Lacan, Book 1: Freud's Papers on Technique, 1953–54* (Cambridge: Cambridge University Press, 1988), pp. 122–23].

45. [Derrida's note:] For example, in "Seminar on *The Purloined Letter,*" in *Écrits,* p. 61 [p. 45].

46. [Derrida's note:] "it is the symbolic order that is constitutive for the subject, by showing you in a story the major determination the subject receives from the trajectory of a signifier" ("Seminar on *The Purloined Letter,*" p. 12 [p. 7]).

sovereignty. The real human sovereign is the signifier. The entry of the subject into the human order of the law presupposes this passive finitude, this infirmity, this defect that the animal does not suffer from. The animal knows nothing of evil, lies, and trickery. What the animal lacks is precisely the lack in virtue of which man is subject to the signifier, subject subjected to the sovereign signifier. But being subject of the signifier is also to be a subjecting subject, a *master* subject, an active and deciding subject of the signifier, master enough in any case, if you will, to feign feigning and thereby to be able to posit one's power of effacement of the trace. This sovereignty is the superiority of man over beast, even if it is based on the privilege of the defect, lack, or fault, a failing that is referred to the generic prematuration of birth as well as to the castration complex—that Lacan, in a text I shall quote in a moment, designates as the scientific (or in any case nonmythological) and Freudian version of original sin or the Adamic fault.

This is where the passage from imaginary to symbolic is determined as passage from the animal order to the human order. This is where subjectity, as order of the signifier from the place of the Other, was supposedly missed by the traditional philosophy of the subject, along with the relations between man and animal. Such at least is Lacan's allegation when he subtly reintroduces the logic of anthropocentrism and firmly reinforces the fixism of the Cartesian cogito as a thesis on the animal-machine in general.

All this has been articulated only confusedly by philosophers, professionals though they be. But it is clear that Speech begins only with the passage from feint to the order of the signifier, and that the signifier demands an other place—the place of the Other, the Other witness, the witness Other than any of the partners—so that the Speech that it supports can lie, i.e. posit itself as Truth.

Thus it is from somewhere other than the Reality that it concerns that Truth draws its guarantee: it is from Speech. Just as it is from Speech that it receives that mark that institutes it in a structure of fiction.[47]

176

This allusion to a "structure of fiction" would send us back to the debate around *The Purloined Letter.*[48] Without reopening that debate at this point, let us note here the reflexive acuity of the word "fiction." The concept toward which it leads is no longer merely that of the *figure* or the simple *feint,*

47. "Subversion of the Subject . . . ," pp. 807–8 [p. 684].

48. [Derrida's note:] See "Le facteur de la vérité," in *La carte postale: De Socrate à Freud et au-delà* (Paris: Flammarion, 1980); trans. Alan Bass as "The Purveyor of Truth," in *The Postcard: From Socrates to Freud and Beyond* (Chicago: University of Chicago Press, 1987).

but the reflexive and abyssal concept of a *feigned feint*. It is via the power to feign the feint that one accedes to Speech, to the order of Truth, to the symbolic order, in short to the human order. And thereby to sovereignty in general, as to the order of the political.

(Before even specifying once more the principle of the reading that I am attempting, I should like to evoke at least one hypothesis. Although Lacan often repeats that there is no Other of the Other,[49] although for Lévinas, to the contrary, from another point of view, the question of justice is born of this quest for the third party and an other of the other who would not be "simply his fellow,"[50] one wonders whether the denied but common implication of these two discourses about the other and the third party does not situate at least one instance of the animal, of the animal-*other*, of the other *as animal*, of the *other*-living-mortal, of the nonfellow in any case, the nonbrother [the divine or the animal, here inseparable], in short of the a-human in which god and animal form an alliance according to all the theo-zoomorphic possibilities properly constitutive of myths, religions, idolatries and even the sacrificial practices of monotheisms that claim to break with idolatry. What is more, the word "a-human" holds no fear for Lacan who, in a postscript to "Subversion of the Subject . . . ," notes that he was not at all upset by the epithet "a-human" that one of the conference participants had used to describe what he said.)

What is Lacan doing when he posits "that the signifier demands an other place—the place of the Other, the Other witness, the witness Other than any of the partners"? Must not this beyond of the partners, and thus of the specular or imaginary duel, if it is to break with the image and the fellow, at least be situated in a place of alterity radical enough (what I earlier called the unrecognizable) that one must break with all identification of an image of self, with any fellow living being, and therefore with all fraternity[51]

---

49. See, for example, "Subversion of the Subject . . . ," p. 818 [p. 693].

50. [Derrida's note:] "Paix et proximité," in *Emmanuel Lévinas*, special issue of *Cahiers de la nuit surveillée*, 1984, p. 345. Cited and commented in *Adieu — à Emmanuel Lévinas* (Paris: Galilée, 1997) [trans. Pascale-Anne Brault and Michael Naas as *Adieu to Emmanuel Levinas* (Stanford: Stanford University Press, 1999)]. In this text, in which Lévinas asks himself the very worried question, in the end left hanging, of what a third party would be that was both "other than the neighbor," "but also an other neighbor and also a neighbor of the other and not simply the other's fellow," it remains clear that the question remains, as he himself says on the same page, in the order of the "interhuman," and even of the citizen.

51. [Derrida's note:] As to the value of "fraternity," as I tried to deconstruct its tradition and authority in *Politiques de l'amitié* (Paris: Galilée, 1994), one ought to study also its credit in Lacan, well beyond the passage we were reading earlier and the suspicion

or human proximity, with all humanity? Must not this place of the Other be a-human? If that were the case, the a-human, or at least the figure of some divinanimality (to say it in one word), even if it were pre-sensed via man, would be the quasi-transcendental referent, the excluded, foreclosed, denied, tamed, sacrificed ground of what it grounds: namely the symbolic order, the human order, the law, justice. Is this necessity not acting in secret in Lévinas and Lacan, who, moreover, so often encounter each other's path despite all the differences in the world? This is one of the reasons why it is so difficult to hold a discourse of mastery or transcendence with respect to the animal and simultaneously claim to do so in the name of God, in the name of the name of the Father or the name of the Law. The Father, the Law, the Animal, etc., the sovereign and the beast—should one not recognize here basically one and the same thing? Or, rather, indissociable figures of the same Thing? One could add the Mother, and it probably would change nothing. Nietzsche and Kafka understood this perhaps better than philosophers or theorists did, at least in the tradition we are attempting to analyze.

178

Of course, once again, my concern is not primarily to object frontally to the logic of this discourse and what it brings with it of the Lacan from the period of the *Écrits* (1966). I must for now leave hanging the question of knowing whether, in the texts that followed or in seminars (published or not, accessible or inaccessible), the frame of this logic was explicitly reexamined. Especially when the oppositional distinction between the imaginary and the symbolic, which forms the very axiomatics of this discourse on the animal, seems to be increasingly left to one side, if not rejected, by Lacan. As always, I am trying to take into account the strongest systematic organization of a discourse in the form in which it gathers itself at a relatively determinable moment of its process. Spanning thirty years, the various texts gathered in one volume, the *Écrits*, strongly bound to itself, give us in this respect a reliable hold and path to follow. Among the published and accessible texts that follow the *Écrits*, one should, in particular, try to follow the path that leads, interestingly but I believe without a break, to the analyses of animal mimeticism, for example, always from the point of view of *view*, from that of the image and the "seeing oneself looked at," even by a can of sardines that can't see me ("First, if it means anything when Petit-Jean says

brought to bear on the parricidal brothers according to the logic of *Totem and Taboo*. In many places, Lacan certainly dreams of an *other fraternity*, for example in these final words of "Aggressivity in Psychoanalysis": "It is to this being of nothingness that it is our daily task to open anew the way of his meaning in a discreet fraternity to which we never measure up" (*Écrits*, p. 124 [p. 101]).

to me that the can can't see me, this is because, in a certain sense, after all, it really is looking at me. It is looking at me at the level of the point of light, which is where everything that looks at me is to be found, and that is not at all a metaphor.")[52]

Instead of objecting to this argumentation, then, I would be tempted to emphasize that the logical, and therefore rational, fragility of some of its articulations ought to commit us to a general reworking of this whole conceptuality.

179

In the first place, it seems difficult to identify or determine a limit, i.e. an indivisible threshold, between feint and feigned feint. What is more, even supposing that this limit is conceptually accessible (and I do not believe it is), it would still remain to find out in the name of what knowledge or what testimony (and knowledge is not a piece of testimony), one can calmly declare that the *animal in general* is incapable of feigning feint. Lacan here invokes no ethological knowledge (the growing and spectacular refinement of which is proportional to the refinement of the *animot*), nor any experience, observation, or personal attestation worthy of belief. The status of the assertion that denies the animal feigned feint is purely dogmatic in its form. But there is no doubt a hidden motivation to this humanist or anthropological dogmatism, and that is the certainly obscure but undeniable feeling that it is difficult, if not impossible, to tell the difference between a feint and a feigned feint, between the ability to feign and the ability to feign feigning. For example, in the most elementary sexual display, how would one distinguish between a feint and a feigned feint? If it is impossible to provide a criterion here, one could conclude either that any feigned feint remains a simple feint (animal, or imaginary, as Lacan would say) or else, to the contrary, and with equal validity, that any feint, however simple it be, repeats itself and posits itself undecidably, in its possibility, as feigned feint (human or symbolic, according to Lacan). As I shall make clearer in a moment, a symptomatology (and of course a psychoanalysis) can and must always conclude that it is possible, for any feint, to be a feigned feint, and for any feigned feint to be a simple feint. The distinction between lie and feint then becomes precarious, along with the distinction between Speech and Truth (in Lacan's sense) and everything he claims to distinguish from it. And therefore between man and beast. The feint requires that the other

52. [Derrida's note:] Jacques Lacan, *Le séminaire livre XI: Les quatre concepts fondamentaux de la psychanalyse* (Paris: Seuil, 1973), p. 89; see especially pp. 70–71 [trans. Alan Sheridan as *The Four Fundamental Concepts of Psychoanalysis (The Seminar of Jacques Lacan, Book 11)* (New York: Norton, 1978), p. 95; pp. 73–74].

be taken into account; it supposes, then, simultaneously, the feint of the feint—of a simple supplementary play of the other in the strategy of the game. This supplementarity is at work from the first feint. Lacan, moreover, cannot deny that the animal takes the other into account. In the article "On a Question Preliminary to Any Possible Treatment of Psychosis" (1957–58), there is a remark that goes in this direction and that I should have liked patiently to link to our network: simultaneously in tension, if not in contradiction, with Lacan's discourse on the imaginary capture of the animal (in this way basically deprived of an other) and in harmony with the discourse on pathology, evil, lack, or defect that mark the relation to the other as such in man but are already announced in the animal:

> To take up a formula that had pleased Freud when he heard Charcot say it, "this does not stop it from existing"—here, the Other in its place A.
>
> For remove it from there, and man can no longer even maintain himself in the position of Narcissus. The *anima*, as though through the effect of an elastic band, snaps back onto the *animus* and the *animus* onto the animal, which, between S and *a,* maintains with its *Umwelt* "foreign relations" that are significantly narrower than ours, without however one's being able to say that its relations with the Other are non-existent, but only that they appear to us only in sporadic sketches of neurosis.[53]

In other words, the beast only resembles man and only enters into relations with the Other (in a weaker fashion, because of a "narrower" adaptation to the environment) to the extent of its illness, the neurotic defect that brings it closer to man, to man as defect of premature animal, as yet insufficiently determined. If there were a continuity between the animal order and the human order, and hence between animal psychology and human psychology, it would follow this line of evil, of fault, and of defect. Lacan, moreover, claimed that he did not hold to a discontinuity between the two psychologies (animal and human), *at least qua psychologies*: "May this digression here dissipate the misunderstanding that we apparently allowed some people to reach: that of imputing to us the doctrine of a discontinuity between animal and human psychology, which is very far from what we think."[54]

What does this mean? That the radical discontinuity between the animal and the human, an absolute and indivisible discontinuity that he nonetheless

180

181

---

53. "On a Question Preliminary to Any Possible Treatment of Psychosis," in *Écrits*, p. 551 [p. 460].

54. "Situation of Psychoanalysis and Training of the Psychoanalyst in 1956," in *Écrits,* p. 484 [p. 404].

confirms and deepens, no longer has to do with the psychological as such, *anima* and *psyche*, but precisely with the appearance of an other order.

On the other hand, an analogous (I do not say identical) conceptual undecidability comes to trouble the opposition, so decisive for Lacan, between *making* and *effacing* tracks [or traces]. The animal can trace, inscribe, or leave tracks, but, Lacan adds, it "does not efface its tracks, which would already mean that it became the subject of the signifier." Now here too, even supposing that we rely on this distinction, Lacan justifies neither by testimony nor by ethological knowledge the assertion whereby "the animal," as he says, the animal in general, does not efface its tracks. Beyond the fact that, as I had tried to show elsewhere (and this is why, so long ago, I had substituted the concept of trace for that of signifier), the structure of the trace presupposes that *to trace* comes down to *effacing a trace* as much as imprinting it, all sorts of animal practices, sometimes ritual practices, for example in burial and mourning, associate the experience of the trace and that of the effacing of the trace. A feint, moreover, and even a simple feint, consists in rendering a sensory trace unreadable or imperceptible. How could one deny that the simple substitution of one trace for another, the marking of their diacritical difference in the most elementary inscription, the one Lacan concedes to the animal, involves effacement as much as imprinting? It is just as difficult to assign a frontier between feint and feigned feint, to draw an indivisible line through the middle of a feigned feint, as it is to distinguish inscription from effacement of the trace.

But let us go further, and ask a type of question that I should have liked, given time, to generalize. It is less a matter of wondering whether one has the right to refuse the animal such and such a power (speech, reason, experience of death, mourning, culture, institution, politics, technique, clothing, lying, feigned feint, effacement of the trace, gift, laughter, tears, respect, etc.—the list is necessarily indefinite, and the most powerful philosophical tradition in which we live has refused *all of that* to the "animal"). It is more a matter of wondering whether what one calls man has the right, for his own part, to attribute in all rigor to man, to attribute to himself, then, what he refuses to the animal, and whether he ever has a concept of it that is *pure, rigorous, indivisible, as such*. Thus, even supposing, *concesso non dato*, that the "animal" is incapable of effacing its traces, by what right should one concede this power to man, to the "subject of the signifier"? And especially from a psychoanalytic point of view? Any man may certainly be *conscious,* within a space of doxic phenomenality, of effacing his traces. But who will ever judge the efficacy of this gesture? Do we need to recall that any effaced trace, in consciousness, can leave a trace of its effacement the symptom of which (be it individual or social, historical, political, etc., and even technical—one can never be sure of having erased something on a computer, etc.) can always guarantee its return? Do we need, especially, to remind a psychoanalyst of this? And to recall that any reference to the power to efface the trace is still speaking the language of the conscious and even imaginary self?

All this does not come down to saying (I've explained this at length elsewhere) that the trace cannot be effaced. On the contrary. It is in the nature of a trace that it always effaces itself and is always able to efface itself. But that it efface *itself*, that it can always efface *itself*, from the first moment of its inscription, through and beyond repression, does not mean that anybody, God, man, or beast, is its master or sovereign subject and can have the power to efface *it* at its disposal. On the contrary. In this respect, man has no more sovereign *power* to efface his traces than the so-called "animal." To efface his traces *radically*, hence just as *radically* to destroy, deny, put to death, even put himself to death.

But one should not conclude from this that the traces of the one and the others cannot be effaced—and that death and destruction are impossible. Traces are effaced, like everything, but it is in the very structure of the trace that it is not in the *power* of anyone to efface *it* or above all to "judge" as to its effacement, still less an assured, constitutive power to efface, performatively, what effaces itself. The distinction can appear to be subtle and fragile, but this fragility fragilizes all the solid oppositions that we are tracking, beginning with the distinction between the symbolic and the imaginary that in the end sustains this whole anthropocentric reinstitution of the superiority of the human order over the animal order, of the law over the living being, etc., where this subtle form of phallogocentrism seems to bear witness in its way to the panic that Freud talks about: wounded reaction not to the *first* trauma of humanity, the Copernican (the earth revolves around the sun), not to the *third* trauma, the Freudian (the decentering of consciousness in view of the unconscious), but to the *second* trauma, the Darwinian.

Before provisionally moving away from Lacan's text, I should like to situate a task and issue a reminder.

The task would commit us, on the basis of everything we have inscribed here under the sign of the Cartesian cogito, to analyze closely Lacan's reference to Descartes. As with the reference to Hegel, and often associated with it, the appeal to Descartes, to the Cartesian *I think*, was constant, determining, complex, differentiated. In a rich set of references and in a broad investigation, a first marker would be imposed on us by our problematic. It would be found in the pages that immediately follow the paragraph on the difference between the nonfeigned feint of the animal and the feigned feint of man capable of effacing his traces. In it, Lacan shares out praise and criticism.

On the one hand, the "Cartesian cogito does not fail to recognize" the essential, namely that consciousness of existence, the *sum*, is not immanent to it but transcendent, and therefore beyond specular or imaginary capture. This comes down to confirming that an animal cogito remains a captive of the identificatory image, a situation one could formalize by saying that the animal accedes to the ego, the "me," only by missing the "I," but an "I" that itself accedes to the signifier only on the basis of a lack: the (animal) self lacks the lack. Lacan writes, for example:

> The ego is thenceforth a function of mastery, a play at being imposing, a constituted rivalry [so many features that are not refused to the animal]. In the capture that it undergoes from its imaginary nature, it masks its duplicity, i.e. that the consciousness in which it assures itself of an incontestable existence (a naïveté to be found deployed in the meditation of a Fénelon) is in no way immanent to it, but indeed transcendent since it sustains itself on the basis of the unary trait of the ego-ideal (which the Cartesian cogito does not fail to realize). Whereby the transcendental ego itself is relativized, implicated as it is in the misrecognition in which are inaugurated the identifications of the ego.[55]

But, *on the other hand,* the *ego cogito* is dislodged from its position as central subject. It loses mastery, central power, and becomes a subject subjected to the signifier.

The imaginary process moves thus from the specular image to "the constitution of the ego on the road of subjectivation by the signifier." This seems to confirm that the becoming-subject of the ego passes via the signifier, Speech, the Truth, etc., i.e. by losing immediate transparency, consciousness as consciousness of a self-identical self. Which leads to an only apparent paradox: the subject is confirmed in the eminence of its power by subverting it and bringing it back to its defect, namely that animality is on the side of the conscious *ego*, whereas the humanity of the human subject is on the side of the unconscious, the law of the signifier, Speech, the feigned feint, etc.:

> The promotion of consciousness as essential to the subject in the historical aftermath of the Cartesian cogito is for us the misleading accentuation of the transparency of the "I" *in actu* at the expense of the opacity of the signi-

55. "Subversion of the Subject . . . ," p. 809 [p. 685].

fier that determines that "I," and the slippage whereby *Bewusstsein* serves to cover the confusion of the *Selbst*, comes precisely in the *Phenomenology of Spirit* to demonstrate, with Hegel's rigor, the reason for his error.[56]

So the accentuation of transparency is said to be "misleading" [*trompeuse*]. This does not only mean the "going astray" [*se tromper*] of error, but a "being misled" [*se tromper*] of trickery, lying, lying to oneself as belief, "making believe" in the transparency of the ego or of self to self. That would be the risk of the traditional interpretation of the Cartesian cogito, perhaps the risk of Descartes' auto-interpretation, of his intellectual auto-biography, one never knows. Whence the Lacanian promotion of the cogito and the diagnosis of lying, trickery, misleading transparency at the heart of the cogito itself.

"Hegel's rigor," he says. We should then have to follow the interpretation that Lacan proposes of the struggle between the Master and the Slave, at the point where it comes to "decompose the equilibrium of fellow to fellow." The same motif of the "alienating dialectic of the Master and the Slave" appears in "Variations on the Standard Treatment" (1955): animal specularity, with its lures and aberrations, comes to "structure durably the human subject," by reason of the prematurity of birth, "a fact in which one apprehends this dehiscence of natural harmony, demanded by Hegel as the fecund illness, the happy fault of life, in which man, by distinguishing himself from his essence, discovers his existence."[57] The reinscription of the question of the animal, in our reinterpretation of the reinterpretation of Hegel by Lacan, could be situated at the point at which the latter reintroduces the reminder about the imaginary, the "specular capture" and the "generic prematurity of birth," a "danger" "unknown to Hegel." Here too, what is at stake is life. Lacan says so clearly, and the move to the human order of the subject, beyond the animal imaginary, is indeed a question of life and death:

> The struggle that establishes him is indeed one of pure prestige [whereby it is no longer animal, according to Lacan], and what is at stake is to do with life, well placed to echo that danger of the generic prematurity of birth, unknown to Hegel, and which we have made the dynamic mainspring of specular capture.[58]

How are we to understand the word "generic," which qualifies with so much force the insistent and determining concept of "prematurity," namely the absolute event without which this whole discourse would lose its "main-

185

186

---

56. Ibid. pp. 809–10 [p. 685].
57. "Variations on the Standard Treatment," p. 345 [p. 286].
58. "Subversion of the Subject . . . ," p. 810 [p. 686].

spring," as Lacan himself says, beginning with the relevance of the distinction between imaginary and symbolic? Is the "generic" a trait of the human genus as animal genus or a feature of the human insofar as it escapes from genus, from the generic, the genetic — by the defect, precisely, of a certain de-generation [*dé-génération*], rather than that of merely degenerating [*dégénérescence*], a de-generation the very defect of which engenders symbolic "generation," the relations between generations, the law in the Name of the Father, Speech, Truth, Trickery, the feigned feint, the power to efface the trace, etc.?

From this question, which we shall leave in abeyance, like a task, at the point where, nonetheless, it proceeds from this traditional logic of the originary defect, I return to what I announced as a final reminder, namely what gathers this whole placing into perspective of the defect in the history of the original fault, an original sin that finds its mythical relay in the Oedipus story, and then its nonmythical relay in the "castration complex" as formulated by Freud. In the following quotation, in which I shall emphasize the lack and the defect, we shall see again all the stages of our journey, Genesis, the snake, the question of "I" and of the "What am I?" ("What am I following?"),[59] a quotation from Valéry's *Sketch of a Serpent* ("the universe is a *defect* in the purity of Non-Being"), etc.:

> This is what is lacking for the subject to be able to think himself exhausted by his cogito, namely what about him is unthinkable. But where does this being come from who appears to be in some sense *at fault* [*en défaut*] in the sea of proper names?
>
> We cannot ask this of this subject as an "I." To know the answer, he *lacks* everything, since, if this subject "I," I was dead, as we said, he would not know it. Therefore that he does not know me to be alive. So how am I to prove it to Myself?
>
> For I can, at a pinch, prove to the Other that he exists, not of course with the proofs of the existence of God with which the centuries have been killing Him, but by loving him, a solution provided by the Christian kerygma.
>
> This is, moreover, a solution that is too precarious for us even to think of grounding in it a detour for what is our problem, namely: What am I?
>
> I am in the place whence it is shouted: "the universe is a *defect* in the purity of Non-Being."
>
> And this is not without reason, for in being maintained, this place makes

187

---

59. [Translator's note:] Derrida's parentheses enclose the words "être et suivre" to draw attention to the ambiguity of "je suis," which can mean both "I am" and "I follow."

Being itself languish. This place is called Enjoyment, and it is the *lack* [*dé-faut*] of this place that would render the universe vain.

So I am responsible for it? Yes, no doubt. Is this enjoyment, the *lack* of which renders the Other inconsistent—is it then mine? Experience proves that it is ordinarily forbidden to me, and this not only, as imbeciles would believe, through a bad arrangement of society, but I would say by the *fault* of the Other if he existed: but as the Other does not exist, all that remains for me is to take the *fault* on "I," i.e. to believe the thing that experience leads us all to, with Freud in the lead: *to original sin*. For even if we did not have Freud's admission, as clear as it is full of sorrow, the fact would remain that the myth that we owe to him, the newest-born in all history, is of no more use than the myth about the accursed apple, with this slight difference (not a result of its status as myth), that, being more succinct, it is considerably less cretinizing.

But what is not a myth, yet which Freud formulated just as early as he did the Oedipus complex, is the castration complex.[60]

60. "Subversion of the Subject . . . ," pp. 819–20 [pp. 694–95]; Derrida's emphases.

January 30, 2002

Once more, alas, as I did last week, with a sadness that knows nothing of repetition, I shall salute the memory of a colleague who was a friend — and to honor Pierre Bourdieu, I neither want nor am able to give in to the genre of encomium or funeral oration — however sincere its pathos may be — at the time when a friend of fifty years has left me, a friend who was also author of the oeuvre you know.

Seeking the right tone and looking for strength on the side of life, or the reaffirmation of life, here and now, and without hiding the element of denial that I accept, I shall recall that it was in this room, in the 1990s, that, with him and a few others, we founded the CISIA, Comité international de soutien aux intellectuels algériens [International Committee for the Support of Algerian Intellectuals], also with the memory and attachment that we both had, though differently, for Algeria and the common concern for the terrible destiny of that country. And still on the side of life, since we are going to speak of Flaubert today, since we are going to bring back the *revenant* Flaubert, I'll behave as though we were inviting Pierre Bourdieu to take part in this seminar with us. I shall quote a passage from his book *Les règles de l'art* (The Rules of Art), which is to a great extent a book on Flaubert and a book based on Flaubert. I have chosen this passage because it deals with literature, knowledge, beasts, and monsters, as well as with the law, with their legitimation. And also, as you will hear, the watchword, spoken like a law, by the father of sociology (Durkheim):

190   But the age is also that of Geoffroy Saint-Hilaire, Lamarck, Darwin, Cuvier, theories on the origin of species and evolution: Flaubert who, like the Parnassians, also intends to go beyond the traditional opposition between art and science, borrows from the natural and historical sciences not only erudite knowledge but also the mode of thought that characterizes them and the philosophy that comes from them: determinism, relativism, histori-

cism. He finds here among other things the *legitimation* of his horror for the preachings of social art and his taste for the cold neutrality of the scientific gaze: "What is beautiful about the natural sciences: they are not trying to prove anything. And so, what breadth of facts and what immensity for thought! You must treat men like mastodons and crocodiles!" Or again: "treat the human soul with the impartiality they use in the physical sciences." What Flaubert learned at the school of the biologists, and especially from Geoffroy Saint-Hilaire, "that great man who showed the legitimacy of monsters," takes him very close to Durkheim's watchword, "social facts must be treated like things," which he puts to work with great rigor in *Sentimental Education*.[1]

What, at bottom? Who, at bottom? At bottom what and at bottom who?[2]

The beast and the sovereign, what is it at bottom? And who? What is there at the bottom of the question, and first of all the question "What is it?" or "Who is it?" at the bottom of the question of being, on the subject of the beast and the sovereign?

What is there, at the bottom of this couple, this strange couple, this *odd couple* as they would say in English.[3] What at bottom? Who at bottom? And what if, at bottom, the distinction between *what* and *who* came to sink into indifference, into the abyss? To die, basically, just as the common condition of both beast and sovereign, qua living beings, is to be exposed to death, and to a death that always risks coming back from *who* to *what,* to reduce *who* to *what,* or to reveal the "what" of "who." Is to die not to become "what" again? A "what" that anybody will always have been.

Who or what *at bottom*? Should we be sure we are devoting a fundamental or profound seminar to this story of "the beast and the sovereign"? Or else, should we be suspicious here more than ever, better than ever, of the seduction of the bottom, the founder, the fundamental, the profound? As

191

1. Pierre Bourdieu, *Les règles de l'art* (Paris: Seuil, 1998), pp. 169–70. Derrida's emphasis. The handwritten opening of this session along with the photocopied extract from *Les règles de l'art* were attached to this version of the session. At the end of the handwritten page (on the back) is this sentence, which indicates how Derrida planned to proceed: "The thing—is it who or what?" A slight variant of the same sentence is also written on the photocopy: "Link. Things—are they who or what?"

2. [Translator's note:] Throughout this session, Derrida exploits the idiomatic possibilities of the French word "fond," which means depth, bottom, fundament, basis, or (back)ground. The verb "fonder" means to found or to ground. I have translated according to the context, and often provided the French in brackets where this seemed necessary.

3. [Translator's note:] The words "odd couple" are in English in the text.

though there were still some *bêtise* in believing in depth, in the profound seating of *what*ever, or of *whom*ever. Perhaps, with the beast and the sovereign, we are put to the test of the vertigo of the bottomless, the bottomless bottom. This vertigo of the bottomless, the abyss, the bottomless bottom can, as vertigo does in fact, make your head spin. The sovereign is the one who is at the head, the chief, the king, the capital, the first, the *arkhē* of commencement or commandment, the prince, but also the one whose head can spin, who can lose his head, in madness or decapitation. And lose, along with his head, meaning. What is there at the bottom of the head? And what do we have at the bottomless bottom of our heads when we speak of the beast and the sovereign?

Perhaps we are going to talk today, without depth, of a certain bottom, a certain bottomless bottom of things, things said to be beast and sovereign.

The beast and the sovereign, that was and remains our title.

Not the *bestiality* of the beast — and the sovereign.

Not the *bêtise* of the beast — and the sovereign.

But the beast *itself* and the sovereign. And when we say the beast *itself*, we are thinking of what is proper to the beast. We are thinking of what makes the proper meaning of the name that names the beast, of what is proper to the beast. And there is no adequate abstract name to designate properly this essence of the beast, the being-beast of the beast. *On the one hand*, because we do not have in French a word such as "bêteté," as we have, for the animal, "animalité." *On the other hand*, because the being-beast of the beast, an expression I have just imprudently used to give an idea of a proper designation of the essence of the beast, has the noun "beast" drift toward the attribute, epithet, or adjective "bête," which, in French, as an adjective, displaces everything and no longer refers at all to the essence of the beast, and is even radically heterogeneous to it, in that it properly applies, or at least has its regime of propriety, as an attribute, in principle, for sense and good sense, only in the order of the human.

What is proper to the beast, if such there be, would be neither *bêtise* nor *bestiality*. Neither *bêtise* nor bestiality, which, if we are to believe good sense and what philosophy makes the most noise about, is rather that which is proper to man, like good sense, the most equally distributed thing in the world among humans.[4] *Bêtise,* which is proper to man, then, unless (this

4. [Translator's note:] French readers would immediately see the reference to the opening of part 1 of Descartes' *Discourse on Method:* "Good sense is, of all things among men, the most equally distributed."

would be my working hypothesis, still in abeyance) it is the proper of the proper *pure and simple*, the proper appropriating itself, the proper *positing* itself, the proper appropriated to itself, *autoposited*, the appropriation or the fantasy of the proper, wherever it comes about, both posits and posits itself, man being only one witness among others, even if he is, as though by definition, an eloquent and talkative witness, by definition the most telling witness of self-proclaimed, autoposited *bêtise,* no doubt the only living being to propose a claim for it that is armed, unionized, even, from a union that would be no other than philosophical culture, or even culture pure and simple.

We have had some trouble avoiding the lure of the beast itself, then, before any *bêtise,* given that in our genelycological doggedness we saw multiplying beneath our steps the steps of wolves and werewolves, on whose track we more often found man himself, man made *bête*, man-*bête*, more often, then, than the beast itself.

When I say man made *bête* or man-*bête* (with a hyphen), you can no longer tell the difference, in the French language that we are speaking by contract, between *bête* the noun and *bête* the adjective. Now between *bête* the noun and *bête* the adjective there is a world in French, because never, I repeat, never, will anyone say, sensibly and meaningfully, understandably for everyone, of a *bête* that it is *bête*. For the moment, speaking French, we are not *using* the word "bête," we are *mentioning* it in quotation marks, according to the well-known distinction between use and mention.[5] When we mention or cite a word in quotation marks, we suspend its use. Our referent is the word itself and not the thing it is supposed to designate. When we quote the word *bête*, we are aiming at the word without yet knowing necessarily what the word designates or means, without yet committing ourselves firmly on that point. And even to know, to determine without error whether, in the act of mentioning *bête,* we are referring to the noun (*la bête*) or <to> the adjective (a man or woman who is *bête*), you see that mention, quotation of the word alone, does not suffice. We already need a sentence, a grammar, a beginning of discourse to decide if I am mentioning the noun (*la bête*) or if I am mentioning the adjective (this man or woman is *bête*, a person is *bête,* a discourse or an action, even an event is *bête*, and according to the subject to which the attribute refers, the sense of the adjective is displaced). The adjective *bête* obviously does not mean the same thing in the sentence "this man or woman is *bête*" and the sentence "this discourse is *bête*," "this action, this way of doing things is *bête*," and still less

5. [Translator's note:] The words "use" and "mention" are in English in the text.

"this event is *bête*," in the sense of "It's *bête*, what's happening" (it's raining, or my car broke down, that's *bête*, I won't be able to go out, in the sense of "it's *ennuyeux* [annoying or boring]"—the *ennuyeux* posing in French semantic problems that are just as redoubtable); it's *bête* means: it is a chance event or occurrence that is undesirable, regrettable, in itself insignificant but damaging in its consequences, without anyone, anyone's *bêtise,* being able to be incriminated. If it is *bête* that I cannot finish preparing my lecture because my computer broke down, it is *bête* although no *bête* is responsible for it, nor anyone's *bêtise.* Only a person, a human person, so it would seem, can be said to be *bête,* but when something *bête* happens, in French, nobody, no person who is *bête,* nobody's *bêtise,* can be held to be responsible for it or guilty of it, can be held to be the cause of this *bête* thing that is happening. The attribute *bête* seems appropriate only to a person (and not to a *bête,* an animal qua *bête*), but there are cases in which the attribute *bête* is appropriate to nobody and refers anonymously to the happening of what is happening, the case or the event. This attribute, the use of this attribute, in a language, already seems very *unheimlich,* uncanny,[6] both strange and familiar, strangely familiar or familiarly strange.

What does *bête* mean? What is *bête*? Who is *bête*? What or who?

So in our dogged determination to hunt down what is proper to man, we were not far from forgetting that more difficult still is the determination of what is proper to the beast, and, a quite different issue, the proper meaning of the word *bête.*

If the proper of man is the properly human, the proper of the *bête* is certainly neither the "properly *bête*" of bestiality nor the "properly *bête*" of *bêtise.* We were not far from considering that, in French at least, bestiality could well be the proper of man.

Indeed, the need to think what has perhaps not yet been thought, namely the proper of man, led us last time, in the exemplary track of Lacan and in the analysis of the presupposition of a psychoanalytic paradigm that is singularly remarkable through many features, but which has a discursive organization and a conceptuality among other possible ones, [led us, then,] to pose the question of a bestiality which, for its part, would be the proper of man: bestiality as cruelty and not as a zoophilic perversion. How this bestiality is possible and what its relation is to the sovereignty of the law: that was basically the question that guided us last week. And we verified what untenable consequences we were doomed to by an anthropocentered and even humanistic logic of the sovereignty of the Law in this respect, that

---

6. [Translator's note:] The word "uncanny" is in English in the text.

is of freedom, *responsibility*, decision, convention, the symbolic, i.e. of the appropriate *response*, as opposed to the supposed (*bêtement* supposed)[7] so-called animal fixity of the programmed, imaginary, specular, hard-wired, coded reaction.

And we verified too what untenable consequences we were doomed to by the human and "supposed to know" logic of a sovereign *responsibility* capable of truth, speech, lie, crime, cruelty, bestiality, feigned feint, and effacement of one's own trace, as opposed to what one is supposed to know, again of a *reactional* irresponsibility of an animality incapable of crime, cruelty, bestiality, lying, feigned feint, or effacement of traces, in short, incapable of becoming a subject of the signifier, the expression "subject *of* the signifier" designating the master subject just as well as the subject subjected to the signifier. And by signifier, the signifier that has become the sovereign's sovereign, one had to understand the linguistic signifier in the last instance, language or speech, even if some pre- or nonlinguistic trace could apparently and provisionally claim some emancipation or some prerogative of seniority.

Today, still trying to think what has perhaps not yet been thought, namely the proper of man and the proper of the beast, and therefore the proper pure and simple, the proper itself, the ipseity of the proper, we might be tempted to wonder, symmetrically, not (as last week): "How is bestiality possible?" but "How is *bêtise* possible?"

This question will have been put, in one form or another, by more than one person. But before coming back to the text I am preparing to quote, before rereading it after a certain detour, and to recall its inscription in the French language, here is a certain shaping of the question by Deleuze, in *Difference and Repetition*.[8] This is a page and a book that antedate *Mille plateaux* [*A Thousand Plateaus*] by almost twelve years, and therefore antedate too the great, rich chapter entitled "1730 — Becoming-Intense, Becoming-Animal, Becoming-Imperceptible" that I talked about two sessions ago, which I still warmly recommend you to read *in extenso,* a chapter that is also traversed by many wolves and from which, last time, I quoted a passage on the Wolf Man and that passage's sarcasm with respect to psychoanalysis. *Mille pla-*

7. [Translator's note:] "Bêtement" is the adverbial form of "bête": here, "stupidly supposed."

8. Gilles Deleuze, *Différence et répétition* (Paris: Presses universitaires de France, 1968), pp. 196–97; trans. Paul Patton as *Difference and Repetition* (New York: Columbia University Press, 1994), pp. 150–51. [Translator's note: I have benefited from being able to consult Patton's translation, but in the interests of literality and consistency with Derrida's commentary I have retranslated all passages quoted from this book.]

teaux, which devotes so many analyses to the becoming-animal, no longer talks about *bêtise*, as did, twelve years earlier, then, *Difference and Repetition*, in a passage to which I shall come in a moment. The only allusion, the only occurrence of the word *bêtise,* that I have found (pending further investigation) concerns, precisely, a certain *bêtise of* psychoanalysis as supposed knowing. The *bêtise* of psychoanalysis, the *bêtises* uttered by psychoanalysis when it talks about masochism and, in a more general way, when it talks about animals. On page 317 [259] of *Mille plateaux* (but reread it all), Deleuze begins a paragraph thus: "We wish to make a very simple point about psychoanalysis: from the beginning, it has often encountered the question of the becomings-animal of the human being" [and we must note immediately that, for psychoanalysis and for Deleuze when he disputes psychoanalysis on this subject, it is always only about man, the becoming-animal of man, the history and stories of man in his becomings-animal, in other words, of the becoming-anthropomorphically-animal of man, and not about the animal and the beast, as it were, themselves].

> We wish to make a very simple point about psychoanalysis: from the beginning, it has often encountered the question of the becomings-animal of the human being. In children, who constantly undergo such becomings. In fetishism and especially in masochism, which constantly confront this problem. The least one can say is that the psychoanalysts, even Jung [this "even Jung" emphasizes and recalls that Deleuze is one of few, on a certain French scene, regularly to declare an admiring interest in Jung], have not understood or have not wanted to understand [Deleuze insinuates in this way that all these psychoanalysts have denied understanding, have behaved as though they did not understand, wanted not to understand what, consequently, they understood perfectly well and found it in their interests not to take on, admit, declare what they understood, what they understood that they understood and still wanted not to understand, wanted to pretend they did not understand, what is more a symptom than a simple failure of learning or knowledge: a symptomatic misrecognition on the basis of an unconscious knowledge. And this active, symptomatic misrecognition is a piece of bad treatment, even a violent and cruel mistreatment of the becoming-animal of man and child, a cruel violence]. They massacred the becoming-animal, in the adult and in the child. They saw nothing. In the animal, they see a representative of the drives or a representation of the parents. They do not see the reality of a becoming-animal, how it is the affect itself, the drive in person, and represents nothing. There are no drives apart from the assemblages [*agencements*] themselves.[9]

9. Deleuze and Guattari, *Mille plateaux,* p. 317 [p. 259].

This concept of affect, like that of machinic assemblage and of "plane," is the central concept of all these analyses and all this Deleuzian strategy. And after a few lines on the becoming-horse of little Hans in Freud, and in Ferenczi, the becoming-cockerel of Arpad, Deleuze comes to the interpretation of masochism. This is where the word *bêtise* imposes itself on him, this time describing discourses of a psychoanalytic type. "Psychoanalysis has no sense of the unnatural participations or the assemblages that a child can build [machines, then] in order to resolve a problem whose exits have been barred for him [so the becoming-animal would here be a ruse, a machination, a war-machine to escape, to undo a snare, a machine built to dismantle another machine]":

> Psychoanalysis has no sense of the unnatural participations or the assemblages that a child can build in order to resolve a problem whose exits have been barred for him: a plane, not a fantasy [critique, then, of the idea of fantasy as natural representer of a deeper and also natural drive, for which Deleuze intends to substitute the more technical, more machinic, less natural, more horizontal and flatter, planer figure of plane. And Deleuze goes on, using, precisely, the word *bêtise*, *bêtise* consisting in believing in the depth of a fantasy where there is really only plane]. In the same way, people would say fewer *bêtises* about pain, humiliation and anxiety in masochism, if they saw that it is the becomings-animal that lead it, and not the opposite. Apparatus, tools, devices intervene, always artifices and constraints for the greater Nature. The fact is that the organs have to be annulled, shut up as it were, so that their liberated elements can enter into new relationships, out of which flow the becoming-animal and the circulation of affects at the heart of the machinic assemblage.[10]

198

In other words, as in spite of everything these machinations of the becoming-animal "lead" adults and children, so their artifices, which remain constraints, affect the affect rather than being voluntarily calculated, and the psychoanalysts would utter fewer *bêtises*, would speak less, on the topic of masochism, for example, about pain, humiliation, and anxiety, if they took on board their knowledge about this subject. Deleuze does not say that psychoanalysts are *bêtes*, but that, mechanically, their statements are so many *bêtises*; they utter *bêtises* on this subject. Which already defines *bêtise* not only as a character (and we'll talk about this again in a moment), as a state, as the essence of what one is, but as the effect of what one does or says: there are events, operations even, *les bêtises*, and not a fundamental essence, *la bêtise*. Psychoanalysts are all the less *bêtes* when they say *bêtises* that they know

10. Ibid., p. 317 [pp. 259–60].

to be such and understand what they "wanted not to understand." They are in on what they want (for reasons to be analyzed) not to understand.

This gesture and this moment, this denunciation of *bêtises*, in spite of this single occurrence of the word in *Mille plateaux*, are the more significant and strategically decisive in this book not only because they are inscribed in the logic of the desiring machine of the *Anti-Oedipus* (1972), but also for the fact that their necessity is announced from the first pages of *Mille plateaux,* around the concept of rhizome and deterritorialization, which are put to the test of examples like the wasp and the orchid ("the wasp and the orchid form a rhizome, in their heterogeneity,"[11] the wasp itself becoming a piece in the reproductive apparatus of the orchid), the example of the baboon and the virus, of the DNA of the baboon and the cat, of the crocodile, etc. And in the second chapter, entitled "1914: One or Several Wolves?" the ironic discourse unleashes its sarcasm against Freud's treatment of the Wolf Man, after a reference to Kafka's story *Jackals and Arabs*. I refer you to this whole chapter from which I must content myself with reading the opening sentences and the conclusion, an indictment of Freud, who is basically ac-cused of not believing in what he said, which also constitutes a machine in which he is hypocritical enough to pretend to believe, but accused of having done everything (and here the condemnation is ethical and even political), done everything, then, to make the patient believe what psychoanalysis was telling him and wanted to have him subscribe to. Have him sign with an-other name, a name other than his own, his name turned into the name of another, the name of the father, patronymic, just when he wasn't that, just when the new name, the brand-new name he'd made for himself, was basi-cally stolen from him, so that we are dealing with nothing less than a theft and the substitution of someone's name by psychoanalysis (a dispossession that calls up from Deleuze a complaint made against psychoanalysis in the name of the Wolf Man, in a style and with a logic of complaint and coun-terindictment that is not far from resembling Artaud's complaint about the theft of his proper, his proper name, his new proper name, and his body proper — supposed to be without organs). Which signifies that these *bêtises* of psychoanalysis are not only poverties of knowledge, nonknowledges or incomprehensions, but ethical violences, machines in turn, and machines of war, subjection, brutalization, ways of making patients more *bêtes*, more brutal or brutish than they are in truth. Hence the sarcastic opening of the chapter entitled "1914: One or Several Wolves." As there is a date, the open-ing is that of a narrative, a chronicle of events, the analysis of the Wolf Man by Freud at the time:

11. Ibid., p. 17 [p. 10].

That day, the Wolf Man got off the couch particularly tired. He knew that
Freud had a genius for brushing against the truth and missing it, then for
filling the gap with associations. He knew that Freud knew nothing about
wolves, or about anuses for that matter. Freud only understood what a dog
was, and a dog's tail [no doubt an allusion to the well-known dogs of the
psychoanalysts Freud and Lacan, whose name before long will be included
in the genealogical series]. It wasn't enough; it wouldn't be enough. The
Wolf Man knew that Freud would soon declare him cured but that it was
not so and that he would continue being treated for eternity by Ruth, by
Lacan, by Leclaire. He knew, finally, that he was in the process of acquiring
a true proper name, Wolf Man, much more proper than his own, since he
was gaining access to the highest singularity in the instantaneous apprehension of a generic multiplicity: wolves—but that this new true proper name
was going to be disfigured, misspelled, retranscribed as a patronymic.[12]

(About this disorthographical violence, and be it said in parentheses for the
flavor of the French and Parisian anecdote, and what was to follow under
Lacan, of whom Deleuze had just said that he inherited and was to increase
Freud's capital of *bêtises* in the violent psychoanalytic domestication and
paternalization of the Wolf Man and what concerns him, allow me to recall
that a few years before *Mille plateaux*, in 1975, if memory serves, when I
had just published a long preface, "Fors" to the book that Abraham and
Torok devoted to the Wolf Man,[13] Lacan had dared to say, in an aggressive
seminar that never has been and no doubt never will be published, that he
believed that I was in analysis with the authors of *The Wolf Man's Magic
Word* and that, in my analysis with them, the subject supposed to know that
Lacan believed himself to be and who though he knew beyond what he was
supposed to know—Lacan said that I "coupled" them, these two analyst
friends. I close this chatty parenthesis on the fantasies, projections, and ban-
tering verbiage of the psychoanalysts of our time and our city.) Here now is
the conclusion of the chapter "One or Several Wolves?" the opening lines of
which I have already read: (Read and comment)

> The Wolf Man, a true proper name, an intimate forename that refers to
> the becomings, infinitives, intensities of a depersonalized and multiplied
> individual. But what does psychoanalysis understand about multiplication?
> The desert hour when the dromedary becomes a thousand dromedaries
> sniggering in the sky. The evening hour when a thousand holes are dug in
> the surface of the earth. Castration, castration, shouts the psychoanalytic
> scarecrow who has only ever seen one hole, one father, one dog where there

---

12. Ibid., pp. 38–39 [pp. 26–27].
13. Jacques Derrida, "Fors" (see session 4 above, n. 12).

are wolves, a domesticated individual where there are savage multiplicities. We are not only reproaching psychoanalysis for having selected only Oedipal statements. For these statements, up to a point, still form part of a machinic assemblage with respect to which they could serve as indices to be corrected, as in a calculus of errors. We are reproaching psychoanalysis with using the Oedipal enunciation to make the patient believe that he was going to make personal, individual statements, that he was finally going to speak in his own name. But everything is a trap from the start: the Wolf Man will never be able to speak. Talk as he does about wolves, howl like a wolf as he does, Freud is not even listening, he looks at his dog and replies: "it's Daddy." While it lasts, Freud says it's neurosis, and when it breaks, it's psychosis. The Wolf Man will receive the psychoanalytic medal for services rendered to the cause, and even the alimentary pension they give to old wounded soldiers. He would have been able to speak in his own name only if the machinic assemblage that produced particular statements in him had been brought to light. But it is not a question of that in psychoanalysis: at the very moment when they persuade the subject that he is going to offer his most individual statements, they take away from him every condition of enunciation. Making people keep quiet, stopping them talking, especially when they are talking, behaving as though they had not said anything: the famous psychoanalytic neutrality. The Wolf Man carries on shouting: six or seven wolves! Freud replies: what? Goats? Kids? How interesting, I take out the kids, a wolf remains, it's your father . . . That's why the Wolf Man feels so tired: he remains lying down with all his wolves in his throat, and all the little holes in his nose, all these libidinal values on his body without organs. The war is coming; the wolves are going to become Bolsheviks, the Man remains choked by everything he had to say. All we'll be told is that he became well brought-up again, polite, resigned, "honest and scrupulous," in short, cured. He takes his revenge by recalling that psychoanalysis lacks a truly zoological vision: "Nothing can be more valuable for a young person than the love of nature and an understanding of the natural sciences, especially zoology."[14]

So much for the single occurrence of the word *bêtises*, in the plural, in *Mille plateaux*. Some twelve years earlier, in 1968, in *Difference and Repetition*, Deleuze opens a long paragraph, more than a page long, with the following proposition: "*Bêtise* is not animality. The animal is guaranteed by specific forms that prevent it from being '*bête*.'"[15] ("*Bête*" is in quotation marks, to

14. Deleuze and Guattari, *Mille plateaux*, pp. 51–52 [pp. 37–38]. The authors state in a note that the last sentence comes from a letter quoted by Roland Jaccard in *L'homme aux loups* (Paris: Éditions universitaires, 1973), p. 113.

15. Deleuze, *Différence et répétition*, pp. 196–97 [pp. 150–51].

mark clearly that the point, once more, is to mention a quite particular use in a certain language: the animal is not *what one calls "bête,"* the animal cannot be called *bête*, qualified or described as *what one calls "bête."*) And the same paragraph, more than a page long, concludes with a question, this time. The question is "How is *bêtise* possible?" or, more precisely, for it's better to read this whole final sequence now, even if we need to come back to it later:

> It would have sufficed that philosophy take up this problem [of *bêtise*] again with its own means and with all necessary modesty, considering that *bêtise* is never that of the other, but the object of a properly transcendental question: how is *bêtise* (and not error) possible?

Two remarks at this point on the very form and first implication of Deleuze's question.

First remark. The great interest of Deleuze's question, and its irony above all, its laugh or smile (and you remember what we were reading a few weeks ago, about a psychoanalysis of animals that, according to Deleuze, would make animals themselves burst out laughing, animals that are too often thought—and I'd say stupidly [*bêtement*]—unable to laugh), the great interest of this ironic as much as serious question—"how is *bêtise* (and not error) possible?"—depends first on the distance marked by the parenthesis "(and not error)." This is a distance taken with respect to the great tradition of "transcendental questions of possibility," of the great criticist questions and first of all the form of the Kantian question in which Deleuze, however, reinscribes the question of *bêtise*. It is the question "How is it possible? On what conditions is it possible? What are the conditions of possibility of what, as a fact, is already possible? On what conditions is science possible? On what conditions is an a priori synthetic judgment possible? etc." But in following this tradition of the criticist transcendental question of the Kantian type, in turning it aside so as to apply it to *bêtise,* which is surprising and has no doubt never been done, Deleuze quite justifiably removes it from its epistemological economy, its usual territory, namely that of knowledge, the judgment as to truth and error, and I'd even say of objectivity (for it is always on the basis of the determination of Being as an object that the transcendental question of the conditions of possibility is determined, not only in Kant, but even in Husserl: it's always a matter of asking, "How is an object in general possible?" How is the objectivity of the object possible?)—Deleuze withdraws his transcendental question from this epistemological regime, from this theory of knowledge, and he does so in parentheses when he specifies, in parentheses, then: "*bêtise* (and not error)," when he excludes error from the question of *bêtise*. *Bêtise* is not a judgment relation to what is, it is not a mode of cognition, it is not an error, nor an illusion, nor a hallucination, nor a failure of knowing in general. One can be in the truth and know everything, and yet be *bête* with *bêtise*. At the limit there could be *bêtise* in absolute knowledge, in particular—and this is the example that everyone who talks about *bêtise* thinks of and gives—when, like Bouvard and Pécuchet, one dreams of that stupid, *bête* form of absolute knowledge that is the encyclopedic knowledge of the totality of beings. So *bêtise,* whatever that means—and we have not finished with this indeterminacy—has nothing to do with knowledge, nor with the adequation or not of a determinative judgment with truth or error. And yet, as we shall see (Deleuze does not say so, but if he takes care to distinguish *bêtise* from error and thereby from judgment, it is because the proximity is great and troubling, even if it does not let itself be reduced to an identity), the use that we make in French of the word *bêtise* implies not an error, a bad judgment, but an aptitude for wrong judgment, a defect in judgment, an inability to judge. Not a nonrelation with judgment (as one might say that a stone does not judge), but a faculty that is dulled, hebetated (which means dulled—we shall have to come back to hebetude), but through a fault, a secret perversion, a poorly oriented or misdirected faculty of judgment, both off the track and inhibited. Someone who is *bête* lacks judgment, where the faculty of judgment—according to that critique of the faculty of judgment that the indictment of *bêtise* always is—where the faculty of judgment is vitiated, but vitiated in the sense that (and the reference to *jus*, to the juridical or the judiciary, to the "just" of both justness and justice obscurely follows every indictment of *bêtise*)—in the sense that *bêtise,* as a supposedly permanent character trait, as an idiosyncrasy (to be distinguished from idiocy, about which we shall also have more to say), affects a certain quality of judgment (where judgment, as Descartes noted, implied both perception and understanding, both intelligence and the intervention of the will, of the voluntary decision, so that *bêtise*, according to this Cartesian nomenclature, would be at the intersection of the finitude of the understanding and the infinitude of the will: precipitation in judging, the excess of the will over the understanding being what is proper to man and leading to *bêtise*, leading one to say *bêtises* through precipitation of the will disproportionate to the understanding; whence the abyssal and properly vertiginous implication, troubling to the point of vertigo, of a *bêtise* that, in this space, always touches, lets itself be touched and moved by a certain infinity of freedom, in the Cartesian sense). Deleuze does not say that, but we shall see later that what he says about the "depth" [*fond*] of *bê-tise*, about that which refers *bêtise* to a certain abyssal depth of the bottom [*profondeur abyssale du fond*], is perhaps not unrelated to what I have just suggested. In any case, this implication of the fault of judgment, where judgment is not only the determinative judgment that leads to the true or the false, but rather the judgment of the judge, the judgment from which one expects some justness as well as some justice.[16] One cannot think *bêtise*, it seems; in any case the use or pragmatics of this word (and that is all that concerns us for now), there is no pragmatic use of the meaning *bêtise* that does not imply some obscure reference to *jus*, with the immense semantic abyss that hollows out that word, that lexical or semantic family (*jus*, jus-tice, justness, judge, etc.).

Another use and thus another meaning and another implication of the category of *bêtise*, and which touches this time not only on the event but on the action, the way of doing things, faultiness, a certain way of doing things badly, is the *bêtise* that one does. Not *bêtise* as an idiosyncratic trait, as an aptitude, a way of being or *exis*, as Aristotle would say, as *habitus*, a hebetudinous habit, but as the accident of what one does. I *did* a *bêtise*, I did something stupid, does not mean that I am *bête* but on the contrary: just when I am supposed not to be *bête*, I let myself go, I surprised myself by doing a *bêtise*. *Bêtise* is not simply an error, although it always implies, later-ally, marginally, but ineffaceably, an insistent reference to the understand-ing of meaning, if not to knowledge of the object, a tenacious reference, then, to a certain opening to meaning, an intelligence that is not only one of knowledge or science, whence the ever-present and ever-threatening risk of confusing *bêtise* with error or illusion, which it is not, whence Deleuze's parenthesis—"how is *bêtise* (and not error) possible?"

In their French usage—and I can never overemphasize (I'll come back to this in a moment) the pragmatics of a French idiom that runs the risk of resisting translation, a resistance to translation with respect to which we shall see what an abyss, what a bottomless bottom, it opens and closes upon—[in their French usage] the adjective *bête* and the noun *bêtise* still no doubt signal toward a truth of meaning, they bank on [*font fond sur*] this truth of meaning, even if this truth, this appearing or this revelation, this patency of meaning, never reduces itself to the objective knowledge of the object. *Bêtise* is always a way of not comprehending, not of not ex-plaining to others or oneself, but of not comprehending, it is of the order, if not of a hermeneutic comprehension of meaning, at least of something like

16. This sentence is incomplete in the typescript.

a *comprenure* [an understanding],[17] like the lack of a *comprenure*, another vaguely popular and almost slangy word that maybe is more in tune with the French idea of *bêtise*, of the word, the adjective *bête*, to which I intend to return at length in a moment.

Second preliminary remark (I say "preliminary" because later we are going to go back over all this). In saying "*bêtise* is never that of someone else," and in calling on philosophy to be modest (I read again: "It would have sufficed that philosophy take up this problem [of *bêtise*] again with its own means and with all necessary modesty, considering that *bêtise* is never that of someone else, but the object of a properly transcendental question: how is *bêtise* (and not error) possible?"), in saying that *bêtise* is never that of someone else, Deleuze suggests that *bêtise* is at the heart of philosophy, which invites philosophy to be modest, and suggests especially that *bêtise,* the possibility of *bêtise*, is never that of someone else because it is always mine and ours, always, then, on the side of "my side," on the side of what is close, proper, or similar [*semblable*] to me.

(In general, be it said in parentheses, *bêtise,* the word "*bêtise*," belongs to the language of accusation, it is a category of accusation, a way of categorizing the other (and you know that in Greek, *katēgoria* itself meant accusation or blame), and I would add, taking a slight distance from Deleuze's text that does not here mention category, that *bêtise,* what's *bête* in *bêtise,* is a funny category because, handled most often as an accusation, a denigration, a blame, an incrimination, a recrimination, which tend to discredit not only a fault of intelligence or knowledge but an ethical or quasi-juridical fault — this category, as we shall not cease to verify, is precisely not a category the meaning of which is ever sure: it is a category without category. I'll now add this, as though in parentheses, without direct bearing on Deleuze's text or intentions when he speaks of a "properly transcendental question of *bêtise*": that if there is a category of *bêtise,* it is a category the meaning of which (I'll come to this in a moment and try to clarify it) cannot be determined. Not, at any rate, like a meaning "as such," the conceptual ideality of which could be translated, in other words, distinguished, however slightly, from the pragmatic and idiomatic body of its occurrences. It is a word which, more than any other word, means something different each time according to the pragmatic singularities (conscious and unconscious)

---

17. [Translator's note:] "Comprenure" is a slang word, perhaps more common in Canadian French, meaning, roughly, an understanding or a grasp; especially in the idiomatic, and rhyming, "être dur de comprenure," to be slow on the uptake.

that engage it or are engaged in it. So *bêtise* is not a category among others, or else it is a transcategorial category. At bottom, I shall try later to say later why and in what way, in my view we will never manage to isolate a univocal meaning of the concept of *bêtise,* in its irreducible link to the French language. If it is indeed a category, *bêtise,* both an accusation and an attribution, an attribute, a predicate, a predication, and if this category does not belong to the regime or the normal series of categories, if it is indeed an exceptional and transcategorial category, then it really does answer to the first literal definition of the transcendental in the Middle Ages, well before Kant: "*qui transcendit omne genus,*" a category that transcends all categories and thus does not belong to the series or table of categories. *Bêtise* would here be in the position of a transcategorial category, a transcendental or, as I would say, a quasi-transcendental. And we should have to draw all the consequences from this.

To which I shall add, since I have just used the word "categorial" and because the word "categorial" is also the word that Heidegger uses, in *Sein und Zeit,* to designate the concepts that concern the ontological structures of the entity that is not *Dasein,* i.e. *Vorhandensein* and *Zuhandensein* (Heidegger calls <what concerns> the analysis and the concepts that refer to *Dasein "existentiell"* and not "categorial") — to which I shall add that one could, without it being unduly artificial, wonder whether the analysis of *bêtise,* as a predicate of man or *Dasein* but referring (in French at least) to something nonhuman (the beast), whether the analysis of this unstable and ambiguous signification, of this structure both human and inhuman, comes under the categorical or the *existentiell.* Obviously, Heidegger never even dreamed of proposing an ontological analysis of *bêtise,* and no one will be surprised at that, but we will soon rediscover the use (categorical, i.e. accusatory, in truth autoaccusatory) he made of a word that is often translated, rightly or wrongly, by *bêtise,* namely *Dummheit.* I close here provisionally this long parenthesis.)

Back to *katēgoreuō,* which in Greek means to decry, accuse, blame, accuse in legal proceedings, speak against, of course; but it also has the logical or epistemological meaning of "make known, reveal, determine by making accessible, visible, and knowable" — to attribute, to say something about someone or something. "S is P" is to categorize: and the *katēgoria* is both the quality attributed, the attribute, the predicate, and the accusation (in opposition to the apology, *apologia,* which signifies conversely praise or defense, justification). How the passage and the affinity works, between attribution and accusation, between the neutral generality of this is that, "S is P," and the accusation, denigration, disqualification (it is *bad* for S to be P),

208

is a profound and significant enigma that I leave to itself for now, after it has allowed us at least to imagine that any definition, any determination, is loaded with a legal action brought, that it already belongs to the language of the examining magistrate, or even the prosecutor, inquisition, or indictment (the "question of being," not only the "What is it?" *ti esti*, but "What about the Being of beings?" "What is the Being of the entity?" and "ontological difference?"; questionality itself, questioning itself, sets some such trial in motion).

In saying that *bêtise* is never that of someone else, Deleuze suggests, then, we were saying, that *bêtise* is at the heart of philosophy, which invites it to be modest, and he declares especially that *bêtise*, the possibility of *bêtise*, is never that of someone else because it is always mine or ours, always, then, on the side of what is on "my side," of what is close, proper, or similar to me. The similar [*le semblable*], the similitude of what resembles me and what I can assimilate because it is on my side, means at least two things.

A. *On the one hand*, an archiclassical motif, that *bêtise* is always human, always that of my fellow, like bestiality. *Bêtise* is a human thing and not that of the beast. And *mutatis mutandis*, we come back here, with this motif of the *semblable* [fellow, similar], of a *bêtise* that is always proper to me or proper to man, a problem analogous (I do not say identical) to the problem we looked at in Lacan last week. Deleuze's gesture remains, however, specific, and to follow the reasoning that leads him to say that *bêtise*, as proper to man, is never that of someone else, we can follow a trajectory that has him associate *bêtise* with three motifs that interest us here more especially:

1. The figure of *sovereignty* called "tyranny" (remember the text from the *Republic* about the tyrant and the wolf, which we were discussing at the very beginning);

2. *Cruelty* (cruel bestiality, which we were talking about last week and have been for years in this seminar);

3. Finally, and indispensably for attributing *bêtise* to man, and understanding the link with philosophy, *bêtise* as a matter of *thought* and of the thinking being that man is (it being understood that animal or beast is not such a thinking being). *Bêtise* is a thinking, *bêtise* is thoughtful, a thinking and thoughtful freedom. It is in this link of thought and individuation that Deleuze is about to uncover the mainspring of *bêtise*, which always presupposes a relation with what he calls the *ground*, in the tradition of Schelling, whom he cites in a note,[18] Schelling the author of the *Philosophical Investi-*

18. Deleuze, *Différence et répétition*, p. 198, note 1 [note 15 to p. 152: the text of the note is on pp. 321–22].

gations into the Essence of Human Freedom. I believe that one would understand nothing of Deleuze's argumentation about a *bêtise* that presupposes thought as human freedom in its relation to individuation, as a phenomenon of individuation (*Vereinzelung*) that stands out from and is determined against a ground [*fond*], without reconstituting Schelling's whole discourse on human freedom and evil, especially concerning that which Schelling calls the ground, the *fond*, the originary ground (*Urgrund*) which is also a nonground (*Ungrund*). This is why I began today by asking:

> What, at bottom [*au fond*]? Who, at bottom? At bottom what and at bottom who? The beast and the sovereign, what is it at bottom? And who? What is there at the bottom of the question, and first of all the question "What is it?" or "Who is it?" at the bottom of the question of being, on the subject of the beast and the sovereign?

In a moment I shall rapidly cite a few lines of Schelling, which Deleuze does not cite but which are clearly the very resource of his argumentation here, when for example he says that *bêtise* "is possible by virtue of the link of thought and individuation,"[19] or again:

> Individuation as such is not separable from a pure ground [*fond*] that it brings up and drags behind it. It is difficult to describe this ground, and the simultaneous terror and attraction to which it gives rise. Stirring up the ground is the most dangerous occupation, but also the most tempting in the moments of stupor of an obtuse will.[20]

Hang on to these words: *stupor*, which we shall relate later to *stupidity*, and *obscure will*, which we shall relate later to *hebetude* but which in any case implies, along with will, freedom: only a free being — and this is very Schellingian — and thus only man as free will, as freedom, can enter into a relation with the groundless ground; and so only a human can be *bête* with *bêtise* (to translate that into French while anticipating the decisive problems of translation that await us). "For this ground," Deleuze continues, "with the individual comes up to the surface and yet does not take form and shape. [. . .] It is there, staring at us, and yet it has no eyes. The individual comes away from it, but it does not come away, continuing to espouse what is divorcing it. It is the indeterminate, but inasmuch as it continues to embrace determination, like earth on a shoe."[21]

And it is at this point that Deleuze distinguishes what is proper to man,

19. Ibid., p. 197 [p. 151].
20. Ibid., p. 197 [p. 152].
21. Ibid., p. 197 [p. 151].

bêtise as proper to man. The animal cannot be *bête*. Deleuze had written earlier: "*Bêtise* is not animality. The animal is guaranteed by specific forms which prevent it from being *bête*."[22] In other words, the animal cannot be *bête* because it is not free and has no will; its individuation, which gives it form, does not come away from a relation to the ground (the *Grund*), which is freedom itself. Here, on the following page, Deleuze writes this, right after the sentence I have just recalled ("It [the ground] is the indeterminate, but inasmuch as it continues to embrace determination like earth on a shoe"): "Now animals are as it were forearmed against this ground by their explicit forms." This is why they cannot be *bêtes*. The formulation, it cannot be denied, is vague and highly empirical, and the expression "as it were" [*en quelque sorte*] introduces a blur into it ("Now animals are *as it were* forearmed against this ground by their explicit forms") and as for the explicitness of a form ("Now animals are as it were forearmed against this ground by their *explicit* forms"), that is question of degree the criteria of which will always remain difficult to fix. From what moment is a form, *as it were, explicit,* and at bottom [*au fond*] what forms is Deleuze thinking about when he designates here in such a general and indeterminate fashion "animals" ("Now *animals* are *as it were* forearmed against this ground by their *explicit forms*")? Do humans not also have *explicit* forms that forearm them, *as it were*, against *bêtise*? The passage from Schelling on the ground, which I wanted to cite, the principle of which seems to me to support the whole of Deleuze's discourse here, is to be found in the *Philosophical Inquiries into the Essence* [or "Nature"] *of Human Freedom*. Schelling is in the process of explaining and attempting to justify his distinction between being (*Wesen*) as ground (*Grund*), and being as existence, existing. Debating this problem (I cannot here reconstitute that debate and I refer you to it), he posits that there must necessarily be a being (*Wesen*) prior to any ground and any existent, and therefore in general before any duality. He then asks,

212

> How can we call it anything other than the original ground [*Urgrund*] or the *non-ground* [*Ungrund*]? Since it precedes all opposites, these cannot be distinguishable in it nor can they be present in any way. Therefore, it cannot be described as the identity of opposites; it can only be described as the absolute *indifference* of both.[23]

22. Ibid., p. 196 [p. 150].
23. See F. W. J. Schelling, *Philosophical Inquiries into the Essence of Human Freedom*, trans. and ed. Jeff Love and Johannes Schmidt (Albany: SUNY Press, 2006), p. 68 (Schelling's emphasis).

Well, in Schelling's logic, and in Deleuze's, man takes form on this ground by retaining a relation to it (a free relation, this is his freedom), which is supposedly refused to "animals," which are, says Deleuze, "as it were fore-armed against this ground by their explicit forms." Reread Schelling, and Heidegger on Schelling,[24] and, in Schelling, especially what he says about that human malady that is stupidity (*Blödsinn*),[25] an allusion that I empha-size because the question of stupidity[26] as *Blödsinn* is at the core of a remark-able book that I shall mention in a moment, with the terrible problems of translation that it poses; I am referring to Avital Ronell's *Stupidity*. Is stu-pidity *bêtise*? Is it exactly the same thing? We are coming to this.

To get back to Deleuze, only the experience of freedom that *bêtise* is, as human freedom, only this freedom as relation to the groundless ground, can explain not only how *bêtise* can be foreign to "animals," but how it can   *213* be linked to those three motifs I pointed out a moment ago, namely sover-eignty, cruelty (and therefore evil—and illness, Schelling would say), and finally thought.

1. Sovereignty in the figure of the tyrant first. Deleuze notes that

the tyrant has the head not only of an ox, but of a pear, a cabbage, or a po-tato. No one is ever superior or exterior to what he profits from: the tyrant institutionalizes *bêtise,* but he is the first servant of his system and the first to be instituted, always a slave commanding slaves.[27] [A literally Platonic motif.][28]

2. <Next,> Deleuze is particularly eloquent and insistent on evil and cru-elty and their essential link with *bêtise*. This is consistent with the gesture that makes of *bêtise* the phenomenon of freedom as human freedom. What is remarkable is that the distinction between *bêtise* and error remains the es-sential condition of this whole interpretation and problematic. For Deleuze writes:

24. [Translator's note:] Martin Heidegger, *Schellings Abhandlung über das Wesen der menschlichen Freiheit*, trans. Joan Stambaugh as *Schelling's Treatise on the Essence of Human Freedom* (Athens: Ohio University Press, 1987).

25. F. W. J. Schelling, "Conférences de Stuttgart" [1810], in "Recherches philosophi-ques sur l'essence de la liberté humaine et les sujets qui s'y rattachent" (1809), in *Oeuvres métaphysiques (1805–1821)*, p. 245.

26. [Translator's note:] "Stupidity" here is in English in the text.

27. Deleuze, *Différence et répétition*, p. 196 [p. 151].

28. Manuscript annotation by Jacques Derrida: "Only a being capable of sovereignty, i.e. free, can become a slave (*bête* ± slave), and *bête* with *bêtise*."

How would the concept of error account for this unity of *bêtise* and cruelty, of the grotesque and the terrifying, which doubles the way of the world? Cowardice, cruelty, baseness, *bêtise* are not simply bodily powers or facts of character or society, but structures of thought as such.[29]

Before coming back to this question of thought, of philosophy and the transcendental, I emphasize with a few quotations the essential importance that Deleuze appears to accord to the link between *bêtise* and cruelty, and thus between *bêtise* and evil, *bêtise* and freedom, *bêtise* and responsibility, so many human rather than animal traits, and the very ones we were discussing last week when we were reading Lacan:

> All determinations become cruel and bad when only grasped by a thought that contemplates and invents them, flayed, separated from their living form, floating on this dismal ground. Everything becomes violence on this passive ground. Attack, on this digestive ground. Here is where we find the Sabbath of *bêtise* and wickedness. Perhaps this is the origin of the melancholy that weighs down on the finest human figures: the presentiment of a hideousness proper to the human face, a rise of *bêtise*, a deformation in evil, a reflection in madness. For from the point of view of a philosophy of nature, madness rises up at the point at which the individual reflects himself in this free ground, and consequently, then, *bêtise* in *bêtise*, cruelty in cruelty, and cannot stand himself any longer. "Then a pitiable faculty developed in their minds, that of seeing *bêtise* and no longer tolerating it" [*Bouvard et Pécuchet*]. It is true that this most pitiable faculty also becomes the royal faculty when it animates philosophy as philosophy of mind, i.e. when it induces all the other faculties to that transcendent exercise that makes possible a violent reconciliation of individual, ground, and thought.[30]

And Deleuze adds in a note: "On evil (*bêtise* and wickedness), on its source, which is like the Ground become autonomous (in essential relation) with individuation, and on the whole story that follows, Schelling wrote some splendid pages, *Philosophical Inquiries into the Essence of Human Freedom*."

3. Third, then, and last: thought. And what is especially interesting in the structural link that Deleuze sees between "*bêtise*" and "thought" (what he calls the "structures of thought as such") is what he denounces as unable to think this thought of *bêtise*. What is accused here, the defect of thought that is here categorically accused, what he basically puts on trial, is a double figure guilty of the same fault: bad literature, pseudoliterature, on the one hand, and philosophy on the other. Both of them have supposedly missed the

29. Deleuze, *Différence et répétition*, p. 196 [p. 151].
30. Ibid., p. 198 [p. 151].

essence of *bêtise*, the essence of *bêtise* as a problem of thought, and Deleuze will explain why. If pseudoliterature and philosophy miss *bêtise* as a thing of thought, the "best" literature, for its part ("best" is Deleuze's word), on the other hand, even if it does not treat thematically and systematically the *bêtise* of thought, *bêtise* as a structure of thought, lets itself be "haunted" by *bêtise*, haunted by the "problem of *bêtise*." And it is this spectral lexicon of haunting that will bear the whole equivocal charge of the difference between pseudoliterature and philosophy, on the one hand, and "the best literature," on the other hand. How does one recognize a haunting? With what signs? Positive, negative? Denegative? Presence of symptoms? Absence of symptoms? Explicit or implicit thematization? To what extent, etc.? (Read and comment)

> Cowardice, cruelty, baseness, *bêtise* are not simply bodily powers or facts of character or society, but structures of thought as such. The landscape of the transcendental livens up: we must put into it the place of the tyrant, the slave and the imbecile — without the place resembling the one who occupies it, and without the transcendental ever being transferred onto the empirical figures that it makes possible. What prevents one from making *bêtise* into a transcendental problem is always our belief in the postulates of the *Cogitatio: bêtise* can no longer be other than an empirical determination, referring to psychology or the anecdotal — worse still, to polemics and insults — and to *sottisiers* as a particularly execrable pseudoliterary genre. But whose fault is it? Is the fault not first of all that of philosophy, which allowed itself to be convinced by the concept of error, even if it borrows that concept itself from facts, but from not very meaningful and highly arbitrary facts? The worst literature makes *sottisiers*: but the best was haunted by the problem of *bêtise,* which it managed to bring to the gates of philosophy, by giving it its full cosmic, encyclopedic, and gnoseological dimension (Flaubert, Baudelaire, Bloy). It would have sufficed that philosophy take up this problem [of *bêtise*] again with its own means and with all necessary modesty, considering that *bêtise* is never that of the other, but the object of a properly transcendental question: how is *bêtise* (and not error) possible?[31]

216

B. *On the other hand*, saying that *bêtise* is never that of someone else does not only mean that it is always reserved for my fellow as a human being. It also means that "I," "myself," as philosopher, theorist or not, always run the risk of having to attribute to myself the *bêtise* I'm talking about or that, dogmatically, *bêtement*, I think I recognize in others. Here, to illustrate

31. Ibid., pp. 196–97 [p. 151].

these remarks of Deleuze's, we are going to follow the track of Flaubert, to whom Deleuze doesn't fail to refer (Flaubert is an obligatory reference on this theme). But this track may gradually lead us toward places that are no longer exactly those of Deleuze.

As to the *bêtise* that can always be mine, and not that of someone else, and which, like the category of accusation, can always betray my fault, my failing, evil, or illness, the defect from which I suffer, well, it would first be necessary to take into account, perhaps, a kind of contagion of *bêtise*, a mimeticism of *bêtise*, which should make us wonder where it comes from and which engenders *bêtise* in the very gaze, in the sustained attention, study, or reflection, the very knowledge we devote to *bêtise*: as though speaking of "the" *bêtise*, claiming to know its essence and its meaning, assuming that there is something like "the" *bêtise*, is already a sign of *bêtise*. And then, to speak of contagion is to recognize—a very important point—that one is never *bête* all on one's own and by oneself, that *bêtise*, *bêtises* in the plural, if such there be, are from the start phenomena of *being-with* or, if you prefer, of the community, intersubjectivity, *Mitsein*, the *socius*, as you will. There have to be several of you at it. You have to speak or, if like me you have doubts about the authority of human speech in this domain as in others, let's say: there has to be some trace. One is never *bête* on one's own, that's how it is, even if this excuses or exonerates nobody. Flaubert doesn't say it this way, but it seems to me he allows us to think it, at the very point of symptom that he admits to, when he writes the following (it is a passage from the *Nota Bene* to *Bouvard et Pécuchet* that I quote in an old article on Flaubert, "Une idée de Flaubert,"[32] in which I approach in my own way this problem of the relations between *bêtise* and philosophy): [Flaubert, then, writes the following:] "Bouvard and Pécuchet fill me up to the point that I have become them! Their *bêtise* is mine and it's killing me!"[33]

"I have become them," "their *bêtise* is mine": this does not merely allude to a sort of contagion, an infection by contact, frequentation, proximity. It does not merely mean that *bêtise* is not natural or idiosyncratic and can be contracted (by means of social frequentation, by the contagion of a symbolic proximity, but also by a sort of contract with the *bêtise* of others), it also

32. Jacques Derrida, "Une idée de Flaubert: 'La lettre de Platon,'" in *Psyché: Inventions de l'autre* (Paris: Galilée, 1998), pp. 305–25; trans. Peter Starr as "An Idea of Flaubert: 'Plato's Letter,'" in *Psyché: Inventions of the Other,* ed. Peggy Kamuf and Elizabeth Rottenberg (Stanford: Stanford University Press, 2007–8), 1:299–317.

33. Gustave Flaubert, letter to Edma Roger des Genettes [15 April? 1875], in *Correspondance*, vol. 4 (January 1869–December 1875), ed. Jean Bruneau (Paris: Gallimard, 1998), p. 920; quoted by Derrida in "Une idée de Flaubert," p. 313 [p. 306].

and above all means that there is no *bêtise* in itself, but a becoming-*bête*, a becoming-*bête* different from, other than, the becoming-animal that Deleuze is talking about.

But there is more, for better or worse: this becoming-*bête* that Flaubert is complaining about, that he accuses in himself, and which cannot then be a simple state, this becoming-*bête* as becoming "them" (Bouvard and Pécuchet) is a transmutation that makes him look not only like two men who are *bêtes*, *bêtes* by the couple contract between them, each more *bête* than the other—no, not only that. Flaubert begins to identify himself with a couple whose *bêtise*, if such there be, whose becoming-*bête*, consists in making *bêtise* their object of knowledge, of reflection, of archivation, of collection, etc. Their *bêtise* consists in their intelligence, in their desire for intelligence, and their compulsion to know *bêtise*. It is this very intelligence 218 that is *bête*, and the more it is developed, and the more Flaubert develops his intelligence of Bouvard and Pécuchet's intelligence, which consists in knowing *bêtise*, the more he becomes *bête* in his turn.

For Flaubert indeed writes (I commented on these passages <in> *Psyché*):[34] "The obviousness of their superiority was hurtful. Since they upheld immoral theses, they must be immoral: people came up with calumnies. Then a pitiful faculty[35] developed in their minds, that of seeing *bêtise* and no longer tolerating it." "Seeing *bêtise* and no longer tolerating it." Their *bêtise*, even in the protest against *bêtise*, even in their intolerance, even in their desire no longer to tolerate it—and so this is the most contagious upping of the ante—consists in seeing *bêtise*, in keeping their eyes fixed on it, in letting themselves be fascinated by *bêtise*, in pursuing it, hunting it down, no longer taking their eyes off it, in knowing it, learning it, making an inventory of it, labeling it—implacably. *Bêtise* becomes their thing.

Let us never forget that all this is said in French and that all the "real" problems are waiting for us at this turn. That the encyclopedia, absolute knowledge, and science and philosophy <are> the very element of the becoming-*bête*, sovereignly *bête*, *bête* to death. "It's killing me," says Flaubert, scared by the *bêtise* that he has made and put to work, by the *bêtise* that he secreted himself, to see, as an enemy of *bêtise*, a *bêtise* he was intelligent and *bête* enough to secrete in order to see, to see it, him too, and no longer tolerate it. The *bêtise* he made in giving life to these two beings of *bêtise*

---

34. *Psyché*, pp. 312ff. [305ff.]. The quoted passage is from Flaubert, *Bouvard et Pécuchet*, in *Oeuvres*, vol. 2, ed. Albert Thibaudet and René Dumesnil (Paris: Gallimard, 1952), p. 915.

35. Derrida's typescript reads "pitiless faculty."

sticks to his skin, invades him, obliges him to tolerate the intolerable that he wanted no longer to tolerate, etc.

Pushing things further in this direction, I would be tempted to say — even beyond Bouvard et Pécuchet, beyond the work that bears this name while bearing the name Flaubert — that *bêtise* is here both the character of what one is and the character of what one does, as when one says *faire une bêtise*: both the *bêtise* of the author of the work and the *bêtise* of the work. And this is what Flaubert suggests when he writes the following in two letters that I quote (p. 315 [p. 427] of *Psyché*), and you will see in them, for once, animals named in the same breath as *bêtise*. This time, becoming-*bête* is also a becoming-animal, but also, as you are going to hear, a becoming-mineral, stony, immune from attack, impassive, invulnerable, a becoming-thing, a becoming-what, like stone or a granite monument.

Two letters then: 1. "*Bêtise* is something unshakable: nothing can attack it without breaking against it. It is of the nature of granite, hard and resistant." And the significant example that Flaubert immediately gives is precisely not the name of the work but the name of the author, the signatory of the work thus bêtified in his monument, in his monumentalization, between the what and the who, in the equivocal becoming-what of the *who* still a *who,* between man, animal, and earth, between the living thing and the lifeless thing:

> *Bêtise* is something unshakable: nothing can attack it without breaking against it. It is of the nature of granite, hard and resistant. In Alexandria, a certain Thompson, from Sunderland, has written his name in letters six feet tall on the Pompey column [. . .] There is no way of seeing the column without seeing the name of Thompson and consequently without thinking of Thompson. The cretin has incorporated himself into the monument and perpetuates himself with it.[36]

<2.> Elsewhere, Flaubert says, and I quote, "masterpieces are *bêtes* [. . .]," "they seem calm like productions of nature, like large animals and mountains."[37] Speculation of the proper name that, essentially credulous as it is, thinks it can increase its capital by betting on *bêtise,* by upping the ante, by making itself even more *bête* than it is.

---

36. Flaubert, letter to his uncle Parain, 6 October, 1850, in *Correspondance I (1830–51)*, ed. J. Bruneau (Paris: Gallimard, 1973), p. 689; quoted in "Une idée de Flaubert," p. 315, note 1 [p. 427, note 10].

37. Letter to Louise Colet, 27 June, 1852, in *Correspondance II (1851–58)*, ed. J. Bruneau (Paris: Gallimard, 1980), p. 119; quoted in "Une idée de Flaubert," ibid., p. 315, note 1 [pp. 427–28, note 10].

But Flaubert also reads otherwise this terrible law of becoming-*bête,* with or without becoming-animal, with or without becoming-thing, this law of the becoming-*bête* as becoming-invulnerable and, if not immortal, at least surviving—reads it otherwise, and one can uncover in it another meaning and another virtuality of the word *bêtise*: the becoming-thing of the proper name, the becoming-what of the who. I analyze it too in the article I mentioned a little bit ago, which I permit myself to refer you to.[38] In a word—and today I would say things differently, in the context that is ours, to push things in the direction that interests me today—the point would be to *define,* to define *bêtise* by plunging into the madness of *definition* itself. Basically, radicalizing things, I would say that definition, where it stops in the "S is P," in the definite article *le* or *la,* is always *bêtise,* the very definition of *bêtise. Bêtise* is defining as much as defined. This is no doubt what Flaubert means when he declares that concluding, stopping, finishing, and defining, concluding by stopping and categorically signing a definition, is a sign of *bêtise.* The category is *bête,* you see where that leads us. The category is a signature of *bêtise.*

After having said all the bad things he thinks about Auguste Comte's *Essai de philosophie positive,* and having flayed its stupidity ("a socialist book," "deadly with *bêtise,*" he says), Flaubert writes: "there are, inside, mines of high comedy, Californias of grotesques [dimensions].[39] There is perhaps something else too. It's possible." And later: "*Ineptitude consists in wanting to conclude* [. . .] It is not understanding twilight, it's wanting only noon or midnight [. . .] Yes, *bêtise* consists in wanting to conclude."[40]

So, to conclude today, *bêtement,* on this *bêtise* of definition, of the definite article that commands the grammar of essence, of what is proper to this or that, proper to "the" *bêtise,* as much as of what is proper to man or the beast or the sovereign, the *bêtise* of the category or the thesis that posits the essence, meaning or truth of this or that, here the *bêtise* that would consist in wanting to say "the" *bêtise,* the proper essence of the being-*bêtise* of *bêtise,* we shall set off again from something paltry but irreducibly obvious. We shall set off again after stopping before an ineffaceable fact, namely that *bêtise* is a word in the French language. *Bête* too. It is also a fact that none of the authors (be they French or not) that we have cited so far has taken

221

---

38. Ibid., pp. 309ff. [pp. 303ff.].

39. [Translator's note:] Derrida's text has the single word "dimensions" in brackets here.

40. Letter to Louis Bouilhet, 4 September 1850, in *Correspondance I,* pp. 679–80; quoted in "Une idée de Flaubert," p. 309 [p. 303].

into account or attempted to reflect on this properly elementary condition of possibility, the condition that I would say is *toute bête*, this condition of the element itself.

As it is too late, I shall say no more about this today. I shall try to argue next time that all this lexicon: *bête, bêtise, bêtise* as structure or state, as character of what one is, or—something different—the *bêtise* that one *does,* or—something else—the *bêtise* that one *says,* but also (and I haven't talked about this so far), *bêtise* or *bêtises* as nothing, almost nothing (little nothings, as when one says: what I'm giving you is nothing, it's only a *bêtise, ce n'est qu'une bêtise de rien du tout,* a bagatelle, *Kleinigkeit* in German, or *Geringfügigkeit, Belanglosigkeit, Nichtigkeit*), all these diffracted senses are radically untranslatable, be it by *Dummheit* or *Torheit,* <by> *Unsinn* or *Blödigkeit,* by *stupidity, foolishness, blunder, silliness,* or *triviality,*[41] etc. And this for many reasons that we shall analyze. These reasons, which are heterogeneous among themselves, these many reasons, do not only concern the relation of significations (signified or signifying) *between* languages: they do not only have to do with the fact that it is only in French that the irreducible diffraction of all these meanings and all these values of *bête* and *bêtise* retains an at least implicit reference to the animal *bête,* a reference one finds nowhere else, that I know of, in the same way. These many reasons depend first of all on a relation, or even a nonrelation, in language and idiom, among the French idiomatic usages themselves. One cannot claim—it would be, precisely, *bête* to claim—to identify among these usages, these ways of saying, of doing in saying, one authoritative and univocal meaning, one meaning, then, a stable meaning distinct from the pragmatic situations of the usages. And this absence of a fundamental or foundational meaning will lead us down two paths, which I'll venture to define here summarily before coming back to them next week.

On the one hand, this impossibility of translation, this limit on the very interior of the French idiom—if it has an interior and if it forms a system—opens onto the absence of a fundamental meaning, a foundational and unalterably idiomatic meaning, [this limit] opens then, in a quite different way, onto the groundlessness [*le sans-fond*] (between who and what) that we were talking about at the beginning.

On the other hand, this abyss of translation obliges us to revise everything about the supposed translation or nontranslation between the so-called animal order and the so-called human order, between the supposed *reaction* and the supposedly *responsible response,* between the so-called language of

41. [Translator's note:] These words are in English in the text.

animals and so-called human language, I prefer to say between the trace of beasts supposedly without *bêtise*, and the *bêtise* of human words supposedly capable of this privilege that is still called *bêtise,* and the right to *bêtise*.

Without concluding from this that *bêtise* is proper to French, even if the word *bêtise* belongs only to the French language (but why, come to mention it?), we shall start out again from this famous comment from a very French work of our time, Valéry's *Monsieur Teste*. This work opens with a sentence that is well known, in France and in *Weltliteratur*: "La bêtise n'est pas mon fort."[42]

Translated into English, you'll immediately see the problem it has presented: "I am not very strong on stupidity."[43]

42. Paul Valéry, "La soirée avec Monsieur Teste," in *Monsieur Teste, Oeuvres*, vol. 2, ed. Jean Hytier (Paris: Gallimard, Bibliothèque de la Pléiade, 1960), p. 15.

43. [Translator's note:] The translation by Jackson Mathews, excerpted in *Selected Writings of Paul Valéry* (New York: New Directions, 1950), has "Stupidity is not my strong point" (p. 236).

February 6, 2002

The [feminine] beast and the [masculine] sovereign.

The beast, first.

Bête, the word *bête*, noun and attribute. Let's imagine, as in a fable, that I am acting *as if* I were betting or *as if*, by a feint, in betting I were throwing down a challenge.

Maybe they're a bit *bêtes*, this bet and this challenge? Perhaps, who will ever know?

According to the fable or the feint of this "as if," I would defy anyone to swear, i.e. to declare under oath, engaging that person's responsibility, and thus to attest solemnly that he or she knows (knows with what's called knowledge and a knowledge conscious of itself), [that he or she knows] what he or she means to say—or means to do—when they say, in French, *bête*, throwing out the adjective *bête*, or even *bêta* (another nuance)[1] or even, then, the noun *bêtise*, the being-*bête* of *bêtise*, or else (we didn't talk about this last week), the adverb "*bêtement*." Try, just to get an idea, try to specify and separate out what you mean to say by these words.

Adjective, noun, and adverb, then. To which you could add, for good measure, the verbs *bêtifier* or *abêtir*, or the old French *bêterie* (for[2] we have to add a historical dimension to this taking account of an idiom, of the use of the French word *bêtise*, which dates only from the sixteenth century and is therefore inseparable from a history of culture, a social history too, a history of the struggles and social forces of so-called French culture, the polemics and rhetorics that marked it and sharpened their weapons on it. For it is certainly significant that the insistent denunciation of *bêtise*, as for

224

---

1. [Translator's note:] In colloquial French, the word "bêta" can be used to refer to someone who is *bête*, a dolt, a dummy, often in the idiom "gros bêta."

2. [Translator's note:] This opened parenthesis does not close. The verbs *bêtifier* and *abêtir* mean to make or render stupid; *bêterie* is an alternative for *bêtise* itself.

instance—to limit myself to literary signs—in Flaubert or Valéry (Monsieur Teste's "La bêtise n'est pas mon fort" [literally: *Bêtise* is not my forte]), should always also be a social or even political accusation, as much as and no doubt more than it is intellectual and individual. It implies a typology and targets types of sociopolitical behavior as much as individual forms of comprehension or lack of comprehension. When Bouvard and Pécuchet, just as much as Monsieur Teste, denounce and take their distance from a *bêtise* that fascinates them, both belong to something *like* (I'm using this notion here in a vague and indicative way), something like a social class or class fraction. The social connotation cannot be effaced from the lexicon and rhetoric denouncing or combating *bêtise*. This is also why I was pointing out last time that one is never *bête* all on one's own, and we have to add that one never mocks *bêtise* on one's own. Not everyone in France can handle, at least not to the same degree, the weapon known as the accusation of *bêtise*.

So I shall act as though I were challenging anyone to swear, and I mean swear (attest by giving the pledge of a sworn faith) that he or she *knows* (and I'm naming thereby *knowledge*, *science* and *responsible conscience*, knowledge that is *communicable, objectifying,* and *determining*), that he or she knows what he or she *means to say* (I'm naming thereby a signified signification, a signified that is identifiable, and therefore idealizable, a *vouloir-dire*, a meaning,[3] *Sinn,* or *Bedeutung* as the stable correlate of a word, a meaning *as such*), what he or she means to say and to do, in saying, but with a meaning-to-do that is not necessarily to be reduced to a meaning-to-say.

In making all this clearer—and you can see that these precisions would rapidly drag us into the abyss if, for quite *bête* and unjustifiable reasons of economy and urgency, of time limits, we didn't cut them short—[in making all this clearer] I am suggesting, I mean to say, I intend to signify in my turn, I am striving to show in my turn that one can always *use* (and I mean use, utilize, or even exploit, implement, or actualize) the lexicon of *bêtise* in a more or less appropriate way, producing more or less the expected effects, *without knowing what one means*. Without being able to answer for it in a theoretically, philosophically, and semantically responsible way. It remains then for us to discover the meaning of "say" and "do," of "try to produce effects," "appropriate," and "expected effects," and of "more or less" (approximately appropriate, approximately expected), when one cannot say *to what* they are appropriate, to what signification *as such*, nor can one objectify the meaning *itself*, the meaning as such, of what is an act or operation of language, in a given pragmatic situation, with a determinate practical

225

3. [Translator's note:] "Meaning" is in English in the text.

strategy. I say with a strategy because the attribution of the attribute *bête,* the attribution of *bêtise,* is always (we've marked this fact quite often so far) a stratagem, i.e. an act of war, an aggression, a violence that intends to be wounding. It is always an injurious, offensive, abusive insult, always *injurious,* i.e. in the order of right, one that runs the risk of being unjust.

I emphasize this juridical vocabulary of injury, and I have it communicate with the act of swearing [*jurer*], and even of the *injurus* (meaning the perjurer), because if I swear that I know what I mean when I say *bête, bêtise,* when I cover with insults [*injures*] the victim of those weapons that words are, then I perjure myself. Who, moreover, does not always feel a little confusedly unjust, unjustly wounding, when accusing someone of *bêtise?* Who does not feel that we are ignoring or denying, through this aggression, that however *bête* the person appears to be or we want to say he or she is, the person is not *that bête*, at bottom, not so *bête* through and through, and that at bottom we are never sure of knowing what we mean, that we are in the dark when we claim that the other is *bête?* (In my Algerian childhood, and I remember well because this expression says clearly that the qualifier *bête* always risks never being a rigorous, objective judgment, sure of its clarity and its distinctive nature, a "yes" or "no" judgment, but always perspectival, always an effect of perspective, of placing in perspective, of point of view, more or less gray and dusky: one is *bête* from this point of view, but not, or less, from that point of view, one is always more or less *bête*; and we would say often, laughing, in my Algerian childhood, with the appropriate accent, "he or she isn't *bête, bête, bête,* but a bit *bête* all the same.")

226

And if the attribution of *bêtise* to someone is not a theoretical gesture, not a neutral gesture but an act of war, if, then, it is an offense and an offensive, sometimes an organized sociopolitical defense (which implies that the accused, the one charged with being *bête,* is always both sociopolitically situated but also supposed to be *bête et méchant,*[4] whether he knows it and wants to be or not: and what is more, nothing is more aggressive, in any case, nothing is less neutral than saying of someone: "You know, he is *bête* rather than *méchant*." "He is not bad, he is not ill-intentioned, but, what do you want, he or she is *bête*" — it is often very *méchant* and wounding to say that; in any case it is never neutral and it accuses the other of something bad, a defect or a malignity). One must then specify as to this war, be it declared or not, the following point, which matters to me here. Taking up for convenience Kant's distinction between *warfare* and *conflict* — conflict (*Streit*)

---

4. [Translator's note:] A common French idiom meaning, literally, "stupid and wicked."

being, as opposed to war (*Krieg*), something that calls for a rational and institutional arbitration — the accusation of *bêtise* is a warlike response, an act of war that would achieve the rational status of conflict only on the hypothesis that someone, a third party or an institution, could determine both the meaning of the word *bêtise* and the justness, justice, justification or not of the accusation. Whence my question, the "as if" of my bet and the fiction of my challenge: Who can swear that he or she knows what or whom they are talking about, what the word *bêtise* means to say or do when it is thus put to work, in act and at arms? What is one saying and doing when one is always doing something in saying something the very meaning of which remains largely indeterminate, plastic, malleable, relative, etc.?

I recognize that this difficulty can affect other words and, ultimately, all usages, all so-called idiomatic implementations of a lexicon, the whole of a language and of languages in general. But the point is to draw a few consequences about a lexicon that puts to work a reference to something, the beast or the being-beast, of which the most common *doxa*, and not only in the greatest philosophical tradition, consists in refusing said animal, the nonhuman beast, access to language as such, to speech, to language, to meaning as such, to response, to the responsibility of response. As if in saying, in French, that someone is *bête,* one were accusing him or her — for it is always, as we were saying the last time and I have just repeated, a categorical accusation, a *katēgoria,* a category and an accusation, even if the accuser can pretend to take pity, even if a movement of compassion ("The poor guy, he's so *bête*," "Don't pay attention, she's *bête*") — even if this more or less affected pity, sometimes affected with affection ("How *bête* you are," "Come on, don't be *bête*, my friend"), can in truth aggravate the accusation: [one was accusing him or her], basically, of being virtually deprived, as is the beast, of all that is supposedly proper to man, beginning with language, but also reason, *logos,* as language and reason, the sense of death, technique, history, convention, culture, laughter, tears, etc., and even work. Heidegger, about whom we shall have more to say as to the animal, not only said that the animal does not die, that it has no language, but also that it does not work; in *Der Ruf zum Arbeitsdienst,* he writes: "*Das Tier und alles bloss Dahinlebende kann nicht arbeiten.*"[5]

So that in this context, using the lexicon of *bêtise* well, using it efficiently

227

---

5. Martin Heidegger, *Der Ruf zum Arbeitsdienst*, in *Gesamtausgabe*, vol. 16 (Frankfurt-am-Main: Klostermann, 2000), p. 239. During the session, Jacques Derrida proposed this translation of Heidegger's sentence: "The animal, and all that is merely living, cannot work."

and appropriately without being able to answer for it theoretically, philosophically, semantically, is using it not only in a bellicose way but using it
bêtement, in some completely *bête* way. And it is from this law, this situation, that we must draw the consequences. Just try to see, try seriously
to ask yourselves: What do I mean, basically, and what am I doing, what
am I claiming to do when I say *bête,* the beast, or especially when I say of
someone or to someone that he or she is *bête,* that he or she says or does a
bêtise, or acts *bêtement* (and this in the form of what is always a proposition, a declaration that would *claim* to be, without ever being able to be,
demonstrably, constative, a judgment, a judicative evaluation, a verdict, a
veridictum supposed to speak the truth and decide as to the truth, but always
remains an irreducibly negative evaluation, as we were saying, and a declaration of war, even if here and there it appears to be attenuated by some
pitying affection)?

I say *judgment,* and such a supposed judgment ought to enter into a theory of true or false judgment: into a *apophantics,* Aristotle would say. Now
try seriously, sincerely, gravely, rigorously, responsibly, to find out and let
us know what you mean and <what> you have in mind or in view, what
you want to say or do, what you want, quite simply. Try seriously, I mean
sincerely and responsibly, try to answer my request, my bet, my challenge,
and thereby try to answer *for* what you are saying and judging in this way,
for what you are doing in saying and judging at that moment.

You would then, I presume, be caught in a sort of apophasis, not in apophantics but in apophatics, i.e. in the vertigo of a sort of negative theology
in which the point would be to approach indefinitely what one is aiming at
by vainly multiplying negations, negative declarations or propositions: for
example, when I say *bête* in the sense of *bêtise,* when I say *bêtise,* someone's
bêtise, the *bêtise* I have done, said, or given (when I give a *presque rien* [a
token gift, a trifle]), I am not saying this, or this, or that, or even that, I am
not saying a whole series of things that are close, related, adjacent, such as
"inanity" [*sottise*], for example. Tons of literature has been written to distinguish *sottise* from *bêtise:* when I say someone or something is *bête,* I do not
mean inane [*sot*], although it is very close (there too, the sociopolitical connotations are noticeable, and not all French people will use the words *sot* or
sottise). When I say *bête,* I am not saying "inane," any more than I am saying
"ignorant," although it's very close: one can be knowledgeable and yet *bête,*
and even when one introduces the apparently animal reference to the ass
and to asininity, in French or other languages, for example Arabic, one is
saying something very close, but being an ass and being *bête* are not the same
thing: the ass is ignorant, either vacant or innocent, does not know what he

ought to know, but *bêtise* is not a defect in the order of knowledge: this is why Deleuze was right to dissociate it from error: one can always know nothing, as it is supposed that the ass knows nothing, and one can commit all the errors in the world, without being *bête* and even without saying or doing a *bêtise*. To be *bête* and to be stupid is not the same thing either, even if, for lack of rigor or in a language that is dull or hebetated (we shall return to this word later), one can take them to be synonyms or take them so as to associate them side by side, as does Rousseau in *Émile* ("You will see him more stupid [*stupide*] and more *bête* than the yokel's son"),[6] this juxtaposition or this contiguity clearly marking that they are not quite synonyms and that the translation of *bêtise* by "stupidity" is not absolutely adequate in English, the more so in that "stupidity" perhaps does not translate quite adequately the use of the French word *stupidité*. Similarly, the use of the attribute *bête*, even where it seems still bound, as I was suggesting last time, to a privation of judgment and of ability to understand, even if this judgment and understanding concern a meaning that is not an object of knowledge (which means that even dictionary definitions are somewhat inadequate, as for example Littré's, which defines *bêtise* as a "defect of intelligence or judgment"), this use of the attribute *bête* is not exhausted by this concept of understanding in the broad sense. It can designate an ethical way of being, a social of even implicitly political disposition (when I say "So-and-so is *bête*," I am beginning, at least virtually, to designate him or her as a class enemy or a political enemy). *Bêtise* is always the object and the target of an accusation, an ambiguous hetero- or self-accusation: I am too *bête*, or you are too *bête*, in the sense of "I am too good," "You are too good," "We are too *bête*," "We're being had," "We're being exploited," "We are good beyond measure or discernment" (and we indeed find here, in a latent state, certainly, an intellectual evaluation, though used to describe in the first place a weakness of the heart, an excess of generosity or charity, of love of one's neighbor). And then there is the *tout bête* (for "quite simple," "easy to understand or easy to do"), etc. We find the same problem with the attribute *con*,[7] more untranslatable than ever, very close to *bête*, and even of *bête* in the sense of "good" (I am too *bête*, I am too *con*), but *bête* and *con*, you can try it out, are not absolutely substitutable synonyms. Neither on the side of the subjects of enunciation nor on the side of the objects or targets of the accusation. One

230

6. Jean-Jacques Rousseau, *Émile* (Paris: Garnier-Flammarion, 1966), p. 149: "vous le verrez cent fois plus stupide et plus bête que le fils du plus gros manant."

7. [Translator's note:] Derived from an obscene word for the female genitalia, "con" (adjective and noun) in current French usage means, roughly, "idiot(ic)."

could write books on the subtle but irreducible differences, even if they can always be neutralized and are always interesting, between *bête* and *con, bête* and *idiot, bête* and *stupide, bête* and *imbécile, bête* and *crétin,* or even *débile* [mentally feeble, "dumb"], *bête* and naïve or *niais* [simpleminded], etc. It is never quite the same thing. But the difference can be felt and marked only in the concrete, situated, contextualized implementation, in the idiom of each situation and each individual, of each group of individuals, each social scene. Which does not mean that one can make this word mean anything at all, and that we would have to give in to an absolute relativism by abandoning the meaningful use of this word to the diversity of contexts and singular usages. But the idealization of an objective and theoretical ideality of meaning, of a "free" ideality, as Husserl would say (and we shall return to Husserl in a moment), cannot be what gives the rule for the use of this lexicon. And you imagine the problems of translation that this can pose: not only from one language to another but—and I'm coming back to this in a moment because it is the argument that matters most to me—within one and the same language, one and the same cultural code.

From one language to another, I very rapidly recalled last time that if, at least in the languages that are not completely inaccessible to me, English and German, *stupidity, foolishness, stupid, foolish, silly, idiotic* did not more adequately translate the being-*bête* of *bêtise* than did *dumm, Dummheit, blöd, blödsinnig* (*Blödigkeit,* which Hölderlin talked about), *albern, Albernheit,* etc., any more than *Kleinigkeit* or *triviality* adequately translated the little nothing *bêtise* or almost nothing bagatelle, the point was not just that the implicit reference to the animal or the beast was absent. I believe I know that in some languages, Greek or Italian, and even Spanish, one can find too a reference to the animal in words or expressions that speak, denounce, or accuse something like *bêtise.* So the point of untranslatability is not that.

So what is the *point of untranslatability* and what is at stake in it here? In the book I have already mentioned, *Stupidity,* Avital Ronell speaks several times (in an English we shall therefore have some difficulty retranslating here and there) of stupidity[8] as a "quasi-concept," i.e. a concept that is so unstable, subject to such variability, such plasticity, such mobility, such a variety of uses that its meaning is not secure. After having studied all the vo-

---

8. [Translator's note:] "Stupidity" is in English in the text. In what follows, the French text of the seminar gives long extracts from Ronell's book, which Derrida read out in English and paraphrased and translated with comments during the session. I have separated out paraphrase (which I have largely omitted) from commentary (which I have translated in brackets).

cabulary of ancient Greek that designates things close to or related to *bêtise,* Ronell writes: "Yet the Greek understanding of what might be regarded as stupidity, taking into account the historical and linguistic mutations of this quasi-concept, holds above all political implications that continue to be significant for us today."[9] And I emphasize, for my part in any case, the word "quasi," in "quasi-concept," because it is not without relation to the fictional logic, the possibility of feint, or even feigned feint, with effacement of the trace and the fabulous element of the "as if," that are important to us today. Why does the question of the *bête* so regularly call for fabulous responses and "as if" concepts, quasi-concepts? Now here is Avital Ronell, twenty-eight pages later, even as she is devoting to it a book that bears this title (*Stupidity*), asking herself, in parentheses, and not without the irony for which she is well known, if one can consider "stupidity" a concept: "it remains to be seen whether stupidity can be viewed as a concept."[10]

After having recalled a whole semantic range of Greek words related to "stupid" (*apaideusia,* not cultivated; *aphronesis,* lacking in judgment; *anaisthetos,* insensitive; *agroikos,* uncouth, an uncultivated man from the country, a peasant, etc.), she turns her analysis around this untranslatability by privileging not a word but a singular occurrence of the word *Dummheit* (*bêtise,* if you will), which Heidegger used to characterize — what? His error? No, something else, more and something other than his error, when he not only joined the Nazi party (he remained a member until the end) but assumed his commitment to Nazism in 1933–34. A political *bêtise,* then. But a *bêtise* as act, operation, moment, accidental faux-pas and not as a permanent and structural character trait. Heidegger did not say: "I am *bête,*" "How *bête* I am," or "I'm always *bête,*" or even, "I am *bête* in politics, always *bête* as to politics or political commitment." No, he said: "That day, I did a *bêtise,* an accidental *faux-pas,*" with the implication, "that I regret even though one is not always entirely responsible for a *bêtise,*" and this is the responsibility, difficult to assign, that we are talking about. Let me read a long extract from Avital Ronell.

> For the ancient Greeks, stupidity cannot be seen as belonging to the domain of the political because it indicates that which lacks politics: it is being-outside-the political. In terms of a political anthropology, the Greek approximation or anticipation of stupidity would have to be located in the prepolitical, in the forgetting of politics. The stupid one is incapable of living in a community. Essentially autarkic, the prepolitical stupid one is

9. Ronell, *Stupidity,* p. 40.
10. Ibid., p. 68.

marked by an absence of relationship or link (*ataktos*). For Plutarch, the term "idiot" expresses social and political inferiority; it is not a certificate of citizenship — the idiot is the one who is not a citizen (*polites*). *Dummheit* retranslated into Greek means a suspension of the political at the very moment when Heidegger offers one of his minimalist utterances concerning his link to the politics of the Third Reich.

At this point, it would be prudent to introduce the problem of untranslatability that will dominate the pages to follow. There was already an internal fissuring within the Greek approximations of "stupidity" — a linguistic instability that could be overcome only by means of considerable rhetorical violence. On another register, the movement between French, German, Spanish, and English appropriations of "stupidity" reveals more than the matter of semantic variance. "Stupidity" resists transfer into *Dummheit*, just as it can hardly inhabit the premises of *bêtise*, with its attendant zoology, the animals or animality that populate the few but noteworthy discussions of stupidity in French. [Here she adds a note: "The French term denoting stupidity is of course *bête*, tying dumbness to the animality of animals. You don't have to be vegan or an animal rights activist to note how unfair this is to animals. Only humans can be, or be predicated as, *bête*." And she continues, no longer in a note:] Still, on another level, there exists a dissociation of meaning and intention that can be said to occur within English usage, a dissociation that compels a second reading of Heidegger's single reference to his own *Dummheit*. And here the matter of untranslatability becomes even more tricky, if equally fundamental. What would happen if we were to translate this avowal of Dummheit according to common usage, as "stupidity"? Would another translation, equally acceptable though less common, alter the horizon of meaning? Let us say that Heidegger referred to his "dumbness" of 1934 rather than to his "stupidity." The date remains the same, but the moral meaning has shifted, taking on another value. This intralinguistic twister repeats the interlinguistic knot tying up "stupid" with *bête*. The difference between avowing stupidity and claiming dumbness for oneself ("That was dumb"; "I was really dumb in 1934") is a significant one. While the disclosure of dumbness leaves no recourse or room for argument, stupidity is linked to an effect of malice; indeed, it calls for judgment. In other words, whereas dumbness might be part of the irreparable facticity of existence, there is an ethics of stupidity, or let us say simply that it calls for an ethics. [Etc. etc.]

[. . .] [A reference to Henri Michaux and "Bonheur bête":]

In "Bonheur bête" Henri Michaux exclaims: "Il n'a pas de limites, pas de [. . .], il est tellement sûr qu'il me désespère" ["He has no limits, no [. . .] he is so sure he leaves me in despair"] [So stupid is he.] The voice narrating is rendered desperate by the boundless certitude of the one who comes off truly as stupid. There are at least two moments in this utterance of which to be aware. First, there is the question of limit: stupidity knows no limit, offering one of the rare "experiences" of infinity. Brecht once noted that intelligence is finite but stupidity, infinite.[11]

What Avital Ronell sees clearly and what matters to us here, is that if "stupidity" (and I must keep the English word) is neither a concept nor a nonconcept but, as she says, a quasi-concept (and this concept of the "quasi," of the "as if," carries the whole charge of the equivocation), this hangs on the fact that it has no status, by which we have to understand both no stability and no legitimacy accredited once and for all: and this nonstatus depends on an undecidability, an indeterminacy, of course, but not any old indeterminacy or any old indecision. It makes your head spin. The point is that it is a matter of an indecision or an indeterminacy between a determinacy and an indeterminacy. So that to link up more visibly and clearly with the problematic of sovereignty that actually has not left us, I would be tempted to say that any decision (and sovereignty is a power of absolute decision) is both mad (every decision is madness, says Kierkegaard) and *bête*, or stupid, that it involves a risk of, or a leaning toward, *bêtise*. Having noted, a little like Deleuze, to whom she often refers, moreover, that there had not been enough philosophical attention paid to the problem of *bêtise*, Avital Ronell insists on this oscillation between determinacy and indeterminacy (once again I am going to cite and translate her at some length, because the book is probably not very accessible in French for the moment):

> While it [stupidity] has not been a great theme among philosophers—there is no tome that would bear the title *Vom Wesen der Dummheit* (*On the Essence of Stupidity*)—"stupidity" can be seen to have settled within the philosophical project. [If I comment rather than translating, this means that if philosophers have never dealt with stupidity, the essence of stupidity, that's perhaps because there was stupidity in philosophy itself.] Defended against the rents in knowing, philosophers are those who dwell in the problem and live by enigmas; though their tone is often superior, it is in their job descriptions to avow that they are confounded by the limits of the knowable, to begin their reflections, if they are true philosophers, in a mood of stupefaction [they begin in stupefaction, that's the origin of philosophy]. Yet this is an aspect of philosophical inquiry that is often veiled by forgetfulness, put away as if a link to fundamental stupidity were unsayable. [In other words, philosophers have never dealt with stupidity, perhaps because there is stupidity in the philosophical project itself, and one gets the impression that, in the description, a link to fundamental stupidity is unspoken,

235

236

11. Ibid., pp. 41–43.

hidden as though ineffable, "unsayable."] There would be no philosophy without this abjected and largely repressed condition of its possibility. One could even pursue the point further by observing that the more successfully repressed philosophy is, the closer it comes to the core stupidity. [The better the philosophy, if you like, the more it represses stupidity. And the theme of stupidity.] Who has not recognized certain philosophical assertions as being stupid in the end? Arguably, there is nothing more stupid, finally, than Hegel's "absolute knowledge" [Etc., etc.] [. . .]. Fundamental stupidity has not really been upgraded to the level of a problem, however, for philosophers have rarely tended to address the question of stupidity (it is therefore not a question but strictly out of the question) or when they have broached the topic, as in the case of Hegel's disciple J. E. Erdmann, their attempts have been greeted with laughter and derision [when a philosopher tried to talk about *bêtise*, he was laughed at [*on s'est foutu de lui*]]. On some level, then, stupidity has no legitimate status in our discursive encounters. [Etc., etc.]

Ronell cites Flaubert, Musil, Baudelaire, Nietzsche, etc. And gets to this point, which I'll translate too:

237

> So we are arriving at some sort of minimal consensus, at least within this community of two writers [Musil and Flaubert], on a determination of stupidity (Baudelaire and Nietzsche pose further problems for the modernist topos in the context of art, artifice, [etc.]). It is certainly difficult, moreover, to speak convincingly of "determination" [i.e. the determination of stupidity] when stupidity appears principally to be of and about indeterminacy — nonetheless, let us continue these ruminations. [In other words, we're going to try to determine stupidity where philosophy has always avoided it and we well know, precisely, that stupidity or *bêtise*, if that's how you translate it, is all about indeterminacy. A little later, p. 69:]
> [. . .] We persistently oscillate between two sides of determination, at once marking both the indetermination and sheer determination of the stupidity cycle.[12]

We are far from having finished with this problem of translation. But you already see clearly that even where we understand, up to a point, even to a great extent, Ronell's text, which is written, basically, in a sort of transfer or shuttle between more than one language (German, and a specific German — that of Heidegger, Musil, Erdmann: *Dummheit*; French, and a specific French — that of Flaubert, Valéry, Deleuze: *bêtise*), but especially English — which dominates and provides the metalanguage and the signi-

12. Ibid., pp. 68–69.

fier of the general equivalent: *stupidity* — the fact remains that this general equivalent is only a general *quasi*-equivalent: this *quasi*-equivalent remains inadequate and we understand it, each in our idiom, only by retranslating it (for example, by *bêtise* in French, and not by *stupidité*), by ceaselessly retranslating it while knowing well or feeling sure, at least confusedly, indistinctly, *bêtement* if you will, *idiotically* if you prefer, that where we are dealing, precisely, with the idiom (i.e. with that extraordinary magnetic field of meaning and uses that link in Greek the *idios* of the particular or singular idiom to the *idiotes*, the idiocy of the *idiotes* who can be the indigenous inhabitant, the simple citizen, and also the ignorant man, without experience, naked, savage, innocent) — [while knowing well and feeling sure, then, at least confusedly, indistinctly, *bêtement* if you will, *idiotically*] that in this retranslation of *stupidity* by *bêtise*, or vice versa, between *Dummheit, bêtise,* and "stupidity," there is a remnant, a remainder that is untranslated and untranslatable. And that this remainder cannot be reduced to the reference made by French alone, or some other language (but rarely) to the beast. What remains absolutely untranslatable, one can say so a priori, what remains untranslatable in the very economy of the word, in the word-for-word or "one word for one word," is the totality of the idiomatic network that coordinates all these values, all these connotations, all these quasi-synonymies or even homonymies (for example, the homonymy between the *bêtise* of someone who is *bête* and the *bêtise* one does, the *bêtise* one says, and the *bêtise,* the "almost nothing," the trifle that one gives or receives, etc.).

So again I ask and again launch the question of a little while ago: what is the point of untranslatability and what is at stake here? Why this syntagm, itself untranslatable, *point d'intraduisibilité*?[13] Well, so as to mark clearly, to mark as well as possible, the absence of all purity and all decidable limits here: neither pure and simple translatability nor pure and simple untranslatability. There is a point of untranslatability, and there is not [*ne . . . point*] untranslatability. What links the meaning and the syntax in the French usage of the word *point* is untranslatable, but relatively untranslatable. The response is always economical, i.e. impure. *Point* is untranslatable by one word when its syntax plays between the point and the negation *ne . . . pas*, but easily translatable if I devote a page of explanation to it, and then it will not be purely and simply a translation.

To sharpen up this question, one must first bear witness to or take stock of the fact that the absence of a general equivalent, namely a univocal con-

13. [Translator's note:] In French, "point d'intraduisibilité" means both "point of untranslatability," and "no untranslatability [at all]."

238

cept absolutely idealizable in its meaning, thus transcendent with respect
to all the practical or pragmatic uses that one can make of a word, of the
lexicon of *bêtise,* of the adjective *bête*, of the adverb *bêtement*, of the noun
bêtise — this absence of a pure general equivalent, as an operator of a translation without remainder, <this operator> does not only not exist between
239   languages, as is only too obvious, but above all exists nowhere, it does not
exist either within each language, in the domestic interiority, itself supposed
to be pure, of a language or an idiom, it does not exist there purely and
rigorously, objectifiable in a pure theoretical knowledge, in an objective science or consciousness: it only exists there in an approximative, relatively
stabilized, stabilizable and more or less decidable manner.

And here you can begin to see what is at stake in this point of untranslatability from the point of view of our problematic: and why I had seemed
to bet, at the beginning of the session, that it is impossible to swear that one
knows what one means to say and what one means to do and know how to
do and make known when one says *bête*. It is because I am making of this
nonknowledge on which I am betting, this "not knowing what one is saying
or meaning" or "has said" or "does," when one says, in French, *bête* — because I am making of this nonknowledge or of the impurity, nonrigor, essential incompleteness of this knowledge, of this science or this conscience
the axiom, the prime mover, the spirit or the inspiration, the *raison d'être*,
if you prefer, of the seminar that gathers us here: this nonknowledge as to
what *bête* (the noun or the adjective, the becoming-adjective of the noun)
means to say, has one say, or does in being said.

The choice of the title for this seminar, *La bête et le souverain*, was designed in the first place to keep bringing us back to this first site of decision,
as to the immense question of the living — at bottom what is irreducibly
bête, we shall have to say this often, is life pure and simple, which is both
infinitely *bête* and cunning, intelligent, *bête* and anything but *bête*: it is the
living in life itself which outplays the opposition between *bêtise* and its supposed contrary, the decidable limit between the two, both in what is called
man and in what is called the animal, the living being in general that is both
bête and not *bête*, idiotic and cunning, naïve and smart, etc.: Nietzsche is
doubtless one of the most eloquent witnesses on this theme — [I was saying
then that the choice of this title for the seminar, *La bête et le souverain*, was
designed in the first place to keep bringing us back to this first site of decision, as to the immense question of the living] and of the relation between
what is proper to the so-called animal living being and what is proper to the
240   so-called human living being, namely the experience of language, sign, or
speech, of manifestation and comprehension, interpretation, etc. That will
always have been the ultimate criterion, let's not forget.

Now if even within a single language, one and the same supposedly coherent, "consistent" idiomatic system, I cannot manage to determine, isolate, objectify, and therefore idealize as the same, a single meaning for the lexicon of *bêtise* (*bêtise, bête, bêtement,* etc.), if each time the use I make of this lexicon is not constative but performative, always both indeterminate and therefore overdetermined, depending on an incalculable number of conditions, protocols, contextual variables, if every occurrence of this lexicon corresponds to an evaluation (for *bête, bêtise, bêtement* is always the axiological correlate of an evaluation that is itself always relative, it is always a negative, depreciative evaluation, an insult, a denunciation, an ironic offense, etc.), then there is no general equivalent that would allow me to say in all rigor: this is the objective and ideal meaning of what I meant to say or do in performatively producing this evaluation, this value judgment, this accusation, this *katēgoria,* this denunciation, this insult, this offense.

Of course, you will say, I am not completely powerless and absolutely without resource in this respect. I can begin to understand and to explain, therefore to translate, to sketch, to test out general quasi-equivalents, more or less satisfactory, consensual, convincing approximations (and that is what we are doing here, basically, and what we were doing in translating approximatively the passages from Ronell I was quoting just now). But you can see that this success is relative, always perfectible, and that in the case of Ronell's book, a large number of contextual conditions were already required, beginning with a certain relative and shared knowledge of three or four languages (Greek, English, German, French), common references, the existence in French of a neighboring word, although one different from "stupidity," etc.

What do I have in view with this point of untranslatability? Well, to say it too briefly: if the accusation of *bêtise*, if the evaluation of *bêtise* (the evaluative and therefore prescriptive or proscriptive, normative, normalizing, and sociopolitical accusation, always perspectival), if this insult as an act of war remains untranslatable because it is always bound and therefore contained, circumscribed, constrained in a singular situation and a contextualized strategy, this is because it does not have as a transcendent rule what, with Husserl, one could call a *free* ideality. Husserl, in a word, calls ideality in general what, as object or signification, is constituted and repeated identically, as the same, across a multiplicity of subjective acts: for example, the number "two" or a literary work or the meaning of a word, or even anything else that remains the same across an infinite number of different subjective acts: it is each time the same number "two," or the same work (ideally such and such a poem) which is intended across the acts or persons who, billions of times, can intend them in the course of different spatiotemporal experi-

241

ences. But among all these ideal objects, among these idealities independent of the empirical subjective acts that intend them, Husserl distinguishes between *bound* idealities (tied up, *gebundene* idealities) which are ideal only in the body, itself ideal, of a particular (not absolutely universalizable) existence, and those that are absolutely free and absolutely independent of their occurrences. For example, the *number*, I repeat, the number 2, the objective number, beyond any language, is an absolutely ideal object, universally intelligible, and so free, detached, unbound, but the words *deux, two, zwei* are the same only each in its own language: they remain the "same" object intended in each language as often as whoever repeats them: but as they remain bound to a language, not universal, they are bound, enchained idealities relatively limited in their ideality or in their process of idealization or universalization. Well, the meaning of the words *bête, bêtise,* as meanings of French words, have an ideal meaning, but one bound to the French language, and so to French history, culture, and society, and thereby in the end, more seriously, always bound to determinate uses and contexts which to that extent limit their translatability or universalization, not only from one language to another but within one language.

I choose phenomenological vocabulary and Husserlian conceptuality to describe this situation because one finds in it this motif of freedom and therefore the correlate of that responsible, free, and sovereign personality that is so often implied to explain to us (for example, as Lacan and Deleuze do close to us, but as has always been done) that cruel bestiality and *bêtise* are proper to man and cannot be attributed to so-called animal beasts. At bottom, what Lacan and Deleuze are telling us about bestiality and (transcendental) *bêtise* is that they are reserved for mankind, that they are the proper of mankind, that the beasts are incapable of them, that one cannot qualify as "bestial" or *bête* (*bête* in the sense of *bêtise*) beasts that have no relation to the law, that they cannot be cruel and responsible, i.e. free and sovereign (sovereignty being, even before defining politically the essence or vocation or claim of a sovereign of a nation-state or a people, the very definition of the juridical person, as a free and responsible person, able to say or imply "I, me," to posit itself as "I, me").

If, then, the *very meaning* of the lexicon of *bêtise* or being-*bête,* of bestiality or *bêtise,* cannot be absolutely translatable, as a free ideality without equivocation, as a semantic object that is pure and independent not only of such and such a language but of pragmatic, performative, polemical, or strategic and violent contexts, then it seems impossible strictly to reserve them to man as sovereign and free. This is why I said last time that this abyss of translation obliges us to revise everything as to the supposed translation or nontranslation between the so-called animal order and the so-called human order, between the supposed *reaction* and the supposed *responsible response*, between the so-called language of animals and the so-called language of man—I would prefer to say between the trace of beasts supposed to be without *bêtise* and the *bêtise* of human speech supposedly capable of this privilege that is still called bêtise, and the right to *bêtise*. A meaning the ideality of which is bound determines a language that participates as much in reaction (within programmatic constraints that can be highly complex and overdetermined, as they are, moreover, both for animals and for humans), as in response. If meaning remains linked to a determinate situation, a warlike or polemical pragmatics, for example, an engagement and a vital investment (of whatever nature: libidinal, hunting, or seductive), to a relation of forces, then the distinction between reaction and response (that everyone from Descartes to Lacan makes the criterion of what is proper to man, of his rationality, freedom, sovereignty, relation to the law)—this distinction loses its rigor and decidability.

243

This is why, without concluding that *bêtise* is proper to French, even if the word *bêtise* belongs only to the French language (but why, in fact?), I also recalled that we should start out again from the famous statement in a very French work of our time, Valéry's *Monsieur Teste*. This work opens with a sentence that is well known, in France and, as we were pointing out last time, in *Weltliteratur*: "La bêtise n'est pas mon fort." Translated into English, you remember, this gave: "I am not very strong on stupidity."[14]

I am not saying this to discredit the discourses that are doing everything they can to specify humanity as much as possible, a properly human character of bestiality and *bêtise*. Nor am I saying it to confuse, to say that there is no difference between animals of a nonhuman type and human animals. On the contrary, it is to refine differential concepts that I am emphasizing a nonpertinence of the concepts and the logic that are employed to reserve the privilege of what one thinks one can define as *bestiality* and *bêtise* [to reserve the right or the privilege, then] to that properly human animality supposedly free, responsible, and not reactive or reactional, capable of telling the difference between good and evil, capable of doing evil for evil's sake, etc.

I should like to clarify here, before concluding for today, the sense of my reservations as to the discourse of the tradition in the original form it takes in Deleuze and Lacan.

244

When, in the Schellingian vein that I recalled, Deleuze says that "*bêtise* is not animality" or that "animals are as it were forearmed against this ground,

14. [Translator's note:] See session 5 above, n. 43.

by their explicit forms," he implies that man, at the very point at which his form, the determination of his "individuation," forearms him against the groundless ground (*Urgrund* as *Ungrund*), [man] nevertheless remains, as an indeterminate freedom, in relation to this groundless ground, and it is from this that this properly human *bêtise* is supposed to proceed.

But what allows one to say this, in this form?

Let us reexamine this statement: "Animals are *as it were forearmed* against this ground, by their *explicit forms*." First, if they are forearmed, then they must be in a relation, in some relation, with this ground and the threat of this ground. And what is more, who is not tempted to perceive in, let's say, many animals, a relation to the groundless ground, a more fascinating and fascinated, worried, anxious relation, one at least as abyssal as in man, and even in what would thus forearm them, a proximity that is pressing, obsessive, threatening, a proximity with precisely the ground against which — but like humans — animals supposedly forearm themselves? And what is more, at the moment at which, in trenchant fashion, Deleuze intends to separate man from animality as to *bêtise,* saying without equivocation, decidedly and determinedly, that *"bêtise* is not animality,"[15] why does Deleuze introduce formulas that are as resistant to trenchant opposition as "as it were," "forearmed" (a notion that always implies a degree, a more or less, a more or less of forearming against something with which one remains in relation, as some animals do with an earthquake still imperceptible to humans) and above all a formula such as "explicit forms"? And what of the implicit, then? This question of the implicit, of the difference between implicit and explicit, opens not only onto gradations, a seamless differential of mores and lesses, but also onto the question of the unconscious, to which we shall return in a moment, and which Deleuze has quickly set aside or not even taken into consideration in this context, presuming, like Lacan no doubt, this time, that animality has no unconscious. Even the human unconscious, repression and resistance, are not taken into account in Deleuze's analysis of *bêtise.* To the point that, however funny and sometimes salutary Deleuze's (or Deleuze and Guattari's) ironic and sarcastic vigilance around psychoanalysis may be, I have already said why it is difficult for me to laugh with them for very long. For conversely, why not recognize that man, inasmuch as he also has explicit forms of individuation, also forearms himself, as it were, against the groundless ground and, to this extent at least, should, like the animal, know nothing of pure *bêtise?* Once again, I do not wish to homogenize things and erase differences, but I believe that the concep-

15. Deleuze, *Différence et répétition,* p. 196 [p. 151].

tuality put forward furnishes no sure criterion to posit clearly that "*bêtise* is not animality" and that man alone is exposed to it. For example, in the following sentences, I don't see in what way the very equivocal figures of "mining," of the work of [under-]mining that comes from the ground, and of "work," of "being worked on by," could not be applied to animals. Unless one supposes, with Descartes and Kant, not only that the animal cannot constitute itself into an I and a Me, but that anthropology, the essence of what is proper to man, is circumscribed by the possibility of the "I, Me," or even by the ability to say "Me, I." That is a question I shall take on immediately after this. Here is what Deleuze says: (Read and comment)

> Now animals are as it were forearmed against this ground by their explicit forms. It is not the same for the I and the Me, undermined by the fields of individuation that work on them, defenseless against a rising up of the ground that holds out to them a distorted or distorting mirror, in which all forms, now thought, dissolve. *Bêtise* is neither the ground nor the individual, but rather this relation in which individuation makes the ground rise up without being able to give it form (it rises though the I, penetrating to the depths of the possibility of thought, constituting the unrecognized of all recognition).[16]

246

This is to recognize that *bêtise* is a thing of the "Me" or the "I," and is not to name something like a form of psychic life (whether one call it ground or not) that would not have the figure of "I Me." Now, without needing to give credit to this or that construction of Freudian metapsychology, one can avoid reducing the whole of psychic or phenomenological experience to its egological form, and one can avoid reducing all life of the Ego, all egological structure, to the conscious self. In psychic or phenomenological experience, in the self-relation of the living being, there is some non-ego, on the one hand, and there is even, Freud would say, some of the Ego that is unconscious. If one does not wish to invoke Freud's authority and discursivity, it suffices to admit that the living being is divisible and constituted by a multiplicity of agencies, forces. and intensities that are sometimes in tension or even in contradiction. I am deliberately, in speaking of a differential of intensities and forces, using a Nietzschean-style language more acceptable to Deleuze. But you see clearly what is at stake around this ego-logics of "I" and "Me."

Given this, not to forget our problem of the beast and the sovereign, if the sovereign is always the agency or a "Me I," of a subject saying "Me I," or

16. Ibid., pp. 197–98 [p. 152].

even "we," a first person, supposed to decide freely, sovereignly, supposed to lay down the law, to respond, to answer for itself, to dominate the rest of psychic life (conscious and unconscious), then who is *bête*? Or what? Me or it [*moi ou ça*]?[17] To whom, to what does *bêtise* belong?

Is this not again the question of the fellow and the other, revisited from another point of view, and from another point of interrogation? To ask the question *bêtement*, am "I, Me" *bête*? Is "Me, I" *bête*? Is *bête* always said of a "Me," of one who says "Me"? Who is more *bête* in me, the one <who> says "Me" or something else, at bottom, at the bottomless bottom of me without me, that the "Me [Ego]" is powerless to dominate, silence, suppress or repress? The commonsense reply, a reply that is always double, with a duplicity that one must know how to hear, would perhaps be that I am always more *bête* than another; one should understand by that that what is *bête,* always more *bête* than another, is me, a "me [ego]," is what says, consciously, me (even if it is to say, like Monsieur Teste, from the start, "la bêtise n'est pas *mon* fort," a proposition in which one hears echoing or welling up, muffled but insistent, from the abyssal depths of a bottom, the pretension of an incorrigible and unfathomable *bêtise*. How *bête* or even *con* do you have to be to dare to say "la bêtise n'est pas mon fort"!).

The "Me, I" is what is more *bête* than another, be it more *bête* than the other in me-I; but the conscious and responsible Me I is also what claims to dominate the beast and the *bêtise* in me. The Me [or the Ego] is always both more *bête* and less *bête* than that [than Id], whatever you put under "that." *Who* is thus always both less *bête* and more *bête* than *what*. More or less *strong* [fort] than what, with only this essential difference that force can be on the side of *bêtise*, that *bêtise* can be, sometimes, force itself, what is strong in force, which obviously complicates everything.

If you take up these formulas again and give full rein to these lapidary statements ("The Me [or the Ego] is always both more *bête* and less *bête* than that [than Id]," whatever you put under "that," or again "I am (or the "I" is) always both more and less *bête* than that"), you will have in a few words the essential part of what I would like to have you hear, at the moment of launching again and putting in question again the assurance of traditional discourses (which I would certainly not call "a little *bête* all the same"), including those of Lacan and Deleuze, so original, though, and, especially in the case of Deleuze, so unusually open to another interpretive experience of animality and *bêtise*—the common assurance, however, of both Lacan

---

17. [Translator's note:] In French "Le Moi et le ça" is the standard translation of Freud's "Das Ich und das Es," "The Ego and the Id."

and Deleuze when they both finally stake everything on a sovereignty of the responsible human Me, capable of responding freely, and not only of reacting, retaining a relation of freedom with the indeterminacy of the ground. The distinction between *response* and *reaction,* between responsible response and irresponsible reaction, and thus between sovereignty and non-sovereignty, freedom and unfreedom, as the difference between man and beast, fails to recognize — which can come as a surprise in a discourse held in the name of psychoanalysis and a return to Freud — at least the possibility of what is called the unconscious. But at this point, we do not need that word, or any theoretical construction (metapsychological or other: ego, id, superego, ideal ego, ego ideal, or RSI, Real, Symbolic, Imaginary). It suffices as a minimal requisite to take into account the divisibility, multiplicity, or difference of forces in a living being, whatever it be, in order to admit that there is no finite living being (a-human or human) which is not structured by this force-differential between which a tension, if not a contradiction, is bound to localize — or localize itself within — different agencies, of which some resist others, oppress or suppress others, trying to implement and have what we shall call, so as not to forget La Fontaine, the reason of the strongest prevail. And in these antagonisms made possible, in every finite living being, by differences of force or intensity, *bêtise* is always necessarily on both sides, the side of the "who" and the side of the "what," on the side of the one that manages to posit itself as sovereign, and on the side of what the sovereign denounces or attacks as the *bêtise* of the other.

Even if it were saying, sovereignly intelligent, something as stupid as "La bêtise n'est pas mon fort" — which has always passed, in French literature, until now, until this evening, for a supreme manifestation of critical intelligence positing itself and proudly claiming its rights, of the pitiless lucidity of the *cogito,* of a hyperconscious and triumphant intellectualism, whereas for my part I hear in it, perhaps, perhaps another *bêtise,* the *bêtise* of the self [*moi*], the *bêtise* of the self itself, of the conscious self-positing self, *bêtise* as such, *my* very *bêtise.* Which posits itself, still triumphant, as intelligent, which is nothing other than the self-confidence and the self-consciousness of a vigilance that is non-*bête,* not so *bête,* inasmuch as it posits itself as such, inasmuch as it posits and posits itself, and finds itself. Positing, thesis, the thesis of self, the triumph of self-positing, reflects and reflects itself as *bêtise. Bêtise* always triumphs, it is always, in the war we are talking about, on the side of the victor. There is a certain *Triumph of Life* in *bêtise.* A certain triumph over which a certain life tries also to triumph. This is why it is vital for *bêtise* not to find itself *bête*: that would be suicidal. Valéry writes in the *Log-book of Monsieur Teste* the following, which one can read simulta-

248

249

neously as a desperate struggle against *bêtise* and the very signature of *bêtise*, its triumphant seal: "I am not *bête* because every time I find myself to be *bête* I deny myself—I kill myself."[18]

What is more *bête*? Where is *bêtise* going to lodge, preferably? Where is there the more characterized *bêtise*, in the conscious self or in the bottom of the unconscious self, in consciousness or in the bottom or nonconscience? The arrogant *bêtise* of whoever dares to declare, basically without enough reflection, already a little like the marionette that he wants to kill within himself, the *bêtise* of the initial statement, of the *incipit*: "La bêtise n'est pas mon fort" is not necessarily that of Valéry; "La bêtise n'est pas mon fort" is not necessarily that of Valéry but no doubt that of his literary quasi-double, even though one can presume in Valéry some admiring and ambiguous fascination for this quasi-double, for his character, his creature, his marionette, Monsieur Teste; one can presume Valéry to be as abyssally attracted, to the point of identification, by a fictional creature busy with intelligence, Monsieur Teste, as Flaubert was attracted, as though toward a gulf and something bottomless, to the point of drowning himself in identification, to Bouvards and Pécuchets besieged by *bêtise*. Fascination, fetishization, conscious or unconscious projections: what is less *bête* or more *bête*, more or less cunning, consciousness or the unconscious? Each says, both say to each other, one is more *bête* than the other. Disaster and triumph. One is stronger than the other. Therefore one is weaker than the other.

This undecidable alternative, both "strange and familiar," uncanny, *unheimlich*, would go just as well for life and death, the living and the dead, the organic and the inorganic, the living being and the machine, the living being and its mechanization, the marionette, the mortal and the immortal: one is always more *bête* than the other. The truth of *bêtise* is no doubt this reciprocal upping of the ante, this denying hyperbole that always adds *bêtise*, a supplement of *bêtise*, to the self-proclamation of its opposite.

Next time, we shall probably set off again from the marionette. Not only that of Monsieur Teste, who, among other declarations that we shall read, is supposed to have "killed the marionette," perhaps in order to deny or kill within him the undecidable internal strangeness, both intestinal and radically other, vertiginous, *unheimlich*, in order to resist, repress, or master a certain *Unheimlichkeit* ("When he spoke, he never raised an arm or a finger: he had *killed the marionette* [these last three words in italics: how can one kill

18. Paul Valéry, "Extraits du Log-book de Monsieur Teste," in *Oeuvres*, vol. 2 (1960), p. 45.

a marionette?] He did not smile, did not say good day or good evening: he seemed not to hear the 'How are you?'").

Not only Valéry's marionette, then, but also the much more thought-provoking one, with respect to the *Unheimliche*, of Celan, whose "The Meridian" begins, as you know, with "Die Kunst, das ist, Sie erinnern sich, ein marionettenhaftes [. . .] kinderloses Wesen," and in the magnificent work of editing, analytic reading, and translation by Jean Launay, which has just appeared at the [Éditions du] Seuil: "Art, you will remember, has the qualities of the marionette and the iambic pentameter. Furthermore — and this characteristic is attested in mythology, in the story of Pygmalion and his creature — it is incapable of producing offspring."[19]

And a little later — but we shall come back to all this — Celan turns toward the vertiginous and abyssal thought of what remains *unheimlich*, in the passage that I shall simply read, and to which we shall be returning no doubt next week: (Read and comment)

> Lenz, that is, Büchner, has — "alas, art" — disdainful words for "Idealism" and its "wooden puppets." He contrasts them — and they are followed by the unforgettable lines about the "life of the most humble," the "movements," the "suggestions," the "subtle, scarcely perceptible play of their facial expressions" — he contrasts them with that which is natural, with all living creatures. And he illustrates this conception of art by relating a recent experience.
>
> "Yesterday, as I was walking along the edge of the valley, I saw two girls sitting on a rock; one was putting up her hair and the other was helping; and the golden hair was hanging down, and the face, pale and serious, and yet so young, and the black dress, and the other one so absorbed in helping her. The most beautiful, the most intimate pictures of the Old German School can convey but the vaguest impression of such a scene. At times one

251

19. Paul Celan, "Le Méridien," in *Le Méridien & autres proses,* bilingual ed., trans. and ed. Jean Launay (Paris: Seuil, 2002), p. 59; trans. Jerry Glenn as "The Meridian," *Chicago Review* 29 (1978): 29–40; reprinted in Jacques Derrida, *Sovereignties in Question: The Poetics of Paul Celan*, ed. Thomas Dutoit and Outi Pasanen (New York: Fordham University Press, 2005). [Translator's note: As the editors of *Sovereignties in Question* point out (pp. 188 and 204), Glenn's translation is the one used by Derrida himself in the U.S. version of the seminar. With occasional slight modifications, it is the version used here and in what follows (although I have also consulted the translation by Rosemarie Waldrop, in *Paul Celan: Collected Prose* [New York: Routledge, 2003], pp. 37–55); page references are to the reprinting of Glenn's translation as an appendix in *Sovereignties in Question* (pp. 173–85).]

might wish to be a Medusa's head so as to be able to transform such a group into stone, and call out to the people."

Ladies and gentlemen, please take note: "One would like to be a Medusa's head," in order to . . . comprehend that which is natural as that which is natural, by means of art!

One would like to, not: I would like to.

Here we have stepped beyond human nature [*Das ist ein Hinaustreten aus dem Menschlichen*], gone outward, and entered an uncanny realm [*ein Sichhinausbegeben in einen dem Menschlichen zugewandten und unheimlichen Bereich*], yet one turned toward that which is human, the same realm in which the monkey, the automata, and, accordingly . . . alas, art, too, seem to be at home.

This is not the historical Lenz speaking, it is Büchner's Lenz. We hear Büchner's voice: even here art preserves something uncanny for him [*die Kunst bewahrt für ihn auch hier etwas Unheimliches*].[20]

20. Ibid., pp. 66–67 [pp. 176–77].

February 13, 2002

The [feminine] beast and the [masculine] sovereign.

Marionette and marionette. There are marionette and marionette, that's the hypothesis, and the wager. There are two experiences, rather, and two treatments, let's say also two arts of the marionette. But also, perhaps, two fables of the marionette. Two marionettes whose fables intersect; two marionettes.

Do marionettes have a soul, as people used to wonder about both women and beasts? Are they merely substitutes and mechanical prostheses? Are they, as is said, made of wood? Insensible and inanimate, spontaneously inanimate, not having sovereignly at their disposal the source itself, *sponte sua*, their animation, their very soul? Or can they, on the contrary, lay claim to that grace that grants life or that life grants? The marionette—*who* or *what*? And what if it, the [feminine] marionette, were between the two, between the two marionettes—between the who and the what—both sensible and insensible, neither sensible nor insensible, sensible-insensible (*sinnlich unsinnlich*, as Hegel and Marx said of time, for example?), sensible insensible, living dead, spectral, uncanny,[1] *unheimlich*?

We have known in any case since the beginning of this seminar that we wouldn't deal with "the beast and the sovereign" without dealing with the immense question of what is called technology, the technology of the living being, political biotechnology, or zoo-polito-technology. What we named, on the basis of Hobbes's *Leviathan*, *prosthstatics* sent us down this track, in which it was no longer possible to avoid the figure of a prosthetic *supplement,* which comes to replace, imitate, relay, and augment the living being. Which is what any marionette seems to do. And any art of the marionette, for, let's never forget this fact, it's a question of art, of *tekhnē* as art or of *tekhnē* between art and technique, and between life and politics. And it is, 254

---

1. [Translator's note:] "Uncanny" is in English in the text.

moreover, art itself, you remember, that Celan, at the beginning of "The Meridian," compares to a childless marionette ("Die Kunst, das ist, Sie erinnern sich, ein marionettenhaftes [. . .] kinderloses Wesen").

There seem to be then, I was saying, two *arts of the marionette*, two marionettes whose fables intersect; two marionettes. Art is perhaps the name of what decides as to what the marionette will have been.

The [feminine] beast and the [masculine] sovereign.

We have not finished with sexual differences. With them [*elles*]. Whereas everywhere, among those who philosophize, people think they've done with them. Done with *elles*.[2]

Even if there are marionettes of both sexes, the association of the name goes more spontaneously, from the start, to the figure or figurine of a girl, of a virgin, since the name marionette comes first from a miniature representation of the Virgin Mary, of "mariolette," a diminutive of "mariole."

Monsieur Teste, for his part, of whom the narrator says that he had "killed the marionette,"[3] is a Monsieur. In other words, a man, as his title indicates. Besides, can one imagine a woman in this role? Could a woman hold this discourse? And say "La bêtise n'est pas mon fort" as her first words, as soon as she opens her mouth, as does the narrator, that other man who is neither Valéry nor Monsieur Teste but who seems to encounter in Monsieur Teste a sort of fascinating double. Because don't make me say a *bêtise,* it is not Monsieur Teste, as you know, nor Valéry, who says "La bêtise n'est pas mon fort," it is another man, the narrator. But a narrator who is a bit of a ventriloquist, who, as a possible double for Valéry, will immediately identify with Monsieur Teste, and will speak in his place, will give voice to the kind of marionette that a character in fable, fiction, or theater always is, here the so supremely, so sovereignly intelligent marionette that Monsieur Teste is, and who, the narrator tells us, "had *killed the marionette*." Like a marionette that was alive enough to kill in itself another marionette alive enough for one to need to kill it. But if the narrator speaks of the marionette that kills this other marionette that Monsieur Teste is as a fictional character, this same narrator is already himself a sort of marionette, both because he is manipulated and ventriloquized, as a theatrical fictional character, by Valéry, and because he identifies himself without de-

255

---

2. [Translator's note:] "Elles" here is the plural pronoun for the feminine noun "différences," but the sense of a less determinate feminine "them" is important here.

3. Paul Valéry, "La soirée avec Monsieur Teste," in *Oeuvres,* vol. 2 (1960), p. 17.

lay with this other marionette, Monsieur Teste, just where Monsieur Teste claims to have killed the marionette within him. There are only doubles of marionettes here, and it's difficult to know who controls them, who makes them speak or who lets them speak, who gives them to speak, who is the boss, the author, the creator or the sovereign, the manipulator and the puppeteer. Just as it's difficult to know what a marionette is, if it is something of the order of the mechanical and inanimate thing (reacting without responding, to pick up our Cartesian-Lacanian distinction again), or if it is of the order of an animated, animal thing (a living being of pure reaction and presumed to be without speech and responsible thought), or if it is already of the human order, and thereby able to emancipate itself, to respond autonomously, as it were, and to take hold, prosthetically, prosth-statically, of a sovereign power. Remember these two moments in Kleist's text "On the Marionette Theater": not only at the end, when the return of grace is possible just where it appears impossible, when consciousness has passed through an infinity and appears in its purest form in an anatomy without consciousness, unconsciousness at that point coinciding with an infinite consciousness, that of a god or a mannequin, but also before, when there is an allusion to a grace of the prosthesis, when there is an allusion to cripples dancing with mechanical and prosthetic legs made for them by artists, specifically English artists. These men dance with "an ease, grace and poise that every thinking person must be astonished by."[4]

256

That the narrator speaks immediately with the voice of Monsieur Teste, his double or his marionette, that he lends him his voice (or borrows it from him)—he says so himself, the narrator, in any case the one who says "I" and who declares, with the comical assurance of quiet strength, "La bêtise n'est pas mon fort," in the very first words of "La soirée avec Monsieur Teste." The narrator has us know that he is speaking of his double: he allows his look-alike to speak, or makes him speak. For as early as the second page, he recounts how he "made the acquaintance of M. Teste," how he was already, even before making his acquaintance, I quote, "attracted by his particular manners"; he had studied, he says, his eyes, his clothes, etc. He recognizes that he is imitating him and he admits: "I would go over again in my mind the sober gestures that he let slip"; "I had nothing left of this sort to learn

4. Heinrich von Kleist, *Sur le théâtre de marionnettes*, traduit de l'allemand par Jacques Outin (Paris: Éditions des Mille et une nuits, 1993), no. 8, p. 13. English translation by David Constantine, in Heinrich von Kleist, *Selected Writings* (London: Dent, 1997), pp. 411–16.

when we entered into relations."[5] He already knows everything about Monsieur Teste when he meets him, he knows him like himself, and it is as if he had made him. As a marionettist knows his marionette. So he is speaking of his double, or it is his double who is speaking in him, ventriloquizing him, or being ventriloquized by him, like a marionettist or like a marionette, as you wish, but undecidably, and the atmosphere is a little — nothing surprising here — like that of one of Poe's fantastic tales (Valéry, in many statements that I'll leave you to read, placed Poe higher than anybody and anything else). In particular at the end of a hyperbolic eulogy of *Eureka* — in the course of which it is written that "*Universe,* then, is only a mythological expression" — where Valéry writes, and it is the last word of this text: "IN THE BEGINNING WAS THE FABLE. It always will be."[6] Not in the beginning was the Act, or the Verb, or the Word, or the Logos, but the Fable, concerning which one must of course recall (but we will talk a lot more about fables) that this Fable is, as its name indicates, first of all Speech.

So the narrator and his double, Monsieur Teste, is or are two men who speak, two substitutes who speak, one in the place of the other. The one for the other. The one has the other say, or lets him say: "La bêtise n'est pas mon fort." I shall return later to my question ("Can one imagine a woman holding this discourse?") by allowing Madame Teste to speak, in giving a voice back to Madame Émilie Teste, at least as Valéry or the narrator hears her, or rather lets her write a letter (for if Monsieur Teste and the narrator of *Monsieur Teste* speak, if they raise their voices, Madame Émilie Teste, for her part, only writes, she is not present, she writes a letter, the "Letter of Madame Émilie Teste").

Monsieur Teste is not only a man, a "sieur," a sire, a sir, he is also, then, a husband. And his double, the narrator of "La soirée avec Monsieur Teste," is also a man who only meets Monsieur Teste at night, and once even in a brothel, "in a sort of b . . . ," says the text.[7]

Before continuing down this track, let me emphasize at least, for I presume it is quite obvious, the general reasons for which I am again focusing on the figure of Monsieur Teste and his double, on someone who not only claims so openly to rise above *bêtise* and who declares, you recall, so as not to be put to death and denied by *bêtise,* that he goes faster than *bêtise* and kills *bêtise* in himself in an odd combat ["Log-book of Monsieur Teste": "I am not *bête* because every time I find myself *bête,* I deny myself — I kill

5. Valéry, "La soirée avec Monsieur Teste," p. 17.
6. "Au sujet d'*Eurêka,*" in Valéry, *Oeuvres,* vol. 1 (1957), p. 867.
7. "La soirée avec Monsieur Teste," p. 17.

myself."[8] So as not to be killed by *bêtise*, he kills it first, as he has killed the marionette in himself. An odd combat, a duel to the death between two living beings. Earlier, from the same "Log-book," we read a remark about *sottise* which is not *bêtise* but is right next to it, and which also finds a dwelling-place in those who are not necessarily the blessed "simple in spirit" or the "poor in spirit" from the Gospels (I recommend that you also read, in the "Log-book," the development entitled "The rich in spirit")]—this remark, then: "Analogy of De Maistre's remark about the consciousness of an honest man! I do not know what is the consciousness of an idiot [*sot*], but that of a clever man [*homme d'esprit*] is full of idiocies [*sottises*]."[9]

If he hastens, I was saying, to kill the *bête* in himself, it is always by positing himself as "*I*": a lucid consciousness, a pitiless intelligence that gives in to no physical or social reflex, to no coded reaction, *I* kill the marionette, i.e. the animal-machine in me, the animal that reproduces, that repeats *bêtement* the coded programs, that is content to react: "Good day," "Good evening," "How are you?," so many idiotic stereotypes and repetitive automatisms, so many stubborn[10] programs and reactions that Monsieur Teste no longer wants to obey for he intends to affirm his liberty, the spontaneous and sovereign liberty of his "*I* think," of his pure egological consciousness, of his cogito, above this form of *bêtise* ("he had *killed the marionette*. He did not smile, said neither good day nor good evening; he seemed not to hear the 'How are you?' ").[11]

How can one kill a marionette, we were asking last time, without assuming it has some life, and therefore some psyche, some animality, some animate desire, and some stubborn, obstinate movement to remain in life? Is a marionette that one wishes to kill still a marionette? Is a marionette of which one can only rid oneself by condemning it to death, by removing its life, still a marionette? A mere marionette? What is a mere marionette? To have to kill it, even if it is inanimate, it must be already an other. And the question then is no longer "What is the marionette in me, that I wish to condemn to death?" but rather "What is the other in me (dead or alive, animate or inanimate) that I want to annihilate so I can finally be myself, alone, sovereign, properly, who and what I am?" How can one kill a mari-

258

259

8. "Extraits du Log-book de Monsieur Teste," in *Oeuvres*, 2:45.

9. Ibid., p. 37.

10. [Translator's note:] "Stubborn" here translates *têtu*. In what follows I shall often translate it as "pigheaded" (in spite of the unwanted denigration of the beast), to allow some of Derrida's play with the figure of the head to emerge. In French, "bête" and "tête" also rhyme.

11. "La soirée avec Monsieur Teste," p. 17.

onette, then, without assuming it has some life, and so some animating psyche, some animate desire and some stubborn [*têtu*], headstrong [*entêté*], obstinate movement to persevere in being? And what if *bêtise* alone had as its distinctive feature stubbornness, stubborn obstinacy, the *conatus* of a perseverance in being? If I had to continue, beyond any pure concept, in spite of all the discouragements and all the trials we were speaking about last time, to seek the essence of *bêtise*, even as I believe I know that it has no qualifiable essence, I would seek on the side of essence, precisely, essence itself, essence as headstrong stubbornness in being, of what in the head gets into its head to continue to be, to be what that is, self-identically, without thinking of anything else, to want perseverance of essence, obstinately to want the essence of the only thing that exists without concept, namely individual existence (which is why Deleuze is right, in spite of everything, to link it to individuation), but individual existence in so far as it *posits*, posits itself and reposits itself with stubborn obstinacy, in pigheadedness [*entêtement*] without concept. *Bêtise* is pigheaded. It has only pigheadedness in its head. At bottom, we certainly have no concept of *bêtise,* in the conceivable and receivable sense of the concept, as I was trying to show last time, but that does not prevent us from having examples, from having no doubt about certain examples, of pigheaded *bêtise. Bêtise* seems to be this strange, *unheimlich* thing, of an example without determinative or reflective concept, a thing without a thing, a pigheaded thing that has no cause, a becoming-thing with nothing, that gets pigheaded, that goes to one's head, that comes from the head and stands head to head, that hits you over the head, always in a pigheaded, capital, de-capital, or even acephalic manner. This is why the question of *bêtise*, so neglected by philosophy, ought to be at the head, ought to come first, like the question of the *arkhē* and of archisovereignty. At the head, like the title or the first chapter, the incipit of the first chapter of every philosophical treatise. Where Monsieur Teste is no doubt right, even if he is wrong to believe that *bêtise* is not his forte, is when he recognizes in fact, in act, that one must begin with *bêtise*, begin by having it out with *bêtise*. Not that one knows in advance what ought to be at the head or what the head is. On the contrary, it is on the basis of conceptless examples of *bêtise* that one can perhaps begin to think what is a head, and for that matter a face, eyes, lips, a tongue, teeth, etc. Can one say of a living being without a head that it is capable of *bêtise*? Perhaps *bêtise* is not what is proper to man or to living beings in general, but the possibility of all living beings that I would call capital beings, the only living beings that have, along with a cerebral or central nervous system, a head, a face, eyes and a mouth. That doesn't mean all living beings and all beasts, but it

260

does include a lot. It includes a lot of beasts and a lot of heads [*beaucoup de bêtes et beaucoup de têtes*], well beyond humanity. A lot of heads, and thus as many virtual *Testes*, because we hear *tête* and *test* in *Teste*, head, examination and pigheadedness, and then all men and beasts with testicles, and then again to test (in justice or law) and testimonial or testament or "testis": the third party (*terstis*) and the witness (we talked at great length about this etymology here a few years ago in the seminar on testimony: as for the word *tête*, it is one of the richest in the French language, and I believe, pending further investigation, that the article on it in *Littré* is the longest of all). As for the testimonial value, Valéry notes it himself in "Toward a Portrait of Monsieur Teste." He states it without commentary in a single sentence: "M. Teste is the witness."[12] On the same page, a little aphoristic series puts the "I" in its place, as it were, and contains the premises for a networking of the many agencies of which the sovereign "I" would be merely a part, constituted by the illusion of being the whole. This sort of three-part aphorism begins with a word in English:

> Conscious — Teste, Testis.
>   Supposing an "eternal' observer whose role is limited to repeating and reprimanding [*remontrer*] the system [I wonder if one should not have transcribed "remonter" [winding up]: the machine of the universe, the mechanical and repetitive system, the universal clock or that of the psychic totality] of which the *I* is that instantaneous part that believes itself to be the Whole.
>   The *I* could never engage if it did not believe itself — to be the whole.[13]

And in the same breath, later, this definition of *bêtise* that seems to flow from what I have just read. *Bêtise* would be a way for that particular thing that the "I" is to take itself for the whole. "The '*bêtise*' [says Valéry, who puts the word *bêtise* in scare quotes] [the *bêtise*] of everything makes itself felt [so no limit on *bêtise*, whence the scare quotes: everything is *bête*, once it consists for everything in taking itself to be everything, for every particular thing to take itself for the whole]. *Bêtise*, i.e. particularity as opposed to generality. 'Smaller than' becomes the terrible sign of spirit." In other words, the spirit, if there is any, in opposition to *bêtise*, consists in being, knowing oneself to be, accepting that one is, "smaller than" everything, than the whole, and it is obviously terrible. To be rich in spirit is to know that one is smaller and therefore perhaps poorer than everything.

12. "Pour un portrait de Monsieur Teste," in *Oeuvres,* 2:64.
13. Ibid.

This whole claim of Monsieur Teste to condemn to death, in himself, the marionette, the automat, the repetition compulsion, the machine or the mechanical, is thus the mark of the self-affirmation of free sovereignty over the social body and one's own body, these two bodies being held, precisely, to be the threatening places of pigheaded *bêtise*. But the paradoxical effect of this duel with the marionette is that it can transform the winner himself into a machine that wants to play the angel—and therefore plays the beast.[14] Monsieur Teste acts as though he didn't live in society and didn't have a body, or again, given that this "as if" can only be an untenable fiction, a fable, he acts like someone who, analogous in this to an absolute monarch, has two bodies, the king's two bodies, one of which is a purely immaterial, angelic body, asexual besides, which rises freely above the other one, the mortal marionette or the living animal, which remains on the ground, eats badly, and screws badly, as we shall see, be it away from home, at the brothel, or at his own place.

262

So there is a sort of quasi-Cartesian politics in *Monsieur Teste*. But if we had time (I don't believe we do have time for this, alas), it would be interesting and highly complicated to articulate the implicit politics of a *Monsieur Teste* with the politics of Paul Valéry, with many other explicitly political, or rather politological, texts by Valéry. To limit myself to a few reminders, let us not forget that Valéry was nevertheless quite scornful with respect to politics and party politicians, as those who are on the side of marionettes and idols. That did not prevent him, in "The Idea of Dictatorship," in 1934, in the preface to a book on Salazar, from offering a prudent but imprudent eulogy of Salazar in a text that begins thus, still in the name of purity, at least of the purity of the concept—and which I am recalling here, among many others, because it names bestiality:

> I know almost nothing about practical politics, in which I assume that everything I flee is to be found. Nothing must be as impure, i.e. mixed with things the confusion of which I dislike, such as bestiality and metaphysics [the word *bestialité* here no doubt covers all the domains of being-*bête*, from animality to *bêtise*, etc., i.e. everything that are often claimed to be the opposite of metaphysics, whereas Valéry supposes for his part some continuity or some contract, some indissociability between bestiality and metaphysics: they would be one and confused together; it is from a spirit of confusion that one ignores this confusion and seeks to distinguish them where they remain indecidably united and complicit: *bêtise* is metaphysical], force and right; faith and interests, the positive and the theatrical, instincts and ideas.[15]

---

14. [Translator's note:] See session 2 above, n. 2.
15. "L'idée de dictature," in *Oeuvres,* 2:970.

And then in numerous texts, all highly interesting (and I cannot analyze them here: I did so a little in *The Other Heading*),[16] Valéry insists on the fictional structure of the social ("Any social state demands fictions");[17] he also insists on Europe, which, he says, "is clearly aspiring to be governed by an American committee"[18] (1927!). He further declares: "The weakness of force is to believe only in force."[19] This is where we would need a close analysis of what is meant by "force" and *mon fort* in "La bêtise n'est pas mon fort," which means not only "I have no taste for *bêtise*, no affinity or complicity, no privileged or specialized alliance with it," but also "I have no weakness for it." Is there a determinable difference between "La bêtise n'est pas mon fort" and "La bêtise n'est pas mon faible" in this sense of "I do not have a weakness for it"? If the two expressions are equivalent, that makes one think about both the untranslatability we were talking about last time (because this equivalence is more untranslatable than ever) and the paradoxical equivalences between strength and weakness [*force et faiblesse*].

In Valéry there are many highly topical reflections, as they say, on idolatry and publicity: "Politics and freedom are mutually exclusive, because *politics is idols* [Valéry's emphasis]"[20]—therefore marionettes. And to limit myself to what touches our theme narrowly (the beast and the sovereign, *bêtise* and *sottise*), here is an insistent distinction between the political [*le politique*] and the politics [*la politique*] that one *does, practical* politics, the politics of politicians, a distinction that takes the form of *sententiae* that could well come from Monsieur Teste in Valéry: "All that is *practical politics* [Valéry's emphasis] is necessarily *superficial*,"[21] and again, same page: "One cannot *do politics* without pronouncing on questions that no sensible man can say he knows. One must be infinitely idiotic [*sot*] or infinitely ignorant [he does not say *bête*, but it is once more very near if not identical] to have an opinion on most of the problems posed by politics."

On the next page we find the wolves, and the lamb, and the ecological paradox of the "reason of the strongest," like the paradox of political struggle as a war between species: "The wolf depends on the lamb who depends on the grass. The grass is relatively defended by the wolf. The carnivore protects the grasses (which feed him indirectly)." Or again, to

16. [Translator's note:] Jacques Derrida, *L'autre cap* (Paris: Minuit, 1991); trans. Michael Naas and Pascale-Anne Brault as *The Other Heading: Reflections on Today's Europe* (Bloomington: Indiana University Press, 1992).

17. "Des partis," in *Oeuvres*, 2:947.

18. "Notes sur la Grandeur et la Décadence de l'Europe," in *Oeuvres*, 2:930.

19. *Mauvaises Pensées et autres*, in *Oeuvres*, 2:900.

20. "Fluctuations sur la liberté," in *Oeuvres*, 2:961.

21. "Des partis," in *Oeuvres*, 2:948.

263

264

moderate what remains political cruelty, but subject to the law: "Among old wolves, the battle is more bitter and more clever: but there are some concessions." Or again: "Right is the interlude of forces."[22]

So we would have to articulate the position and the fiction of Monsieur Teste with Valéry's politics or metapolitics. The fact remains that Monsieur Teste, to come back to him, this fictional character, this marionette, is, like his narrator, not only a man qua man (*homo*) who has sworn the death in himself of the pigheaded *bêtise* of the marionette, he is also a man qua man (*sieur, vir*), a Monsieur (in the filiation of *sieur*, a contraction of *seigneur* [lord]), he is a sir, or even a bourgeois sovereign, a Monsieur, a man whose virility never misses a chance to call attention to itself or to call to order.

What order?

Well, the order of the sexes.

The narrator and he, as we noted, sometimes meet in a brothel.

As soon as he has said, and they were his first words, "La bêtise n'est pas mon fort," the narrator or spokesman of Monsieur Teste enumerates, as though he were reaching the end of his life as he is writing his memoirs, everything he has *done*. And indeed they are acts, doings [*faits et gestes*], that he always recalls in the first person. With active and transitive verbs in the first person. Things don't happen to him, he does them and makes them happen, he is an "I," an "*I*," who always acts, always does this or that. And among all that "I have done," all that the "*I*" does, there is a "I have touched on women" [*j'ai touché à des femmes*], the grammar of which is, once again, difficult to translate. He does not even say: "I have touched women," but "I have touched *on* women." Listen to all these connotations in the narrator's mouth. From the start, from the opening, as soon as the narrator opens his mouth — because all this is principally a question of the mouth, as you are going to see — it is to say:

> *Bêtise* is not my strong point. I have seen many individuals; I have visited a few nations; I have played my part in diverse enterprises without loving them; I have eaten almost every day; I have touched on women.[23]

This sequence is full of symptomatic signatures. Through the disappointed and condescending disdain of the blasé Monsieur, the gentleman with no illusions, who says in the past tense: [Oh], I've seen *many* individuals [anonymous and sexually undifferentiated crowd]), I've visited *a few* nations, I've played *my part* in diverse enterprises *without loving them* [admire the statis-

265

22. Ibid., pp. 949–50.
23. "La soirée avec Monsieur Teste," p. 15.

tical curve of the decreasing degrees of participation: *many* individuals, *a few* nations, *my part* in enterprises],[24] the whole without love ("I played my part in enterprises without loving them"), you clearly perceive a lovelessness, a lack of love and desire that colors and connotes by contagion the whole series of doings, of acts, for they are always actions rather than passions; and the decreasing statistical series of little participation will become more accentuated: after "many," after "a few," and "my part" comes the "almost" of "almost every day" ("I have eaten almost every day"). This allusion of the narrator as double of his creature or *alter ego* will find its echo on the following page, when it will be said of Monsieur Teste, who is married though never seems to eat his meals at home: "He took his meals in a little restaurant in the rue Vivienne. There he ate as one purges oneself, with the same kind of energy. Sometimes he allowed himself elsewhere a slow, refined meal."

And finally, to come back to the opening, before the final point of the serial collapse, finally, after "I have eaten almost every day" [a semicolon and before the period]: "I have touched on women." Not "I have touched women," but "I have touched *on* women," just as, one scarcely touches [on] one's food, hardly tastes it, with a look of distaste.[25] He has "eaten almost every day," not every day, and has "touched [on] women." Scarcely touched, and not touched, transitively, but touched [on] women. As though from afar, distractedly, mechanically, without desire, in passing, passing flings with passersby whom one scarcely touches, whom one brushes against or fondles, and with whom, touching [on] them, one barely flirts.

One senses here not love but distaste [*On ne sent pas l'amour ici mais la moue*]. Touching *on* women, whom clearly he loves no more that his "part in diverse enterprises" ("I have played my part in diverse enterprises without loving them"), rather than touching women, he touches on women, he takes them on [*les entreprend*], for it's a kind of enterprise, he takes them on without loving them; he doesn't make love, or scarcely, so little, he doesn't love, he doesn't make love, he shows distaste [*il ne fait pas l'amour, il fait la moue*].

La moue is a very interesting word, and as untranslatable as it is interesting. *La moue* is always something one *does*, moreover (*on fait la moue*) and it is, among other things, this terrible proximity (signifying the insignificant) between *faire l'amour* and *faire la moue* that forever resists translation. In

266

24. Derrida's emphasis.

25. [Translator's note:] "Faire la moue," which Derrida will gloss in the following paragraphs, means to purse one's lips, to pout, to pull a face, to look disgusted or have a look of distaste.

French, *la moue* is always what one does with one's mouth, while speaking or not, with one's lips; *la moue* is a sort of coded grimace to signify the insignificant, lack of interest, scant taste or even distaste that the thing inspires in us. We may say that Monsieur Teste's double *fait la moue*, we

267   see his mouth *faire la moue*, we see a kind of disgusted grimace accompany everything he says. This can go as far as repulsion, aversion, a silent but eloquent manifestation of impotent rejection, sometimes in situations of utter extremity. Montaigne says that among the North American Indians, "the prisoner [spits] in the faces of those who kill him and *fait la moue* at them.[26] And so Monsieur Teste recognizes,[27] after having said "I have eaten almost every day," that "I have touched [on] women."

This man who has sovereignly touched [on] women is the double or spokesman of Monsieur Teste, who is not only a man but a husband. And the narrator is not only the double of Monsieur Teste, he presents himself as doubled, tripled, multiplied. Read carefully all that follows, the two pages before the narrative of the encounter with Monsieur Teste, in particular what concerns his self-multiplication, this "arithmetic" (his word) that counts with self, counts out the self, calculates or tallies up his own multiplicity. For example, in the paragraph that follows the one we have just read, and after speaking of something that remains ("what could remain did so"), the narrator tells of the profit, the saving, the economy that he finds in this arithmetic. This accounting of the self, as you will hear, not only allows him a certain economy of self, a wisdom that allows him to tolerate himself and grow old with himself, but also discreetly opens the quasi-infinite field of a hyperbolic upping of the ante that gives him a right and a power superior to sovereignty, superior to that of superior men, more than sovereign, in sum, more than superior, as it were. This is a superiority that can no longer restrain itself, both infinitely cunning and infinitely *bête*. This is in any case how I would interpret the following lines: (Read and comment)

> I have retained neither the best nor the worst of these things: what could remain remained.
>
>   This arithmetic spares me from being astonished at growing old. I could

268   > also tally up the victorious moments of my spirit, and imagine them to be

---

26. Montaigne, *Essais* (Paris: Gallimard, 1950), book 1, chap. 31, p. 251 [my translation].

27. [Translator's note:] Strictly speaking, the narrator of *Monsieur Teste,* not Monsieur Teste "himself."

unified and welded, composing a *happy* life . . . But I believe I have always judged myself well. I rarely lost sight of myself; I have detested myself, I have adored myself;—then, we grew old together.

[. . .]

If I had decided like most men, not only would I have believed myself superior to them, but I would have appeared so. I preferred myself. What they call a superior being is a being who has been mistaken. To be astonished at him, one must see him—and to be seen he must show himself. And he shows me that the idiotic mania of his name possesses him.[28]

Read what follows, and you will see that the only company, the only society, that the narrator or the double seems prepared to tolerate (and it will begin soon with that of Monsieur Teste) is that of those absolute solitary types who bear multiplicity within them, who double, triple, and multiply. And what seems most interesting here is that this incalculable arithmetic, this economy of a fathomless escalation, has the effect of transforming these supermen, in sum (in the sense that Nietzsche places the superman beyond the superior man), of transforming these supermen into things, making these "whos" mutate into "whats." Arithmetic, even hyperbolic and incalculable arithmetic, number itself, suffices to transform the "who" into "what." Whence what Valéry calls "the admirable mathematical kinship of men"[29] (I encourage you to reread this whole sequence, itself admirable, about the Thing, the One, and the Self).

"What," the "what": one can call that the thing, the *res,* or the nothing [*rien*] of the thing, a thing that is not someone, neither a subject nor a self, nor a consciousness, nor a human being, nor a *Dasein,* the thing that does not think, does not speak and does nothing, the thing that remains silent [*coite*], if you want to play on this homonym whereby the *quoi* remains *coi* (c.o.i.), i.e. mute and immobile, a tranquil force, and *coite, coite* meaning not *coitus* [*coït*] but coming from *quietus,* which means "at rest, tranquil, impassive." Well, the arithmetic we are speaking about, even hyperbolic and incalculable arithmetic, number itself, suffices to transform the "who" into "what" [*le "qui" en "quoi"*]. To count, to calculate is to produce the becoming or the re-becoming *what* of *who,* the becoming-thing of the person.

269

They were, invisible in their limpid lives, solitary people who knew before anybody else. They seemed to me to double, triple, multiply in the dark every famous person—they who disdained to publish their chances and

28. "La soirée avec Monsieur Teste," pp. 15–16.
29. "Extraits du Log-book de Monsieur Teste," p. 41.

particular results. They would, in my view, have refused to consider themselves as anything other than things.

These ideas came to me during October '93, in the instants of leisure in which thought plays merely at existing.

I was beginning to think about it no more, when I made the acquaintance of M. Teste. (I think now of the traces that a man leaves in the small space in which he moves each day.)[30]

This internal multipli-city, the self-accounting, of all these doubles and shadows [*doubles et doublures*], these third-party witnesses and witnesses of witnesses with whom we have been counting for a while (Valéry, the narrator, Monsieur Teste, so many "selves" and agencies themselves multiplied up and engaged in an escalation of sovereignty, rising above superior men and seeking to subject all the others to them, to ventriloquize them or silence them), this battlefield between agencies short on sovereignty — this is already like an inner society, a war or a contract, an alternation of war and peace, of selection and election, of competition, rivalries, jealousy even, of actions and reactions, shared responsibilities or limited responsibility, in the way we speak of shared sovereignty or a limited liability company. And Valéry is aware of the political or quasi-political character of this field. He says, for example, in the "Extracts of the Log-book . . ." appended to *Monsieur Teste*[31] — (if I'd picked up this interesting use of the word *cap* [cape or head], I would have cited it in *L'autre cap,* where I already took into account a number of *caps* in Valéry, who decidedly wagers a lot, stubbornly or pigheadedly, on this word.[32] Valéry constantly has in his head this word, which bespeaks a head, all heads):

Man always standing on Cape Thought [le cap Pensée], wide-eyed before the limits, either of things, or of sight . . .

["Man always standing on cape Thought," an extraordinary figure, because of the cape, of course, which is a head on which the man is standing, but also because the name of this cape is "Thought," like a proper name, with a capital letter: not the thinking cape or the cape of thought or the thought cape or cape thought, but "cape Thought," with a capital for Thought. Valéry continues:]

---

30. "La soirée avec Monsieur Teste," p. 16.
31. "Extraits du Log-book de Monsieur Teste," p. 39.
32. *L'autre cap,* op. cit.

It is impossible to receive the "truth" from oneself. When one feels it form-ing (it is an impression), one forms by the same token an *other unaccustomed self*... of which one is proud—of which one is jealous...

[So one can be jealous of oneself as of another, and it is always the most invincible jealousy, by definition, and it is the moment of truth, the mo-ment when the truth comes to us like a guest, like a visitor: we "receive" it, says Valéry, and immediately after having said this and used three suspen-sion points ("It is impossible to receive the "truth" from oneself. When one feels it forming (it is an impression), one forms by the same token an *other unaccustomed self*... of which one is proud—of which one is jealous..."), Valéry adds in parentheses:]

(It is a high point of internal politics.)[33]

There's certainly politics here because there's what I amuse myself by call-ing a multipli-city, a city as multipli-city of agencies or a plurality of worlds and of "selves" [*moi*], of subjects who, like countable citizens, share out and fight over the truth, nothing less than the truth, argue about a truth, but a received truth, a truth always received: but this politics, this apparently internal politicity, this inner multipli-city, this multipli-city of self, here reaches its high point ("high point" [*comble:* acme] is Valéry's word: "high point of internal politics") not only because it is full, fulfilled, accomplished, saturated, but because, since it's a matter of the other in the self, and of the other in the self of whom one is forever jealous, this internal politics reaches its high point in the excess that exceeds and un-counts it, namely the other and the outside. Jealousy is always the high point that simultaneously com-pletes me, supplements me, and exceeds me precisely because it receives, welcomes, and can no longer chase out the other in me, the other me in me. One is only ever jealous of oneself, of the selfsame, and that doesn't fix anything, and it doesn't merely explain passional dramas but explains all the loves and all the wars in the world. Which take place between the same, the others as the same. And that happens as soon as there is any cape—and some "man always standing on Cape Thought."

"Man always standing on Cape Thought." This figure, this turn [*le tour*] of the phallic erection, this turn of the double erection (standing, and be-ing on a cape), the turn of this double erection of Capital, of this capital-ized erection that is here called Thought, this double turn that makes one

271

33. "Extraits du Log-book de Monsieur Teste," p. 39.

think of the double tower [*la tour*] of some World Trade Center,[34] towers or turns jealous of themselves, this double surrection, this re-surrection of the standing position, recalls us not just to the human but to the virile, and so to the point from which we started out and on which I shall conclude today (I had thought I would finish with Valéry and move from his marionettes to Celan's marionette, or even Kleist's, have them chat among themselves, but I shall do that only next time) — [the point from which we started out and on which I shall conclude today] namely that Monsieur Teste and his doubles and his third parties and his witnesses (Valéry, the narrator, etc.) are men, are male, are husbands. It is men who speak and have the right to speech. And when they consent to allow a woman, Madame Émilie Teste, to speak, it is so that she will write, among other things, these three or four motifs, from which I'll have to content myself for the moment with a few quotations (we shall come back to them next time, but I recommend that you read them all, because you will find much more than I can bring out here, in the little time left).

272

First motif, the hardness of Monsieur Teste according to Madame Émilie Teste, but a hardness so hard that it changes back into its opposite:

> The machine of his monotonous acts explodes; his face shines; he says things that very often I only half understand, but which never fade from my memory. But I wish to hide nothing from you, or almost nothing: *he is sometimes very hard*. I do not think anyone can be as hard as he is. He breaks your spirit with one word, and I see myself as a failed vase, which the potter throws into the trash. He is as hard as an angel, Monsieur. He does not realize his force: he says unexpected things that are too true, that annihilate people, wake them up in the middle of their *sottise*, face to face with themselves, completely trapped in what they are, living so naturally on idiocies.
>   [...]
>   But do not imagine that he is always difficult or overpowering. If you only knew, Monsieur, how he can be quite different! ... Of course he is hard sometimes; but at other times he adorns himself in an exquisite and surprising sweetness that seems to come down from heaven. His smile is a mysterious and irresistible gift, and his rare tenderness a winter rose. However, it is impossible to foresee either his ease or his violence. It is in vain that one expects his rigors or his favors; he outplays by his profound distraction and by the impenetrable order of his thoughts all the ordinary calculations that humans make as to the character of their fellows. I never know

34. [Translator's note:] "World Trade Center" is in English in the text.

what my kindnesses, my indulgences, my distractions, or my little failings will get from Monsieur Teste.[35]

2. Second motif: this hardness deprives Madame Teste of love and trans-   273
forms her into a beast:

> I believe this is not a good thing, but I am like that, in spite of reproaching myself for it. I have confessed to myself more than once that I thought I would prefer to believe in God than to see him in all his glory, and I have been blamed for it. My confessor told me that it was a *bêtise* rather than a sin.
>
> [. . .]
>
> I cannot say that I am loved. You should know that this word love, so uncertain in its ordinary meaning, hesitating between many different images, is completely worthless if applied to the emotional relations [*rapports du coeur*] of my husband toward myself. His head is a sealed treasure, and I do not know if he has a heart. Do I even know if he thinks me special; if he loves me, or studies me? Or if he studies through me? You will understand if I do not emphasize this. In short, I feel that I am in his hands, in his thoughts, like an object that sometimes is the most familiar, sometimes the strangest in the world, according to the variable type of gaze that adapts itself to it.
>
> If I dared to communicate to you my frequent impression, as I tell it to myself, and which I have often confided to M. l'Abbé Mosson, I would say metaphorically that I feel as if I live and move in the cage in which the superior spirit locks me—*by its existence alone*. His spirit contains mine, like the spirit of a man contains that of a child or a dog.
>
> [. . .]
>
> I am a fly that buzzes and gets by in the universe of an unwavering gaze; sometimes seen, sometimes not seen, but never out of sight. I know at every minute that I exist in an attention that is always vaster and more general than all my vigilance, always more prompt than my sudden and most prompt ideas. Are the greatest movements of my soul little insignificant events to him? And yet I have my own infinity . . . which I feel.
>
> [. . .] Back to my fate: I feel that he is what he must be; I tell myself that I *want* my fate, that I choose it anew at every instant; I hear within me the clear deep voice of M. Teste calling me . . . But if you knew by what names!
>
> There is no woman in the world named as I am. You know what ridiculous names lovers exchange: what dog and parrot names are the natural   274
> fruit of carnal intimacy. The words of the heart are childlike. The voices of

35. "Lettre de Madame Émilie Teste," in *Oeuvres*, 2:27–28.

the flesh are elementary. What is more, M. Teste thinks that love consists in *being able to be* bête *together* — a full license for idiocy and bestiality. And so he calls me in his way. He almost always designates me according to what he wants from me. All by itself, the name he gives me makes me understand in a word what I should expect, or what I must do. When he desires nothing in particular, he calls me *Being*, or *Thing*. And sometimes he calls me *Oasis*, which I like.

But he never tells me that I am *bête,* — which touches me very deeply.[36]

3. Third motif: the centaur, Monsieur Teste as a centaur:

"His heart is a desert island [it is the Abbé speaking] . . . All the extent and all the energy of his spirit surround him and defend him; his depths isolate him and guard him from the truth. He flatters himself that he is quite alone . . . Patience, dear lady. Perhaps one day he will find a certain print in the sand . . . What a happy and sacred terror, what salutary terror, when he knows from this pure vestige of grace that his island is mysteriously inhabited! . . ."

Then I said to M. l'Abbé that my husband often made me think of a *mystic without God* . . .

"What insight!" said the Abbé, "what insights women sometimes draw from the simplicity of their impressions and the uncertainties of their language! . . ."

But immediately, to himself, he replied:

"Mystic without God! . . . Luminous nonsense! . . . Easy to say! . . . False light . . . A mystic without God, Madame, but there is no conceivable movement that does not have its direction and its meaning, and that does not finally lead somewhere! . . . Mystic without God! . . . Why not a Hippogriff, a Centaur!"

"Why not a Sphinx, Monsieur l'Abbé?"[37]

4. Fourth motif: death and botany: (Read)

275

We go, in the end [. . .] to this antique garden where all people with thoughts, cares, and monologues go as evening comes [. . .] They are scientists, lovers, old men, the disillusioned and priests; all possible *absent ones*, of all sorts. It is as though they are seeking their mutual distances [. . .] in this place worthy of the dead. It is a botanical ruin. [. . .] Monsieur Teste lets himself be distracted by these large living drops, or else he moves slowly among the green-tagged "beds," in which specimens from the vegetable

36. Ibid., pp. 28, 31–33.
37. Ibid., p. 34.

world are more or less cultivated. He enjoys this somewhat ridiculous order and amuses himself spelling out the baroque names:

> Antirrhinum Siculum
> Solanum Warscewiezii!!!

And this Sisymbriifolium, what lingo! . . . And the Vulgare, the Asper, Palustris, Sinuata, and the Flexuosum and the Præaltum!!!

"It is an epithet garden, he said the other day, a dictionary and cemetery garden . . ."

And after a time he said to himself: "Die learnedly . . . Transiit classificando."[38]

The incalculable multi-plicity[39] of these marionettes that double and triple has something strange and disquieting about it and, I would say in German, to translate this being-at-home-with-the-other, something *unheimlich* (I use this word to graft on all the Freudian and Heideggerian problematics of *Unheimlichkeit* and the *deinon* that we studied here some time ago). But one feels that, in Valéry, everything tenses up in a movement of intellectual vigilance to master this *Unheimlichkeit,* sovereignly to neutralize its affect, and this neutralization undoubtedly has a political import. Things may be different, perhaps, with other marionettes, those of Kleist and especially those of Celan, which we shall speak about next week.

But the contrasts may not be as simple or trenchant in this multipli-city of marionettes summoned to appear in court.[40]

38. Ibid., p. 36.
39. Hyphenated thus ("multi-plicité") in the typescript.
40. The last half hour of the session was devoted to discussion.

February 20, 2002

The phallus, I mean the *phallos*, is it proper to man?

And if said phallus were proper to the sovereign, would it still be proper to man? Would it be the proper in what sense? And of man in what sense, proper to man in what sense? And what if the phallus were *bêtise* itself?

Let's leave these questions to prepare themselves in the wings or in their dressing rooms, they will come back on stage and into the glare of the lime-light, and surprise us when the moment comes.

That's it too, the art of the marionette — or the marionette theater.

As if a marionette, far from being content to react after the fashion of a beast, supposed, by our classical thinkers, able only to react rather than respond — as if a marionette, then, rather than being content to react and even to respond, still had the power to ask us questions, in the wings. As if it were still asking us:

The [feminine] beast and the [masculine] sovereign, so *what*? So *who*?

Between the two, between the beast and the sovereign, would be the art of the marionette, the two arts of the marionette, that we're keeping waiting, and the wolves, so many wolves! Not weather fit for dogs, but so, so many wolves [*Non pas temps de chien, mais tant et tant de loups!*].[1]

278 Wolves of the world — I leave you to complete or supply . . .

Wolves of the world, there's a call that seems to have been resounding for months across the spaces of this seminar. So many wolves have already responded, from so many different places, countries, and states, so many different cultures, mythologies, and fables. Every wolf in this genelycology or this politic-eco-lycology could hear this call, both as beast and as

---

1. [Translator's note:] "Tant" and "temps" in French are homophones. "Un temps de chien" is terrible weather.

sovereign, as Beast and Sovereign, be the wolf an outlaw or be he above the laws like the werewolf, be he outside the law insofar as he makes the law or above the law like the sovereign possessing the right of pardon, of life or death over his subjects.

The wolf is then also the sovereign, the lord, the sire, the sir, Mon Sieur or His Majesty.

His Majesty the wolf, Sir Wolf. "Sire," "Your Majesty" . . .

This is what the lamb calls him, you remember, *Sie erinnern sich*, this is how the lamb addresses the wolf when he speaks in La Fontaine's *The Wolf and the Lamb*:

> Sire, replies the lamb, may Your Majesty
> > Not grow angry;
> > And rather consider
> > That I am slaking my thirst
> > > In the current
> > More than twenty paces below Him.[2]

It was with this fable that we began ("IN THE BEGINNING WAS THE FABLE," says Valéry), in order to ask on the threshold of the seminar the question of force and right; not force and justice but force and right, the right which, Kant reminds us, with good sense itself, already in its concept implies the means, and thereby the coercive force, of its application and its implementation: a right without force is not a right worthy of the name; and it is primarily for this reason that the troubling problem imposes itself, which is the very problem of sovereignty (the sovereign always representing the most powerful power, the highest, greatest power, all-power, the strongest strength, the most eminent capital or capitalization, the extreme monopolization of force or violence—*Gewalt*—in the figure of the state, the absolute superlative of power)—the troubling problem of a force, then, that because it is indispensable to the exercise of right, because it is implied in the very concept of right, would give right or found right, and would give reason in advance to force, as is said in the first line of this fable, as the first line of the fable with which we opened this seminar:

> The reason of the strongest is always the best
> As we shall shortly show.

2. La Fontaine, "Le loup et l'agneau" (see session 1 above, n. 10), p. 51. [Translator's note: In the French text, the capitalized pronoun is the feminine "Elle," corresponding to the grammatical gender of "Votre Majesté."]

279

"Always" (in "always the best") bespeaks universality and recurrence or regularity: *always* thus, everywhere and all the time, every day, in all places and at all times; *always* already bespeaks the law, the day, and the phenomenal appearing of the universality of the law, the daylight of all the days of the law, or a natural and observable law, *describable* (in fact this is always how it is, it's clear even if it is not just) or on the contrary the other light of a *prescriptive* law: it must be thus, it is good and just that it be thus, one must act so that it remain always thus.

This equivocation of the concept of the law, of a law described or a law prescribed, prescribing, this equivocation that concentrates the whole problem and thus lurks in the "always"—this equivocation had already marked the use—there too highly idiomatic—of the word "reason" (in "the reason of the strongest is always the best"). The word "reason" denotes or designates both and equally two things: *on the one hand*, the reason given, alleged, presumed by the stronger, whether or not he be right [*avoir raison*], whether or not this reason be rational or not (I can advance a reason, my reason, even if I am not right); and "reason," *on the other hand*, can name the right that he has [*la raison qu'il a*], the good and just reason he has to exercise his force and make it predominate, his greater and higher power, his sovereign power, his all-power, his superlative power, his sovereignty. Whence this third meaning or third implication of the idiomatic use of the word "reason," namely that the sovereign (or the wolf in the fable) acts as if he had reason to judge just and legitimate the reason he gives because he is the strongest, i.e. because, in the relation of force that here makes right, that here gives reason, the strongest one, the sovereign, is he who, as we say in French, *a raison des autres* [prevails over the others],[3] who wins out over the less strong, and treads on the sovereignty or even the reason [or sanity] of the others.

Is there any point recalling so many examples from our modernity when, as Hannah Arendt insisted, it is the most powerful sovereign states which, making international right and bending it to their interests, propose and in fact produce limitations on the sovereignty of the weakest states, sometimes, as we were saying at the beginning of the seminar, going so far as to violate or not respect the international right they have helped institute

3. [Translator's note:] Derrida exploits several possibilities of the French "raison" in what follows. In the most general sense, "raison" is reason. "Avoir raison" is literally to have reason, but idiomatically to be right. "Avoir raison de . . ." is to prevail, to win out over.

and, in so doing, to violate the institutions of that international right, all the while accusing the weaker states of not respecting international right and of being rogue states,[4] i.e. outlaw states, like those animals said to be "rogue" animals, which don't even bend to the law of their own animal society? Those powerful states that always give, and give themselves, reasons to justify themselves, but are not necessarily right, have reason of the less powerful; they then unleash themselves like cruel, savage, beasts, or beast full of rage. And this is just how La Fontaine describes the sovereign wolf in the fable. The wolf is described as, I quote, "that animal full of rage," ready to launch punitive, even preventive or vengeful expeditions. Listen to the wolf when he takes the lamb to task and prepares a preventive offensive against the one who might take over his wells or food sources:

> Who makes you so bold as to muddy my drink?
> Said this animal full of rage;
> You will be punished for your temerity.

Punishment and penal law. The motif of revenge comes to close and seal the fable, as if at bottom the penal law exercised by the strongest, as if the punishment it inflicts ("You will be punished") were always retaliation or revenge, *talio,* an eye for an eye, rather than justice. "I must avenge myself," says the wolf at the end.

Note, with what are called "current events" in mind, that in La Fontaine's fable revenge has to unleash itself blindly against all those who are presumed to be related, allied, socially or by blood, by a link of fraternity, with the presumed guilty party, be it a child, a powerless lamb that is basically accused of being guilty before even being born. The lamb is accused of having muddied the wolf's water, his source or his resource, before even being born. And when the lamb argues back and says, "I wasn't born yet," the wolf replies forthwith and without a moment's hesitation the famous phrase that accumulates all the perversions of collective, transgenerational, familial or national, nationalistic and fraternalistic accusation: "If not you, your brother, then" [*Si ce n'est toi, c'est donc ton frère*]. You are therefore guilty at birth, by your birth, guilty for being born what you were born. Originary culpability, responsibility, or liability, *ursprüngliche Schuldigsein* of the lamb the figure of which you can, if you like, reinterpret either on the basis of the Bible and the Gospels (the Christly lamb), or against a Greek background (you remember the passage from Plato's *Phaedrus* that I quoted

4. [Translator's note:] "Rogue States" is in English (capitalized) in the text.

at the beginning of the seminar: it also put on stage, in an erotic scene this time, the appetite of the lover who loves his beloved as the wolf loves the lamb, to the point of eating it).

At this point I can only encourage you to read a text that ought to be quoted and studied *in extenso* for an infinite amount of time. This text is entitled "The Love of the Wolf," "The Love *of* the Wolf," ten pages by Hélène Cixous published in the theater review *La Métaphore*.[5] Through readings of a very large number of texts, from Pushkin to Shakespeare, from Tsvetaïeva to Ingeborg Bachmann and Afanassiev, via Little Red Riding Hood and the Eumenides, or . . . , Hélène Cixous deploys all the paradoxes, reversals, and hyperbole that are at work in the genitive in "love *of* the wolf," the ambiguous expression "love *of* the wolf," which gives her text's title all its potential: objective genitive or subjective genitive, love of the wolf by the lamb or love of the lamb by the wolf, the lamb loves the wolf who loves the lamb, love *of* the wolf that sometimes drives to "renunciation," she says, among so many other things, with "Christly love," those are her words, and "sacrifice of the wolf."[6] Hélène Cixous makes very clear, and this is precisely the strength of her text and her argument, how the love of the wolf can be inseparable from love of fear. And all the force of force, the force of desire, the force of love, the force of fear conjugate here. The text says: "We love the wolf. We love the love of the wolf. We love the fear of the wolf . . ."[7] The fear of the wolf can also be heard according to a double genitive: the fear of the wolf who has fear of the lamb who has fear of the wolf. We have fear of the wolf who has fear of us and that is the whole love *of* the wolf. "But happiness is when a real wolf does not eat us."[8] So read "The Love of the Wolf."

I would say, diverting a bit, that the wolf boasts of[9] loving the lamb, of loving his enemy's weakness, of loving it to the point of taking it into himself, consum(mat)ing his love, consuming himself with love in consummating his love, i.e. in eating him with one bite. The wolf boasts of loving the lamb, who loves him back. The love of the other is their strength, and you see where it leads them . . . Nothing is stronger than love, save death.

In La Fontaine's fable, when the lamb protests his innocence and says that he could not have muddied the water and the drink of His Majesty the

5. Hélène Cixous, "L'amour du loup," *La Métaphore* (Lille), no. 2 (Spring 1994); reprinted in *L'amour du loup et autres remords* (Paris: Galilée, 2003).

6. *L'amour du loup et autres remords,* p. 32.

7. Ibid., p. 23.

8. Ibid., p. 33.

9. [Translator's note:] "Se fait fort de": boasts of, but literally "makes himself strong by."

Wolf because he is lower, so much lower than He, His Majesty the Wolf replies, and you are going to see once more the association between the motif
of sovereignty and that of cruelty, of the "cruel beast":

> —You are muddying it, replied this cruel beast,
> And I know that you spoke ill of me last year.
> —How could I if I was not yet born?
> Replied the Lamb; I still suckle my mother.[10]
>   —If not you, your brother, then.
> —I have no brother. —So one of your people:
> For you scarce spare me,
> You, your shepherds, and your dogs.
> People have told me so: I must take my revenge.
> And with this, to the depth of the forests
> The Wolf carries him off, and then eats him,
> Without further ado.

283

"Without further ado" [*sans autre forme de procès*: without any other form
of trial]: an exercise of force, then, as punitive justice in the interests of the
sovereign who sets up no tribunal, not even an exceptional or military tribunal and who, in the name of his self-defense,[11] his self-protection, his supposed "legitimate defense," annihilates the defenseless enemy, the enemy
who doesn't even have the defense given by a defense counsel in a regular
trial, etc.

In this fable dedicated, in 1668, like La Fontaine's other fables—like
the whole volume of *Fables* — to Monseigneur le Dauphin—in this fable,
then, *The Wolf and the Lamb* [of which Chamfort already said, "Everyone
knows this fable, even those who know only this one"],[12] in *The Wolf and the
Lamb,* then, the wolf is called "Sire" and "Your Majesty." The wolf figures
the King, the grandeur and highness of King and Dauphin, a grandeur and
highness that the dedication evokes literally. Once we have allowed for convention and a generic law for this type of dedicatory address, we cannot fail
to notice a certain analogy or magnetic attraction of vocabulary in recalling
The Wolf and the Lamb, and especially the language of the lamb, a humble
citizen addressing the sovereign, His Majesty the Wolf:

284

> Sire, replies the lamb, may Your Majesty
> Not grow angry;

10. This line was omitted in Derrida's transcription.

11. [Translator's note:] "self-defense" is in English in the text.

12. Chamfort, quoted in La Fontaine, *Oeuvres complètes,* vol. 1: *Fables, contes et nou-
velles,* ed. Jean-Pierre Collinet (Paris: Gallimard, 1991), p. 1067.

And rather consider
That I am slaking my thirst
In the current
More than twenty paces below Him.

[One cannot fail to notice] the dedication or rather the *envoi* in prose, before the dedication in verse. This *envoi* also names the Majesty of the father King, the father of the Dauphin, who is six and a half years old at the time, the Majesty of the father, the King, Louis XIV, known as Louis le Grand; and the same *envoi* to Monseigneur le Dauphin insists on these figures of highness and grandeur which are proper to majesty, to *maiestas*. La Fontaine speaks humbly of "him on whom His Majesty [and so your father] cast his eyes to instruct you." Casting an eye is what a lord does, from high to low. There follows the praise of the Monarch, of the "qualities that our invincible Monarch gave you with your birth." What follows is all about the great European designs of Louis le Grand, of his wars, wars that are always imposed upon him by aggressions but that are always in the end triumphs for him; Louis le Grand is also compared to Augustus and Alexander (Alexander the Great, and "Alexander" also means the great man). Everything converges, we may well say, on the figure of grandeur, on the eminent erection, the eminently phallic, excellently eminent and excellently phallic erection of sovereign highness, its transcendence, political grandeur, but also the "grandeur of soul" that the Dauphin has inherited from his father ("I invoke as testimony those noble worries, that vivacity, that ardor, those marks of spirit, of courage and of grandeur of soul [the kid is six and a half] that you show at every moment.")[13]

285   And the metaphor of grandeur, highness, erection (i.e. of phallic eminence) comes close to the signature, almost to conclude the *envoi*; the irresistible growth and erection of an immense tree, a ligneous line that dominates and covers its whole domain: "It is a highly agreeable spectacle for the universe to see growing thus a young plant that will one day cover with its shade so many people and nations."[14]

Grandeur and highness, erection, majesty.

In *The Wolf and the Lamb*, the expression "twenty feet below Him" [capital "H"], this precision as to the inferior place in which the lamb is humbly situated, clearly signifies, like the capital letter on Sire or Majesty, that what

13. La Fontaine, "À Monseigneur le Dauphin," in *Fables*, ed. Fumaroli (see session 1 above, n. 10), pp. 3–4.

14. Ibid., p. 4.

marks Majesty is grandeur and highness. Sire is not far from Sir and *sieur* and the Monsieur Teste that we were talking about last time.

Even before *The Wolf and the Lamb,* and still on the theme of "the reason of the strongest is always the best," or at bottom the theme of might making right, might giving right, the "right of the stronger," in the fable entitled *The Heifer, the Goat, and the Ewe in Society with the Lion*, this latter, the lion, attributes to himself, along with the right to divide up the stag, their common prey (and in so doing he *makes* the law, he is the law, he is the law above the laws, the law is always a law of dividing up, *nomos, nemein*)—[the lion attributes to himself, along with the right to divide up the stag], the right to keep everything for himself, to monopolize everything, and he does so in his capacity as Sire. And it is as Sire that he declares the right of the strongest, that he says what he is doing in doing what he says, authorizing himself with the very performative that he declares himself.

> Then into so many parts the stag he cut;
> Took for himself the first in his capacity as Sire:
> It should be mine, said he, and the reason

I emphasize again this appeal to reason, to a reason that is not one, which is only, as reason given, as reason alleged, the *fact* of the name and the force of the stronger.

> Is that I'm called Lion:
> Nothing to be said to that.

286

Arbitrariness of the name, which has no sense or justification: I am who I am, my name is lion, that's my quality as Sire, and from my birth no one could change anything about it, not even I: nothing to be said.

> The second by rights should fall to me too:

the second portion of the stag: he's just taken the first

> This right, as you know, is the right of the strongest.
> As the most valiant I claim the third.
> And if any one of you girls touches the fourth,
> I'll strangle her right now[15]

And so, progressively, one, two, three, four, on the pretext of sovereignly making the law of the division into four, he appropriates it all in the name

---

15. La Fontaine, "La génisse, la chèvre et la brebis, en société avec le Lion," Livre premier, fable VI, in *Oeuvres complètes*, 1:37.

of the right of the strongest, a right of the strongest that moreover he states, emits, both produces and performs himself. *First,* the first portion, in his quality as Sire, in the name of his name ("Lion"); then, *second*, the second portion, by right (common right, indeed, since they are four of them sharing it, he is also like the others: so he is both king and subject; the king has the same rights, he has no fewer rights than his subjects even if he also has more rights than they and in fact every right, and he also posits this right to every right as "right of the strongest"); *third*, the third portion, the courage and valiance he shows and that give him the right to take and do what he has the courage to take and do in saying so: the courage of the absolute performative; finally, *fourth*, the fourth portion, the threat or fear that he inspires in the others (remember Hobbes: one becomes subject to the sovereign out of fear, here not fear of the wolf but fear of the lion):

287

> And if any one of you girls [*si quelqu'une*] touches the fourth,
> I'll strangle her right now.

This "quelqu'*une*" reminds us that the lion possesses and subjugates to himself, hence subjects to himself, while violating their rights, three beasts the names of which, in French, are feminine and all three of which have a certain relationship, a certain family resemblance, to the lamb: *la* génisse, *la* chèvre, and *la* brebis. *La* bête and *le* souverain: *la* génisse, *la* chèvre, and *la* brebis in society with *le* lion. *La* bête in society with *le* souverain, the beasts and the sovereign, who is the only one to name himself, to refer himself, *ipse*, to himself, to his title, to his name, and to his might. To his ipseity.

The beast and His Majesty the sovereign, his grandeur the sovereign, his highness the sovereign. What is majesty? You know that this Latin word (*majestas*, which comes from *magnus, major*), signifies grandeur, highness, dignity (at bottom, Kant's *Würde* is a majesty of man, a dignity attached to the human person as an end in itself). In Latin, in Roman, *majestas* is also sovereignty, that of the state or that of the Roman people. Jean Bodin, who passes for the first great theorist of sovereignty, opens chapter 8 of his book (*The Six Books of the Republic*), entitled "Of Sovereignty," by recalling that "Sovereignty is the absolute and perpetual power of a Republic, which the Latins call *majestatem*, the Greeks *akran exousian*, and *kurian arch'* and *kurion politeuma*, the Italians *segnoria*, [. . .] the Hebrews call it *Tismar schabet*, etc."[16] "Majesty" is thus another name for the sovereignty

16. Jean Bodin, "De la souveraineté," in *Les Six Livres de la République*, book l, chap. 8, p. 111 [*On Sovereignty*, p. 1]. Derrida again quotes from the Livre de Poche edition,

of the sovereign. And *Majestas* indeed names, as the superlative of magnitude or grandeur, the majority of the great, of the *magnus*, the *major*, the male erection of a grandeur grander than grandeur. The king, the monarch, the emperor is upped [*majoré*], erected (and I mean "erected" for a reason that will come out in a moment when we speak about marionettes again) [erected] to a height that is majestic, upped, augmented, exaggerated, higher than the height of the great, incomparably higher than height itself, even sublimely higher than height, and this is already the height of the Most High: the Sovereign in its Majesty is most high, greater than great. He is great like Louis the Great. This standing, erect, augmented grandeur, infinitely upped, this height superior to every other superiority is not merely a trope, a figure of rhetoric, a sensory way of representing the sovereign. First, it is not just sensory, since the majestic Most High rises above all comparable and sensory height (whereby it is also sublime, or in any case lays claim to being meta-metaphorical and meta-physical, more than natural and more than sensory). So this is not a figure, but an essential feature of sovereign power, an essential attribute of sovereignty, its absolute erection, without weakness or without detumescence, its unique, stiff, rigid, solitary, absolute, singular erection. And concretely, this translates, in the political effectivity of the thing, not only as an all-power of the state over life-death, the right of pardon, generation, birth, sexual potency as generative and demographic power, but also the height from which the state has the power to see everything, to see the whole, having literally, potentially, a right of inspection over everything. I was quoting a moment ago the praise of Louis le Grand and his Dauphin by La Fontaine. This was praise of majestic height that covers not only, like a tree reaching to the sky, the whole national territory of its subjects but virtually the whole world ("It is a highly agreeable spectacle for the universe to see growing thus a young plant that will one day cover with its shade so many people and nations"). And today, the sovereign power, the international power of a national sovereignty is also proportionate to its power to see, power to have under surveillance, to observe, take in, archive from a superterrestrial height, by satellite, the whole globalized surface of the earth, to the centimeter, and this in the service of the economic strategy of the market as well as of military strategy. This erection toward height is always the sign of the sovereignty of the sovereign, of the head of state or simply the Head, the Dictator we were talking about recently, *Il Duce*, the *Führer,* or quite

288

289

---

with its inaccuracies. As in the second session, we have corrected the Greek terms here transliterated. See session 2 above, n. 10.

simply the political leader, his "leadership."[17] Of course we shall soon see
how and why this erection to the heights, to the height of the head or the
capital, can give rise to the marionette, to a becoming-marionette. Translated into the theatrical space of the politics of our time, namely the public
space called televisual media, all political leaders, heads of state, or heads
of parties, all the supposedly decisive and deciding actors of the political
field are consecrated as such by the election of their erection to the status
of marionette in the puppet show,[18] translated as it happens into French as
the *Bébête Show*,[19] so many animal marionettes, anthropo-zoological puppets, so many fables for our time, the most significant feature of the thing
being the desire of said notables to be elected to this erection to the status of
marionettes. Election to the erection. Their ambition, the declared sign of
their ambition, is the urgency of the desire with which they hope, expect,
demand, sometimes with considerable edginess, champing at the bit to appear on the *Bébête Show*, as though this election to the status of marionette
was the true and ultimate selection, as though the metamorphosis into a
bête bébête were the supreme legitimation: "As long as you don't appear,"
they seem to say to themselves, "as a *bête bébête* on the *Bébête Show*, you
have no chance of becoming sovereign, prime minister or Head of State."
That's what Ovid's *Metamorphoses* have become today on Canal Plus.

The word "Majesty" (*Majestät*) appears at least once in Celan's "Meridian,"
which we are getting close to.[20] The word *Majestät* appears at least once in

290

17. [Translator's note:] "Leadership" is in English in the text.
18. [Translator's note:] "Puppet show" is in English in the text.
19. An allusion to the *Bébête Show*, a satirical program inspired by *The Muppet Show*
and broadcast on the French TV station TF1, from 1983 to 1995. *Les Guignols de l'Info*,
a satirical program first broadcast in 1988 on [the subscription channel] Canal Plus, was
for a time a rival of the *Bébête Show* until the latter's disappearance. [Translator's note:
Bébête, meaning "childish," "silly," derives from *bête*, and the conceit of the show was
to have politicians appear in the form of animal puppets. *Les Guignols de l'Info* is something like "The Punch and Judy Newshour."]
20. This part of the session (pp. 217–20 and then 225–35) and part of the next session
(pp. 259–73), which both concern Derrida's reading of Celan's text "The Meridian"
from the point of view of political and poetic sovereignties, were translated by Outi
Pasanen, in a modified and abridged version (especially in the quotations from Celan
commented by Derrida), under the title "Majesties," in Jacques Derrida, *Sovereignties in
Question: The Poetics of Paul Celan*, ed. Thomas Dutoit and Outi Pasanen (New York:
Fordham University Press, 2005), pp. 108–34. [Translator's note: I have retranslated
these passages in the interests of consistency.]

the German text, and we shall see it later picked up or repeated a second time in the [French] translation of this text by Jean Launay, the exemplary translator and editor of this admirable volume.

In "The Meridian," the word "Majesty" stands in the vicinity of the word and the lexicon of "monarchy," which was so much at issue in this speech, the monarchy decapitated during the French Revolution, but this vicinity is there for contrast, as we shall see, to mark a difference between the majesty Celan is talking about and the majesty of monarchy. But it is too soon to make this clear: we have to wait a little. And proceed by slow and prudent approaches, for things are more complex and subtle and evasive, more undecidable even, than ever.

Let us return to the marionette. There is more than one of them, we were saying. We are going to approach Celan's (*"Die Kunst, das ist, Sie erin-nern sich, ein marionettenhaftes [. . .] kinderloses Wesen"*) at the point where, as I was suggesting last time, the marionette of "The Meridian" comes to us, gives itself to be read and thought, through an experience of the foreign (*das Fremde*) and of the *Unheimliche* (*das Unheimliche*) that all Monsieur Teste's marionettes and marionettes' marionettes *seemed most often* (I want to be prudent) — seemed most often to try to reduce or suppress, repress, purify of equivocation.

Marionette and marionette. There is marionette and marionette, that's the hypothesis and the wager I risked last time. There are two experiences, rather, let's also say two arts of the marionette. But also, perhaps, two fables of the marionette. Two marionettes whose fables intersect, two marionettes.

If I place so much emphasis on the fable and the fabulous, it is undoubtedly, and too obviously, because of fables, like La Fontaine's, that put on the political and anthropological stage beasts that play a role in civil society or in the state, and often the statutory roles of subject or sovereign. But there's another reason for my emphasizing the fabulous. The point is, as the fables themselves show, that the essence of political force and power, where that power makes the law, where it gives itself right, where it appropriates legitimate violence and legitimates its own arbitrary violence — this unchaining and enchaining of power passes via the fable, i.e. speech that is both fictional and performative, speech that consists in saying: well, I'm right because yes, I'm right because, yes, I'm called Lion and, you'll listen to me, I'm talking to you, be afraid, I am the most valiant and I'll strangle you if you object. In the fable, within a narrative that is itself fabulous, it is shown that power is itself an effect of fable, fiction, and fictive speech, simulacrum. Like that law, that force of law that Montaigne and Pascal said was essentially fictional, etc.

Between the two fables of the marionettes, one would perhaps be a poem, the other not: one perhaps make one think, the other not. I always say perhaps. Perhaps two: it's never certain.

The difference between the two would be, perhaps, almost nothing, scarcely the time or the turn of a breath, the difference of a breath, the turning of a scarcely perceptible breath (*Atemwende*, Celan would say, precisely. *Atemwende* is not only the title of one of his collections of poetry, it is the word he uses in "The Meridian" to attempt a definition of poetry: "*Dichtung: das kann eine Atemwende bedeuten*"[21] ("Poetry: that can mean a turning of breath")). But we are never sure of this. And the poem, if there is any, and thought, if there is any, depend on this improbability of breath. But breath remains, among certain living beings at least, the first sign of life but also the last sign of life, of living life. The first and the last sign of living life. No doubt there is no speech and no speaking silence without breath, but before speech and at the beginning of speech there would be breath.

292   Not only is the certainty of this distinction between the two (marionettes or arts of the marionette) never achieved in any living present, but perhaps one *must* never be certain of it. This *must* or *must not* [*ne faut pas*] or *must avoid* [*faut ne pas*] perhaps disqualifies or discredits the presence, the self-presence, of any living presence. If I use, and emphasize, the expression "living present" (*lebendige Gegenwart*: living now), an expression to which Husserl, as you know, gave a phenomenological status and a sort of letter of nobility in philosophy, it is of course in order to make a strategically essential and necessary reference to Husserlian phenomenology and the transcendental phenomenology of time; it is also for reasons that will appear later, in the course of an attempted reading of Celan and what he says about the present or the now, of its "Majesty," precisely. But it is above all to interrogate one more time this way of naming life, or more precisely the living being: not Life, the Being or Essence or Substance of something like LIFE, but the living being, the presently living being, not the substance Life that remains in life, but the attribute "living" to qualify or determine the present, the now, a now that is supposedly essentially living, presently living, now as living (*die lebendige Gegenwart*). As those who have been following

21. Paul Celan, "Le Méridien," in *Le Méridien & autres proses*, p. 73 [p. 180]. [Translator's note: bracketed page numbers here and in subsequent notes refer to Glenn's translation; see session 6 above, n. 19.]

this seminar for a few years know well, through what we have tried to think together under the title of forgiveness, pardon, the death penalty, and sovereignty, what we were attached to was always that which I would not say presents itself as what is living in life, the enigma of the living being—on the side of *zōē* as much as of *bios, life, Leben, Lebendigkeit*, as Husserl has it, again, livingness [*vivance*], what now maintains [*maintenant maintient*] life in life, but that which stands back a little at the very place where the question "What is living in life?" holds its breath before the problematic legitimacy of a subjection of the question of life to a question of Being, of life to Being.

To think a difference between marionettes, to think the marionette *itself* is to try to think the living in life, and a living "being" that perhaps "is" not—a *living without being*. As I wrote long ago, "God without Being,"[22] an expression to which Marion gave the majestic form and force of the title of one of his books.[23] Of a "living without being"—or what "is" only a simulacrum of a being. Or what is only a prosthesis. Or what is only a substitute for the being of the thing itself, a fetish. The marionette is all that: life death at the same time [develop], a simulacrum, a prosthesis (remember Kleist's allusion to the art of the English artist who produces a wooden leg that one can dance gracefully with)—a simulacrum, a prosthesis, a fetish. Man can and should produce marionettes and even a marionette theater. Will we rush to say that those we call animals cannot do so? No. Of course, most of them, and most men too, don't produce a puppet show or Kleist's marionette theater. But are certain nonhuman animals capable of producing and getting attached to simulacra, to masks, and to meaningful prosthetic substitutes? The reply would then be "yes," and this would be easy to argue either on the basis of our everyday experience, or on the basis of ethological or primatological knowledge.

It is along this a-venue[24] that I was proposing, already last time, to attempt a timid or intimidated, partial, highly selective reading, after *Monsieur Teste*'s marionettes, of Celan's marionettes in "The Meridian." I already twice quoted, the last two times, the first words of this "Speech," which you know was given in October 1960, in Darmstadt, on Celan's reception of the Georg Büchner prize, which explains and largely justifies, because of the context, the central and organizing character of the references to the works

293

22. See session 2 above, n. 16.

23. Jean-Luc Marion, *Dieu sans l'Être* (Paris: Fayard, 1982); trans. Thomas A. Carlson as *God without Being* (Chicago: University of Chicago Press, 1995).

24. [Translator's note:] "A-venue" in Derrida's typescript.

of Büchner, to *Danton's Death, Woyzeck*, etc. I already twice quoted, the last two times, the opening words of this "Speech" (*"Die Kunst, das ist, Sie erinnern sich, ein marionettenhaftes* [. . .] *kinderloses Wesen"*).[25] But before going further to encounter what is said about the encounter (*Begegnung*, the secret of the encounter, *im Geheimnis der Begegnung*) in this speech, and what is there called "Majesty"—and it is not just any majesty, but the majesty of the present, of the *Gegenwart* we were just talking about with respect to *die lebendige Gegenwart*, and the present of man or the human ["The homage here rendered is to the majesty of the present, testimony to the presence of the human, the majesty of the absurd" (*"Gehuldigt wird hier der für die Gegenwart des Menschlichen zeugenden Majestät des Absurden"*)[26]]—[before going further, then, to encounter what is said about the encounter in this speech, and what is there called "Majesty"] I want finally to tell you what I had in mind not only in talking to you insistently about the erection of grandeur in the vocabulary and semantics of sovereign majesty but in insisting, since last time, on the fact that there are two marionettes, two arts and two meanings of the marionette, and thus a difference in the very body and heart of the marionette. And this difference between two marionettes in the marionette is again one of the sexual differences we have been talking about since the beginning of the seminar.

Last time I recalled that most often, in our typical representation of the marionette, what insistently came to the fore was the feminine figure of the small and the young, the little girl, the touching young girl, even the virgin, the Virgin Mary (*mariole, mariolette*). With the grace, innocence, and spontaneity that usually go with that.

But as you have no doubt already sensed, things are not so simple. In truth, they are less simple than ever. As always when sexual differences are in play. (Incidentally, I'll venture to say to all those who—often in the press, as you know—speak ironically of people who, like me for example, are fond of issuing warnings, saying, "Things are not so simple," those to whom irony comes easily when they are faced with this systematic warning, I believe it's primarily because they want to hide from themselves, forget or deny something to do with sexual differences. There's always a clandestine debate raging about sexual differences.) So, as I was saying about the marionette as little girl or young innocent virgin full of grace, things are not so simple. And if they are not simple, it is because of the equivocality of the living being, precisely, where the living being concentrates, as though into

25. Celan, "Le Méridien," p. 59 [p. 173].
26. Ibid., p. 64 [p. 175].

a single value, spontaneity (the "what goes of itself" and flows from the source, what moves by itself, spontaneously, *sponte sua* — this is how the living being in general is defined: the living being is spontaneous and moves of itself, it is automotive), the living being concentrates in a single ambiguous value this automotive spontaneity that gives itself its law, its autonomy and which, by the same token, is right up close to automotive autonomy but also signifies its opposite, namely automaticity, or in other words the automat's mechanics of action and reaction — without spontaneity, precisely, and with no autonomous liberty. The living being is automotive, autonomous, absolutely spontaneous, sovereignly automotive, and at the same time perfectly programmed like an automatic reflex. I insist on this paradox to put back on stage the eminently phallic figure of the marionette, the phallic erection that comes to inhabit, haunt, and double that of the virgin girl. The virgin girl is inhabited by motion, movement, the essentially phallic law of the marionette. What does this mean?

The point is not just to say that the marionette is erect, because it is upright, tensed, hard as wood, made of wood (hard, as Madame Émilie Teste insisted, like the hardness of her husband Monsieur Teste, hardness, i.e. also stiffness, rigidity, or again, as in "The Meridian," quoting Büchner: "Nothing but art and mechanics, nothing but cardboard and springs!"[27]): we should not only say that the marionette is erect, because it is upright, tensed, hard as wood and that it stands on the stage, etc., like an instrument, a thingamajig [*machin*], or an operated machine, content to react mechanically, always a little stiffly, to what is mechanically acting on it. Like an actor too, an actor or a mask, a simulacrum, a substitute actor that is acted as much as it acts, operated, hard-wired (as they say about animal behavior) down to the slightest reaction, etc. This is true, of course, and one could go far in this direction of straight and direct erection, and compare the quasi-mechanical automatism of the marionette machine in the hands of its puppeteer to the reflex, one might almost say the reflex and quasi-automatic reaction of the phallic erection, what presents itself as hard, straight, standing, stiff, and rigid. And from this facile comparison one could indeed conclude that the marionette is a sort of metaphor or figure, a sort of phallic trope. It makes you think of the phallus, even though it's sometimes still a girl, and the taste, fascination, modes, and genres that cultivate the marionette or the marionette theater would thus be participating in the cult of the phallus. One could indeed follow things quite a long way down this road.

But in truth it is also the very opposite that we now have to recall. What,

296

27. Ibid., p. 61 [p. 174].

then? Well, even before holding the marionette to be a phallic figure, a simple figural representation of the phallus, one should remember to the contrary that the phallus is itself originally a marionette. As you know, the *phallos*, which is not the penis, first designated in Greece and Rome for certain ceremonies, that simulacrum, that figured representation of an erect penis, hard, stiff, rigid, precisely like a gigantic and artificially made-up puppet, made of tensed springs and exhibited during rituals and processions. The *phallos* is, itself, like the thing itself that it is, a sort of marionette. I will not here — merely for lack of time, because it would be highly interesting, even from the point of view of this seminar — get into the history of this culture or this fetishistic cult of the phallic simulacrum, which honored fecundity or the generative potency in the Dionysiac mysteries. I mention only a few features that make this phallus into a marionette *avant la lettre*: on the one hand, we are dealing with a simulacrum, a fictional figure: we are not dealing with the organic penis but with a prosthetic representation of the penis in permanent erection, a penis that is hard, stiff, and rigid but detached from the body proper, just like a prosthesis, a prosthetic and automatic machine; on the other hand, this detached representation is mechanical, it is made of artificial springs that respond by reaction to the orders that operate it: it is a rigid automat, but just as the erection itself is or seems to be, at least through an enigmatic collusion of the desire of the other and the mechanical reflex, [the erection] seems to be automatic, independent of will and even of desire; and then this male or female phallus as mechanical puppet is *bête,* both *bête*, inanimate (it's made of nonliving, inorganic matter) and cut from man, from both the *aner* and the *anthropos* to which one would like to reattach it. Whence my initial question: if the phallus is automat and not autonomous, if there is something in its stiffness and hardness that is machinelike or mechanical, already in itself prosthetic, and that withdraws it from human responsibility, is it proper to man or else, already cut from man, is it a "something," a thing, an a-human, inhuman *what,* which is, moreover, scarcely more masculine than feminine? Neither animal nor human?

If, then, the *phallos*, the phallic erection, is a machine but also the attribute of sovereignty, one would be tempted to say that this attribute of sovereignty, of its majesty, its grandeur or its erect highness, its Most Highness, this attribute of the sovereign is not an attribute of man, of something proper to man, nor indeed proper to anyone, not to the animal and not to God.

I am emphasizing this phallic simulacrum of the marionette and the sovereign, as also the mechanized, machinelike and therefore marionettiform structure of the phallus itself, because in "The Meridian"—which I'm creeping up on like a wolf, slowly, discreetly—a whole reading, one possible reading among others (a reading that to my knowledge has not yet been attempted of this great and majestic text of Celan's), another possible reading could elect, privilege, select what I shall call a phallic dramaturgy, and even a dramaturgy of phallic sovereignty. To limit myself provisionally to vocabulary, we know that we are going to find the marionettes again, of course, more than once, and heads, many heads, monarch's heads in particular, and revolutionary decapitations, we know that we are going to find again the majesty I was just talking about, and above all a Medusa's head, which I don't need to recall—though I will in a moment—the apotropaic relation it has (and that Freud recalls in *Das Medusenhaupt*)[28] to petrified erection and the threat of castration.

298

Here perhaps, in the comic or derisory aspect of erection, is where the experience of *bêtise* returns. In what remains comic about it, enough to make you die laughing. One cannot think of the Greek phallus without associating it with Priapus, or even priapism. I note first that Freud, who often speaks of the phallic, the phallic phase, the phallic mother, etc., rarely speaks, in fact almost never, of the phallus itself under this common noun. He uses the adjective "phallic," and almost never the noun "phallus." One of the very rare occurrences, if not the only exception, is precisely in a historical reference to Priapus's phallus in "The Taboo of Virginity."[29] To show that people were fearful of the threat that weighed on whoever deflowered girls, Freud recalls that in India young wives had first to sacrifice their hymen on a wooden lingam (again a kind of marionette) and that this custom can also be found among the Romans. He then mentions Saint Augustine's comment that the newlywed wife at least had to sit on what Freud calls "a gigantic stone phallus of Priapus." You know that the principal attribute of Priapus, who was often held to be the son of Dionysus and Aphrodite or a nymph, was that he was endowed, even afflicted, with an outsize phallic member, and we must say phallus rather than penis because this penis was outsize precisely because it was, or insofar as it was, uncontrollable by the subject, in permanent and irrepressible erection, that is, ithyphallic as it is sometimes called and as one should always call it: the *ithyphallos* is the hardness of the straight, rigid, standing phallus (*ithus* is straight, incidentally also in the sense of rectitude). The ithyphallic is the phallus in erec-

28. Sigmund Freud, "Medusa's Head," in *The Standard Edition*, 18:273–74.
29. Sigmund Freud, "The Taboo of Virginity," in *The Standard Edition*, 11:193–208 (p. 204).

tion, as it was represented in Dionysiac or Bacchic feasts. An immense, tall,
high, hard, stiff, and rigid phallus. Terrible (*terribilis* says Columella in his
Agriculture, 10.33),[30] terrible, terrifying, terrorizing, and comic all at once.
There would be a lot to say about this derision, this comic or mocking dimension in the effigies of the ithyphallic god sometimes daubed with red
and shouting obscenities. It was said of this quasi-god in constant erection
that he was born of an ass and was like an ass. Lactantius tells of a competition to see which of the two, Priapus or the ass, has the bigger member. The
ass wins, beats Priapus, but to avenge himself Priapus kills the ass.[31] Here,
insinuating itself, we see the hypothesis that a mark of *bêtise* always threatens the presumed superiority of a constant and imperturbable erection. I
shall call this, very seriously, ithyphallic *bêtise*, the essential, nonaccidental
bêtise that characterizes the phallic as such (and so sovereignty as such, of
which the ithyphallic is the attribute). It is like a marionette whose reflex
spring and uncontrollable automaticity never let up. The ithyphallus is a
marionette, whose hyperbolic desire is both nil and empty of thought and of
its own drive, of course, but it is this void that nonetheless pushes it, pulses
and compulses it, it is what promises, promotes, and makes one think of a
drive that is absolutely *bête, entêté,* that never gives anything up, that is an
absolute stranger to all thought.

I am not sure that Aristotle suspected this, but it is he who, intrigued by
the phenomenon of erection, worried about what might happen if by misfortune (and it is this misfortune I am venturing to call *bêtise*) the erection
became permanent. That would be not only ridiculous and would not only
make us laugh, as in the rituals and jokes I have just been talking about,
but, says Aristotle (in *The Parts of Animals* 689a 25–27), it would constitute an unnatural hindrance. Perhaps tolerable for beasts and for demigods,
this imperturbable and impassive erection would produce in men only im-
potence without the emission of semen, and thus without generative power,
and would produce only pain without enjoyment. The pathology called
priapism leads to death. And priapism is infinite ithyphallism, ithyphallism
foreign to that detumescence that is the finitude of erection and that, as such,
makes possible the time of erection — which it threatens, of course, but to

30. Quoted by Maurice Olender, "Priape, le dernier des dieux," in *Dictionnaire des
mythologies,* 2:312; trans. as "Priapus: The Last of the Gods," in *Mythologies,* comp. Yves
Bonnefoy, 1:629.

31. Handwritten addition: "As if he had found in the ithyphallic ass something more
bête than himself, intolerably more *bête* than himself."

which it also gives its opportunity. A priapic, i.e. permanent and indefinite, erection is no longer even an erection—and it is a mortal pathology.

But is detumescence castration? Instead of taking on this immense question frontally, it's time to return to "The Meridian," which we have, in fact, kept obliquely in view since the beginning of this session. What is said in it about the marionette, about the Medusa's head, about heads in general, and about majesty allows for a fairly well-justified transition. But I should also like to emphasize the Foreigner (*Fremde*), the Other (*Andere*), and the familiar or worrying estrangement (*Unheimliche*). I had to choose between a continuous reading of Celan's "Speech," an interpretation that would follow the apparent order and linear time of the text, its very consecution, and another, less diachronic, more systematic reading, which would be concerned, for the purposes of demonstration, to bring out a configuration of motifs, words, and themes, figures that usually do not appear in this order. I have of course taken this second course, [on the one hand] because we won't have time to read together, in a linear way, the whole text from A to Z (though I recommend that you do so yourselves), and, on the other hand, because the actively interpretative, selective, and directed reading I am about to propose to you requires it. You understand that I do not hold this interpretative reading to be the only or even the best possible one, but it doesn't seem impossible, and it is important to me in the perspective of this seminar.

Even before looking (too quickly, of course) at the motifs that I am proposing to articulate together (even though Celan does not do so explicitly)—namely art, the marionette or the automat, the Medusa's head, heads in general, and majesty, the Foreigner, and the *Unheimliche*—I have two preliminary remarks.

First preliminary remark. There is a lot about dates in this text, which is also a sort of poetics of the date. When I devoted a little book to it some fifteen years ago (*Schibboleth*),[32] I made it into a privileged object of reflection and analysis or interpretation, especially around a certain *January 20* that recurs regularly, at least three times, in the text (Büchner's Lenz, "the Lenz who 'on January 20 was walking through the mountains,' "[33] then "Perhaps we can say that every poem keeps inscribed within it its 'January 20,' "[34] then

301

---

32. [Translator's note:] Jacques Derrida, *Schibboleth: Pour Paul Celan* (Paris: Galilée, 1986); trans. Joshua Wilner and Thomas Dutoit, in Derrida, *Sovereignties in Question*, pp. 1–64.

33. Celan, "Le Méridien," p. 71 [p. 179].

34. Ibid., p. 73 [p. 180].

"I had myself written from a 'January 20,' my 'January 20' ").[35] I insistently elaborated on these dates, on the question of anniversaries and the calendar, and on this example of the "January 20" in *Schibboleth*. But it is thanks to Jean Launay's edition (so precious and exemplary, as I have said) that I was able to discover a further import to this "January 20." Referring to Celan's manuscript, Launay tells us in a note[36] that "January 20 is also the day in 1942 of the so-called Wannsee conference in Berlin, during which Hitler and his collaborators drew up the plans for the 'final solution.' " And here is the translation of the passage from Celan's manuscript: "We are still writing, still today, January 20 — *this* January 20 [*this* underlined, 'diesen 20, Jänner'], to which has been added since then the writing of so much [so many days of] ice" ("*zu dem sich [seitdem] soviel Eisiges hinzugeschrieben hat*"). "January 20," an anniversary of death, then, of crime against humanity, of a sovereignly, arbitrarily genocidal decision. "January 20," the eve of the anniversary of the decapitation of the monarch, Louis XVI, about whom a lot is said, between the repetitions of "Long live the King" of Lucile and Lenz, to which we shall return.

    Second preliminary remark. The apparently surprising contiguity between our readings of *Monsieur Teste* and "The Meridian," texts that are, however, so different, so distant through so many features — this contiguity or proximity of two texts that are apparently so anachronistic with respect to each other is justified not only, beyond mere juxtaposition, by the fact that they both, each in its own way, treat of the marionette and everything that is attached to it. The fact is that Valéry is not simply absent from "The Meridian." Celan wonders at a certain moment, on the subject of a radical questioning of art, if one must not "think Mallarmé through to his ultimate consequences?" ("*Mallarmé konsequent zu Ende denken?*"). Here too a long note by Launay[37] puts us on the track of a manuscript of Celan's that refers to a passage by Valéry in *Variétés*. Here, Valéry quotes something Mallarmé said to poor Degas, who was complaining about not finishing his little poem when he was "full of ideas." Mallarmé, as Valéry reports, replied: "But Degas, it is not with ideas that poetry is made, but with words." And Valéry concludes: "That is a great lesson."[38]

    Let us now try, around or through the configuration I have announced

302

---

35. Ibid., p. 81 [p. 184].
36. Jean Launay, in Celan, *Le Méridien & autres proses,* p. 107, note 50.
37. Ibid., p. 105, note 43.
38. Paul Valéry, *Variétés*, in *Oeuvres*, 1:784.

(art, the marionette, the Medusa's head or the automat, heads in general and majesty, the Foreigner and the *Unheimliche*), to decipher a certain poetic signature, I don't say a poetics or an *ars poetica*, not even a poem, but rather what I shall call a certain poetic signature, the unique signature of a unique poem, always unique, that tries—so as to express, not the essence, the presence, or how it *is* with the poem, but where the poem is coming and going—to free itself, by art, from art.

What line shall we follow toward the unique encounter with a unique poem? You know that the concept of encounter, the "secret of the encounter" we were just talking about (*Geheimnis der Begegnung*), is the secret of the poem, of the presence or the putting into presence or the presentation of the poem, the secret of the encounter as secret of the poem in the double sense of the term "secret of": in the sense of what, *on the one hand*, first, makes a poem, in the sense of its manufacture, its making, its possibility of taking form, if not of its art and its know-how, I prefer to say its signature (that is, the secret as genesis of the poem, its condition of possibility, as when we say, "That guy has the secret," implying the art of something or other, though here it is not essentially art that holds the secret of this act or rather this event, it is the encounter) and then—the double sense of secret—*on the other hand*, secondly, as what in the present itself—in the very presentation of the poem, in this present now on which Celan insists so much, in the experience of the encounter—still remains secret, at bottom like a present that does not present itself, a phenomenon that does not phenomenalize itself. Nothing shows up, the nothing, the absurd shows up in manifesting nothing. We shall get to this manifestation as nonmanifestation.

But I think I know from having read this poem so often that its trajectory follows a line that defies all reconstitution in the form of logical or narrative exposition. The few initial sketches or sidesteps [*esquisses ou esquives*] that I am proposing to you today are really only an invitation to take a look, to go get your eyes and hands involved in it yourselves, to encounter the poem. The line (I keep the word "line," but we shall have to say "link" in a moment, for the line is a link, *Verbindende*), the line as a link that links to the other, the Thou in the encounter, the line as link that I am seeking to draw or reconstitute is, moreover, the very thing that is being sought, that Celan admits having sought for during this journey, on this path that he describes at the end—and I shall basically be setting out from this, i.e. at the end, from the end—[that Celan describes, then] as an "impossible path" or a "path of the impossible." Moreover, an "impossible path" and a "path *of* the impossible" are not exactly the same thing. One might imagine that

303

the path *of* the impossible, for its part, as a path, as the pathway of the path, remains possible, which would by the same token make the impossible path possible in its turn: and it is no doubt deliberately, and with a view to the inextricable knot that holds them together, though distinct, that Celan says, juxtaposing and crossing them, "impossible path" *and* "path *of* the impossible":

> Ladies and gentlemen, I find something that offers me some consolation for having traveled in your presence [*in Ihrer Gegenwart:* and this *in Ihrer Gegenwart*, which looks like a conventional banality, a standard piece of politeness addressed to the audience on prize day, this *in Ihrer Gegenwart* is all the more noticeably serious for the fact that the whole text will have turned around the enigma of the "now," *Gegenwart*, and of presence; in a moment I shall take only *three* examples *by making three returns* among others that are possible, after having quoted the end of this sentence] this impossible path, this path of the impossible [*in Ihrer Gegenwart diesen unmöglichen Weg, diesen Weg des Unmöglichen gegangen zu sein*].[39]

It is this impossible path of the impossible that constitutes, as link, the line that he *believes* he has found, even *touched* (*habe ich ihn soeben wieder zu berühren geglaubt*: these are the very last words), and which will soon be called the Meridian. This line is a link that leads to the encounter (*Begegnung*), to your encounter, the encounter of you, the nomination of Thou, whereby he will more than once have named the poem and the present of the poem. But before continuing this quotation to the end, I would like, via a few returns, *three returns*, as I said, to show you how this "in your presence" (*in Ihrer Gegenwart*) was not a conventional concession (there are none in this extraordinary text). This "in your presence" (*in Ihrer Gegenwart*) was already invested, charged, made more serious by the question of the poem, the poem in its difficult and tumultuous settling of scores with art, the question that bears on art and the question that bears on poetry ("*Frage nach der Kunst und nach der Dichtung*," said Celan earlier, adding, "I have approached Büchner, consciously, if not voluntarily, with my question about art and literature — one question among many — in order to identify his question").[40] Now this question becomes that of the poem, determined by Celan as present and presence, as now and presence.

First return, toward what exactly the word "Majesty" implies in the very essence or rather the event, the chance, of poetry. After several appearances

39. Celan, "Le Méridien," p. 84 [p. 185] .
40. Ibid., p. 67 [p. 177].

of art, to which we shall return (art as marionette, art as monkey, etc.), here is Lucile from *Danton's Death*, the one who is "blind to art" (*die Kunstblinde*), who surprises us by shouting, "Long live the King!" You see, as if I needed to tell you, that with this scene from the French Revolution and the putting to death of the king, right by the scaffold, but also this evocation of marionettes and the monkey, we are indeed as close as can be to our great question, "the beast and the sovereign."

Lucile shouts, "Long live the King!" and Celan emphasizes with an exclamation point how surprising this cry is, right by the bloody scaffold and after he has recalled the "artful words" (*kunstreiche Worte*) of Danton, Camille, etc. — she, Lucile, who is blind to art, shouts, "Long live the King!" Celan calls it a counterstatement (*Gegenwort*):

> After all these words spoken on the platform (the scaffold [*es ist das Blutgerüst*]) — what a statement [*welch ein Wort!*]!
>
> It is a counterstatement [*Es ist das Gegenwort*], a statement that severs the "wire," which refuses to bow before the "loiterers and parade horses of history." It is an act of freedom. It is a step. [*Es ist ein Akt der Freiheit. Es ist ein Schritt.*][41]

To support this claim, namely that this "Long live the King" from the one who is blind to art is a "step" and an "act of liberty," a manifestation without manifestation, a countermanifestation, Celan must withdraw this cry, this "counterword," from its political code, namely its counterrevolutionary meaning, and even from what a countermanifestation may still owe to this political code. Celan thinks that, on the contrary, he can recognize the cry, it being an act of liberty, as a poetic act — or, if not a poetic act, a poetic doing or still less an *ars poetica* on the part of one who is "blind to art" — he thinks he can recognize it as "poetry" itself (*die Dichtung*). And it is in order to hear the poetry in this "act of freedom," in this "step" (and the reference to a step, to walking, to coming or going, is always decisive in "The Meridian") [it is in order to hear the poetry in this act of freedom, in this step], that Celan advances the thought that the homage in this "Long live the King," the taking sides, the profession of faith, the salute (*gehuldigt*) is not pronounced, politically speaking, in favor of the monarchy, of His Majesty the King Louis XVI, but in favor of the majesty of the present, of the *Gegenwart*. This *Gegenwort* speaks in favor of the majesty of the *Gegenwart*. And in the passage that I shall read in translation, I shall emphasize *four*

306

41. Ibid., p. 63 [p. 175].

words for reasons that are too obvious and that I scarcely need to comment on: these are words that come under the vocabulary of "witnessing," "majesty," the "present," and the "human":

> To be sure, it sounds like an expression of allegiance to the "ancien régime" [. . .]. But these words [. . .] are not a celebration of the monarchy and a past that should be preserved.
>
> They are a tribute to the majesty of the absurd, which bears witness to mankind's here and now. [*Gehuldigt wird hier der für die Gegenwart des Menschlichen zeugenden Majestät des Absurden.*]
>
> That, ladies and gentlemen, has no universally recognized name, but it is, I believe . . . poetry [*aber ich glaube, es ist . . . die Dichtung*].[42]

(This "I believe," so close to the "majesty of the absurd"—the word "absurd" comes back more than once in the text to bespeak no doubt what stands beyond meaning, idea, theme, and even the tropes of rhetoric, beyond all the logic and rhetoric to which one thinks a poetics should bend itself—[this "I believe," so close to the "majesty of the absurd,"] seems to imply: "I believe where, I believe because, it is absurd, *credo quia absurdum*." Faith in poetry as faith in God, here in the majesty of the present.) Celan's gesture in resorting to the word "majesty"—and this is what matters most to me here, at least in the context of this seminar—is a gesture that consists in placing one majesty above another, and thus upping the ante with respect to sovereignty. An upping that attempts to change the meaning of majesty or sovereignty, to make its meaning mutate, while keeping the old word or while claiming to give it back its most dignified meaning. There is the sovereign majesty of the sovereign, the King, and there is, more majestic or differently majestic, more sovereign or differently sovereign, the majesty of poetry, or the majesty of the absurd insofar as it bears witness to the presence of the human. This hyperbolic upping of the ante is inscribed in what I shall call the dynamics of majesty or of sovereignty, in its *dynamics* because we're dealing with a movement where precipitation is ineluctable, and a *dynamics* (I choose this word deliberately) because we are dealing with the sovereign, specifically with power, with potency (*dynamis*), with the deployment of the potentiality of the dynast and the dynasty. That is to say, "there is something more majestic" than the majesty of the king, just as Monsieur Teste, you remember, was described as superior to the superior man, or Nietzsche's superman as above the superior man. As in Bataille, sovereignty, in the sense he intends and means to give it, exceeds classi-

307

42. Ibid.

cal sovereignty, namely mastery, lordship, absolute power, etc. (We'll come back to this later. Insist on this "more," and the void.)[43]

But then, why keep the word?

What counts most here, with Celan, is that this hypermajesty of poetry, beyond or outside the majesty of the king, the sovereign, or the monarch, this supreme majesty of the absurd, as majesty of *Dichtung*, is determined by four equally serious values, among which I believe we must still privilege one, or rather recognize among them the privilege of one only, and it is that of the present (*Gegenwart*). These four serious values or meanings are that of *testimony*, of course; that of *majesty* insofar as it bears witness (*zeugenden Majestät*); that of the *human* for which it bears witness; but above all, in my view, because it is continually confirmed and repeated, that of the present ("*Gehuldigt wird hier der für die Gegenwart des Menschlichen zeugenden Majestät des Absurden*"). Majesty is here majestic, and it is poetry, insofar as it bears witness to the present, the now, the "presence," as Launay translates it, of the human. Just as to bear witness is always to perform an act of presence, through speech addressed to the other, attesting to a presence, so what counts here, and what signs, is a presence attesting to a presence or rather to a present, qua human.

I would not privilege to this extent the present, the presence of this present, if, beyond all the reasons you easily imagine, Celan himself did not return to it with an insistence that is obvious and, I believe, undeniable. I shall be briefer, for lack of time today, on the other two promised examples or returns.

Second return. Around ten pages later, after a trajectory that I cannot reconstitute but from which we'll follow a few essential stages next time, Celan says this about what he calls "language actualized" (*aktualisierte Sprache*), under the sign of a "radical individuation": he says this, then, adding the present to the now, making *Gegenwart* more serious with *Präsenz*:

> Then the poem would be—even more clearly than before—the language of an individual which has taken on form; and, in keeping with its innermost nature, it would also be the present, the here and now. [*Dann wäre das*

308

---

43. Handwritten addition: "Insist on the essential hyperbole. More and more of . . . [+ *et* + *de*]." In the bibliographical notes written for the American version of the seminar, Derrida gives several references to Bataille: "'Hegel, la mort et le sacrifice,' in *Deucalion*, 5; *L'expérience intérieure* ('Post-scriptum au supplice'); 'Genet,' in *La littérature et le mal*; 'Méthode de méditation,' etc. See also, if you like, my article on Bataille in *Writing and Difference*."

*Gedicht — deutlicher noch als bisher — gestaltgewordene Sprache eines Einzel-
nen, — und seinem innersten Wesen nach Gegenwart und Präsenz.]*[44]

309   *Third return.* On the following page, Celan specifies something essential as
to, let's say, the structure of this now-present, and it is from this specification, which risks complicating everything, that I shall begin again next
time. He specifies that this now-present of the poem, *my* now-present, the
punctual now-present of a punctual *I*, my now-present must *allow* the now-
present of the other, the time of the other, *to speak*. It must *leave* time, *give*
time to the other.

To the other, it must leave or give *its* time. *Its own time.*

To the other, it must leave or give *its* time. To the other, it must leave or
give *its* own time. This formulation is not literally Celan's, but I imprint
on it this ambiguous or even *unheimlich* grammar, in which we no longer know to whom the possessive adjective belongs, to self or other (to the
other, leave or give *its* time), I give or leave it this grammatical equivocity to
translate what I believe to be the truth of what Celan is saying: to the other,
leave or give its own time.

Which of course introduces into the now-present a divisibility or an alterity that changes everything. It gives over to a total rereading of the pre-
dominant authority, even of the majesty of the present, that becomes that of
the other or that of a dissymmetrical division with the other, turned toward
the other or come from the other. I now read the passage in question, literally, sometimes, when necessary, in both languages.

> The poem becomes—and under what conditions!—a poem of one who—
> as before—perceives, is turned to [*zugewandt,* I emphasize this turn, the
> turn of this "turned"] that which appears [*dem Erscheinenden Zugewandten*].
> Who questions this appearing and addresses it [*dieses Erscheinende Befragen-
> den und Ansprechenden:* this *Ansprechen* — the turning-oneself toward the
> other to speak to him, to address, speak to the other, even to apostrophize
> the other—is no doubt the *turning* and the *turn* that answers for everything
> in this passage, and even in "The Meridian": and I say this "turn" less to
> suggest a figure, a turn of phrase, or even one of those rhetorical figures
> of which Celan is very wary, than to signal toward *Atemwende,* the turn or
> turning of breath, which is so often, literally, inspiration itself, the spirit of
310   "The Meridian"]. It becomes dialogue—it is often despairing dialogue [*es
> wird Gespräch — oft ist es verzweifeltes Gespräch.*][45]

44. Celan, "Le Méridien," p. 76 [p. 181].
45. Ibid., p. 77 [p. 182].

So the poem is a speaking-with-two (*Gespräch*, a speaking together), a speaking with more than one, a speaking whose maintaining now maintains [*dont le maintenant maintient*] more than one in it, a speaking that *gathers* more than one in it (I say "gather" because what is maintained in this maintaining is now, as you will hear, a movement of gathering, a being-together, a chance of gathering, *Versammlung*—once again a very Heideggerian motif—a movement, an impulse, a step that gathers more than one in it, and the address of the one to the other, even if it fails, even if the address is not received or does not arrive at its destination, even if the despair of the other, or as to the other, is always lying in wait, and even if it must always lie in wait, as its very possibility, for the possibility of the poem). Celan continues:

> Only in the realm of this dialogue does that which is addressed [*das Angesprochene*] take form and gather [*versammelt es sich*] around the I who is addressing and naming it. But into this present [*Aber in diese Gegenwart*], the one who has been addressed [*das Angesprochene*] and who, by virtue of having been named, has, as it were, become a thou [*zum Du Gewordene*], also brings its otherness along [*bringt [. . .] auch sein Anderssein mit*]. In the here and now of the poem [*Noch im Hier und Jetzt des Gedichts*] it is still possible—the poem itself, after all, has only this one, unique, punctual present [*diese eine, einmalige, punktuelle Gegenwart*]—only in this immediacy and proximity does it allow the most idiosyncratic quality of the Other, its time, to participate in the dialogue [*noch in dieser Unmittelbarkeit und Nähe lässt es das ihm, dem Anderen, Eigenste mitsprechen: dessen Zeit*].[46]

What the poem allows to speak at the same time (*mitsprechen*: allows to speak *also*, says Launay's translation, and the *mit* of the *mitsprechen* merits a stress mark, this speaking is originally, a priori, a speaking *with* or *to* the other, even before speaking alone, and this *mit* does not necessarily break the solitude, one could say that it is also its condition, as it is sometimes that of despair), what the poem allows to speak with it, allows to share its speech, what it allows to co-loquate, con-voke (so many ways of translating *mit-sprechen*, which says more than a dialogue), what it allows to speak, or even sign with it (co-sign, consign, countersign), is the time of the other, *its* time in what is most proper to it: the most proper and therefore the most untranslatably other of the time of the other.

One ought to comment to infinity on every word of these phrases. You can see that it is not just a matter of a dialoguing gathering. It is not even, here, a poetics, still less a politics of dialogue, a dialogue during which, with

311

46. Ibid., pp. 77–78 [p. 182].

help from experts and communication counselors, one would laboriously learn to let the other speak. It is not a matter of a democratic debate, during which one leaves the other his speaking time, timed by one of those clocks that incidentally are also discussed, along with the calendar, in "The Meridian." It is not a matter of speaking time but of letting the other, and thus of giving the other, without there being any act of generosity, effacing oneself absolutely, of *giving* the other its time (and to give is here to leave, for one is then giving the other only what is proper, irreducibly proper, to the other), it is a matter of leaving the other not only speech, but of letting time speak, the other's time, what its time, the time of the other, has as most proper to it. It is the time that one must let speak, the time of the other, rather than leaving the other speaking time. It is a matter of letting the time speak, the time of the other in what is most proper to the other, and therefore in what in the other is most other — and which happens, that I let happen, as time of the other, in the present time of "my" poem. And that I *let* happen, that I let happen what happens (of the other) — this "letting" neutralizes nothing, it is not a *simple* passivity, even if some passivity is required here: it is on the contrary the condition for an event to advene and for something to happen. What I would *make* happen instead of *letting* happen — well, that wouldn't happen. What *I make* happen does not happen, obviously, and one must draw the consequences of the apparently paradoxical necessity (but obviously the *lassen* in Celan's German means both *let* [*laisser*] and *make* [*faire*] . . . ["*. . . noch in dieser Unmittelbarkeit und Nähe lässt es das ihm, dem Anderen, Eigenste mitsprechen: dessen Zeit*"].)

Starting there, as it were, but I must stop here, "The Meridian" starts up again, and we make a U-turn. After saying that the poem seeks this place (*Ort*), Celan approaches the question of the place (*Ort*, rhetorical place, *Bildern und Tropen*), the question of *topoi* and of u-topia, while reminding us that he's talking about a poem that is not, an absolute poem that cannot be ("*das gibt es gewiss nicht, das kann es nicht geben!*").[47]

I announced that after these three returns and three examples, I would read to the end this conclusion I had begun to quote. I will do so, and then next time I shall come back again to "The Meridian" (which I ask you to reread meantime). So I shall come back, hoping that their necessity will be clearer, to the motifs of the Other and the Foreigner, the *Unheimliche*, the head ("The Meridian" moves between heads and decapitations, often speaks of falling into the *Grund* and the *Abgrund*); and then we shall come back, among other heads, to the Medusa's head (in its relation to erection

312

47. Ibid.

and castration), and finally we shall head back toward the monkey, toward the marionette as question of art ("*Die Kunst, das ist, Sie erinnern sich, ein marionettenhaftes [. . .] kinderloses Wesen*"). (Read and comment)

I am also seeking the place of my own origin [*den Ort meinen eigenen Herkunft*], since I have once again arrived at my point of departure.

I am seeking all of that on the map with a finger which is uncertain, because it is restless — on a child's map, as I readily confess. None of these places is to be found, they do not exist, but I know where they would have to exist — above all at the present time — and . . . I find something! [*und . . . ich finde etwas!*]

Ladies and gentlemen, I find something which offers me some consolation for having traveled this impossible path, this path of the impossible [*diesen unmöglichen Weg, diesen Weg des Unmöglichen gegangen zu sein*], in your presence [*in Ihrer Gegenwart*].

I find something which binds and which, like the poem, leads to an encounter. [*Ich finde das Verbindende und wie das Gedicht zur Begegnung Führende.*]

I find something, like language [*wie die Sprache*], abstract, yet earthly, terrestrial, something circular, which traverses both poles and returns to itself, thereby — I am happy to report — even crossing the tropics and tropes. [*sogar die Tropen Durchkreuzendes*[48]] I find . . . a *meridian* [*ich finde . . . einen* Meridian].

With you and Georg Büchner and the state of Hesse I believe that I have just now touched it again [*habe ich ihn soeben wieder zu berühren geglaubt*].[49]

313

---

48. Derrida's commentary, during his reading: "Crossing out (*Durchkreuzende*) is Heidegger's crossing out of the word 'Being.' Here it is crossing out tropes, figures of rhetoric, but also the earth's tropics."

49. Celan, "Le Méridien," pp. 83–84 [p. 185].

February 27, 2002[1]

It is time, then, that we had a real discussion: questions, objections, back and forth. As I promised, we are going to spend the whole session doing that. And then next week I'll pick up the course of the course again . . .

Before turning it over to whoever wants to speak, I want to say two things. First, I received a written question, a very long and differentiated one that I'll read to you in a moment and to which I shall try to respond. And then, as an exergue, before beginning, to give you time to prepare your first questions, I wanted to read you a text that I had thought I might read before this, without tying it in to anything very specific, even though, as you'll see, it concerns just about everything we've approached directly or indirectly. It's a text by D. H. Lawrence, a poem called "Snake."[2] Now naturally, in this seminar, as you have already sensed and seen coming, especially given the time limits we face, although we can't unfold in all its breadth the history of the relations between what is called man and animal, and the socialization of those relations—the question of hunting, of taming, of training (which is something different), the question of domestication (we shall talk

316

1. We should like to remind the reader that there is no written version of the following pages. This ninth session is entirely oral, and has been transcribed on the basis of a recording of the session, which was in part devoted to discussion with the participants in the seminar, not transcribed here (see Editorial Note above, p. xv). The way the session is presented is, then, wholly the responsibility of the editors, who have decided to remain as close as possible to the commentary here improvised by Jacques Derrida as an introduction to that discussion session, and to restitute it as fully as possible. The reading of the Lawrence poem, sometimes very attentive to detail, sometimes more cursive, or interrupted by commentaries, is inseparable from the *tone* of the voice and the very lively manner of *speaking* the text. The reader will find an uninterrupted version of Lawrence's poem at the end of the session.

2. Derrida alludes to this text and comments on it briefly in the "Envoi" at the beginning of *Voyous* (see session 1 above, n. 10), p. 23 [p. 5].

next week about taming, training, and domestication, which are very different things, when we broach the question of the zoo, the zoological park or the menagerie)—but, then, although it's impossible for us to unfold in all its breadth the question of the relations between man and beast, man and animal, we have already seen in outline a kind of typology in the form of a bestiary, a typology of animals that in the limited field that is ours here, that of politics and animality, political sovereignty and animality, [we've seen in outline a typology or bestiary of animals that] plays a particularly significant role in this domain: the wolf is not the only one, the wolf got there first, but there is also the monkey (which we'll have more to say about), there's the bee, the queen bee, the dolphin (which we'll also be talking about next week)—and then there's the snake. The snake, not only because of original sin, all the virtues and vices that are attributed to the snake . . .

The question is whether the snake has a head—since the question of the head has also come back regularly—a head, i.e. a face and a visage, and I had recalled, I think, the question that Lévinas sent back to a questioner who asked him: "Can one say of the animal what you say of man in his ethical dimension?"—and you know that for Lévinas, the other, in its ethical dimension, is what he calls a face, a "face," the face being not only what is seen or what sees, but also what speaks, what hears speech, and therefore it's to a face that our ethical responsibility is addressed, it's from a face that it receives from the other, and therefore it's to a face that our ethical responsibility is addressed, from a face that it receives something from the other, that I receive the imperative: "Thou shalt not kill," which, for Lévinas, is the first commandment ("Thou shalt not kill" is the first commandment, not the sixth as in the biblical order, and this command comes to me from the face: what the face of the other signifies to me before any other manifestation is "Thou shalt not kill"). And so to the question that was asked him one day: "Does the animal have a face?" and thus, does the animal belong to this space of the ethical that Lévinas analyses and proposes, Lévinas's awkward response was: "I don't know . . . ," and then, to emphasize the expression of that awkwardness, he returns the question: "Would you say that the snake has a face?"[3] This example doesn't come up by chance. One might wonder: OK, the snake has eyes, it has a tongue, it has a head to some extent, does it have the face? What about the snake's face? And it's under the sign of this

317

---

3. Jacques Derrida had mentioned this exchange in his lecture to the 1997 Cerisy conference, *L'animal autobiographique*. See *L'animal que donc je suis*, pp. 148–49 [trans. David Wills, pp. 107–8]. The version of the story given here is very slightly different from the earlier one.

serious, poetic question (especially for Lévinas's ethics), that I wanted to read you this text by D. H. Lawrence, "Snake."[4]

SNAKE

A snake came to my water-trough
On a hot, hot day, and I in pyjamas for the heat,
To drink there.

In the deep, strange-scented shade of the great dark carob-tree
I came down the steps with my pitcher
318 And must wait, must stand and wait, for there he was at the trough
before me.

And "he" is the snake, "for there *he* was," it's already a personal pronoun,[5] "he was" (in English, animals are sometimes "he," sometimes "she": cats are "she") "for there *he* was at the trough before me":

He reached down from a fissure in the earth-wall in the gloom
And trailed his yellow-brown slackness soft-bellied down, over the edge
of the stone trough
And rested his throat upon the stone bottom,
And where the water had dripped from the tap, in a small clearness,
He sipped with his straight mouth,
Softly drank through his straight gums, into his slack long body,
Silently.[6]

Someone was before me at my water-trough,
And I, like a second comer, waiting.

"Someone" (a question we've been asking from the beginning of the seminar: who or what? The animal, who or what? The marionette, who or what? The snake here is "someone." And so "someone" is somebody, not as much *qui* as *quelqu'un* in French, but you don't say "someone" about a stone), "Someone was before me at my water-trough, / And I, like a second comer, waiting." So, he waits for the first to pass. He says . . . and here, to return to Lévinas—I don't want to place the whole poem under the sign of Lévinas, but reading it I remember something Lévinas often says, namely that morality, ethics, begins with an "After you." After you. The first sign
319 of respect for the other is "after you." This doesn't just mean something like "go ahead" at the elevator, etc., it means "I come after you," and I come to

4. D. H. Lawrence, *Birds, Beasts and Flowers! Poems* [1923] (Santa Rosa: Black Sparrow Press, 2007), pp. 127–31.

5. Derrida says "prénom" (forename).

6. Jacques Derrida repeats more quietly: "silently."

myself, to my responsibility as an ego, in some sense, only from the other. The other is there before me, and I receive the order from the other who precedes me. That is the situation when faced with the other, and he not only goes ahead of me, must go ahead of me, but is there before me. So I say "After you," and it's my first address to the other as other.

"Someone," the snake, was "at my water-trough, / And I, like a second comer, waiting." And here the French translation, "Et moi, arrivé en second, j'attendais," is OK, but a "second comer" is not the second to arrive. There is the first comer, the first comer is the snake and one has to say, naturally, that morality, ethics, the relation to the other, is not only coming after the other, helping oneself after the other, but after the other *whoever it be,* before even knowing who he is or what is his dignity, his price, his social standing, in other words, the first comer. I must respect the first comer, whoever it be. When he says "a second comer," I am "a second comer," I am the one who comes afterward, not the one who happens to have come second, I am a second comer, I come afterward. And I, *like,* the "like" also falls like a second comer, and "I" like an "after-comer," someone who comes afterward by contrast to the first comer, I as though coming second, waiting.

He lifted his head from his drinking, as cattle do,

Cattle is not only an animal society, it's a set of beasts that are grouped together, watched over and mastered and appropriated as beasts for consumption, beasts that are raised. Just now I mentioned taming, training, and domestication, but there is also raising: cattle are a set of beasts raised with a view to use and human consumption. "He lifted his head from his drinking, as cattle do," it's a plural, a collective verb, not "cattle does": there are several, cattle is a collective, many in one.

And looked at me vaguely, as drinking cattle do,
And flickered his two-forked tongue from his lips, and mused a moment,[7]
And stooped and drank a little more,
Being earth-brown, earth-golden from the burning bowels of the earth
On the day of Sicilian July, with Etna smoking.

The voice of my education said to me
He must be killed,
For in Sicily

320

7. [Translator's note:] The French translation has "rêva" [dreamed] for "mused": Derrida comments: "*Rêva* is 'mused,' it means he daydreams [*rêvassa*], not dreaming in the sense of *Traum*: 'mused,' meditated a moment."

We are in Sicily, Etna . . . smoking. "Smoke" is an extraordinary word. In French as it is in English. One can smoke transitively, pipe, cigar, cigarette, and then one can smoke. With Etna smoking . . . "The voice of my education said to me He must be killed . . ."

For in Sicily the black, black snakes are innocent, the gold are venomous.

Let me recall—because you are listening and you don't have the poem in front of you and it's difficult to keep things straight—that he said earlier, describing this snake, "earth-brown, earth-golden." So it's a golden snake, not a black one, "For in Sicily the black, black snakes are innocent, the gold are venomous." So he's dealing with a poisonous snake. But one that comes before him. Moral question: must I respect and leave the first comer to do as he will, even if I see that he is dangerous? Hospitality. Someone comes, he's there before me, he asks . . . Must I welcome him in, leave him, not kill him, even if I can sense or foresee or fear that he might kill me himself? The scene described by Lawrence is immediately the scene of a fight to the death. "The voice of my education said to me / He must be killed," because if you don't kill him he will kill you. "For in Sicily the black, black snakes [I emphasize 'black'] are innocent, the gold are venomous."

And voices in me said,

So what were the voices saying . . . more than one voice? He started by saying, "The voice of my education" . . . He's already presenting himself as someone with lots of voices in him, isn't he. There is the voice of his education that says, "He must be killed," and now there are voices in the plural, "And voices in me . . . ," other voices in me, saying:

If you were a man
You would take a stick and break him now, and finish him off.

"If you were a man . . . ," initially it's a hypothesis; "If you were a man . . ." evidently in the sense of a human being, but also of courage, of the virile man who, in a duel, must annihilate his victim. "And voices in me said, If you were a man / You would take a stick and break him now, and finish him off."

But [there's a space before this line] must I confess how I liked him
How glad I was he had come like a guest in quiet,

This is why I was talking a moment ago about the code of hospitality. He is the first comer, and whether or not he wants to or might kill me, I owe him, I ought not to kill him, I ought to respect him. He is therefore a guest:

321

this is a classic scene, a classic biblical scene, a classic Middle Eastern scene: it happens near a source of water, the scene of hospitality takes place near a source of water, in an oasis or near a well, and the question of hospitality is posed as to water, as to the disposition of the water source.

> How glad I was he had come like a guest in quiet, to drink at my
>   water-trough
> And depart peaceful, pacified, and thankless,
> Into the burning bowels of this earth?
>
> Was it cowardice, that I dared not kill him?
> Was it perversity, that I longed to talk to him?

322

The desire to speak . . . All he talks about, when it comes to this snake, and despite the voices he hears in him, the many voices he hears in him, his first desire, he who loves the snake, is to talk to him. "Was it perversity, that I longed to talk to him?"

> Was it humility, to feel so honoured?

Honoring the guest: here the host feels honored by the guest,[8] by the one who comes, who is the first comer. He is honored, that's the first experience, the first affect. He is there, he is there with me, before me, ahead of me, and I am grateful to him for that. That he exists for me makes me feel honored.

> Was it humility, to feel so honoured?
> I felt so honoured.
>
> And yet those voices:
> If you were not afraid, you would kill him!

If you were a man, a man, a real man isn't scared, you would kill him.

> And truly I was afraid, I was most afraid,
> But even so, honoured still more
> That he should seek my hospitality
> From out the dark door of the secret earth.
>
> He drank enough
> And lifted his head, dreamily, as one who has drunken,
> And flickered his tongue like a forked night on the air, so black;
> Seeming to lick his lips,

323

---

8. [Translator's note:] "ici l'hôte (*host*) se sent honoré par l'hôte (*guest*)": Derrida parenthesizes the English words, exploiting the ambiguity of the French word *hôte*.

And looked around like a god, unseeing, into the air,

So you have here the human race, the signatory of the poem, the one who says "I" and who hears voices saying to him: "If you were a man . . . ," the humanity of man, [and] there is the beast, the snake . . . but the beast resembles a god.

And looked around like a god, unseeing, into the air,
And slowly turned his head,
And slowly, very slowly, as if thrice adream,

The dream again: *as if thrice adream*, *thrice adream,* three times *adream*, three times dreaming, adream in one word, you see, *thrice adream*, three times in a dream.

Proceeded to draw his slow length curving round
And climb again the broken bank of my[9] wall-face.

And as he put his head into that dreadful hole, [There's the head . . . This snake has a head.]
And as he slowly drew up, snake-easing his shoulders, and entered farther,
A sort of horror, a sort of protest against his withdrawing into that horrid black hole,
Deliberately going into the blackness, and slowly drawing himself after,
Overcame me now his back was turned.

You get the scene: the snake is withdrawing, returning into its night, and the horror submerges [the narrator], "A sort of horror . . . overcame me now his back was turned."

324

I looked round, I put down my pitcher,
I picked up a clumsy log
And threw it at the water-trough with a clatter.

I think it did not hit him,

Which leads one to suppose that he threw his pitcher[10] like a projectile, an offensive weapon, at the snake's head.

But suddenly that part of him that was left behind convulsed in undignified haste,

9. Derrida emphasizes the possessive adjective.
10. Derrida says "cruche" [pitcher] instead of "bûche" [log].

Writhed like lightning, and was gone
Into the black hole, the earth-lipped fissure in the wall-front,
At which, in the intense still noon, I stared with fascination.

And immediately I regretted it.
I thought how paltry, how vulgar, what a mean act!
I despised myself and the voices of my accursed human education.

He despised himself for having in the end given in to the aggressive gesture by throwing his pitcher, not knowing if he hit him or not, but in any case he could not resist the human pulsion or compulsion, dictated by the voices in him, including the voice of education, voices that commanded him: "Kill it." He does so and is immediately submerged with horror and shame. And regret. "And immediately I regretted it. / I thought how paltry, how vulgar, what a mean act! / I despised myself and the voices of my accursed human education." So he curses his education. His education is accursed. These voices in him are accursed, the voices that basically tell him to kill, or to try to kill a guest, a first comer, one who had not yet, as it were, attacked. Out of fear he kills the other, the guest.

And I thought of the albatross,   325
And I wished he would come back, my snake.

"My" snake: it becomes *his* snake from this moment on, precisely because of the scene of the murder, the at least virtual or aborted murder. He couldn't resist the drive to kill, he carried out the gesture of killing and is immediately submerged by remorse, of course, but also by the desire for the snake to return. His snake, "my snake": his love for the snake is declared, made manifest, after the guilty act of murder. "And I thought of the albatross, / And I wished he would come back, my snake."

For he seemed

And here's sovereignty: that's why I chose to read you this text.

For he seemed to me again like a king,
Like a king in exile, uncrowned in the underworld,
Now due to be crowned again.

The snake, the beast, becomes the sovereign after having been, if not assassinated, at least the target of an attempt on his life, an act of hatred on the part of the man. The beast becomes the sovereign, the king. "Uncrowned," but waiting for the crown, on the way to being crowned. "For he seemed to me again like a king, / Like a king in exile, uncrowned in the underworld, / Now due to be crowned again."

> And so, I missed my chance with one of the lords
> Of life.
> And I have something to expiate;
> A pettiness.

326   And so morality, ethics, the "Thou shalt not kill" with respect to anyone at all, the first comer, the first living creature to come, be it a God, a snake, a beast, or a man, and that's a question we ought to discuss, and this is one of the questions posed by the person[11] who handed me this text last time: "Does morality tell us to respect solely or primarily man, the humanity of man, or life, the living being in general, including the animal?" Here, visibly, the poet, the signatory, Lawrence if you will, the one to whom this thing happens in some sense awakens to ethics, to the "Thou shalt not kill," in a scene of hospitality, before the first comer, the snake, who can perhaps be threatening (it doesn't say that he was perhaps threatening, he could always be threatening, always be murderous). So his ethics is announced or awakened in this scene of hospitality before a first comer whoever it be, and this ethics was formalized, confirmed [. . .].[12] He becomes aware . . . , he truly thinks what duty would have obligated him toward the living creature in general, in the figure of the snake, the snake's head, this snake that is a nonhuman living creature, who becomes in some sense the sovereign as other, as guest [*hôte*]; it is the guest [*hôte*] that commands, the other as guest [*l'autre comme hôte*] who commands. And so one of the questions among many others that are posed to us here is a double question: 1. Does an ethics or a moral prescription obligate us only to those like us—you remember the question of the *semblable* we were asking when rereading Lacan—i.e. man, or else does it obligate us with respect to anyone at all, any living being at all, and therefore with respect to the animal? 2. The second question, wrapped up in the first, is this: Once we have recognized that the sovereign is in the end the first comer, the one who comes before me, the other before

327   who is before me, are we going to reconstitute a logic of sovereignty, a scene of sovereignty, by simply displacing sovereignty from me to the other—I become subject to the other, but the other is sovereign—in other words, should the deconstruction of sovereignty limit itself to deconstructing sov-

---

11. We were unable to identify the name of this person on the recording of the session.

12. There is a short break in the recording here.

ereignty as my sovereignty, but in order to transfer it to the other, or should the idea of sovereignty in general be contested here? Hence the question of the fellow [*semblable*] and the question of sovereignty as sovereignty of the other or not. Of course, as ethics as such, the formalization of ethics clearly appears after the fact, i.e. after the transgression of ethics, after the murder, after he tries to kill the snake, the question is that of knowing if the origin of the moral law is linked or not to a murder or to remorse. As you know, when Freud—the transpositions are easy here, of course—when Freud explains the origin of the moral superego via the murder of the father, when the sons agree on equality between them after the murder of the father, Freud—and this is one of the contradictions in what he says—specifies that it is when the sons or the brothers feel remorse after the murder of the father that morality is born.[13] In other words, the moral law is born of remorse. But the contradiction is that in order for there to be remorse, the moral law would already have to be in place. And so for him to have anything to "expiate," "and I have something to expiate," means that he knew ahead of time that the moral law was already there, without which there would have been neither remorse nor expiation. This is why, as you will have noticed, I pointed out, however difficult this may seem, two moments in this epiphany of the moral law, this appearing of the moral law: there is a first moment in which the moral law is there, already there but virtual, potential, always already there, then, and then it is actualized as such, it appears as such after the murder. Before the murder it is already there, without which there would be no remorse: he would have killed the snake without remorse. For there to be remorse, the moral law had already to be there. But it is in the moment of expiation, or remorse, the moment of guilty conscience, that the moral law appears as such. And then—well, if we wanted to dwell longer with this poem, we'd spend more time looking at the other animals, such as the albatross. Why the albatross? The snake is a reptile, the low, an animal of the earth, of humus (humility, *humus*), and that is why he keeps emphasizing the earth. The motif is that of the earth. So there is the low, the animal that is the lowest, the snake, and then the albatross, the animal of the heights. And as you have already noticed, in particular last week, our question, which we'll come back to next week, is that of the opposition between low and high. The sovereign, in principle, and I'll come back to this, is the being of height, of grandeur, of erection, his Highness. The albatross:

328

---

13. Sigmund Freud, *Totem and Taboo*, in *The Standard Edition*, 13:1–161.

And I thought of the albatross,
And I wished he would come back, my snake.

For he seemed to me again like a king

I was thinking that if we had the time, we'd pause over this "like." Why is the snake not a king but "like a king," resembling what a king is in human politics? But not only is he only analogous to a king, he is "like a king," he is not a king, but he is like a king who is not a king, for two reasons (you remember the three lines): because he is in exile, he's a king not exercising power, a king without power, a king dethroned in a sense — and the scene of exile, obviously, is consonant with the scene of hospitality (they go together, exile and hospitality, those asking for hospitality are exiles), it is the scene of the home, of what is at home without being at home, *unheimlich* (we'll come back to that next week), *unheimlich,* all this is *unheimlich,* the most familiar and the most strange, the most disturbing, the most terrible also (*unheimlich* is a word with which, often in fact, I'll come back to this too next week, Heidegger translates the Greek word *deinon* in Sophocles, i.e. the terrible, the terrifying, he says that man is what is most *unheimlich,* most disoriented and disorienting [*dépaysé, dépaysant*], at-home-not-at-home), this whole scene is *unheimlich,* and obviously *Unheimlichkeit,* the fact of being at home away from home is a scene of both exile and hospitality: the exiled, those asking for asylum and hospitality are not at home, they are seeking a home, and here is the man who takes them in or not, at his water-hole that is a water source, a resource for the guests or guest-exiles or those seeking asylum — so he is like a king, but he is not a reigning king, for he is in exile and he has no crown, he is

329

Like a king in exile, uncrowned in the underworld,
Now due to be crowned again.

Provisionally in exile, the snake signals toward a kingdom to be restored, from his exile, i.e. a scene that banished him. What is striking in this poem, which is clearly an ironic or perverse translation of the Garden of Eden, is that what is banished, exiled, is the snake, not Adam and Eve but the snake. The victim in all this, Adam's victim ("Adam" means the earth), the victim is the snake. We need to reread the Bible because, at bottom, the one to be sorriest for in this whole story is the snake! (Laughter.) That's not usually how it gets read! And there is no woman here, no woman, just a man and a snake.

[Questions.]

SNAKE

A snake came to my water-trough
On a hot, hot day, and I in pyjamas for the heat,
To drink there.

In the deep, strange-scented shade of the great dark carob-tree
I came down the steps with my pitcher
And must wait, must stand and wait, for there he was at the trough
    before me.

He reached down from a fissure in the earth-wall in the gloom
And trailed his yellow-brown slackness soft-bellied down, over the edge
    of the stone trough
And rested his throat upon the stone bottom,
And where the water had dripped from the tap, in a small clearness,
He sipped with his straight mouth,
Softly drank through his straight gums, into his slack long body,
Silently.

Someone was before me at my water-trough,
And I, like a second comer, waiting.

He lifted his head from his drinking, as cattle do,
And looked at me vaguely, as drinking cattle do,
And flickered his two-forked tongue from his lips, and mused a moment,
And stooped and drank a little more,
Being earth-brown, earth-golden from the burning bowels of the earth
On the day of Sicilian July, with Etna smoking.

The voice of my education said to me
He must be killed,
For in Sicily the black, black snakes are innocent, the gold are venomous.

And voices in me said, If you were a man
You would take a stick and break him now, and finish him off.

But must I confess how I liked him,
How glad I was he had come like a guest in quiet, to drink at my
    water-trough
And depart peaceful, pacified, and thankless,
Into the burning bowels of this earth?

Was it cowardice, that I dared not kill him?
Was it perversity, that I longed to talk to him?
Was it humility, to feel so honoured?
I felt so honoured.

And yet those voices:
If you were not afraid, you would kill him!
And truly I was afraid, I was most afraid,
But even so, honoured still more
That he should seek my hospitality
From out the dark door of the secret earth.

He drank enough
And lifted his head, dreamily, as one who has drunken,
And flickered his tongue like a forked night on the air, so black;
Seeming to lick his lips,
And looked around like a god, unseeing, into the air,
And slowly turned his head,
And slowly, very slowly, as if thrice adream,
Proceeded to draw his slow length curving round
And climb again the broken bank of my wall-face.

And as he put his head into that dreadful hole,
And as he slowly drew up, snake-easing his shoulders, and entered
    farther,
A sort of horror, a sort of protest against his withdrawing into that horrid
    black hole,
Deliberately going into the blackness, and slowly drawing himself after,
Overcame me now his back was turned.

I looked round, I put down my pitcher,
I picked up a clumsy log
And threw it at the water-trough with a clatter.

I think it did not hit him,
But suddenly that part of him that was left behind convulsed in
    undignified haste,
Writhed like lightning, and was gone
Into the black hole, the earth-lipped fissure in the wall-front,
At which, in the intense still noon, I stared with fascination.

And immediately I regretted it.
I thought how paltry, how vulgar, what a mean act!
I despised myself and the voices of my accursed human education.

And I thought of the albatross,
And I wished he would come back, my snake.

For he seemed to me again like a king,
Like a king in exile, uncrowned in the underworld,
Now due to be crowned again.

And so, I missed my chance with one of the lords
Of life.
And I have something to expiate;
A pettiness.

Taormina
D. H. Lawrence

March 6, 2002

The [feminine] beast and the [masculine] sovereign, so *what*? So, *who*?

And the marionette, is it *what* or *who*? Something or someone? And then, is it living or dead? Living animal or living human?

I'm going to inscribe something today—by way of exergue—a date, then a quotation. I do so to recall a calendar but also a historical chronicle the sense and necessity of which will become clear only progressively. I'm calling it an exergue, certainly, to designate an *hors-d'oeuvre* [literally, "an outwork"] (the *ex-ergon* stands, like the parergon, outside the work, on the borders of the work or the operation, like one out of work, inoperative, and at loose ends [*désoeuvré*], but that makes work happen, another figure of capital, and, like capital, the exergue comes at the head); but I call it an exergue primarily to recall that in an exergue, in those medals, sometimes royal medals, that were called exergues, what was inscribed was often not only words but a date.

The date, here, is 1681. This is the text:

> Never perhaps was there a more imposing anatomical dissection, judged
> by the enormity of the animal, by the precision with which its several parts
> were examined, or by the quality and number of those present.

(Read it twice.)

I shall say no more about it for the moment, save this: apart from the very large beast being talked about here, namely an elephant (the text emphasizes "the enormity of the animal," its dimensions, its size, the large and high stature of the enormous animal subject to dissection), apart from the immense beast, among "those present" (the text says "the quality and number of those present") you should know that there was a great, immense sovereign, Louis le Grand himself, the Sun King, who, says the text to which I shall return in a moment, "deigned to honor with his presence" such a "ceremony." You can picture that "ceremony": a very large animal, an elephant, and a very great sovereign, the beast and the sovereign were there together, in 1681, in the same room, for the same anatomy lesson, the one alive and the other dead, the living observing the dead, in the space and time of a "ceremony" that was a dissection, i.e. an operation of knowledge, a violence on the dead to see and to know. We'll find out more about it later.

The [feminine] beast and the [masculine] sovereign, so, what? So, who?

The [feminine] beast and the [masculine] sovereign together, in the same place, one dead one alive, one looked at by the other, so, what? So, who? Something or someone?

You had already suspected, seeing in the last few sessions all those heads go by, crowned heads, capitals, capital and decapitation, that with the royal *majesty* of the sovereign a certain dated revolution was becoming our subject.

This dated Revolution is that of the guillotine and the Terror, of the decapitation of the king and of many revolutionaries, the very ones who set up and justified the revolutionary Terror. You remember the "Long live the King!" from Lucile, the wife of Camille, Camille Desmoulins, "that Camille" who, in Büchner's *Danton's Death*, says Celan, "dies theatrically, then, not to say iambically"[1] (*iambisch,* an allusion to the first sentence, the opening phrase of "The Meridian," which itself made a quasi-citation of a remark of Camille's in *Danton's Death*: "Art, you remember, is a species of marionette, a being with five iambic feet"—and the question of art that weaves through the whole of the "The Meridian," the question of poetry as art, is also all the more the question of technology for being linked to this appearance, one of three appearances, three comings or three returns of art, namely the appearance of art as a marionette, i.e. a sort of technical *who* and *what*. Who will deny that the marionette is a technical thing, and even a sort of allegorical personification of technical power itself, of machinality? So it is indeed a question of interrogating art between the *tekhnē* of the fine arts and the *tekhnē* of techniques, and, as we shall verify, that is not the only proximity or intersection with Heideggerian questions, worries, stylistic motifs, at least),

339

1. Celan, "Le Méridien" (see session 6 above, n. 19), p. 62 [p. 175; translation modified].

"that Camille," then, dies theatrically, not to say iambically, a death that only two scenes later, on the basis of a word that is foreign to it—that is so close [a word both foreign and close, remember this: "*von einem ihm fremden — einem ihm so nahen — Wort*"]—we can feel it to be his own death, then, whereas all around Camille pathos and phrases attest to the triumph of the "marionette" and "strings" ["*Puppe" und "Draht*," this time, it's a quotation that I'll come back to], here now is Lucile, the one who is blind to art, the same Lucile for whom speech has something person-like about it ["*etwas Personhaftes*," in opposition, I suppose, to the marionette: comment] something that one can see, perceive ("*etwas Personhaftes und Wahrnehmbares*"), here is Lucile, once again, with her sudden cry: "*Es lebe der König!*"[2] ("Long live the King!").

The allusion, with quotation marks, to the marionette (*Puppe,* this time) and the "strings" is a quasi-quotation from Büchner's play (act 2, scene 5), where those condemned to death compare themselves to marionettes manipulated by history, by the sovereign powers of history: they no longer feel themselves to be responsible persons, free subjects, but figures, or even mechanical figurants in the invisible hands of those supposed to make history; but they suspect that there is not even a puppeteer and a subject of history to pull the strings in this theater of political marionettes; and they say and think so at the moment they die, saying, "Marionettes, that's what we are, pulled by strings in the hands of unknown powers, nothing by ourselves, nothing!"[3]

You recall, then, the "Long live the King!" of Lucile, who, close to the scaffold or the guillotine, declaimed "The Meridian" and, marking in it a major difference between two values of *Majestät*, guided our reading of this poem. All this could only confirm our hypothesis. In this Revolution it's certainly a matter of head, capital, and decapitation. The Medusa head and everything in it that signals toward erection as well as castration would be enough to remind us of that.

Although I didn't present things to you in this way and in this order, I'm sure that it won't have escaped you that the last session moved between two singular sovereigns, two kings of France, Louis XIV and Louis XVI, between his majesty Louis le Grand or the Sun King on the one hand, and his Majesty Louis Capet the decapitated, Louis XVI, on the other. While following a certain marionette theater, from Kleist and Valéry to Celan, we had therefore observed, as vigilantly as possible, the intriguing devel-

2. Ibid., p. 59 [p. 175].
3. Cited by J. Launay in Celan, *Le Méridien & autres proses,* p. 103, note 31.

opment of the word "majesty," from the sovereignty it designates in Latin (*majestas*, as Bodin reminded us) up to its occurrence in *The Wolf and the Lamb* and La Fontaine's dedication of the *Fables* to the Dauphin.

[In brackets, when I pronounce the word *Dauphin*, I think of the animals thus named by man, all the dolphins [*dauphins*], those beasts that are held to be so human, so intelligent, almost as intelligent as man, a species a large number of whom, two or three weeks ago, seem to have lost their sense of direction, and, doubtless through the fault of men and human pollution of the ocean depths as well as the water close to the coast, and thereby disoriented by man, those poor dolphins lamentably but obstinately became beached, and died, on the beaches of northern France. Do not forget that dolphin, *delphis* in Greek, *delphinus* in Latin, is first of all the name given by man to that other great [*gros et grand*] animal, that carnivorous cetacean whose blubber furnishes a precious oil (*delphinus delphis*) and which passes for being so close to man, so benevolent and friendly a matter toward us that La Fontaine, who dedicated his *Fables* to "Monseigneur le Dauphin," wrote its eulogy: he praised the animal, did La Fontaine, an animal not so *bête*, as you'll see, and an animal friendly to man, in a fable I'm going to read to you, after recalling that the French title "Dauphin," used to designate the king's son and thus the heir to the throne, has a very French, purely French history, as in the calendar of the monarchy and the revolution we are interested in at the moment. *Dauphin* was originally a name borne by the lords of the French province of the Viennois at the time the Dauphiné was ceded to the king of France. Now the proper name at the origin of the Dauphiné was *Delphinus*, the name of the fish, quite simply because the lords had chosen three dolphins to figure on their coat of arms. Which means, if one interprets this heraldic symbolism as a sort of totemic effect, that the title *Dauphin* for the elder son and royal heir is, at least by a drift toward a royal beach, a totemic title. If now I read *in extenso* the fable of La Fontaine entitled *The Monkey and the Dolphin*, it's not merely because of the irony whereby the subject citizen La Fontaine dedicates all his fables to his virtual sovereign, Monseigneur le Dauphin. It is for many other reasons: for if all the animals in the fables are anthropomorphic figures, and in one way or another human figures, as positive or negative heroes, here the animal is not only human like all the others but embodies, among the human animals, among animals in human form, among the anthropoids in the broad sense of this word, one of those that are naturally more human and above all friendly to man, "a strong friend of our species," as the fable says. And then there is the monkey, the other hero of the fable. The monkey is not just any animal, in our problematic and among the animals that

341

342

are more human than others, as I do not need to emphasize: above all, in Celan's text to which I shall return in a moment, there is also a monkey: and we are enriching our bestiary with the principal roles for our theater of "the beast and the sovereign" (the wolf, the dolphin, the monkey, and, let's not forget—we'll probably have an opportunity to talk about her—the queen bee). In this fable, the dolphin saves men, ensures their safety: just as a man would be, the dolphin is struck by the resemblance between a monkey and a man, and he is fooled before disabusing himself and recognizing his error when he perceives the monkey's *bêtise*: and then this dolphin laughs (which people think animals can't do), he is capable of friendship for men, for "our species," he laughs, he laughs at the monkey, he finds the monkey *bête*; as would a man, he finds the monkey both similar and *bête* precisely because, though able to communicate and react with signs, the monkey doesn't really know how to speak, doesn't really know how to respond, how to hear names and the meaning of questions. Cunningly, the dolphin feigns and asks him a trick question, as you'll hear, and the *magot* falls into the trap (*magot*, in one of its usages, means a monkey, a Barbary ape, a monkey with a small tail, a rudimentary tail, a monkey of the species of the macacas: "Magot" is an interesting name because it comes from the Apocalypse, Magog). You will see that the dolphin's final judgment on the monkey that he has tricked is a judgment that falls under Cartesian logic. This seventeenth-century dolphin, a Cartesian dolphin, says to himself: this monkey is *bête*, it's not a human although it looks like one, it's a machine, it's not a human because it doesn't know how to respond, it merely reacts, instead of responding it's content to react *bêtement*.

THE MONKEY AND THE DOLPHIN

It was the custom of the Greeks
For passengers over sea to carry
Both monkeys full of tricks
And funny dogs to make them merry.
A ship, that had such things on deck,
Not far from Athens, went to wreck.
But for the dolphins, all had drowned.
They are a philanthropic fish,
Which fact in Pliny may be found;—
A better voucher who could wish?
They did their best on this occasion.
A monkey even, on their plan
Well nigh attained his own salvation;
A dolphin took him for a man,

343

And on his dorsal gave him place.
So grave the silly creature's face,
That one might well have set him down
That old musician of renown.
The fish had almost reached the land,
When, as it happened, — what a pity! —
He asked, "Are you from Athens grand?"
"Yes; well they know me in that city.
If ever you have business there,
I'll help you do it, for my kin
The highest offices are in.
My cousin, sir, is now lord mayor."
The dolphin thanked him, with good grace,
Both for himself and all his race,
And asked, "You doubtless know Piraeus,
Where, should we come to town, you'll see us."
"Piraeus? yes, indeed I know;
He was my crony long ago."
The dunce knew not the harbour's name,
And for a man's mistook the same.
The people are by no means few,
Who never went ten miles from home,
Nor know their market-town from Rome,
Yet cackle just as if they knew.
The dolphin laughed, and then began
His rider's form and face to scan,
And found himself about to save
From fishy feasts, beneath the wave,
A mere resemblance of a man.
So, plunging down, he turned to find
Some drowning wight of human kind.][4]

344

While following, as I was saying, a certain marionette theater, from Kleist to Valéry to Celan, we analyzed the intriguing fate of the word "majesty," from the sovereignty that it designates in Latin (*majestas*, as Bodin reminded us) up to its occurrence in *The Wolf and the Lamb* and the dedication of La Fontaine's *Fables* to the *Dauphin*, and finally to the distinction

---

4. La Fontaine, "Le singe et le dauphin, " Livre quatrième, fable VII, in *Oeuvres complètes* (see session 8 above, n. 12), 1:149–50; trans. Elizur Wright in *The Fables of La Fontaine* (Boston, 1841). During the session, Derrida added after the quotation, "He wants to save 'humans'! Not a 'beast' . . . That would be a 'crime against humanity' for the dolphin!" The long bracketed section opened on p. 253 closes here.

proposed by Celan between the majesty of the monarch and the poetic majesty of the present, of the absurd that bears witness to the human present ("*für die Gegenwart des Menschlichen zeugenden Majestät des Absurden*").

You also recall that this question had taken a number of relays last time. From Kleist to Valéry's *Monsieur Teste* — who had wished, says the narrator, to "kill the marionette in him" — and then to Celan's "Meridian," the question of marionettes keeps coming back, undecidably "whats" and "whos," feminine and masculine, taking on all forms, from marionette as virgin girl, little Mary, to phallic erection, the prosthesis of the phallus *as* marionette and the priapism of the erection without detumescence, erection unto death, the cadaverized erection, tragic and comic: all of which sketched out the *unheimlich*, worrying, and undecidable figure of the marionette as life *and* death, life-death, life death, both the spontaneous and graceful autonomy of the living and the rigid automatism of machine and death, machine of death or of *bêtise*.

The phallus, let's see, we wondered, is the *phallos* proper to man?

345 And, we also wondered, if said phallus were proper to the sovereign, would it be for all that proper to man? Proper in what sense? And of man in what sense? Proper to man in what sense? And what if the phallus were *bêtise* itself? Where had this question of the sovereign, the standing position, the grandeur or highness of the Most High led us?

The *Majestas* of sovereignty no doubt signifies high stature, highness. Moreover, one doesn't only say Your Majesty but also Your Royal Highness, and I even found "Your Altitude" in a seventeenth-century document by Antoine Galland, author of a *Voyage to Constantinople*, who was one of the first translators of the *Thousand and One Nights* — one also talks of great Lords, Grand Dukes, Grand Viziers, and His Eminence, an expression that also bespeaks the highness of excellence.

Before proceeding in this direction, namely that of the majestic and sovereign erection as impulse toward the greatest, highest, and most rigid, the most inflexible state of a station or a stance, a stable state, I would like to add a logical precision, as it were, and forestall a misunderstanding that might have crept in. A misunderstanding as to what *grand* and *high* mean in this case — in this *case* in which precisely there would be neither case, nor *casus*, fall, falling off, detumescence, fall back toward the low. In this case, which is not one case among others, we made clear that the logic of sovereignty not only tended toward the greatest and the highest but also, through a hyperbolic and irrepressible upping of the ante, through a constitutive *hybris* — which sometimes makes it sublime, precisely — tends toward a height that is higher than height, if such an expression ("higher than height") doesn't lose meaning (but it's this loss of meaning, this excess of meaning, that we are talking about with sovereignty), a height higher than height, then, a grandeur grander than grandeur, and superior to superiority (and so several times, concerning the example of *Monsieur Teste,* precisely, we recalled the *topos* of the Nietzschean superman who overcame even the superior man and rose above his height). What is essential and proper to sovereignty is thus not grandeur or height as geometrically measurable, sensible, or intelligible, but excess, hyperbole, an excess insatiable for the passing of every determinable limit: higher than height, grander than grandeur, etc. It is the *more*, the *more than* that counts, the absolutely more, the absolute supplement that exceeds any comparative toward an absolute superlative. And the erection we are talking about is a superlative, absolute erection, beyond any sensible and growing erection. At which point the attribute of "grandeur" or even "highness" must be relativized. It is only one more example or figure of the "more," the maximum, a maximum that, in spite of its name (which, like *majestas,* also comes from *magnus,* from *majus,* greater), a maximum that is no longer a maximum of grandeur but perhaps—and this is what I was trying to get to—a maximum of smallness: the smallest possible, the more as more small can also do the job for the sovereign—or the erection of what is also called in French, let us note in passing, *le petit* [the little one], the male sex organ. (See Bataille and his "Le petit.")[5] What counts here for sovereignty, which is first of all a power, a potency, an "I can," is the maximum of potency, the greatest potency, an absolute power, and this absolute power can be figured by the grandeur of the grandest but also by smallness, arch-smallness, the absolute diminution of the smallest. Of the microscopic, and thus the almost invisible, the *minus,* the minuscule reduced to its smallest diminutive. As for highness, it can situate just as easily the greatest as the smallest. The smallest can be found very high, as well as the greatest, and, moreover, the extenuation, the diminution of the sensible and comparative figure that is found just as well in the majestic sovereignty of the Most Great or the Most High, of the infinitely great or the infinitely high as well as in the sovereignty of the infinitely small, that diminutive extenuation that tends asymptotically toward the disappearance of the sensible figure, seems sometimes to be more easily satisfied by shrinking, reduction, shriveling diminution than by aggrandizement.

346

5. Georges Bataille, "Le petit," in *Oeuvres complètes,* vol. 3: *Oeuvres littéraires* (Paris: Gallimard, 1971), pp. 33–69.

347   I am clarifying this point, among other things, to account for the fact that the political power that is today trying to make its sovereignty prevail thanks to its economic and techno-scientific resources (I was mentioning last time the satellites of worldwide surveillance, whose information is sometimes bought by the United States) does so through the refinement of what are now called *nanotechnologies*, i.e. a technical know-how that excels, sometimes in vertiginous fashion, in the miniaturization of instruments: this nanotechnology has made in recent years — and promises to make in years to come — fabulous progress. This art, this techno-science, is deploying itself without limit toward the ever smaller (hence the least visible, the microscopic, the least sensible, the most invisible, the lightest, the least apparent, the hardest to find out, the most easily displaceable or transportable by the body or within the human body, etc., in connection with computers, transistors, biological prostheses of all sorts). And these nanotechnologies are deploying their power as much in the space of all markets in general as in the space of military strategy and the surveillance of world territories or again in the field of biology, medicine, and surgery.

     And there, since I'm talking again about satellite and surveillance, the smallest in miniaturization dissociates itself from the largest, but can continue to be associated with the highest: the smallest can be the highest or even, beyond earth, in the supraterrestrial, higher than the highest. There is no more reason to call a supraterrestrial God great ("God is great") than small. Why does one not say, to describe the absolute power of God, "God is small," "really small," instead of saying "God is great"? I leave you to reply to this question. There must be untold answers already tried and available. Some would defy geometrical topology, to the point of recognizing that if God is in us, more intimate with us than we are ourselves, then he must

348 be in us insensibly, invisibly, both greater and smaller than we in us. He is simply more . . . in us than we. Other responses would recall that in certain religions the manifestation of divine presence or sovereignty passes though the small, the smallest: the weakness and smallness of the baby Jesus for example, or the lamb, these two examples being of great consequence for what matters to us here.

     What I retain for the moment from this detour via nanotechnologies is that the more, the supreme, the maximum that characterizes sovereignty is a more of power and not of size, and so of quality or intensity and not of magnitude. And the being-potential, the possible, the *dynamis* can be as small as possible without ceasing to be potential, precisely. And the scheme of erection, or even of phallic erection that we have associated with sovereign majesty is a schema of potency, not of size. More potent cannot be re-

duced to "bigger" nor "smaller." Potency in general, sovereign potency, like
any potency in particular, cannot be determined within the oppositional
grid of the large and the small. Here potency can be exercised by the force
of the larger, there by the force or cunning (which is also a force, the force of
the fox we discussed in connection with Machiavelli) of the smaller: which
comes down to saying that the small is not the contrary of the large in this
case. What counts is the *more*, the economy of the *more*, the economy of
the surplus or the economy of the supplement, the smaller able to be more
powerful or even larger than the largest: another logical effect of that law
according to which, remember what Nietzsche says about it, the weaker
can be stronger than the stronger — and that's the whole of history. Don't
forget the exergue, to which I shall return in a moment, which gathered in
the same ceremony, a *postmortem* ceremony, after a putting to death, a dissection ceremony — gathered in the same place a very great animal and a
very great king.

And so we are brought back with this enigma of a potency, a power, an
"I can" that can grow or intensify, gain in "more" via figures or determina-
tions of the "less" or the "lesser," [we are brought back] toward the row we
have been hoeing here for years, namely that of a thought of the possible as
im-possible, and conditions of possibility as conditions of im-possibility. Or
of im-potence. But I will not continue frontally in this direction today.

This question of the sovereign, the standing position, the grandeur or
the highness of the Most High had also led us last time not only from Roman *majestas*, as sovereignty of the Roman state or people, to the majesty
of one of La Fontaine's fables, *The Wolf and the Lamb*, to His Majesty the
Wolf, but also to a double division, as it were, a division of division itself, in
what I dare to call, through this poem on poetry, "The Meridian," [what I
would also dare to call] before or through the poem, Celan's discourse, the
discursive logic or axiomatics, that underlies and scans his poem, a double
division, then, namely:

On the one hand, a first difference, dissociation, or division between the
majesty of the Monarch (here the monarch Louis XVI, the one who will
lose his head in a Revolution) and the majesty, let's say, of the present or
of poetry (*Dichtung*, since as you remember, after Celan has spoken of the
"*für die Gegenwart des Menschlichen zeugenden Majestät des Absurden*," adds,
"but I believe it is . . . poetry" ("*aber ich glaube, es ist . . . die Dichtung*"): this
last majesty, this last sovereignty, poetic sovereignty is not, says Celan, the
political sovereignty of the monarch.

And, on the other hand, the division in the point, the pinpoint, the very
punctuality of the now, as the very presence of the present, in the very maj-

349

esty of the poetic present, in the poem as encounter — the dissociation, then, the partition that is also a parting [*partage*], between my present, the present itself, the very presence of the present, of the same present, in the present of the same [*le présent même, la présence même du présent, du même présent, le présent du même*], and, on the other hand [*d'autre part*] — and this is the other part of the partition and the parting — the other present, the present of the other to whom the poem makes a present of its time, thus, in a *Mitsprechen*, letting the time of the other, its own time, speak (*"das Gedicht selbst hat ja immer nur diese, einmalige, punktuelle Gegenwart — noch in dieser Unmittelbarkeit und Nähe lässt das ihm, dem Anderen, Eigenste mitsprechen: dessen Zeit."* [In the here and now of the poem it is still possible — the poem itself, after all, has only this one, unique, limited present — only in this immediacy and proximity does it allow the most idiosyncratic quality of the Other, its time, to participate in the dialogue.])[6]

We specified at length what the time of this speaking left to the other was, in the encounter of the poem, beyond its politico-democratic interpretation, beyond calculable speaking time or vote counting on the occasion of electing a sovereign.

Having reached this point, so as not to lose sight of our question as to what is proper to man, on phallic majesty and the revolutionary decapitation of the sovereign, I should like, privileging these motifs along with those of the animal, the monkey, the marionette, and above all the Medusa's head, to reconstitute as quickly and schematically as possible the trajectory that leads back to what Celan refers to as a stepping outside the human (*"ein Hinaustreten aus dem Menschlichen"*).[7]

This stepping outside the human, the human for which the poetic majesty of the Absurd bears witness, *could be* (we must keep the conditional here, you'll see why we must always say "perhaps"), *could be* what is proper to art according to Büchner, but proper to an art that would be *unheimlich* (the word, as you will hear, already appears twice, once translated [by Jean Launay] as "strange" [*étrange*], once by "strange, unsettling" [*étrange, dépaysant*]) — an art that would be *unheimlich* because in this art one would find at home (*zuhause*) these apparently inhuman things, these three apparently inhuman or a-human things in whose form art has been making its appearances since the beginning of the speech — three appearances as follows: 1. a Medusa's head (we were just hearing about it from Büchner's Lenz, through whom Celan prefers to hear the voice of Büchner himself; 2. "the

350

351

---

6. Celan, "Le Méridien," pp. 77–78 [p. 182].
7. Ibid., p. 67 [p. 177].

figure of the monkey" (*die Affengestalt*), which also appears earlier; and 3. automata or marionettes.

Here, as always, one must be very attentive to ellipses or furtive slippages, to cursory allusions. The character that Celan allows this stepping outside the human, which Celan describes as one describes a gesture or movement of the other — Büchner's Lenz or Büchner himself — which he allows, attributes, or confers, is that of *unheimlich*. You know that this word has two apparently contradictory and undecidable meanings — we have spoken a very great deal about it here (cf. Freud and Heidegger[8]): the familiar but as nonfamiliar, the terribly worrying aspect of the foreigner but as the intimacy of one's own home. The word appears twice in one passage, and much more often elsewhere: (Cite and comment and bring out the *Unheimlich*.)

> Yesterday, as I was walking along the edge of the valley, I saw two girls sitting on a rock; one was putting up her hair and the other was helping; and the golden hair was hanging down, and the face, pale and serious, and yet so young, and the black dress, and the other one so absorbed in helping her. The most beautiful, the most intimate pictures of the Old German School can convey but the vaguest impression of such a scene. At times one might wish to be a Medusa's head so as to be able to transform such a group into stone, and call out to the people [*Man möchte manchmal ein Medusenhaupt sein, um so eine Gruppe in Stein verwandeln zu können, und den Leuten zurufen*].

> Ladies and gentlemen, please take note: "One would like to be a Medusa's head," in order to . . . comprehend that which is natural as that which is natural, by means of art! [*um . . . das Natürliche als das Natürliche mittels der Kunst zu erfassen!*]
>
> One would like to, not: I would like to.

> Here we have stepped beyond human nature [*Das ist ein Hinaustreten aus dem Menschlichen*], gone outward, and entered an uncanny [*unheimlichen*] realm, yet one turned toward that which is human, the same realm in which the monkey, the automata, and, accordingly . . . alas, art, too, seem to be at home.
>
> This is not the historical Lenz speaking, it is Büchner's Lenz. We hear Büchner's voice: even here art preserves something uncanny for him [*etwas Unheimliches*].[9]

352

8. See, among other places, the ninth, tenth, and eleventh sessions of the unpublished seminar "Répondre du secret" (1991–92).

9. Celan, "Le Méridien," pp. 66–67 [pp. 176–77].

The word *unheimlich* here bears all the weight, precisely where it remains equivocal and so hard to translate, it says the essential bearing of "The Meridian," or so it seems to me. It reappears elsewhere in the text, associated with a word that is just as frequent, the foreigner.[10] (Cite and comment.)

> And poetry? Poetry, which, after all, must travel the path of art? In that case we would in fact be shown here the path to the Medusa's head and the automaton!
>
> At this point I am not searching for a way out, I am just asking, along the same line, and also, I believe, in the line suggested in the Lenz fragment.
> Perhaps — I'm just asking — perhaps poetry, in the company of the I that has forgotten itself, travels the same path as art, toward that which is uncanny and alien [*zu jenem Unheimlichen und Fremden*]. And once again — but where? but in what place? but how? but as what? — it sets itself free [*wieder frei?*]?[11]

Although the strangeness of the *Unheimliche,* of *Unheimlichkeit* — which is a familiar strangeness because the figures of the automat, the monkey, and the Medusa's head are at home (*zuhause*) — [although the strangeness of the *Unheimliche*] is often associated with the foreigner, it is not all by chance that it should also be close to what makes the secret of poetry, namely the secret of the encounter. For in German, "secret" is *Geheimnis* (the intimate, the folded back on itself, what has withdrawn in withdrawal, the hidden inside of the house and home), and this secret of the encounter is at the most intimate heart of what is present and presence (*Gegenwart und Präsenz*) in the poem.

> Then the poem would be — even more clearly than before — the language of an individual which has taken on form; and, in keeping with its innermost nature, it would also be the present, the here and now. [*Dann wäre das Gedicht — deutlicher noch als bisher — gestaltgewordene Sprache eines Einzelnen, — und seinem innersten Wesen nach Gegenwart und Präsenz.*]
>
> The poem is alone. [*Das Gedicht ist einsam.*] It is alone and underway. [*Es ist einsam und unterwegs.*] Whoever writes it must remain in its company. [*Wer es schreibt, bleibt ihm mitgegeben.*]
> But doesn't the poem, for precisely that reason, at this point participate

353

---

10. [Translator's note:] Derrida translates "Fremde" and its cognates as "étranger," which, like the German term, corresponds to the English "strange(r), "foreign(er)," "alien."

11. Celan, "Le Méridien," p. 69 [p. 178]. Derrida comments: "listen to all the 'perhaps's' [*vielleicht*], there are going to be dozens of them."

in an encounter [*in der Begegnung*] — in the secret of an encounter [*im Geheimnis der Begegnung*]?

The poem wants to reach the Other, it needs this Other, it needs a vis-à-vis. It searches it out and addresses it.

Each thing, each person, is a form of this Other [*eine Gestalt dieses Anderen*] for the poem, as it makes for this Other.[12]

Before coming back to this concept of the Foreigner thus associated with the strange, the strangeness of what is *unheimlich*, I should like at least to indicate the path of a long detour via some texts of Heidegger's. In this very place, a few years ago, I emphasized the decisive importance (scarcely noticed, if at all) of the vocabulary of the *Unheimliche* and of *Unheimlichkeit* in Heidegger (an importance as great as in Freud, though at least apparently different).[13] Now without wanting nor being able to reopen wide the question of the *Unheimliche* in Heidegger, from *Sein und Zeit* up to the end, I shall content myself with pointing out — precisely because it has to do with the human and the inhuman — a passage from the *Introduction to Metaphysics* (1935), which resonates strangely (*unheimlich*) with what Celan says about the *Unheimliche* as what at home in art seems to exceed the human in the human, seems to step outside the human in human art.

I reopen the *Introduction to Metaphysics* rather violently, guided by what matters to us at the moment, at the point where Heidegger relaunches the question "What is man?"[14] Let me put down a couple of essential markers before coming on to what interests us here in this journey, namely the *Unheimliche*.

1. *First marker.* Heidegger begins by asserting the secondary character, the fundamentally derived, late-on-the-scene, and (from the ontological point of view) fundamentally very unsatisfactory character of a definition of man as *animal rationale* or as *zōon logon ekhon*. Incidentally, he interestingly and unassailably calls this definition "zoological," not only but also in the sense that it links the *logos* to the *zōon* and claims to render account and reason (*logon didonai*) of the essence of man by saying of him that he is first of all a "living thing," an "animal" ("*Die genannte Definition des Menschen ist im Grunde eine zoologische*"). But the *zōon* of this zoology remains in many

354

---

12. Ibid., pp. 76–77 [p. 181].

13. See n. 8 above.

14. Martin Heidegger, *Einführung in die Metaphysik* (Tübingen: Niemeyer, 1976), pp. 108ff.; trans. Gregory Field and Richard Polt as *Introduction to Metaphysics* (New Haven: Yale University Press, 2000), pp. 150ff.

respects questionable (*fragwürdig*). In other words, so long as one has not questioned ontologically the essence of being alive, the essence of life, it remains problematic and obscure to define man as *zōon logon ekhon*. Now it is on this unquestioned basis, this problematical basis of an unelucidated ontological question of life that the whole of the West, says Heidegger, has constructed its psychology, its ethics, its theory of knowledge, and its anthropology. And Heidegger then describes with irony and a superior air the state of the culture in which we live, in which one can receive books bearing on their cover the title *What Is Humanity?* without even a hint of a question being asked beyond the cover of such a book, which, he notes (in 1935), the *Frankfurter Zeitung* praises for being a book that is "unusual and courageous."[15]

355   2. *Second marker.* Henceforth the reply to the question "What is man?" cannot be a reply but a question, a questioning, an act and experience of *Fragen*, for in this question it is man himself who is determining himself by questioning about himself, about his being, discovering himself in this way to be of a questioning essence in the *Fragen*. From which Heidegger draws *two conclusions in one*, namely that—I'm citing the [French] translation that seems to me not very illuminating and that I shall attempt to clarify later: "It is only insofar as he comes forth in questioning that man comes to himself and is a self" ("*Der Mensch kommt erst als fragend-geschichtlicher zu ihm selbst und ist ein Selbst*" [comment]). And that therefore this *Selbst*, this self, this ipseity (as *Selbst* is translated) that is not yet an "I," nor an individual, nor a "we," nor a community, is a "who" before any "I," any individual, any person, any "we," and any community (a fortiori, I would add for what is of interest to us, nor a subject or a political animal, for Heidegger's suspicion about man as *zōon logon ekhon, animal rationale,* would be the same as to man as political animal, an expression of Aristotle's to which we shall return at length later). So that—second conclusion wrapped up in the first—the question of man as to his own being (*nach seinem eigenen Sein*) is transformed, is no longer "What is man?" *What* is man? (Was *ist der Mensch?*), but "*Who* is man?" (Wer *ist der Mensch?*).

    Having recalled these two markers, you will see, if you reread this text as I ask that you do, that Heidegger, provisionally abandoning Parmenides, whom he is reading, and turning to Sophocles' *Antigone*[16] to look for the poetic sketch of what could be the Greek way of listening to the essence of man

15. Ibid., p. 109 [p. 152].
16. Ibid., pp. 112–26 [pp. 156–76].

(a poetic sketch in the interpretation of which he advances a return toward what he holds to be a more originary sense of the Greek *polis,* the full sense ("*dies trifft nicht den vollen Sinn*") of which is not rendered by the translation as city or [city-]state, *Stadt und Stadtstaat.* Before the state, and thus before what we call the political, the *polis* is the *Da,* the *là* [there] in which and as which *Da-sein* is *geschichtlich,* advenes as history, as the historial origin of history. To this historial site belong not only sovereigns (*Herrscher*), the men who hold power, the army, the navy, the council, the assemblies of the people, but also gods, temples, priests, poets, thinkers.[17] But what matters most to us here, in the paths of these readings of Sophocles, is the moment when Heidegger translates the *deinotaton* of the *deinon,* the most terrible, most violent, or most worrying in the worrying, spoken of in lines 332–75 of *Antigone,* which also say that there is nothing more *deinon* than man, as *das Unheimlichste des Unheimlichen,*[18] of which he will say that it resides in conflict, in the antagonistic relation (*im gegenwendigen Bezug*) between justice (*dikē*) and *tekhnē.* Heidegger himself asks, "Why do we translate *deinon* as *un-heimlich*?"[19] The principle of his reply is that the sentence (*Spruch*) that says, "*Der Mensch ist das Unheimlichste* [*deinotaton,* then]" ("Man is the most *unheimlich*") gives the authentic, proper, *Greek* definition of man (*gibt die eigentliche* griechische *Definition des Menschen*). Why? Why translate it this way? Not to add a meaning after the fact to the word *deinon* (which is often translated as "violent" or "terrible"), nor because we hear the *Unheimliche* as a sensory impression, as an affect or what makes an impression on our sensibility, but because there is in the *Unheimliche* something that expels us from the *heimliche,* from the peaceful quiet of the domestic, the *heimisch,* the usual (*Gewohnten*), the current and the familiar (*Geläufigen*). Man is the most *unheimlich,* because he steps outside the familiar, the habitual frontiers (*Grenzen*) of habit, etc. When the chorus says of man that he is *to deinotaton* or *das Unheimlichste,* the point for Heidegger is not to say that man is this or that, and only then *unheimlichste*: the point is much more, much earlier [*bien plutôt, bien plus tôt*], more originarily, to say that the essence of man, what is proper to man (his fundamental feature, his *Grundzug*), is this being foreign to everything that one can identify as familiar, recognizable, etc. What is proper to man would be, basically, this way of not being secure at home (*heimisch*), even with oneself as with one's proper essence. As if, according to what is now basically quite a traditional motif, Heidegger were

356

357

17. Ibid., p. 117 [p. 163].
18. Ibid., p. 124 [p. 171].
19. Ibid., p. 115 [p. 160].

saying that what is proper to man is the experience that consists in exceeding the proper in the sense of what can be appropriated in familiarity. In saying which, Heidegger does not go so far as to say <that> "there is nothing proper to man," but rather that this proper has as its fundamental feature, if not a certain impropriety or expropriety, at least the property of being apprehended, as property, as strange, not appropriate, or even inappropriable, foreign to the *heimisch*, to the reassuring proximity of the identifiable and the similar, to familiarity, to the interiority of the home — in particular beyond all the definitions, that Heidegger calls "zoological," of man as *zōon logon ekhon*.

Leaving there, for lack of time, everything that in and beyond these pages resonates in Heidegger around the statement "*Der Mensch ist to deinotaton, das Unheimlichste des Unheimlichen*,"[20] I emphasize only, before returning to what in Celan seems to echo it strangely, that the superlative (*das Unheimlichste*) does not count less than the equivocal and unstable meaning (*das Unheimliche*) that it thus superlativizes and hyperbolizes and extremes. Man is not only *unheimlich*, an essence already as equivocal and strange as what *unheimlich* means (see, I repeat, what Freud says in the article that bears this title, *Das Unheimliche*, on the contradictory meanings of this word in German, that designates both the most familiar and the most strange), man, what is called man, is not only *deinon* and *unheimlich*, he is *to deinotaton* and *das Unheimlichste*, the most *unheimlich* being, meaning that he sovereignly excels in this, he is more *unheimlich* that everything and everyone, he reaches, I would say — but this is not expressly Heidegger's language and word — a sort of exceptional excellence, a sort of sovereignty among *unheimlich* beings and the modalities of *Unheimlichkeit*. The superlative is the sign of the hyperbolic, it wears the crown of the sovereignty of human *Dasein*. And this sort of sovereignty, as you have heard, concerns, under the sign of the *Unheimliche*, a certain experience of foreignness, not only of the strange, but of the Foreigner (a figure who will be relayed later in the texts on Trakl, in *Unterwegs zur Sprache*, which I studied in earlier seminars, a long time ago).[21]

If now, keeping in one's memory this indissociable couple of the *sovereignly* and *superlatively unheimlich* and the foreigner, or foreignness, we come back to "The Meridian" and the moment in the journey where Celan

358

---

20. Ibid., p. 114 [p. 159].

21. See, among other texts, "La main de Heidegger (Geschlecht II)," in *Psyché: Inventions de l'autre* (see session 2 above, n. 16), 2:35–36 [2:29], and the unpublished seminar "Nationalité et nationalisme philosophiques: Le fantôme de l'autre" (1984–85).

has just evoked this stepping outside the human (*ein Hinaustreten aus dem Menschlichen*) and the movement that consists in "transporting oneself to a domain that turns toward the human its strange face" (the three appearances of art: the automats, the figure of the monkey, the Medusa's head): this moment of stepping outside the human must be summonsed to appear with the moment that, earlier, had implied that "perhaps" ("I believe," says Celan), poetry was that homage rendered to the majesty of the absurd insofar as it bore witness to the present of the now of the human (*für die Gegenwart des Menschlichen zeugenden Majestät des Absurden*). Celan also wonders, as you have heard, if poetry ought or ought not to take the path of an art that would also be that of Medusa and the automat. From this moment, the value of *unheimliche* can no longer be separated from that of the foreigner, not only of the strange but of the foreigner, and all the — many — approaches of what poetry might be are all approaches not toward an essence but a movement, a road and a step, a direction, a turn in the direction of the step, like a turn in breath itself (*Atemwende*).

We could find an example of this on almost every line, at least starting at page 70. I shall quote only a few, in order to suggest that this insistence on the step that liberates, crosses, comes and goes in this or that direction, commands us to think poetry as a path (*Weg,* and this is so often Celan's word that we have, for right or wrong, difficulty dissociating it from an incessant and insistent work of meditation on the path, the *Bewegung* of the path, on the movement of the *Weg* in Heidegger), a path, according to Celan, for what comes or goes, and which is less something that *is* than an event, the coming of an event that happens [*arrive*]. I very rapidly stress this privilege accorded the path, the going and coming, the step. But in reading these lines, I shall not be content to mark time [*marquer le pas*: literally, to mark the step], I shall also mark time on three other words for reasons I shall give in a moment, namely the I, the Foreigner, and the bottomless abyss (*Abgrund*):[22]

359

---

22. In the interests of legibility, we have placed in this note a passage bracketed by Derrida in the typescript: "[Read and comment pp. 70–72 [pp. 178–79], up to '*Himmel als Abgrund unter sich* [sky below, as an abyss]' (announce that we are going to insist on topology and direction, place and step. I and abyss (*Abgrund*): the bottomless (refer to Schelling, *Ungrund, Urgrund*, etc.). On this subject, see Heidegger at the beginning of *Introduction to Metaphysics* (p. 2 in German, p. 3 in the [English] translation) concerning the question 'Why are there beings? What is the basis of the entity?' Heidegger wonders then if this ground in an originary ground, *Urgrund*, or whether this originary ground refuses all foundation and becomes *Abgrund*, or else a ground that is not one, an

In that case art would be the path traveled by literature — nothing more and nothing less.

I know, there are other, shorter paths. But after all, literature too often shoots ahead of us. *La poésie, elle aussi, brûle nos étapes.*

360

I will take leave of the one who has forgotten himself, the one concerned with art, the artist. I think that I have encountered poetry in Lucile, and Lucile perceives language as form and direction and breath [*und Richtung und Atem wahr*]. Here, too, in this work of Büchner, I am searching for the very same thing. I am searching for Lenz himself, I am searching for him, as a person, I am searching for his form: for the sake of the location of literature, the setting free, the step [*um des Ortes der Dichtung, um der Freisetzung, um des Schritts willen*].

Büchner's "Lenz," ladies and gentlemen, remained a fragment. Would it be proper for us to search out the historical Lenz, in order to learn which direction [*Richtung*] his existence took [*welche Richtung dieses Dasein hatte*]?

"His existence was an inescapable burden. — So his life went on." Here the story breaks off.

But literature [*Dichtung*], like Lucile, attempts to see form in its direction; literature shoots ahead. We know where his life went, and how it went on. [*Wir wissen,* wohin *er lebt, wie er* hin*lebt.*]

"Death" — one reads in a work about Jakob Michael Reinhold Lenz by the Moscow academician M. N. Rosanow which appeared in Leipzig in 1909 — "Death the redeemer was not slow in coming. Lenz was found dead on one of the streets of Moscow during the night of May 23–24, 1792. A nobleman paid for his burial expenses. His final resting place is unknown."

So his life had gone on. [*So hatte er* hin*gelebt.*]

This person Lenz: the true Lenz, Büchner's Lenz, the one we were able to recognize on the first page of the story, the Lenz who "walked through the mountains [*durchs Gebirg ging*] on the 20th of January" — this person, and not the artist and the one concerned with questions about art — this person as an I [*er als ein Ich*].

Can we now, perhaps [*vielleicht*], find the place where strangeness was present, the place [*Finden wir jetzt vielleicht den Ort, wo das Fremde war, den Ort*] where a person succeeded in setting himself free, as an — estranged — I? Can we find such a place, such a step [*einen solchen Ort, einen solchen Schritt*]?

". . . but now and then he experienced a sense of uneasiness because he was not able to walk on his head [*dass er nicht auf dem Kopf gehn konnte*]." —

---

appearance of ground, *Schein von Gründung, Ungrund:* ' . . .)]." This last parenthesis is incomplete in the typescript.

That is Lenz. That is, I am convinced, Lenz and his step, Lenz and his "Long live the King!"

"... but now and then he experienced a sense of uneasiness because he was not able to walk on his head."

Whoever walks on his head, ladies and gentlemen, whoever walks on his head has heaven beneath him as an abyss [*wer auf dem Kopf geht, der hat den Himmel als Abgrund unter sich*].[23]   361

There here comes about, in Celan's path or poetic speech, but, as always with decisive events, under the category or the reserve of the "perhaps" (*vielleicht*), in truth between two "perhaps's" and even three "perhaps's" and even four, five, six, seven, eight "perhaps's" (in about twenty lines and two paragraphs), there here comes about, then, between two and three and four, five, six, seven, eight "perhaps's" the event of an unheard-of turning, the riskiness of which I would like to experience with you and, so to speak, re-connoiter the corner turned. Celan has just referred to the obscurity proper to poetry as the place of an encounter to come from the horizon of the distant and the foreign. Here is a first *perhaps*: (Read and comment)

Ladies and gentlemen, nowadays it is fashionable to reproach poetry for its "obscurity." [. . .] That is, I believe, if not the inherent obscurity of poetry, the obscurity attributed to it for the sake of an encounter — from a great distance or sense of strangeness perhaps of its own making [*vielleicht selbst-entworfenen*].

And then, still under the reservation of a second *perhaps*, there is a strange division of the strange itself: perhaps there are two sorts of strange, right up close to each other:

But there are perhaps two kinds of strangeness, in one and the same direction — side by side. [*Aber es gibt vielleicht, und in einer und derselben Richtung, zweierlei Fremde — dicht beieinander.*]

And now, to specify this duality at the very heart of the foreigner, here is a sort of revolution in the revolution. You remember that Lucile's "Long live the King!" had been saluted as a counterstatement (*Gegenwort*) which was,   362 perhaps ("I believe," Celan says at that point), poetry, in which a homage was rendered, far from the political code of reactionary countermanifestation, to the (nonpolitical) majesty of the absurd that bore witness to the present or the now of the human. Now another "Long live the King," the "Long live the King!" of Lenz, i.e. Büchner, is supposed to go a step further

23. Celan, "Le Méridien," pp. 70–72 [pp. 178–79].

than Lucile's. And this is no longer, this time, a word, nor even a counter-word (*Gegenwort* bearing witness to a *Gegenwart*), it is, more particularly, no longer a majesty but a terrifying silence, an arrest that strikes speech dumb, that cuts off breath and cuts off speech.

> Lenz — that is, Buchner — has here gone one step further than Lucile [*ist hier einen Schritt weiter gegangen als Lucile*]. His "Long live the King" no longer consists of words [*Sein "Es lebe der König" ist kein Wort mehr*]. It has become a terrible silence [*es ist ein furchtbares Verstummen*]. It robs him — and us — of breath and speech [*es verschlagt ihm — und auch uns — den Atem und das Wort*].
>
> Poetry: that can signify a turn-of-breath [*Dichtung: das kann eine Atem-wende bedeuten*]. Who knows, perhaps [*Wer weiss, vielleicht*] poetry travels its path — which is also the path of art — for the sake of such a breath turn-ing [*um einer solchen Atemwende willen zurück*]?[24]

What I should like to bring out, still privileging the thought that concerns us here, namely the thought of sovereignty and its majesty in the figure of present and self-present ipseity, sometimes present to itself in the form of the ego, the living present of the ego, the "I" — that "I," that power to say "I" that, from Descartes to Kant to Heidegger has always been liter-ally, explicitly reserved to the human being (only man can say or mean "I," "myself I," while referring in autodeictic fashion to himself — those three, *363* Descartes, Kant, Heidegger, all wrote that) — [what I should like to bring out], if possible, is the way Celan signals toward an alterity that — within the "I" as punctual living present, as point of the living self-present present, an alterity of the wholly other — comes along not to include and modalize another living present (as in Husserl's analysis of temporalization, of the protention and retention of another living present in the living present now, the ego holding in itself, in its present, another present), but here, which is quite different, letting the present *of the other* appear, that "leaving the most proper of the time of the other" we were talking about last time.

I'll first read this long passage peppered with I know not how many "perhaps's," which all ultimately aim to withdraw these poetic statements about the event of the poem from the dimension and authority of knowl-edge. (Read and comment)

> Perhaps [*Vielleicht*] it succeeds, since strangeness [*das Fremde*], that is, the abyss and the Medusa's head, the abyss and the robots, seem to lie in the same direction — perhaps it succeeds here in distinguishing between

24. Ibid., pp. 72–73 [pp. 179–80].

strangeness and strangeness, perhaps [*vielleicht*] at precisely this point the Medusa's head shrivels, perhaps the automata cease to function for this unique, fleeting moment? Is perhaps [*vielleicht*] at this point, along with the I—with the estranged I, set free at this point and in a similar manner [*mit dem* hier *und* solcherart *freigesetzten befremdeten Ich*]—is perhaps at this point an Other set free [*vielleicht wird hier noch ein Anderes frei*]?

Perhaps [*Vielleicht*] the poem assumes its own identity as a result [*Vielleicht ist das Gedicht von da her es selbst*] . . . and is accordingly able to travel other paths, that is, the paths of art, again and again [*wieder und wieder gehen*]—in this art-less, art-free manner [*und kann nun, auf diese kunst-lose, kunst-freie Weise*]?

Perhaps [*Vielleicht*].

Perhaps [*Vielleicht*] one can say that every poem has its "20th of January"? Perhaps [*Vielleicht*] the novelty of poems that are written today is to be found in precisely this point: that here the attempt is most clearly made to remain mindful of such dates?

But are we all not descended from such dates? And to which dates do we attribute ourselves?

But the poem does speak! It remains mindful of its dates, but—it speaks, to be sure, it speaks only in its own, its own, individual cause. But I think—and this thought can scarcely come as a surprise to you—I think that it has always belonged to the expectations of the poem, in precisely this manner, to speak in the cause of the strange—no, I can no longer use this word—in precisely this manner to speak in the cause of an Other—who knows, perhaps in the cause of a wholly Other [*wer weiss, vielleicht in eines ganz Anderen Sache*].

This "who knows" [*Dieses "wer weiss"*], at which I see I have arrived, is the only thing I can add—on my own, here, today—to the old expectations.

Perhaps [*Vielleicht*], I must now say to myself—and at this point I am making use of a well-known term—perhaps it is now possible to conceive a meeting of this "wholly Other" and an "other" which is not far removed, which is very near.[25]

Naturally I can now only leave you to read and reread the whole of "The Meridian." But perhaps we are starting here to think this subtle *unheimlich* difference between the two foreigners, a difference that is like the place for the narrow passage of poetry that Celan will soon mention. This is the difference, in the punctuality of the now, in the pinpoint of the present moment, of *my* present, between, *on the one hand*, my other living present (retained or anticipated by an indispensable movement of retention and pro-

364

25. Ibid., pp. 73–74 [p. 180].

tention), and, *on the other hand*, wholly other, the present of the other the temporality of which cannot be reduced, included, assimilated, introjected, appropriated into mine, cannot even resemble it or be similar to it, a present or proper time of the other that I must surely let go, radically giving it up, but also the very possibility of which (the *perhaps* beyond all knowledge) is

365 the chance both of the encounter (*Begegnung*) and of this event, this advent, of what is called poetry. An improbable poetry ("who knows") but a poetry to take one's breath away and turn it, and so also turn life and path, which can still be a path of art both wider and narrower.

I'll read a final passage, before taking, not without some brutality, a jump backwards and sideways toward the scene of dissection from which we began, the dissection of the great animal, the elephant, in the presence of His Majesty Louis le Grand. (Read and comment)

> *Elargissez l'Art!*[26] This question comes to us with its mysteries [*mit ihrer neuen Unheimlichkeit*], new and old. I approached Büchner in its company — I believed I would once again find it there.
>
> I also had an answer ready, a "Lucilean" counterstatement; I wanted to establish something in opposition, I wanted to be there with my contradiction.
>
> Expand art?
>
> No. But accompany art into your own unique place of no escape [*in deine allereigenste Enge*]. And set yourself free [*Und setze dich frei.*].
>
> Here, too, in your presence, I have traveled this path. It was a circle. [*Es war ein Kreis.*]
>
> Art — and one must also include the Medusa's head, mechanization, automata; the uncanny [*das Unheimliche*], indistinguishable, and in the end perhaps [*vielleicht*] only one strangeness [*letzten Endes vielleicht doch nur eine Fremde*] — art lives on [*die Kunst lebt fort*].
>
> Twice, in Lucile's "Long live the King" and as heaven opened up under Lenz as an abyss [*als Abgrund*], the breath turning seemed to be there. Perhaps [*vielleicht*] also, when I attempted to make for that distant but occupiable realm which became visible only in the form of Lucile.[27]

366 As you have clearly understood, in this division between two strangers, two ways of thinking the other and time, in this very division between the two "Long Live the King's" — of which only the first is called *majestic*, of which only the first, Lucile's, requires the word *majesty*, *poetic* and not *political* majesty — we have now (perhaps) moved beyond *all majesty, and therefore*

26. In French in Celan's text.

27. Celan, "Le Méridien," p. 80 [p. 183].

beyond all sovereignty. It is as if, after the poetic revolution that was reaffirming a poetic majesty beyond or outside political majesty, a second revolution,
the one that takes one's breath away or turns one's breath in the encounter
with the wholly other, came to try or to recognize, to try to recognize, or
even — without cognizing or recognizing anything — to try to *think* a revolution in the revolution, a revolution in the very life of time, in the life of the
living present.[28] This discreet, even unobvious, even minuscule, even microscopic dethroning of majesty exceeds knowledge. Not to pay homage to
some obscurantism of nonknowledge, but to prepare perhaps some poetic
revolution in the political revolution, and perhaps too some revolution in
the knowledge of knowledge, precisely between the beast, the marionette,
the head, the Medusa's head, and the head of His Majesty the sovereign.
Which is no doubt signed by the repetition of the "perhaps's" and the "who
knows" (*wer weiss*).

Well, to conclude for today, to mark a provisional punctuation or a few
points of suspension in our history or in our fable entitled "The Beast and the
Sovereign," to make a signal that is still indeterminate, in waiting, in two directions, *both* toward the revolution that de-crowns the majesty, *and* toward
several ages in the history of knowledge, a knowledge of the living animal
being that objectifies or produces objects for the gaze of the sovereign, be
that sovereign a great king or be it the people, here then are two signals to
end today, two signals we shall have to learn to decipher. They both concern
mastery, both political and scientific, indissociably political and scientific,
over an animal that has become an object of knowledge — knowledge of
death, anatomical knowledge above all — for the sovereign, the king or the
people. In both cases, the one prerevolutionary, the other postrevolutionary,
we are dealing with a political organization of the field of knowledge, in the
form of the anatomy lesson or the lesson of natural science.

I take these two signals, these two reference points, from a book and
especially an article that I recommend to you. The book is by Henri F.
Ellenberger, translated into French under the title *Médecines de l'âme: Essais
d'histoire de la folie et des guérisons psychiques.*[29] These are texts gathered and

367

28. On the printout of this session, Derrida has added: "Poetic revolution no less
than political revolution (develop)."

29. Henri F. Ellenberger, *Médecines de l'âme: Essais d'histoire de la folie et des guérisons
psychiques*, ed. Élisabeth Roudinesco (Paris: Fayard, 1995). [Translator's note: I quote
the essay to which Derrida refers from its original English publication, "The Mental
Hospital and the Zoological Garden," in *Animals and Man in Historical Perspective,* ed. J.
Klaits and B. Klaits (New York: Harper and Row, 1974), pp. 59–93.]

translated by Élisabeth Roudinesco. One of the articles, to which I am now referring, "The Mental Hospital and the Zoological Garden," proposes a fascinating parallel between these two histories (that of the zoo and that of the asylum), especially in France. I shall come back to this next week in more detail. But I wanted today to take from it the two signals or indices that I mentioned above.

The first, the prerevolutionary one, is the one that I placed as an exergue at the beginning of this session. It is indeed an anatomy lesson. Following very closely a famous book by Gustave Loisel, *Histoire des ménageries de l'Antiquité à nos jours* (Paris, 1912, 3 vols.), Ellenberger reconstitutes this dissection scene and this sort of anatomy lesson objectifying[30] the dead body of a large elephant on the institutional initiative and under the gaze of a great sovereign. Here's the passage from which I took a fragment at the beginning of the session:

> In his curious work *The New Atlantis,*[31] written between 1614 and 1617, Francis Bacon described an imaginary land where life was dominated by the cult of scientific research. The parks there contained specimens of all the known animals, which were used in experiments in physiotherapy, including the fabrication of monsters, hybrids, and new species. Here was the foreshadowing of a new trend: the utilization of the zoo for scientific research.
>
> It was in France that this new kind of establishment saw the light of day. In 1662 Louis XIV created the Menagerie of Versailles, intended from the outset to be the biggest and most magnificent in the world. Although this was primarily a display establishment reserved for the visits of the king and the court in full ceremonial, Louis XIV also made it a research center. Upon arrival each animal was painted or represented in miniature by a known artist. Scientific exploitation of the menagerie was placed in the hands of the Académie des Sciences, whose members did many animal dissections and produced the first important work in comparative anatomy. Loisel tells the famous story of the ceremonial dissection of an elephant in 1681, an event which the Sun King deigned to honor with his presence: "Never perhaps was there a more imposing anatomical dissection, judged by the enormity of the animal, by the precision with which its several parts were examined, or by the quality and number of assistants." But Loisel also

368

---

30. Derrida's pencil annotation: "Objectifying to death of the object (develop)."

31. [Ellenberger's note:] Francis Bacon, *The New Atlantis,* Great Books of the Western World, no. 30 (Chicago: Encyclopaedia Britannica, 1952), pp. 199–214.

rendered the sad account of the decline of the menagerie under Louis XV and Louis XVI and its inglorious end during the Revolution.[32]

After this decadence of the zoo, it was still in the name of knowledge, in the name of scientific objectivity, that the French Revolution, without emancipating the animals in the name of the rights of man and citizen, and speaking in the name of the sovereignty of the people, would invent new zoological institutions, still well known to all Parisians, including those who, like me, nevertheless remain enamored of the Jardin des Plantes.

> The era of the French Revolution inaugurated a new conception of the zoo-logical garden. Until that time menageries, even those such as Versailles' where important scientific work was done, served primarily as diversions for the monarch and his courtiers. This is why the Encyclopedia declared: "Menageries must be destroyed when people have no bread, for it is scandalous for animals to feast while around them men starve." Whence followed the destruction of the menagerie of Versailles by the revolutionaries. Bernardin de Saint-Pierre had the remnants of the menagerie transported to the Paris Jardin du Roi, of which he was intendant, and proposed the creation of a new institution. A report on this subject was prepared by three members of the Natural History Society of Paris, Brongniart, Millin, and Philippe Pinel. One would like to know just how much Pinel, the famous alienist, contributed to the report of 1792, which concluded: "A menagerie like those that princes and kings are accustomed to maintain is nothing but a costly and unnecessary imitation of Asiatic pomp; but we think that a menagerie without frills could be extremely useful to natural history, to physiology and to the economy." The new institution would serve both scientific progress and public instruction. Thus was created, in the rebaptized Jardin des Plantes, the National Menagerie of the Museum of Natural History of Paris, the zoo that served as a model for all similar institutions throughout the nineteenth century. There one of its first directors, Frédéric Cuvier (brother of the more famous zoologist Georges Cuvier), made numerous pioneering and unjustly neglected observations of animal psychology.[33]

---

32. Ellenberger, "The Mental Hospital and the Zoological Garden," pp. 63–64.
33. Ibid., pp. 64–65.

March 13, 2002

No doubt you are curious—you are probably curious—to know what the principal point at stake will be in this session, since there is one every week.

Well, I can tell you for your curiosity, which will nonetheless have to be patient for a while, [I can tell you] that the point at stake will be, precisely, a curiosity, not only this or that curiosity, several curiosities, but just curiosity. Curiosity itself, if any such thing exists. Can one ask a question, ask oneself a question about curiosity, without curiosity?

It's a very fine word, a fine verbal animal, *curiositas*, for a seminar such as ours, and it's a verbal animal, a vocable that, according to one of the traditions that is occupying us and that we are analyzing, we will perhaps set to work. A curious vocable of burden. But let us leave it there for now, let's leave *curiositas* to wait and rest. Let's pretend in the meantime to distract ourselves with other questions.

For example: What is an *autopsy (autopsia)*?

And an *autopsy* of oneself?

In the *autopsies* of which we have so many images, and so many films, one always imagines an operating table or even a laboratory workbench. This table has become the base, the support, the subjectile of a body in some amphitheatrical theater. (This very room, this seminar room, was until recently, as you know, before its remodeling, just such a theater for work in natural history, for you have noticed—I believe the inscription is still legible on the way in—that these buildings were until recently used for zoology and natural science laboratories, for the study of living organisms or minerals. I think it's still written on the outside wall.) The autopsy table in anatomy lessons also looks like a cathedra, like this table, like a rostrum [*chaire*] on which the flesh [*chair*] of a living being that is no longer living, be it beast or sovereign, is exposed, dissected, and analyzed.

What does the word *autopsy* mean, and what does it set in motion, in the becoming-*what* of the *who*? In the becoming-object of a living being? That is, so often, in the becoming-dead of a *zōon*? This is the very question that one must try, and must take the time, to submit to autopsy, or even an autopsy of autopsy.

The [feminine] beast and the [masculine] sovereign, so, what? So, who?

By beginning and then beginning again in this way with a question, and a question in this form, "The [*la*] beast and the [*le*] sovereign, so, *what*? So, *who*?" I could let it be understood, I could let it be expected, that the expected response, rightly understood, would be of the order of knowledge. The [*la*] beast and the [*le*] sovereign, so, *what*? So, *who*? Well, the virtual response to this series of implicit or explicit questions would be supposed to make me know, give me to know, this or that about the beast and the sovereign. One presumes that this response, like any response, could enrich my knowledge, my science, or my conscience; it would be supposed to give me more to know, make me know more by teaching me, by revealing to me, unveiling to me, teaching me by example and *in truth,* what the one and the other *are*, the beast and the sovereign, the one or the other, the one as seen by the other, or if they are, the one and the other, the one or the other, beings of the "who" type or beings of the "what" type. Supposing that this distinction were to stand up for long.

Under the title of knowledge, science, or conscience, as to "the beast and the sovereign," one can arrange all the fields of theory and ontology. Theory and ontology are, precisely, kinds of knowledge or sciences: for example, as to the sovereignty of the sovereign, as to the essence of the sovereign, politology or political onto-theology is a *-logy*, a logic, a knowledge, the supposedly rational discourse of a knowledge; as for animality or bestiality, biology or zoology, these also are kinds of knowledge, discourses of knowledge. The ontology of the living being, of the living being in general, be that ontology regional or general, is a theoretical knowledge, with its *logos*, its logic, its rational and scientific order. And theoretical knowledge is, at least in its dominant figure, a seeing, a theatrical *theorein*, a gaze cast onto a visible ob-ject, a primarily *optical* experience that aims to touch with the eyes what falls under the hand, under the scalpel—and this optical model can be a sovereign autopsy, as in the case of the great elephant autopsied, inspected, dissected under the gaze of Louis XIV during the ceremony or lesson of anatomy in 1681.

373

Why recall these obvious facts that one would be within one's rights to judge trivial?

For *two reasons* at least, besides the one that is always *de rigueur* for whoever philosophizes or would simply like to know what he's saying and what people are talking about, namely the good reason there is to try to know what is meant by the knowledge in question.

What does "knowledge" mean? What is it to "know"?[1]

Before even pretending to think the possibility or not of an *absolute knowledge*, don't we have to know, absolutely, in its absoluteness, i.e. in general, before any other determination, the meaning of the word or the experience that is so imperturbably called "knowledge"? Knowledge in general? Whatever is it, to know? And what if "the beast and the sovereign" were not only one example among others to put to the test the suspended and openmouthed astonishment thus figured in the form "Er, what is it — knowledge?" And what if "the beast and the sovereign" were primarily an incitement, a provocation not only to know, but to know knowledge otherwise or for the first time or, more precisely, to *think* knowledge, to determine it, and thus also to reconnoiter it and so know its limits? What could that mean, to know the limits of knowledge?

Against the background of this general horizon, which will constantly border but also un-border, will exceed our procedure and proceeding, I was saying that there are at least two specific reasons for recalling obvious facts that some would quite rightly judge to be extremely banal.

First. Without returning either broadly or minutely to what we have already done, one of the movements or gestures that we have learned to recognize, in its possibility as well as in its necessity, on reading together Celan's "Meridian" (its animals, its monkey figure, its marionettes, its Medusa head, all its heads, all its decapitations, its questions on art, its "perhaps's" on the *pas* of poetry, its revolutions in the revolution, its displacements, the *Gegenwort* and the *Atemwende* of the cries of "Long live the King" and then its disqualifications of sovereign majesty, etc., its thinking of the encounter, the "secret of the encounter," the abyss (*Abgrund*), *Unheimlichkeit,* the Strange, etc.), [one of the movements or gestures that we have learned to recognize, in its possibility as well as in its necessity] was precisely the *pas*, the movement of a *pas* that consists in suspending with a "who knows" (*wer weiss*) and with so many "perhaps's" (*veilleicht*), [suspending] the order and the authority of a sure knowledge, precisely, a knowledge sure of itself, determined and

---

1. [Translator's note:] In French, the word *savoir* is both the infinitive of the verb "to know" and the noun meaning "knowledge."

determining, and this not to produce an apology for obscurity, praise of nonknowledge, or to give oneself over to some improper propaganda in favor of obscurantism, but to begin to think the order of knowledge, the delimitation of knowledge — and to think that, perhaps, neither thought nor poetry was to be reduced to it *without* remainder, to this order of knowledge, precisely at the point where sovereign majesty and a certain bestiality consisted in a superlative upping, in an excess or a *hubris* of the more, the *more than*; of the absolute more, going outside the law to make the law. All the "perhaps's" that multiplied in order to do right by, and justice to, the possibility of the *pas* and advent of the event, all the "who knows's" that liberated, cleared, disengaged by wagering [*dégageaient, désengageaient en la gageant*] the possibility of thinking poetically the event of an *Atemwende* and a revolution in the revolution, all those "perhaps's" and that "who knows" without facility and without concession were inviting us, without ordering us, to go over the limit of knowledge, to go over — were it only in order to know and to know knowledge — the limit of knowledge, and especially of that figure of knowledge that is called the sure certainty of the *ego cogito*, of the present and indivisible punctuality of the *ego cogito* or the living present that claims to escape, precisely, in its absolute certainty, from the "perhaps" and the "who knows." The fact that this movement should take place on a revolutionary and ultrarevolutionary, political and ultrapolitical stage, on which kings were next to monkeys, Medusa heads, and marionettes, made us think that these "perhaps's" and this "who knows" were raised, motivated, inspired as close as can be to our linking or separating hyphen between "the beast *and* the sovereign."

Second, the second reason: in the improbable and even undecidable wake of a *perhaps* that would discern between the possible-im-possible and power, we have the presentiment, or even the suspicion, that the order of *knowledge* is never a stranger to that of *power*, and that of *power* [*pouvoir*] to that of *seeing* [*voir*], willing [*vouloir*], and having [*avoir*]. It is not original but it is not false, no doubt, to recall that the scene of knowledge, and especially of knowledge in the form of the objectivity of the ob-ject, of the knowledge that has what it knows or wants to know at its disposal in the form of an object disposed before it — [that this scene of autopsic/autoptic knowledge] supposes that one disposes, that one poses before oneself, and that one has taken power over the object of knowledge.

Without wanting or needing to deploy here in all its scope the immense question of the ontological determination of the entity as ob-ject (cf. Heidegger versus Husserl, etc. Develop at length), nor even the question of the existential analytic in the style of Heidegger, which would distinguish between several types of entity (*Da-sein, Zuhandensein, Vorhandensein*) of which only the *Vorhanden-sein* (what is before, there, to hand, in reach) could be called object, I shall recall only the crucial difficulty that there is in situating in Heidegger an ontology of the living being, and a thought of animality (to which I hope one day to return at as great a length as is necessary), I shall set off again here from the difficulty that there is in Heidegger, in *Sein und Zeit* and elsewhere, in situating not only the animal but the dead body in the field of the three types of entity. The dead body of the living being, animal or man, is strictly speaking neither *Dasein* nor *Zuhandensein* nor *Vorhandensein* . . . No more is the living animal, as such, as living, the beast, either *Dasein,* or *Vorhandensein*, or *Zuhandensein*.

376

So I shall set off, instead of opening wide again the windows of these immense questions, I shall set off or approach by narrowing the angle, from the dead body of the animal or the dead body of the beast, to ask again the question of knowledge as wanting-to-be-able [*vouloir-pouvoir*] and first of all as wanting-to-see [*vouloir-voir*] and *wanting-to-have* [*vouloir-avoir*]. Knowledge is sovereign; it is of its essence to want to be free and all-powerful, to be sure of power and to have it, to have possession and mastery of its object. And this is why, as you had understood, I began and ended last time with a dead body, an immense dead body, by pushing this huge dead body onto the stage or the table of this seminar, and by quoting this dated scene of an anatomy lesson in the seventeenth century, one among so many others, so many other well-known pictures, where this time the dead body in the picture is animal and not human: I'm speaking, then, of the picture of the dissection of an elephant *under* the orders and *under* the gaze of the greatest of kings, His Majesty Louis le Grand. The beast and the sovereign is here the beast as dead ob-ject, an enormous, heavy body under the gaze and at the disposal of the absolute knowledge of an absolute monarch. Ellenberger says:

> Loisel tells the famous story of the ceremonial dissection [hang on to this word "ceremonial," which implies more than a scientific experiment: it also has elements of cult, ritual, celebration, and festival, of a festive and vaguely funereal wake] of an elephant in 1681, an event which the Sun King deigned to honor with his presence: "Never perhaps was there a more *imposing*[2] anatomical dissection, judged by the enormity of the animal, by

---

2. [Translator's note:] The French translation of Ellenberger that Derrida is using renders "imposing" here as *éclatante*, "glittering," and Derrida comments: "hang on to this word 'glittering,' which we shall encounter again among other glitters [*éclats*]." *Éclat* also means radiance, sparkle, or glare. See n. 25 below.

the precision with which its several parts were examined, or by the quality and number of assistants."[3]

Four remarks on this point before going any further.

1. We have in spite of everything, faced with this scene, this picture im-   377
mobilized under the eye of a painter, the striking impression of a hand-to-
hand combat [*un corps à corps*]. Hand-to-hand between whom and whom,
whom and what? First, between two very great bodies, the beast and the
sovereign, of course. Between two immense living beings first of all: the
king of kings, the greatest of kings, Louis le Grand, and the greatest animal.
Next, this hand-to-hand is a duel, or rather the end, the aftermath, of a duel
(a warlike duel, perhaps, or unconsciously amorous, therefore narcissistic,
after a scene of seduction, hunt, or capture, captation or predation). The
scientific scene, the scene of knowledge, takes place in the aftermath, or the
day after, the defeat of one of the two living beings, on a battlefield but also
<on> the magnetic field of a narcissistic attraction that opposed the two
great living beings, the one surviving and the other become cadaveric object at the disposal of the other, at the hand of the other, manipulable by the
other, captive of the other after having been captured by the great king or
his servants, soldiers or merchants, in the course of expeditions.

2. This scene of knowledge is as *phenomenal* as the elephant. This is a phenomenal beast, a phenomenal elephant, i.e. an object that appears, in its
phainesthai, to the gaze not only of the learned observers but of a Sun King,
a king of light and a source of light, a king who is the condition of possibility of appearing and of knowledge, a phenomenological, phenomeno-
poetical, phenomeno-political king, source and producer of light who, from
most high, like Plato's Good, sun, and *agathon*, gives being and appearing to
things. Here, everything is subject to the Sun King, knowledge, and being,
and the phenomenal elephant is both subject and object under the king's
gaze. The king keeps, owns, has in his possession the immense beast, he
has the immense cadaver at his disposal, like an object for his power, for his
knowledge, for his having and his seeing, and for his pleasure [*pour son pouvoir, pour son savoir, pour son avoir et pour son voir, et pour son bon vouloir*].

3. This setup (wanting to have the power to see and to know [*vouloir avoir
le pouvoir de voir et de savoir*]—and you can manipulate this chain in <all>
directions), is mediated by institutions. This whole scene of dissection and   378

3. Loisel, quoted by Ellenberger in "The Mental Hospital and the Zoological Garden," p. 64. Derrida's emphasis.

anatomy lesson (an anatomy lesson that always presupposes some cadaver subject to the hand, the instrument and the gaze of man; anatomical inspection always presupposes some cadaver docile to autopsy) unfolds under the authority of an Academy of Sciences, itself created, like the Académie française, by a sovereign monarch. To whom it remains very docilely subjected. And the other institution of the same power is the one that was put in place fewer than twenty years before the spectacular and theatrical dissection of the elephenomenelephant, namely the Menagerie of Versailles instituted in 1662. One thinks of this elephenomenelephant that was no longer looking at them but that could have seen them, with its own eyes seen the king see it in its own autopsy.

4. Finally, as I suggested with a quotation last week, the structure of this setup of knowing-power, power-to-know, knowing-how-to-see, and sovereign being-able-to-see is not, fundamentally, revolutionized by the French Revolution. It is not interrupted, and at the death of the king one can still say: "The King is dead, long live the King!" One has simply changed sovereigns. The sovereignty of the people or of the nation merely inaugurates a new form of the same fundamental structure. The walls are destroyed, but the architectural model is not deconstructed — and will, as you will see, continue to serve as a model and even as an international model. The destruction of the menagerie of Versailles is only an episode, a simple transfer of power, since Bernadin de Saint-Pierre, who was the intendant of the King's Garden, had the debris transported and proposed that a new establishment be founded. I recalled last time that a report was then ordered by the Paris Society for Natural History, and written among others — which as we shall see is far from being insignificant — by the alienist Pinel. This report, written at the height of the Revolution, in 1792, concluded:

> A menagerie like those that princes and kings are accustomed to maintain is nothing but a costly and unnecessary imitation of Asiatic pomp [we shall see shortly, or next time, why "Asiatic": the point is, then, for the Revolution, to put an end to the luxury and idleness of the rich, which does not entail putting an end to the popular curiosity of all, but also to bend to European and Western rationality a monarchy that was supposedly merely aping the Asian despots]; but we think that a menagerie without frills [a democratic and popular menagerie, then, a popular-democratic menagerie, secular and republican, in conformity with the new sovereignty, that of nation and people] could be extremely useful to natural history, to physiology and to the economy.[4]

379

4. Quoted by Ellenberger in ibid., p. 65.

So one moves from luxury and useless expense, one transitions from sump-
tuary beasts to useful beasts, to a viable and profitable menagerie: profitable
to knowledge but also profitable, as you've just heard, to economy, economy
as knowledge, first, no doubt, as theory of economy, that of the physiocrats,
for example, but also to economy pure and simple — economy, *oiko-nomia,*
the *nomos* of the *oikos*, i.e. the law of the house; once again I emphasize this
not out of a concern for semantics or etymology, but because in this reform
of the zoo, the zoological garden, and the zoological in general, not to speak,
as we shall in a moment, of circuses and private houses [and in any case we
shall see that zoological gardens, even when they are instituted for the purpose of knowledge or for the protection of animals, have in common with
circuses that, being open to the public, they are also places of spectacle, the-
aters — as, indeed, were insane asylums for a long time] — *oikonomia*, then;
for the ecological or economic concerns will pass through a know-how that
consists in furnishing a house, a habitat for beasts in a process that oscillates,
sometimes accumulating them simultaneously, between domestication (and
thus appropriation to the laws of the family home, the *domus*, the house of
the master [*dominus*], or the mistress — *domus, Heim, home*, domesticity),
taming, training, stock raising, so many modalities of master and sovereign
power, power and knowledge, knowing how to, knowing in order to see
and seeing in order to know and to be able, having [*du pouvoir et du savoir,
du savoir pouvoir, du savoir pour voir et du voir pour savoir et pour pouvoir,
de l'avoir*], possession, appropriation, and the property of beasts (through
capture, h,unting, raising, commerce, enclosure), *oikonomia* also being the
general condition of this *ipseity* as sovereign mastery over the beast, in this
one and the same experience that binds together, with the beast, power,
knowledge, seeing, and having [*le pouvoir, le savoir, le voir et l'avoir*]. The
fields of knowledge that were supposed to benefit from this new institution
thus went well beyond zoology in the narrow sense. As, moreover, was the
case in the anatomy lessons under the gaze of the sovereign Louis le Grand,
the interest was not only anatomical knowledge that had become accessible
under the skin of the pachyderm subject to dissection, was not only physio-
zoological knowledge as to the functioning of the animal organism, but was
already a comparative knowledge that was to clarify the analogies between
human anatomy and physiology and animal physiology. This is already a
real anthropo-zoology. (When I was a student in ethnology, there was a discipline and an examination at the Musée de l'Homme, where I was working
then, that bore the strange name of zoological anthropology: it was a field of
comparative knowledge in which one studied the analogies and the differences between anthropoid apes and men. One of the exercises, for example,
consisted in being able to distinguish — it was sometimes difficult — to dis-

tinguish between, on the one hand, a male or female skull, dolichocephalic or brachycephalic, prognathic or not, with or without a supra-orbital brow ridge, and, on the other, skulls of male or female chimpanzees; or between shoulder blades, femurs, or teeth of various species, races, sexes, and ages.)

This comparative concern was certainly not absent from the institutional places and the experiments of prerevolutionary zoology. In the dissection of the great elephant under the gaze of Louis le Grand, a scene around which we ought to sojourn much longer (imagine, just imagine, think about it, represent it—for all this is a representation [*une représentation*: also, "a performance"]—represent to yourselves the enormous, heavy, poor beast, dead or killed I know not how, dragged in from I know not where on its side or its back into a luxurious room, a beast no doubt bloody, among doctors, surgeons, or other armed butchers, impatient to show what they could do but just as impatient to see and give to be seen what they were going to see, trembling with lust for autopsy, ready to get to work, to get their hands, scalpels, axes, or knives onto the great defenseless body in spite of its ivory tusks [*défenses:* literally, "defenses"] still intact, and its detumescent trunk, at the moment that the little king, who was not as big as his name implied, the king smaller than his name, smaller too than his huge hat, which we know well, doubtless smaller still than a baby elephant, this little king making his entrance in great pomp, with all the crowd and the courtesans, the doctors and the academics bowing to the ground, imagine all that, represent to yourselves this whole ceremony, which we didn't see in the fine film about Louis XIV,[5] you know, a film to which we should add this episode, the dissection, done with great pomp and sovereignly academic, of probably the largest beast on earth: an episode, a political picture, that in any case remains more interesting and greater, of a type to spoil the appetite for sovereignty that always slumbers in us, more interesting, greater, then, so much more stylish that a Salon of Agriculture at the Porte de Versailles, well, well, the Porte de Versailles . . . , a Salon of Agriculture in the midst of an election campaign,[6] when those pretending to the throne, of all [political] families (for the thing is more familial than ever) [when those pretending to the throne, of all [political] families] stroke the cows' rear end (consenting cows, of course, as thieves and rapists always say, by definition)

381

5. Probably an allusion to Rossellini's *Rise of Louis XIV.*

6. [Translator's note:] The Salon de l'agriculture is an annual, highly mediatized event in French cultural and political life. March 2002, when Derrida gave this session, was also the height of the French presidential election campaign, during which a visit to the Salon was *de rigueur* for all the candidates.

and walk around candidly, candidately among the stands, their mouths full of foie gras, beer, presidential *pâté de campagne* ["country pâté"; also, literally, "campaign pâté"], their mouths also full of verbiage, which never stops them from stuffing themselves and kissing babies, in a crowd in which it would be harder than ever to tell a beast from a sovereign). In this dissection of the great elephant under the luminous gaze of Louis le Grand, the point was also no doubt to recognize in this great cadaver, right in the open body of a giant animal whose consent no one ever asked and who is at the mercy of the surgeons, of their scalpels, their gazes — [the point was also no doubt to recognize] in this great animal (great but not the king of the animals, the lion) — to recognize anatomo-physiological analogies: the brain, the heart, the kidneys, the circulation of the blood, etc.

To reconstitute properly all these historical possibilities, we should have to go in many directions, well beyond what we would have time to do here. First, and minimally, into the analysis of what in this way makes visible an animal being, a *zōon* henceforth lifeless but previously alive, the submissive cadaver laid out, exposed, carved up, explored, the cadaver of one of the greatest, if not the greatest, animal in the world and, opposite, a little above it no doubt, the living body of a king who holds himself to be the greatest in the world; the living body of a king, then, but also the mortal body of a king who has at his disposal another body, that double body (earthly[7] and mortal, and celestial, sublime, eternal, that of the function or the majesty, of the royal sovereignty supposed to survive eternally the mortal body — and sovereignty always presupposes this, in some way or another and in general, a priori, I would say, because it is in the structure of the concept of sovereignty, [sovereignty always presupposes] that double body the structure of which Kantorowicz analyzed in *The King's Two Bodies*[8] (195<7>), the double body that the Revolution naïvely thought it could end by decapitating the terrestrial body of Louis Capet. So I refer you to Kantorowicz and to the earlier book by Marc Bloch, *Les rois thaumaturges* (1924),[9] about those theories of canon law that distinguish two persons and thereby two bodies in the person of the sovereign, the "personal person," as it were, and as it was indeed called, the *persona personalis* of the mortal king, and the "ideal

7. The parenthesis opened here does not close in the typescript.

8. Ernst Kantorowicz, *The King's Two Bodies: A Study in Mediaeval Political Theology* (Princeton: Princeton University Press, 1957).

9. Marc Bloch, *Les rois thaumaturges* (1924; Paris: Gallimard, 1983); trans. J. E. Anderson as *The Royal Touch: Sacred Monarchy and Scrofula in England and France* (London: Routledge and Kegan Paul, 1973).

person," the *persona idealis,* of the immortal king.[10] These two persons and these two bodies are united during life but separated after death, as are the "dignity" of the king during his lifetime and the "sovereignty" or the "majesty" of the king that survives him and is inherited from one king to another. There is a royal dignity, exercised in the present, the *regia dignitas,* and there is a royal majesty, *regia Maiestas,*[11] that survives and is inherited, as sovereign function, from king to king. But during the lifetime of the king, the two bodies, the two royalties, the personal and the ideal, dignity and majestic sovereignty, are united. Well, the king who was present at the ritual and ceremonial dissection of the great animal and deigned to honor it with his presence was present in his two bodies and his two capacities, he was present in person but in his double person, his duplicitous person, present as *persona personalis* and as *persona idealis,* in his dignity but also in his majesty, and thus in his sovereignty.

One must not forget that at the same moment — read Louis Marin on this subject, especially "Du sublime à l'obscène" and "La césure du corps royal," in *Lectures traversières*[12] — [one must not forget that at the same moment] the king's doctors were busy around his suffering body, his *persona personalis,* his moral and threatened person, on the lookout for every symptom, daily studying his excrements, sweats, humors, even keeping a journal of the king's health that can still be consulted, which is entitled *Journal de la santé du Roi Louis XIV de l'année 1647 à l'année 1711.* These archives are under the responsibility of the Société des Sciences morales, des lettres et des arts de Seine-et-Oise. The king's doctors looked after the king's body as two bodies at once. They were looking after the king's body both as the body of a respected, admired, venerated, feared, all-powerful, and omniscient God, and as the objective, objectified, coldly regarded and inspected body of an animal with irresponsible reactions (one cannot help but think of the role and discourse, and sometimes the publications of such doctors at or after the death of our presidents of the Republic, Pompidou and Mitterrand).[13] When I say that they were looking after and over the body of the king, I mean it literally since they kept vigil even over his sleep, when the king, supposed to see and know everything, to have all power and have everything [*tout voir*

10. See Kantorowicz, *The King's Two Bodies,* p. 400.

11. Ibid., p. 408.

12. Louis Marin, *Lectures traversières* (Paris: Albin Michel, 1992), pp. 171–78 and 179–93.

13. [Translator's note:] French presidents Georges Pompidou and François Mitterrand both notoriously had serious health problems that were concealed from the public during their terms of office.

et tout savoir, et tout pouvoir et tout avoir], could no longer see them, his own doctors, seeing him. Just this one passage from the *Journal de la santé du Roi Louis XIV,* describing the Sun King's unsettled nights, provides evidence: (Read and comment)

> His sleep, amid so much good health, was always agitated and unquiet, a little more than ordinary, speaking often and even sometimes rising from the bed, which was to me a convincing indication of some heated bile as well as the effect of the great affairs he decided during the day and the images of which would return during the night and awaken the actions of the soul during the repose of the body [. . .]. One must add to this the heat of his intestines as a disposition of the subject very susceptible to being shaken at the slightest occasion [. . .] heated face, heaviness of head and nonchalance of the whole body, chagrin even and melancholy without reason, accidents [. . .] the causes of which are contracted by the little rest he allows himself, awake too long and sleeping insufficiently for a man whose mind is as active as his.[14]

I also encourage you to read Louis Marin's *Le portrait du roi,*[15] especially the chapter "Le récit du roi ou comment écrire l'histoire." It is of course still about Louis le Grand. Although Marin, to my knowledge, does not discuss the relation to animals, or the elephant autopsy, or the menagerie at Versailles, he nonetheless provides many fascinating and illuminating details for the perception and analysis of the many implications of this extraordinary scene. Since I've just said that Marin provides details that are "illuminating," that cast light on this optical, autoptical scene, which, I recall, makes use of an absolute power over the beast with a view to seeing and knowledge, in the name, at bottom, of Enlightenment, but of light, always that of the Sun King, light that in the end never dissociates theoretical observation in the service of knowledge, here for example the optics of the autopsy—[never dissociates it] from spectacle, theater, ceremony as representation, and representation as representation *of* the king (a double genitive again), both the spectacular representation given by the king, ordered by him, organized by him in view of himself, and the representation *of* the king that represents the king, that presents him, shows him in his portrait, or recounts him in action. And I would say, under the title "the beast and the sovereign," that the ceremony of the dissection of the elephant, the im-

385

---

14. Marin, *Lectures traversières*, p. 173. *Journal de la santé du Roi Louis XIV de l'année 1647 à l'année 1711* (Société des Sciences morales, des lettres et des arts de Seine-et-Oise, 1862), year 1673, p. 117; year 1680, p. 135.

15. Louis Marin, *Le portrait du roi* (Paris: Éditions de Minuit, 1981).

mense anonymous beast, that act that Loisel calls, precisely, a "ceremony," is indeed such a representation; it is designed — showing the elephant and the learned subjects of the king, the doctors, anatomists, academicians — to show the king in a picture, but also to enrich the archive of a narrative on the body and actions, the splendor or the effulgence of the Sun King.

From this point of view, I will select from Marin's book *Le portrait du roi*, and from the chapter entitled "Le récit du roi ou comment écrire l'histoire," [The Narrative of the King or How to Write History] certain passages that, revolving around the work and *Project* of the king's appointed historian (Pélisson, official historiographer, author of a *Project for the History of Louis XIV* addressed to Colbert) — I will select, then, what Pélisson calls the "delicious spectacle" that he intends to offer the reader-spectator of his history of the Sun King.[16] The point is to behave as though the spectacle, as it were, when read, were taking place from the point of view of absolute knowledge, as though the reader knew in advance what was going to happen, since everything is known in advance by the king. And here is the return of the marionette that I did not want to miss out, because as soon as there is absolute knowledge, everything happens as though it were known in advance and therefore all but programmed, providentially prescribed (for the Sun King, the sovereign who sees and knows and fore-sees everything is in essence pro-vidential, and he pre-writes, pre-describes as much as he prescribes), and as soon as there is such a providential pre-vision, everything moves as though mechanically, everything unwinds as one unwinds or holds tight on to a string, and thereby on to a marionette. And the point would be, in such a history, for the historiographer of this history of the sovereign to create in the reader-spectator (and thus in the king's subject) the simulacrum, the illusion, that he is the one who is pulling the strings of the marionette of history (remember that in Büchner, too, the revolutionaries admitted at a certain moment that they felt themselves manipulated by history like marionettes).

Marin writes, on the subject of this effect of mastery and sovereignty:

> The pleasure of reading is born in this contrariness, this coming and going between the representation and what is represented: a rhythm of expectation-foresight and surprise-novelty; surprising familiarity, foreknowledge of the known; desire of mastery and power accomplishing itself in the imaginary of reading; pleasure-trap of the narrative. Everything happens *as if* [Marin's "as if's," so judicious and lucid, once provoked impatience in a classical

386

16. [Translator's note:] The translation of this sentence reflects the syntactic incompleteness of the original French.

historian: what do all these "as if's" mean, they mean nothing for a historian, a historian knows what really happened, what really happened or didn't happen, but never "what happens as if," never "everything happens as if": did it really happen or not? That's what interests the historian: this historian was, I won't say *bête*, a little *bête*, but deaf and blind to all the fabulous "as if's" that effectively, performatively make history: back to the quotation from Marin]—[everything happens *as if*] the spectator-reader were himself pulling the strings of the mannequin-marionette that the narrator has given him, *as if* he were presiding over the historical destiny of the characters, as though he were bringing about sovereignly, necessarily, the chances and contingencies of their actions, *as if* [my emphasis again], like the Platonic gods, he were pulling the strings of the mannequins in the story, and at each gesture of the marionette he discovered—divine surprise of contingency—the effect of his own act.[17]

What Marin is suggesting, if I am interpreting or rather following and extending him appropriately, is that the narrative or the representation here don't come *after* the event, to report, recount, depict, or represent the providential power of the sovereign, but that the narrative and this representation are a structural part of this sovereignty, its constitutive structure, its dynamic or energetic essence, its force, its *dynamis,* or even its dynasty. But also the *energeia*, which means the act, actuality, but also the *enargeia*, which means a certain effulgence of evidence, a certain shining that we shall talk about again. Fiction is the *dynamis* and the dynasty of the dynast, but also the radiant *energeia* and *enargeia* of his actions, his powers, his potency. His possibility and his power: both virtual and actual. Hidden and visible. There would be no sovereignty without this representation. The illusion or fiction to which the reading or watching subject is subjected are the very exercise and effect of sovereign power to which they are subject as subjects of the king. Sovereignty is this narrative fiction or this effect of representation. Sovereignty draws all its power, all its potency, i.e. its all-powerful nature, from this simulacrum-effect, this fiction- or representation-effect that is inherent and congenital to it, as it were co-originary. Which means that, and this is a paradox, by giving the reading or watching subject of the narrative representation the illusion of himself pulling sovereignly the strings of history or of the marionette, the mystification of representation is constituted by this simulacrum of a true transfer of sovereignty. The reader, the spectator of this "history of the king" has the illusion of knowing everything in advance, of sharing absolute knowledge with the king, and of

387

17. Ibid., pp. 80–81. Derrida's emphasis on each "as if."

himself producing the story that is being recounted to him. He participates in sovereignty, a sovereignty he shares or borrows. This is also what Marin regularly calls the trap, the trap narrative, which is also, I would say, the very trap of sovereignty, of shared sovereignty, and it will later be the trap of the transfer of sovereignty of the monarch to that of the nation or the people. The trial of the king and his decapitation would be, in my opinion or according to one of the readings I would be tempted to propose, one of these transfers of sovereignty, a transfer that is at one and the same time fictional, narrative, theatrical, representational, performative, which does not for all that prevent it from being terribly effective and bloody. In all these deployments of ceremonial representation and theatrical cult, in all these simulacra, blood flows nonetheless, no less cruelly and no less irreversibly — the blood of the elephant like the blood of the absolute monarch. The beast and the sovereign bleed, even marionettes bleed.

388

As for the transfer of sovereignty, for example, the revolution as transfer of sovereignty, however violent and bloody it might be as a taking of power (and a political revolution that was not a revolution of the political and a poetic revolution in the nonrestrictive sense I was defining the other day — a political revolution without a poetic revolution of the political is never more than a transfer of sovereignty and a handing over of power) — what I am here designating as transfer of sovereignty clearly situates the essential features of the problem. If most often what is at stake in politics and wherever else a drive to power is exercised (*Bemächtigungstrieb,* as Freud calls it, before or beyond the other drives and the death drive), a drive to power that orders even the drive to see and to know, the scopic and epistemophilic drive — [if most often what is at stake in politics and wherever else a drive to power is exercised] is not only an alternative between sovereignty and nonsovereignty but also a struggle *for* sovereignty, transfers and displacements or even divisions of sovereignty, then one must begin not from the pure concept of sovereignty but from concepts such as drive, transference, transition, translation, passage, division. Which also means inheritance, transmission, and along with that the division, distribution, and therefore the economy of sovereignty. Economy is a distributive division not merely because of the *oikos* of which it is the law, but because the law (*nomos, nemein*) also means division. Rather than on sovereignty itself, which at bottom perhaps never exists as such, as purely and simply itself, since it is only a hyperbolic excess beyond everything — and so it is nothing, a certain nothing (whence its affinity with effects of fiction and simulacrum) — [rather than on sovereignty itself], it is on these properly mediate words and concepts, impure like middles or mixtures (words and concepts such as transfer, translation, transition, tradition, inheritance, economic distribution, etc.) that we must bring the charge of the question and of decisions that are always median, medial transactions, negotiations in a relation of force between drives to power that are essentially divisible.

For in fact, as we know well, wherever—today more than ever but for a long time now—wherever we think we are up against problems of sovereignty, as if we had to choose between sovereignism and antisovereignism, whether it occurs in sophisticated debates in political or juridical theory or else in the rhetoric of the local café or the Salon of Agriculture, the question is not that of sovereignty or nonsovereignty but that of the modalities of transfer and division of a sovereignty said to be indivisible—said and supposed to be indivisible but always divisible.

If I emphasize the scene, the picture, the theater, the visibility of the autopsy, the autoptic of the elephant, I do so because we are dealing with what I called so long ago, in a 1963 text on Lévinas, a "violence of light."[18] The blood I've just been speaking about always shines in the light, in the *enargeia* of seeing and knowing. There too, read Marin, especially what you will find in the same chapter under the subtitles "Shining(s): The place of the king," and "Scopic Machinations."[19]

Marin's demonstration insists on the major concern of the future historiographer of the king, of the future-perfect historiographer of the king, as I would say. Pellisson wants to define and describe the "place of the king," and this "place of the king" must be a place that should shine or from which the character of the king should shine in the sense of a resplendence or explosion of light, of *enargeia*: fulguration of the sun, splendor of the eye, the Sun King should appear for what he is, in his narratives, i.e. a source of light but a source that one cannot look at directly, any more than one can look at the sun (as Plato already said). "The portrait of the king," says Marin, "is not only the sun in the central place of the narrative, it is also light spread everywhere, posed in splendor on everything and everyone, *making* them be seen."[20]

Here, as he does several times, Marin refers to Descartes, here to the fifth part of the *Discourse on Method* and the *Dioptrics*, but I think—this would

389

390

18. Jacques Derrida, "Violence et métaphysique: Essai sur la pensée d'Emmanuel Levinas," in *L'écriture et la différence* (Paris: Seuil, 1967), pp. 125ff.; trans. Alan Bass as "Violence and Metaphysics," in *Writing and Difference* (Chicago: University of Chicago Press, 1978), pp. 79–153 (p. 117).

19. Marin, *Le portrait du roi*, pp. 81–91.

20. Ibid., p. 81.

be my suggestion, at any rate—that one would have to coordinate all this, everything we're talking about here, with very many other historical developments, well beyond what we can do here, coordinate it all not only with the entire history of medicine, of anatomical painting and drawing of the human body at that time and previously (think of Leonardo da Vinci and all the *Anatomy Lessons*, the two, for example, that Rembrandt painted twenty years apart, including the 1632 one, I believe, of Professor Nicholas Tulp—anatomy lessons often represented with a science book in sight and replacing the Bible in the painting, and remember that Rembrandt, the painter of these anatomy lessons, also painted so many animals, flayed oxen, for example, presented like the body of Christ, etc.), coordinate with all this and with the Cartesian moment, and not only with the *Dioptrics* or more still with Descartes' *Treatise on Man,* which, as you know, as though it were an autopsy or an anatomo-physiology, treats the human body as a "machine of earth" that "God forms expressly" and that Descartes compares to machines made by men (clocks, artificial fountains, mills, and "other similar machines"). Particularly interesting and relevant from this point of view and from the point of view of what must be linked up with the autopsy ceremonies that we are interested in would be what concerns the brain, the eye, and above all the circulation of the blood, especially what Descartes calls the "animal spirits,"[21] that very subtle wind, that very quick and pure flame that circulates between the veins, the arteries, the heart, and the brain. Above all, above all (but I won't do it here because I did it elsewhere, although in a still unpublished form (it was a lecture at Cerisy)),[22] the whole theory of animal-machines in Descartes. Read it all, it is accessible and well known, but worth rereading from a political point of view also.

391

In short, Marin is right to emphasize the analogy with the system of Cartesian physics and that "like the sun in the discourse of physics, the portrait of the king is, by itself, the resplendent and privileged moment of the narrative scene, and like Cartesian light, it is also what brings to light and allows the spectator-reader to see all the subjects who are actors in the story by striking them with its radiance [*éclat*]."[23]

Another feature that must be emphasized in the optics of this hyperoptics is, from the point of view of the beast and the sovereign, the motif

21. Descartes, *Traité de l'homme*, in *Oeuvres et Lettres*, ed. André Bridoux (Paris: Gallimard, 1952). The quoted passages are on pp. 807, 814–15, 818–19ff.

22. *L'animal autobiographique,* Colloque de Cerisy, 1997. Subsequently published in Derrida, *L'animal que donc je suis* (see session 1 above, n. 20).

23. Marin, *Le portrait du roi*, p. 81.

of dissymmetry. Or asymmetry. One can push a long way the logic of reflection, of the reflective effects of these lights, gazes, and mirrors. There is a point where the symmetry is broken and where sovereignty is marked by the power to see, by being-able-to-see *without* being seen, what I called elsewhere, in *Spectres of Marx* on the subject of *Hamlet*, the visor-effect.[24] The king or the king's specter sees without his gaze, the origin of his seeing, without his eyes being seen. Here it is the same thing and Marin does not fail to recall this "asymmetry":

> One would be wrong to think that this position puts in return the king into the position of a seen object. In truth it is the opposite. This position is only what it is by being under the gaze of the king, in the optical cone of his eye. [And Marin gives many references to this all-seeing and panoptical eye of the sovereign, in La Bruyère, Racine (in a Discourse given, precisely, at the Académie française in 1685, four years after the autopsy of our elephant), etc.] The gaze of the "I-one" is the plural, indefinite and nonpersonal eye in the sovereign gaze, resplendent sun and fulgurant light [*soleil éclatant et lumière éclatée*] of His Majesty [you see that the word *éclat* bespeaks both the brilliance of the beam [*éclat*] that strikes and, also, the ubiquitous dispersion which disperses or only disperses the better to invade everything].[25] Asymmetrical reciprocity of eyes and gaze, of eyes that see what the king does, says and thinks, and of the gaze that makes them see what he does, says, and thinks: perfect representation without excess or loss in this play of reflections or recognition, in spite of the double polarity of the historical agent and the narrator, but which operates its effects only at the price of the simulation of this spectacle.[26]

392

Marin certainly talks of *autopsy* but not about the working of the anatomy lesson with the violent opening up of the body of a living-dead, an animal or a man, and especially a dead animal. Marin uses the word *autopsy* in what is indeed its original sense, the "seeing by oneself," inspecting with one's own eyes. That's what *autopsia* originally means: the experience that consists in seeing with one's own eyes, and thus of being able to bear witness (and this is the sense to which Marin limits himself when he says that Pellisson is inspired by the "ancient demand of autopsy as guarantee of the

---

24. [Translator's note:] See Jacques Derrida, *Spectres de Marx* (Paris: Galilée, 1993), pp. 26–27; trans. Peggy Kamuf as *Spectres of Marx* (London: Routledge, 1994), pp. 5–6.

25. [Translator's note:] The French word *éclat* can mean a shining or a brilliance, but also a shard or a fragment. The verb *éclater* can mean to shine out, but also to break up or explode.

26. Marin, *Le portrait du roi*, pp. 87–88.

authenticity of the narrative of the past event and the absent place," making the narrator a "witness" or even a "martyr"[27] (originally the same thing).

But *autopsia* later acquired *two meanings* in Greek, which Marin has the right not to take into account but we for our part must take seriously:

1. A rare meaning, that of a participation in the all-powerfulness of the gods and an intimate commerce with them;
2. A meaning that became current and even dominant, like a metonymy or an authorized abbreviation, the meaning we are using here to designate the ceremony of dissection, namely the autopsy of a cadaver. Littré says that it is an improper use, and that one ought to say "cadaveric autopsy" or "necropsy."

What amuses me here (assuming I am amused), in the virtual play between these two last meanings, is that in the autopsy of the elephant, where it is the gaze of the greatest of kings, of the sovereignissimus, that directly and indirectly sees the cadaver of the greatest of beasts, a cadaver that also represents the mortal animal that is one of the bodies of the king, there is, in all the meanings, autopsy (in the third sense) as resplendent and reflecting participation, autopsy in the second sense, a symbolic and fictional and phantasmatic division of all-powerfulness, that of the dead elephant as well as that of the eternal, but also sur-viving and mortal, king. This dead elephant, put to death or held at bay, because of being dead, by the king, is also to some extent, in this necropsy, the denied, averted, vaguely totemic representation of the dead king, the mortal king, the king dead from a death of the king that everyone both fears and hopes for, and that every subject projects into the autopsy or the necropsy of sovereignty. A funeral oration whose refrain never ceases: Long live the king, the king is dead long live the king the king is dead long live the king the king is dead. A funeral oration that resounds from the century of Louis XIV to the Revolution to Büchner to Lucile and to Lenz.

Remember that other throne [*chaire*] from which a Bossuet delivered, ex cathedra, his autoptic funeral orations. Instead of quoting funeral orations by the great Bossuet—the theorist of Providence, don't forget—I prefer to re-cite a passage from one of his sermons on the duties of kings, which Marin quoted at the beginning of his book. So far we have been speaking of an indissociable chain, the chain *pouvoir, voir, savoir, avoir*: it was missing the *devoir* [as a noun: duty; as a verb: to have to, to owe], it was necessary to have to name *devoir*.

27. Ibid., p. 89.

Let me recall first that Marin, just before quoting Bossuet and Pascal, proposes to add, as it were, another body to the king's two bodies, the theory of which was made famous by Kantorowicz. In classical absolutism, suggests Marin, the king's body is divided or multiplied by *three*:

1. The historical and physical body, and thus the mortal body, the one around which the king's doctors (but also subjects and mistresses) busy and concern themselves;
2. The juridical and political body (in sum, I would say, though Marin does not put it like this, the body of the sovereign in the strict state and political sense);
3. Finally, the semiotic sacramental body, this third body being the one that primarily interests Marin since, through the portrait of the king (that's why he calls it semiotic: you know Marin's fine work on portraits and medals), [through the portrait of the king] the sacramental body is supposed to ensure the exchange, "without remainder," says Marin, between the three bodies.

394

For my part, I would suggest that this sacred or sacramental body, sworn in and legitimated by God himself, by divine sovereignty itself, is indeed the place of exchange, the pact or alliance between the politico-juridical sovereignty of terrestrial all-powerfulness and the celestial sovereignty of the all-powerful God. In any case, having put forward the hypothesis of these three bodies, Marin quotes in support of his conjecture the following texts by Bossuet and Pascal. As they are very beautiful and say what is essential as to the structures and laws that matter to us here, I shall read them: (Read and comment)

> In 1662, in his sermon on the duties of kings, Bossuet exclaims: "To establish this power that represents his power, God places on the forehead of sovereigns and on their face a mark of divinity. [. . .] God has made in the Prince a mortal image of his immortal authority. You are gods, says David, and you are all children of the Most High. But, O gods of flesh and blood, O gods of earth and dust, you will die like men. No matter, you are gods even though you die, and your authority does not die; this spirit of royalty passes entire to your successors and imprints everywhere the same fear, the same respect, the same veneration. Man dies, it is true: but the king, we say, never dies: the image of God is immortal."
>
> A few years earlier, on a little scrap of paper, Pascal had analyzed the mechanisms of the representational apparatus, describing the effects produced and discerning their reasons in the configurations they sketch out on the political, juridical and theological planes: "The custom of seeing kings

accompanied by guards, drums, officers, and all the things that bend the machine toward respect and terror, means that their face, when perchance alone and without these accompaniments, imprints on their subjects respect and terror, because one does not separate in thought their persons from their entourage, seeing them ordinarily together. And society, not knowing that this effect comes from this custom, believes it comes from a natural force; whence these words: 'The character of Divinity is imprinted on his face,'" etc.[28]

395   If the French Revolution, as we have seen, transferred the Menagerie de Versailles as it transferred sovereignty, if it destroyed its reality without deconstructing the model (objective *savoir-pouvoir-avoir à voir*), this old new model (let's call it *autopsic*) became the globalized model of all nineteenth-century zoological gardens. Globalization of the autopsic model, as I call it, charging the attribute "autopsic" with all the features we have emphasized until now: the objectifying inspection of a knowledge that precisely inspects, sees, looks at the aspect of a *zōon* the life and force of which have been neutralized either by death or by captivity, or quite simply by ob-jectification that exhibits there before, to hand, before the gaze, and de-vitalizes by simple objectification, a learned objectification in the academic service of a learned society, certainly, but a society for which, between the autopsic seeing of theoretical knowledge and the autopsic seeing of the theatrical spectacle, between the theoretical and the theatrical, between inspection and spectacle, the passage and transfer are more than tempting, in truth organized and institutionalized, whence the two other senses of *autopsia*: that of the necropsic relation to the cadaver and that of participation in divine power. I am specifying this point before coming to what in this "theoretico-theatrical," let's say *inspectacular* structure, autopsic and objectifying, de-vitalizing, also ensures a certain analogical passage between the modern and postrevolutionary zoological garden and psychiatric institutions, insane asylums. I propose, in order to give a common title to this space of analogy, to make use — reawakening it, reactivating it with a certain inflection — of the word "curiosity." To be curious, *curiosus*, is to be both avid for knowledge — *curiositas*, curiosity, is primarily the desire to know, to see, and to inform oneself — but also to take care, to provide care (*cura*, treatment both domestic and therapeutic, hospital-based), to inspect with care, and to care for. But we know that this curiosity that takes account in taking care can, in its epistemophilic autopsy, or in its hurry to verify its spectating mastery, [it can] degenerate into indiscreet or unwholesome curiosity (*Neugier,*

28. Ibid., p. 21.

Neugierde, as Heidegger would say, Heidegger who, as you know, saw in it an inauthentic form of Dasein's relation to knowledge, in the "They" (*das Man*): see *Sein und Zeit*). And the word *curiosity* (as is the case in both English and French, but not for the Latin *curiositas*) can designate the subject, as it were, as well as the object. One speaks of someone's curiosity, but also of something or someone who becomes a curiosity, a curious thing for the spectator or the enthusiast.

Well, "curiosity" is the word I was looking for to formalize the whole field of analogy that gathers the beast and the madman, in postrevolutionary zoological gardens and insane asylums: they become, in all senses of the words, *curiosities* for the eager, compulsive *curiosity* of, let's say, those who are outside and approach them only to within a certain distance to observe or inspect them in a sovereign manner from outside after having locked them up.

In his article "The Zoological Garden and the Mental Asylum," which I have already quoted, Ellenberger insists a great deal on what he calls a "general comparison" between these two institutions. I shall say in a moment, and no doubt next time too, why I have some reservations as to the philosophy (others would say the ideology) that orients Ellenberger's work, especially in its conclusions, but I shall begin by following him, in my own way, in the material he provides for us. He recalls that the French model (the one I called *autopsic*) became globalized after the Revolution: zoos in London (1829), Amsterdam (1838), Berlin (1844), Anvers (1848), etc. Sometimes subventioned by the state, sometimes the object of a worldwide commerce and speculation, these zoos were places both of study and of popular outings for the Sunday crowds and the curious, who also included artists, draftsmen, and scientists such as Darwin and Galton in London, for example.

What is remarkable in the nineteenth century in the institution of these zoological gardens, and what makes them comparable, up to a certain point, to be determined, with psychiatric hospitals, is that the enclosure that is common to them, the new system of territorial limits and uncrossable frontiers, was not incompatible with the appearance of what I shall call a planning of the menagerie, a certain ecological progress, the economy of a new ecology, an ecosystem that was not without a certain improvement in the living conditions of both animals and the mentally ill. This economy, in the planning of menageries that turned into zoological gardens, was sometimes primarily economy in the capitalistic sense, and a source of revenue for merchants practicing the globalization of the market before the term was invented and two centuries ahead of time. There is the case of a real

396

397

family of animal merchants who also instituted progressive zoological gardens, as it were. A certain Hagenbeck was famous in Germany for furnishing circuses with animals from all around the world (for spectacle and curiosity, for taming and performance: the animals, captured and transported, became curiosities for the curiosity of the curious who wanted and henceforth were able to see and observe them with their own eyes, autoptically), but for furnishing menageries too. His son, Carl Hagenbeck (1844–1913), was a writer, the author of an autobiography entitled *Von Tieren und Menschen* (1908), and he extended his father's business, globalized it further in the tracks of colonization, sending expeditions all over the world. Better still, this writer-merchant was also a founder of institutions and of a school. With the help of a Swiss architect and sculptor, Urs Eggenschwyler, he had the huge zoological park in Hamburg constructed, which became famous, among other reasons, for the system of limits it innovated — or with which it was surrounded, as one surrounds with care by surrounding with limits. It's certainly the concept of care, concern, solicitude, *cura,* that we are talking about here, and the question of knowing whether it's possible to surround with care, as we say, without surrounding with reappropriating limits. Inventing limits, installing limits, that's the art we are speaking of here. And it is an art of both caring and locking up. Between the beast and the sovereign, it's merely a question of limits, and knowing whether a limit is divisible or indivisible. For knowing how to install a limit is both an art and a technique, perhaps *tekhnē* itself. *Tekhnē* is perhaps always an invention of limits. Since the point here is always to limit the freedom of movement of these living beings, the strategy of the Hamburg zoo consisted in transforming the visible form and structure, the phenomenon, the phenomenality of these limits in order to render them all but unnoticeable, thus giving the captive animals the illusion of an autonomy of movement: these new limits, then, are no longer unbreakable metal railings (railings that already limited movement while letting both sides see: so railings were already not an absolute and indivisible limit) [these new limits, then, are no longer unbreakable metal railings] but deep ditches that no longer appear as fences, ditches that disappear as they hollow out, that are formed and appear only hollowly [*en creux*], in sum, and that become negativized, hollowed-out [*en creux*] limits, *in absentia*, as it were, even more uncrossable than railings but as invisible as an interiorized and freely consented-to limit, as if these poor captive and dumb animals had given a consent they never in fact gave to a violence more sure of itself than ever, to what I'll call repressive violence with a liberal, idealist, and spiritualist grimace.

This does not prevent Ellenberger from saying that Hagenbeck was "not

398

only a businessman of genius but knowledgeable in animal psychology, as is indicated by his founding a school for animal trainers," and that his "innovations were adopted by many zoological gardens. The first result was an improvement in the biological condition of animals. Many species that had never reproduced in captivity began to do so in modern zoos."[29]

This question of the reproduction of life will be decisive here, in particular so as to distinguish, in their very analogy, between zoological gardens and psychiatric asylums, at least in the dominant interpretation, in particular that of Ellenberger. In the joint, synchronic, and, up to a point, parallel improvement of the two institutions, the zoological park and the psychiatric hospital, if one allows the beasts to reproduce, one prevents the humans from doing so, at least within the walls of the psychiatric asylums. But let's wait a little.

The culture of curiosity thus organizes the showing of curiosities for curious crowds, but the same culture of curiosity also had ambitions to *treat,* to care for, if not to cure. Or even to liberate by locking up differently. The *cura* of this curious curiosity always hesitated between two forms or two aims of what is always a *treatment.*

Treat, treatment: I propose to privilege this vocabulary of treatment because I find it quite appropriate here, precisely because it is equivocal, appropriate *because of* its equivocality, and this because of a certain essential im-propriety, a certain constitutive ambiguity in an experience of treatment, or even trade [*la traite*] (and the white slave trade obeys an analogous logic), of treatment, tractation, or trade without contract, which consists, precisely, in a strange and equivocal economy, a strange and equivocal ecology that consists in expropriating the other, appropriating the other by depriving the other of what is supposed to be proper to him or her, the other's proper place, proper habitat, *oikos*. And time, Celan would say. For in this *tekhnē* of limits, it is as much a matter of time as of space. Which is also a certain *Unheimlichkeit* in this treatment of the habitat of the other — or even in the concept of treatment in general. Having proposed it, I propose we keep this word *treatment*, and that we keep the two other words we have brought back to themselves, *autopsy* and *curiosity*.

One treats, well or badly, with good or ill treatment, and the treatment can be a therapeutic cure or not. This *cura*, this therapy, can cure or not cure: it can, without curing, produce or not an improvement in the quality of life, even well-being. (You know that there are now shops, boutiques, on the boulevard Saint-Germain for example, that sell, it's written on their

399

29. Ellenberger, "The Mental Hospital and the Zoological Garden," p. 66.

sign, it's their title, that do commerce in "well-being": they are well-being shops, as you can read on their storefronts, not the good life in the Greek ethical sense (*eu zēn*), or for the art of living, but well-being: these are neither pharmacies, nor organic stores for macrobiotic or dietetic products, nor furniture or clothes stores that would allow you to feel better in your skin, but stores which, between body and soul, sell you well-being, unclassifiable products that go from books on sexuality — soft or hard[30] — to so-called essential oils, to advice as to how to avoid back pain, how not to suffer from noise on the plane, etc., to incense and all kinds of massage instruments, etc.: this is neither medicine, nor surgery, nor pharmacy, nor herbalism, nor orthopedy, nor food science, nor psychology or psychoanalysis, it is none of these but slides between all these disciplines, for your well-being.) So one treats, well or badly, according to good treatment or ill treatment, and this treatment can be a therapeutic cure or not: this *cura*, this therapy, might or might not cure, but in any case power treats beasts and the mentally ill, and in any case the treatment, whatever its goals, whether they are openly declared or not, whether beneficial or maleficent, whether they are followed or not by the desired or alleged outcome, consists in enclosing, depriving of freedom of movement and, hence, of freedom itself, hence of power, of power to see, to know, to have beyond certain limits, and hence of sovereignty. By enclosing within idealized limits, or limits in any case that have become less visible, tending to become quasi-internal, by one of those fictions or fables we have been analyzing since the beginning and which are also the element of force, power, violence, and lies, this culture of curiosity, then, also had the ambition or the pretension to treat, to care for, to take great care (*cura*) of what it was enclosing and objectifying and cultivating to ends of enrichment and curiosity.

As I've just been speaking, with regard to enclosure, about the common enclosure of the zoological gardens and psychiatric hospitals of a certain postrevolutionary modernity — [as I have just been speaking] of freedom, of limitation of the freedom of movement, and thus of the freedom to *pouvoir voir savoir*, and thus of sovereignty, I want to emphasize once more, briefly but heavily, this terrible logic.

Which logic?

Well, that of a double bind, the extreme tension, weight, and gravity of which we should not hide from ourselves — a gravity all the heavier and all the harder to exonerate oneself from in that it is at the center, indeed at the center of gravity, of all decisions and all responsibilities, all strategies

30. [Translator's note:] The words "soft" and "hard" are in English in the text.

and all transactions, that need treating, be they political or not — the tension between the political and its others being only one of the tensions, both supplementary and intrinsic, in the double bind to which I refer. I'm using the English expression "double bind" deliberately and not facilely, because the contraction or the tension I'm about to recall concerns not only a double binding, a double injunction, but a duplicity in the very concept of binding, obligation, bind, bond, ligament, more or less tight ligature, stricture rather than structure (as I said in *Glas*),[31] that stricture that precisely comes to limit liberty along with sovereignty or sovereignty along with liberty. For we must not hide from ourselves that our most and best accredited concept of "liberty," autonomy, self-determination, emancipation, freeing, is indissociable from this concept of sovereignty, its limitless "I can," and thus from its all-powerfulness, this concept to the prudent, patient, laborious deconstruction of which we are here applying ourselves. Liberty and sovereignty are, in many respects, indissociable concepts. And we can't take on the concept of sovereignty without also threatening the value of liberty. So the game is a hard one. Every time, as seems to be the case here, at least, we appear to be criticizing the enclosure, the fences, the limits, and the norms assigned to the free movement of beasts or the mentally ill, we risk doing it not only in the name of liberty but also in the name of sovereignty. And who will dare militate for a freedom of movement without limit, a liberty without limit? And thus without law? For anybody, any living being, human or not, normal or not, citizen or not, virtual terrorist or not?

The double bind is that we should deconstruct, both theoretically and practically, a *certain* political ontotheology of sovereignty without calling into question a certain thinking of liberty in the name of which we put this deconstruction to work. 402

Which supposes a quite different thinking of liberty: *on the one hand*, a liberty that binds itself, that is bound, heteronomically, precisely to the injunctions of this double bind, and therefore, *on the other hand, responsibly putting up with* (but we would also need to think the concept of responsibility as not resisting the questions we have posed as to the opposition man-animal as opposition between responsibility and reaction, it being understood that the limits that the powers we have just been talking about — powers of all sorts, political, police, economic, psychiatric, etc. — intend to impose on the movements both of the animals in the zoological garden and of the mentally ill in the psychiatric hospital are limits supposedly assigned to irresponsible

31. See Jacques Derrida, *Glas* (Paris: Galilée, 1974); trans. Richard Rand and John P. Leavey Jr. as *Glas* (Lincoln: University of Nebraska Press, 1990).

living beings, pure reactional machines), [which supposes, then, returning to my proposition, a quite different thinking of liberty: *on the one hand*, a liberty that binds itself, is bound, heteronomically, precisely to the injunctions of this double bind, and therefore, *on the other hand*, the responsibly putting up with] this difficult but obvious fact: namely that the choice and the decision are not between indivisible sovereignty and indivisible non-sovereignty, but between several divisions, distributions, econ*omies* (*-nomy*, *nomos, nemein* meaning, let me remind you, distribution and division), economies of a divisible sovereignty. Another dimension or another figure of the same double bind would be — I have tried to formalize this question elsewhere, especially in *L'université sans condition*[32] — that of thinking an unconditionality (be it a question of liberty, gift, pardon, justice, hospitality) without indivisible sovereignty. It's more than difficult; it's aporetic, given that sovereignty has always given itself out to be indivisible, and therefore absolute and unconditional.

403   If ever this double bind, this implacable contradiction, were lifted (i.e. in my view never, by definition, it's impossible, and I wonder how anyone could even wish for it), well, it would be . . . it would be paradise.

Should we dream of paradise? How can we avoid dreaming of paradise? If, as I have just said, it's impossible and I wonder how one could even wish for it, this can mean that we can only dream of paradise and that at the same time the promise or memory of paradise would be at once that of absolute felicity and of an inescapable catastrophe.

I am not speaking of paradise here for fun. As you no doubt know, and as Ellenberger reminds us, everything didn't begin with an earthly paradise, with the garden of Eden that the Bible tells us about, with the story of the snake I was talking to you about recently when reading Lawrence's "Snake," and I will talk more about it next week, with all sorts of animals to be named and mastered by man, on the orders of God — [as you know], everything didn't begin with this earthly paradise, or even earlier with what was to become the model it inherited, the Persian *paradeisos* (*paradeisos* is originally a Persian word), namely a vast enclosed territory where many beasts lived in semiliberty under the surveillance of man, for pleasure and according to the pleasure of a monarch. These animals were tamed; many

---

32. Jacques Derrida, *L'université sans condition* (Paris: Galilée, 2001); trans. Peggy Kamuf as "The University without Condition," in Jacques Derrida, *Without Alibi* (Stanford: Stanford University Press, 2002), pp. 202–37.

were given to the king or taken from those he gave to his friends. There were animals there destined for the royal hunt, for official parades, or to serve as artists' models. The Persian *paradeisos* had a function that Ellenberger calls "mystical": the king was the incarnation of the supreme god or the master of creation, and so he received the offering or homage of these animals in a garden forbidden to the common mortal. It was less forbidden for the animals to leave than for the men and subjects of the king to enter.

Well, this *paradeisos* itself was not original. It dates from the great empires of Babylon and Assyria that themselves followed epochs of tribal political organizations whose potentates already gathered for themselves collections of wild animals with no obvious purpose, apparently for pure play, and sometimes ending by massacring them. We shall talk again about all this, the more so because Ellenberger, with a confidence I don't share, concludes his article by asking himself whether, at the end of a transformation, a happy progress under way — a progress both of zoological gardens and of psychiatric hospitals — "Will we one day," he asks, "see the revival of the Persian *paradeisos,* and will that revival produce a new ethical system?"[33]

What I shall retain for today is, provisionally, this: the garden of Eden, the paradise that the Bible and Dante (and D. H. Lawrence the other day) tell us about, was not original, any more than the sin that bears that name. I refer you here in conclusion, still provisionally, to the words of Lacan that we quoted a few months ago, in the questioning reading we attempted. We have to read them again and question them again differently. In "Subversion of the Subject and Dialectic of Desire," Lacan said this, in which I shall content myself with emphasizing the word "experience," which bears all the weight of the problem, the word "I," the word "believe," and the vocabulary of *bêtise* (the words "imbeciles" and "cretinizing"):

> Is this enjoyment, the *lack* of which renders the Other inconsistent — is it then mine? *Experience* proves that it is ordinarily forbidden to me, and this not only, as the imbeciles [*bêtes* or not?] would *believe,* through a bad arrangement of society, but I would say by the *fault* of the Other if he existed: but as the Other does not exist, all that remains for me is to take the *fault* on "I," i.e. to *believe* the thing that *experience* leads us all to, with Freud in the lead: *to original sin.* For even if we did not have Freud's admission, as clear as it is full of sorrow, the fact would remain that the myth that we owe to him, the newest-born in all history [the Oedipus myth], is of no more use than the myth about the accursed apple, with this slight difference (not a

---

33. Ellenberger, "The Mental Hospital and the Zoological Garden," p. 92.

result of its status as myth) that, being more succinct, it is considerably less cretinizing [*abêtissant?*].[34]

But what is not a myth, yet what Freud formulated just as early as he did the Oedipus, is the castration complex.[35]

405   Is everything that we are dealing with, including the castration of domestic animals and the more or less virtual sterilization of the mentally ill, part of the logic of castration? Does this discourse on castration belong more to science than to myth and belief? Those are enough questions for our curiosity, or even for our autopsy today.

34. [Translator's note:] Derrida's interpolation.
35. Jacques Lacan, "Subversion du sujet et dialectique du désir," in *Écrits* (see session 4 above, n. 2), pp. 819–20 [pp. 684–85].

March 20, 2002

Will we ever manage to untangle, in our tangles, will we succeed in unraveling, disintricating, as it were, unscrambling things between *zoology* and *biology*? Between the zoological and the biological, between these two Greek words which are more than words, and are both translated as "life," *zōē* and *bios*? Isn't it too late to try, and aren't all efforts in that direction doomed, essentially, to failure? Especially in French, but also in German and English and many languages in which there is no distinction between the two words, or even the two concepts, for saying "life" and "living"? And isn't philology too poorly equipped, too unequal to the task, in spite of the grand airs that the lesson givers and the pseudo-experts in this domain sometimes take on? Too unequal to the task, philology, not up to this question, which is more than a question as to meaning and word, between *zōē* and *bios*, between *zoo*logy and *bio*logy, the logic of the *logos* fixing nothing and simplifying nothing, as we shall see, for whoever cares to try to untangle things. And in French, what are we saying when we say "life" (ah, *la vie!*), and the living? Are we talking of the zoological or the biological? And what would be the difference? To what are we obstinately signaling here with the word "life"?

There is a line of Heidegger's that I like, even though I'm not always ready to follow him on the question of death. The question of life and death. And still less on the question of the animal. It's the moment when he says, with his rather arrogant smugness, that sometimes irritating condescension that we know him for: "*Den Eigensinnigen ist Leben nur Leben* [For those who are stubborn [*têtus*] (*entêtés, den Eigensinnigen:* for those who have only one idea in their heads), *ist Leben nur Leben* (life is merely life)]." For the stubborn, life is merely life, life is only life or life is all of life. You'll find this witticism in the *Introduction to Metaphysics*,[1] which we'll talk about again in a moment. Heidegger continues:[2] "*Den Eigensinnigen ist Leben nur Leben*," for the stubborn, then, the obstinate, for him who has only one idea in his head—in German there is no reference here to the head [*la tête*], but in French that gives us one more head in our tally of chiefs, heads, caps, and decapitations; and here the stubborn obstinacy of him who has only one idea in his head is something of a definition of *bêtise*; and when Heidegger goes for those who are *eigensinnig*, one can say without risk of being too far wrong that he is not far from finding them *bête*; it is *bête* to think that life is simply life, without asking oneself the question, as Heidegger will immediately do, of a death that is life, a life that is death, a death that belongs to the very being of life: but *eigensinnig* is an interesting word here to bespeak the *bêtise* of stubbornness and obstinacy, in that it marks on the one hand, as you will see, that stubborn *bêtise* consists in not asking any questions.

(This is difficult and worth a brief parenthesis, because one might indeed be tempted to say that *bêtise* consists in an inaptitude for the question—that's an easy thought: we tend to think that people who don't ask themselves any questions are rather stupid, don't we, lacking in critical spirit and reflection: he or she doesn't ask questions, that means *bêtise*; but there is also a strange and troubling affinity between a certain form of *bêtise* and a certain obstinacy, on the contrary, in asking or asking oneself questions, wanting to know (*wissen wollen:* "*Fragen ist wissen-wollen*," says Heidegger,[3] and that brings us back to the question of knowledge and the curiosity we were talking about last week; but here Heidegger is talking about questioning as wanting-to-know, before it becomes degraded into curiosity, and provided, he says, that one remembers that the question on Being or the question of Being presupposes that willing is not an acting (*Agieren*) but is grounded in a "leaving" (*Lassen*), leaving Being to be what it is. *Bêtise* here, stubborn *bêtise*, I would say without further commenting on Heidegger, would be not to know how to leave Being to be what it really is, but to rush excitably toward the question, giving in to the compulsion, to the question as excitable, nervous compulsion, wanting-to-know [*vouloir-savoir*] by accumulative curiosity; for there is without doubt a *bêtise* of the question, as there

409

---

1. Heidegger, *Einführung in die Metaphysik* (see session 10 above, n. 14), p. 100 [p. 139]. [Translator's note: The English translation systematically translates *Eigensinn* as "caprice."]
2. Derrida really only continues Heidegger's sentence two pages later.
3. Heidegger, *Einführung in die Metaphysik*, p. 16 [p. 9].

is of affirmation, as there is of negation: *bêtise* that is nothing, that has no essence, we were saying, even transcendentally, but that can traverse and threaten—by reassuring them, precisely—the three modalities (question, affirmation, negation), but traverse-threaten-reassure them in a positive way, and *bêtise* is perhaps positivity itself, positing, to which affirmation, the "yes," is not to be reduced: *bêtise* would rather resemble self-positing across each of these three modes (question, affirmation, negation), it would be positivism, in sum, self-positivism in general, that positivizes—and no one is immune to or sheltered from this, not even those who denounce *Eigensinn*. I close this parenthesis.)

This last word, I was saying, *Eigensinn*, where, following Heidegger, it marks the fact that stubborn *bêtise* consists in not asking oneself any questions, this word makes at least an elliptical reference to the proper (*eigen*) and to meaning (*Sinn*). At bottom, I would say, playing a little, the obstinate *bêtise* of the *Eigensinnige* is having the obstinacy of one's opinion that consists in believing that something has one proper meaning and one only: life is life, period, that's my opinion and I believe it. That's my opinion and I'm sticking to it, period. Against this *Eigensinnigkeit,* Heidegger continues: "[For these *Eigensinnigen*] *Tod ist ihnen Tod* [death is for them death] *und nur dieses* [and nothing else, and only that, death. But the Being of life, Heidegger then adds, is at the same time death]. *Aber das Sein des Lebens ist zugleich Tod.* [Everything that enters into life also already begins by that fact to die, to go to its death, and death is at the same time life]. [. . .] *und Tod ist zugleich Leben. Heraklit sagt Frgt. 8*[4]: [. . .]" (There follows a definition of contradiction and of the *logos* as gathering of contraries.)   410

Let's leave this short treatise on *bêtise*, a *bêtise* that perhaps always comes down to sticking to some stubborn opinion about life death. Where I would be tempted (I won't insist on this because I have talked about it elsewhere) to find Heidegger a little *eigensinnig*, if not a little *bête* himself on this subject, is where he holds so firmly to the opinion, to what I believe to be no more and no less than an opinion, that only man or only *Dasein* has an experiential relation to death, to dying, to *sterben as such*, to his *own* death, his own being-able-to-die, to its possibility, be it the possibility of the impos-

---

4. Ibid. The German text reads as follows: "*Den Eigensinnigen ist Leben nur Leben. Tod ist ihnen Tod und nur dieses. Aber das Sein des Lebens ist zugleich Tod. Jegliches, was ins Leben tritt, beginnt damit auch schon zu sterben, auf seinen Tod zuzugehen,und Tod ist zugleich Leben. Heraklit sagt Frg. 8: 'Das Gegeneinanderstehende trägt sich, das eine zum anderen, hinüber und herüber, es sammelt sich aus sich.'*"

sible, whereas the animal, that other living being (*zōon*) that we call the animal, perishes but never dies, has no relation worthy of the name to death. For my part, at the risk of being stubborn about it — I've talked about it elsewhere, and we shall come back to it later concerning Heidegger and the animal — I don't believe a word of it, it's not at all certain in any case that man has a relation to death or an experience of death *as such*, in its possible impossibility, or that one can say, properly, in the proper sense and simply, calmly, that the animal is deprived of it. But let's leave that here — it in any case requires a complete recasting of the conceptuality, the recasting we are engaged in here.

The end is near: I mean the end of this year's seminar. Hoping to continue it further next year, I can see clearly, you can see clearly, that we are still on the threshold.

411   Yes, the threshold: what is a threshold?

The threshold is one of the names for what was occupying us at the end of the last session when, busying ourselves around logics of closure and enclosure, it was actually the threshold we were worrying about, the threshold to be crossed or not crossed, the forbidden threshold, *le seuil interdit,* in both senses,[5] both for the animals in the zoological garden and for the mentally ill in the psychiatric asylum. And for the curious spectators of both. And in the Iranian *paradeisos*, more original that the garden of Eden, more original than its supposed sin of the same name, both gardens, however, marked by interdicts, [in the Iranian *paradeisos*] it was forbidden for men to enter rather than for beasts to leave.

The threshold, then, crossable or not — what is it? Basically, it could be shown that all our seminars that have, for more than ten years now — all of them — been bearing on the meaning of responsibility, bearing, then, on the meaning and structure of certain limits, on what one must or must not do, that to which one must and must not respond — that they all stood, still stand, on the threshold, I do mean all the seminars and not just the seminar on hospitality a few years ago, which literally named the threshold and the passage of a threshold at every step. The question of responsibility is a question of the threshold, and in particular, as we again verified this year, a threshold at the origin of responsibility, the threshold from which one passes from reaction to response, and therefore to responsibility, a threshold which, according to the humanist and anthropocentric, in truth logocentric,

---

5. [Translator's note:] The French adjective "interdit" means both "forbidden," and "speechless" or "dumbfounded."

tradition that we are deconstructing here—and we are going to talk at length about the *logos* today—[a threshold that] marks, that is supposed to mark, the indivisible *limen*, the indivisible limit between animal and man. And we recalled last time that this limit, this threshold of responsibility, is the same as that of liberty, without which there is no responsibility and therefore no sovereignty. Responsibility, like liberty, implies something of that indivisible sovereignty accorded to what is proper to man and denied the beast.

Always the threshold, then. What is the threshold? And once we say "threshold," THE threshold, the uncuttable and atomic unity of the threshold, one single threshold, we suppose it to be indivisible; we suppose that it has the form of a line of demarcation as indivisible as a line without breadth that one could cross or be forbidden from crossing only in a punctual instant and in a step itself indivisible. *412*

What we were saying last week concerned, under the names of park or hospital, a kind of treatment of the threshold and of hospitality, of the hospitality of menageries or hospitals, continuing the seminar on incarceration and the death penalty [1999–2001], and therefore sovereignty, just as much as the one on hospitality [1995–97]. I remember too that in the intervening seminar on pardon [1997–99], the question was asked whether certain animals could feel guilty or be in mourning, if they were sensitive to shame and had any capability of repentance and of asking pardon (a question to which we answered yes). As for the seminar on the secret [1991–92], which was, par excellence, a seminar on limits not to be crossed, on the separation of *secernere*, of *secretum*, we reencountered its track with the *Geheimnis der Begegnung,* the secret of the encounter in Celan and the whole poetico-political problematic of *Unheimlichkeit,* the *Abgrund*, the *Urgrund* and the *Ungrund*.

So it's still the same seminar, and when I say that we are still on the threshold of it, that means not only that *we don't have the key*, or that we don't have a key, but that the question on the threshold that we are lingering on is indeed that of the key, and that of knowing if there is some key, the <key> to the door, to the gate, the key to the zoo, the key to the hospital, the key to the crypt to be decrypted. Not only do we risk remaining eternally on the threshold, but what we are really doing is doubting the existence of a threshold worthy of the name. The threshold not only supposes this indivisible limit that every deconstruction begins by deconstructing (to deconstruct is to hold that no indivisibility, no atomicity, is secure), the classical figure of the threshold (to be deconstructed) not only supposes this indivisibility that is not to be found anywhere; it also supposes the solidity of a

413 ground or a foundation, they too being deconstructible.[6] The word "threshold" [*seuil*, sill, sole] itself signifies this solidity of the ground: it comes from the Latin *solum*, which means the soil or more precisely the foundation on which an architectural sill or the soles of one's feet rest: *solum* is the lowest part, the bottom or the sole; *solea* means sandle, etc. Now when we say that in these seminars we are remaining on the threshold, that doesn't mean that we are lingering on it or attesting to the existence of a threshold, whether to remain on it or to cross it interminably. Rather, it would mean, in my view — and this is the gesture of a deconstructive thinking — that we don't even consider the existence (whether natural or artificial) of any threshold to be secure, if by "threshold" is meant *either* an indivisible frontier line *or* the solidity of a foundational ground. Supposing that we dwelled on the threshold, we would also have endure the ordeal of feeling the earthquake always under way, threatening the existence of every threshold, threatening both its indivisibility and its foundational solidity.

And if there is no threshold, how could one have a key to open an entrance door on the threshold?

Lacking a key, a lost or nonexistent key (as in those zoological gardens, you remember, surrounded by deep ditches substituted for fenced-in enclosures, ditches that also couldn't be crossed because there was no longer any key, or any question of a key), [lacking a key, a lost or nonexistent key] is also not knowing where to enter or exit, where to lift the blockade, and even where to begin. Almost all zoological gardens and psychiatric hospitals have keys, but isn't it true that every house, every habitat (be it familial, urban, or national), every place of economy and ecology also presupposes thresholds, limits, and therefore keys, bunches of keys? The keys of the city, of the house, or the national territory are indispensable for getting in or for deciphering a code. This seems to remain true, even if keys made of metal or some solid material are today replaced by digital codes, telephone codes, computer codes, by enciphering and signaling techniques, so many *414* secrets that allow one to enter a territory, to penetrate a place (*sol, solum*), or even to invade it without ever setting foot or the sole (*solea*) of one's shoe in it, and even more efficaciously, more irresistibly, than by setting foot in it. There are now locks, padlocks, with no key, devices for enclosing, that open only for those who have the code, and thus one or more numbers [*chiffres*, ciphers]. Even prisons are beginning to be replaced, in the USA, by electronic bracelets that allow the prisoner to be located at all times, and thus to leave him, wherever he goes, at supervised liberty. Supervised lib-

---

6. In the session, Derrida corrected this to "they too being undeconstructible."

erty is, moreover, the most common condition, and therefore supervised sovereignty—and which of us would dare to claim that we can escape it or even, which is more serious, that we want to escape it?

Of course, we also desire a certain enclosure, some limits and some threshold for our "well-being." What is more, in the materials provided by Ellenberger as to the comparison between animals parked in zoological gardens and patients interned in psychiatric hospitals, there were remarks on the logic of this desire for territorialization that made people love the ecosystem of limits in which both animal and madman, and, I'd add, everybody, all the mad animals that we are, are as happy to stay as we are to get out. We love the threshold, both crossing it and not crossing it. A certain Bernhard Grzimek, the author of "Gefangenhaltung von Tieren" (1950) ("Detention of Beasts," or the incarceration, the incarceration behavior, of beasts), cited by Ellenberger, notes that the animal that leaves the zoo, which we would be inclined to say has escaped or liberated itself, in fact feels homeless, *heimatlos*, and does everything it can to return "home" (*zuhause*) to its cage.[7] I don't know to what extent this can be generalized or taken at face value, but it's quite probable that it happens in certain conditions. According to the same logic, when it has taken possession of its new incarcerating territory, the animal will become more dangerous and aggressive with respect to the intruder and more peaceful with respect to whoever respects the threshold and only feeds it from outside. This law seems to have its human equivalent. And Dr. Daumézon, a French psychiatrist from Sainte-Anne [Hospital] (whom I knew quite well—I recall that some fifty years ago, Foucault, whom we shall be talking about in a moment, [Foucault] took me with some other students to see him as part of the exercises leading to a certificate in psychopathology, to be present at his examinations and case presentations—the examination of the patients and the examination of young interns who had to go through diagnostic exercises in front of Dr. Daumézon and us—fascinating, terrifying, and unforgettable moments)—Dr. Daumézon, then, was the author of an article entitled "Rootedness of Cured Patients in the Asylum," in which he mentions, among others, frequent cases of patients adapted to the asylum, apparently cured, who, as soon as anyone talks to them about leaving, about the end of treatment, present new symptoms or the return of old symptoms, symptoms that are really designed to make them remain in, or return to, the asylum, an asylum they basically don't want to leave. They

415

7. Bernhard Grzimek, "Gefangenhaltung von Tieren," *Studium Generale* 3 (1950): 1–5. Quoted by Ellenberger in "The Mental Hospital and the Zoological Garden," p. 84.

no longer want to cross the threshold of the asylum and leave what has become their "home."[8]

The threshold, then. What is a threshold? What constitutes its indivisibility, be it punctual or linear? And its solidity — foundational or terrestrial, territorial, natural, or technical, architectural, physical, or nomic?

For a while now, I have been talking about the threshold as a supposedly indivisible line across which one enters or exits. So the threshold is always a beginning, the beginning of the inside or the beginning of the outside. As we approach the end of this year's seminar, as we were saying — hoping to continue it next year — I see clearly, you see clearly, that we are still on a threshold the very possibility of which we are interrogating, where that possibility is bound up with the very possibility of beginning.

The threshold: to ask oneself, "What is the threshold?" is to ask oneself "How to begin?" "How to begin?" we are asking ourselves very close to the provisional end of our first meridian, our first circle or return of the line. How to begin again? A question of commencement and commandment, an archaic question of the *arkhē* that means, I recall once again, both commencement and commandment, principle and prince, the One of the first. The *arkhē,* the archon, is a figure of the sovereign himself. And it's about the one, the one and the other, that we are speaking here.

The beast and the sovereign, the one and the other, I was suggesting last time, were already two, and the one *commanded* the other, even before paradise, even before our paradise, before the garden of Eden and even before the Iranian *paradeisos,* the model of which already preceded our Bible's garden of Eden.

We no longer know, between the beast and the sovereign, where to begin tackling this question of the paradisiacal or pre-paradisiacal commencement or commandment. Our *trousse* [case, kit], our *trousseau* [bunch (of keys), reserve, bottom drawer] of quasi-canonical references . . .

(Parenthesis: since we are speaking of threshold and keys, well, about *trousse* and *trousseau, trousser* [to truss, to bunch up], etc. (or terms such as *trousse-galant* [a devastating illness], *trousse-pied* [horse-tying], *trousse-queue* [tail tie], *troussequin* [saddle part], *trousse-traits* [harness-rings], etc.), I would say that these are words and a vocabulary to which I would have liked, if it were reasonable, to devote a whole year's seminar: and it might not have been all that unreasonable, because, and here's my advice, if you read

---

8. G. Daumézon, "L'enracinement des malades guéris à l'asile," *L'Hygiène Mentale* 36 (1946–47): 59–71; quoted in Ellenberger, "The Mental Hospital and the Zoological Garden," p. 84.

some dictionary carefully, for example, the *Robert* or better still the *Littré,* on this family of words around *trousse, trousser, trousseau,* you will have in a few pages the whole network of themes and problems that is occupying us here, you will have the whole kit and caboodle [*la trousse et le trousseau*] of everything we are trying to get into here, the bunch of keys being only one resource among others, especially if the key should be missing or replaced by a code, to deal with the structures, the strictures, and thus the locks I was talking about in connection with the double bind and paradise, as I was concluding last time. End of parenthesis on the *trousseau*.)

As I was saying, we don't know, between the beast and the sovereign, how to get going on this question of the paradisiacal or pre-paradisiacal commencement and commandment. Our kit, our bunch of quasi-canonical references, namely Genesis, its very "In the beginning," *Bereshit,* which also means, as Chouraqui translates it, "at the head" (and there we have the commencement, the commandment, the performative *fiat* of Elohim, and the head in the so-called Old Testament that begins, we're coming to it, with a *fiat,* the commencement of a commandment, the order of a *fiat*). But before exploring the *trousseau* of all the commencements that we have at our disposal, we Europeans, descended from both the Abrahamic religions and Greek philosophy, here are at least three commencements:

1. Genesis, *Bereshit,* and the creation of the animals before man, with what follows from that, which we'll talk about again.

2. The beginning of the Gospel of John, *En arkhē en o logos, In Principium erat verbum,* "In the beginning was the Word (*logos*) and the *logos* was God." To say that God was *logos,* as sovereign all-powerful creator of everything, was basically to confirm the first words of Genesis, of the Head, where God by means of speech, by saying "Let there be light," by this archperformative, effected that light was and came. John continues, "The *logos* was in the beginning with God" (*outos ēn en arkhē pros to theon*), everything existed through it [through the *logos*] and nothing that existed existed without it. In it [the *logos*] was life (*zōē*) and life was the light (*phōs*) of men."[9] Retain this for now: sovereignty equals *arkhē, arkhē* equals *logos,* the *logos* that creates, that causes to come or advene, and that creates the living being, the life of the living (*zōē*), the evangelic *logos,* which basically repeats genesis and speaks of an origin of the world created by the sovereign, God, by an all-powerful *fiat,* which is, let's say, *zoological,* the *fiat* of a *logos* producing *zōē,* a *zōē* that is light, appearing, *phōs, photology* for mankind. This zoo-

9. John 1:1–4. Derrida's translation.

417

logy needs to be understood in a special sense, as you can well imagine, but one that cannot be radically foreign to the current sense. If, no doubt, what I'm here calling zoo-logy concerns a life that is in the *logos*, a *zōē* that is, says John, in the *logos* like a life that is the light of mankind, if of course he is not speaking of the *logos* of *zōē* as a science of life or a discourse on life, the fact remains that if there can be zoology as discourse, reason, or science of life, it's certainly because there seems to be some ontological affinity between *life*, *zōē*, and *logos*.

3. Third and finally, still to make sure that the classical bunch of abrahamo-philosophical keys is still in our pocket, there was the other beginning, the other key, one that is chronologically earlier that the gospel of John, and it's what Aristotle's *Politics* also tells us about *logos* and *zōē*, in statements that are just as famous but can never be reread often enough.

I believe it's my duty to begin with this today and to return right now to a passage in Aristotle's *Politics* that you no doubt all know well, which has remained behind everything we've said until now but which may be opportune to reopen just when, between the performative *fiat* of Genesis, just on the threshold of an already inherited garden of Eden, and, further, the evangelical and Johannine *en arkhē ēn o logos* and *ēn autō zōē ēn* (at the commencement and the commandment was the *logos* and in it life) — it is, then, opportune to reopen the text from the *Politics* where we find another configuration of *zōē* and *logos*, another essential inherence of *logos* in the living or the living in the *logos*, another *zoology* or another *logozōēy* which are situated, are supposed to be situated, at the *arkhē*, at the commencement, at the sovereign principle of everything that concerns what appears and grows in the light, the *physis* of light, *phōs*, of life, *zōē,* and of *logos*, of speech.

When Heidegger — you remember the text we read from *Introduction to Metaphysics* — seemed to be denigrating this determination that he called, somewhat scornfully, a "zoological" determination of man as *animal rationale* — that is, and this is Aristotle's expression, *zōon logon ekhon* — in fact he might have been indirectly taking aim at the biblical statements, from Genesis to the Gospel of John. We shall see in a moment that he did not fail to do so, too.

But as Aristotle's text comes before the Gospels and above all remains the more political, in truth the only one that is explicitly and literally political, in the first, i.e. Greek, sense of that word, the only one that conjugates *logos* with the political, I should like (since with sovereignty we are above all talking about the political), [I should like], at risk of belaboring paths that have already been cleared many times, to return a little to the letter of this passage, a passage that is in the end quite tortuous, twisted, thorny, resistant to clearance as much as to decipherment and decrypting.

Let us first of all take into account the textual situation of this definition of man as a political animal, or, more literally, of man who is *by nature* (*physei*) a political animal (*politikon zōon*).[10] This definition comes up at the very opening, the beginning, the commencement of politics, at the commencement of the first book of Aristotle's *Politics*. The definition of man as a political animal, a definition that never fails to specify "by nature" (*physei*)—and this insistent, recurrent, literal reference to *physis* is not the least obscure—this definition of man as a political animal will reappear, in the same form, in book 3 (at 1278b) at the moment when Aristotle is defining the purpose of the state (*polis*) and of constitutions. Aristotle there says: "*kai oti physei men estin anthrōpos zōon politikon*" ("and man is by nature a political living being") (1278 b19). It is in this passage that, on the basis of a single occurrence of the word *bios,* in the midst of many uses of *zōē* or *zen* (to live)—we shall no doubt come back to this—Agamben, at the beginning of the book I have already mentioned, *Homo Sacer*, thinks he can find a distinction between *bios* and *zōē* that will structure his entire problematic. It is in the name of this distinction that Agamben, while situating himself in the tracks of Foucault, cites the latter and then proposes, as he puts it, to "reconsider" his affirmation:

> In Foucault's statement according to which man was, for Aristotle, a "living animal with the additional capacity for political existence" it is therefore precisely the meaning of this "additional capacity" that must be understood as problematic.[11]

Two pages later, Agamben goes further than to "reconsider": he says "corrected and completed." I quote:

420

> The Foucauldian thesis will then have to be corrected or, at least, completed [this is not at all the same thing, but let's pass over this strategy or this rhetoric], in the sense that what characterizes modern politics is not so much the inclusion of *zōē* in the *polis* — which is, in itself, absolutely ancient—nor simply the fact that life as such becomes a principal object of the projections and calculations of State power. Instead the decisive fact is

10. Aristotle, *Politics*, 1.1253 a3.

11. Agamben, *Homo Sacer* (see session 3 above, n. 25), p. 7. [Translator's note: The French translation used by Derrida (trans. Marilène Raiola, Paris: Seuil, 1997) uses the verb "reconsidered" in translating this passage.]

that, together with the process by which the exception everywhere becomes the rule, the realm of bare life—which is originally situated at the margins of the political order—gradually begins to coincide with the political realm, and exclusion and inclusion, outside and inside, *bios* and *zoé*, right and fact, enter into a zone of irreducible indistinction.[12]

We have to reconstitute this whole context before returning to Aristotle himself, if we can still say that, the better to measure what is at stake today in this rereading, from the point of view that is ours here. All of Agamben's demonstrative strategy, here and elsewhere, puts its money on a distinction or a radical, clear, univocal exclusion, among the Greeks and in Aristotle in particular, between bare life (*zōē*), common to all living beings (animals, men, and gods), and life qualified as individual or group life (*bios: bios theōrētikos*, for example, contemplative life, *bios apolaustikos*, life of pleasure, *bios politikos*, political life). What is unfortunate is that this distinction is never so clear and secure, and that Agamben himself has to admit that there are exceptions, for example in the case of God, who, says Aristotle's *Metaphysics*,[13] has a *zōē aristē kai aidios*, a noble and eternal life. Such an insecure semantic distinction cannot serve to determine a historical periodization, which causes Agamben to say, I quote again:

421

> What characterizes modern politics is not so much the inclusion of *zōē* in the *polis* — which is, in itself, absolutely ancient—nor simply the fact that life as such becomes a principal object of the projections and calculations of State power. Instead the decisive fact is that, together with the process by which the exception everywhere becomes the rule, the realm of bare life—which is originally situated at the margins of the political order—gradually begins to coincide with the political realm, and exclusion and inclusion, outside and inside, *bios* and *zoé*, right and fact, enter into a zone of irreducible indistinction.[14]

What is difficult to sustain, in this thesis, is the idea of an entry (a modern entry, then) into a zone of irreducible indifferentiation, when the differentiation has never been secure (I would say Agamben furtively admits as much); and, above all, what remains even more difficult to sustain is the idea that there is in this something modern or new; for Agamben himself, as you are about to hear, taking the Foucauldian idea of a specifically modern biopolitics seriously, [Agamben] is keen to recall that it is as ancient as can

12. Ibid., p. 9.
13. Book Λ, 7, 1072b 28; quoted by Agamben, ibid., p. 1.
14. Ibid., p. 9.

be, immemorial and archaic. I will read the paragraph, then, that, on the one hand, constitutes a particularly abrupt questioning of Foucault's thesis on the modernity of the biopolitical, just when Agamben seems to want to inscribe himself, with some reservations, in Foucault's tracks, where Foucault will have been *almost* the first, as Agamben, for his part, will have been the first to say that Foucault was almost the first to say, that what appears to be modern, as you will hear, is in truth immemorial. I will read, then, but after a long detour, the paragraph that, on the one hand, gives up on any specifically modern determination of a biopolitics of the state, that supposedly only picks up what is archaic and most immemorial. I mention all these texts less because I understand them (I admit I often have to give up on that) than because they mark at least the currency of the problems and concerns that are ours here.

In a moment I shall first quote Agamben, and then quote Foucault. But not without having first pointed out that neither the one nor the other refers, as I believe it would have been honest and indispensable to do, to the Heidegger who, I remind you, in the *Introduction to Metaphysics*, said that it is only tardily, after the event (*Geschehnis*), after the conscious, knowing, knowledgeable appearance (*die wissende Erscheinung des Menschen als des geschichtlichen*) of man as historial man, only after this historial eventness, and thus tardily, did one define (Heidegger puts the word in scare quotes: *"definiert"*) man by a concept (*in einem Begriff*), and this concept was, as Heidegger says without even having to name the signatory of this literal definition—Aristotle—*zōon logon ekhon*, *animal rationale,* living being endowed with reason, *"vernünftiges Lebewesen."* In this definition of man, Heidegger makes clear, the *logos* appears, of course, it comes forth (*kommt vor*), but it appears in a form or a figure that is unrecognizable, unknown (*in einer ganz unkenntlichen Gestalt*) and in a very curious, very remarkable environment (*in einer sehr merkwürdigen Umgebung*): and this is what interests Heidegger, who, in the course of what is also a reading of Parmenides, Heraclitus, Aristotle, and Hegel, is attempting to rethink in an original way the relation between *logos* and *physis* (*physis,* of which he says, at the beginning of the *Introduction to Metaphysics*, that its Latin translation as *natura*, which also speaks of "birth," has turned away from the originary sense of the Greek *physis*, as ethics, in the sense of morality, has degraded the originary sense of *ethos*).[15]

Five questions had earlier been posed by Heidegger, and we should keep them in mind during this whole reflection:

422

---

15. Heidegger, *Einführung in die Metaphysik*, p. 108 [p. 151].

1. *"Wie west die ursprüngliche Einheit von Sein und Denken als die von* φύσις *und* λόγος*?"* ["How does the originary unity of Being and thinking essentially unfold as the unity of *physis* and *logos?"*]

423

2. *"Wie geschieht das ursprüngliche Auseinandertreten von* λόγος *und* φύσις*?"* ["How does the originary disjunction [secession, divorce] of *logos* and *physis* come to pass?"]

3. *"Wie kommt es zum Heraustreten und Auftreten des* λόγος*?"* ["How does one come to the se-cession [the exit (from the stage)] and to the procession [the appearance, the entry onto the stage] of the *logos?"*]

4. *"Wie wird der* λόγος *(das 'Logische') zum Wesen des Denkens?"* ["How does *logos* (the 'logical') become the essence of thinking?"]

5. (This is a question to which I shall be giving a certain privilege, for reasons I shall give), *"Wie kommt dieser* λόγος *als Vernunft und Verstand zur Herrschaft über das Sein im Anfang der griechieschen Philosophie?"* ["How does this *logos*, as reason and understanding, come to reign (to exercise its mastery, its authority, its sovereignty (*Herrschaft*)) over Being at the beginning of Greek philosophy?"][16]

In other words, how, not the *logos,* the *logos* itself, but the *logos* determined, interpreted, understand travestied, disguised, one might almost say corrupted into the form of reason and understanding, the *logos as* reason and understanding, in fact as "logic"—how, in this disguise or in this guise, does it come to dominate being, to become stronger than being, from the beginning of Greek philosophy? I am not forcing things with the word *force* on this relation of force and forcing, domination or hegemony. It is Heidegger's discourse and explicit intention that I am respecting, for Heidegger speaks of *Herrschaft* here (one could already translate *Herrschaft* by sovereignty as much as by mastery or lordship); it really is a question of a violently imposed sovereignty of *logos as* reason, understanding, logic: it

424

really is a question of a force of reason that overcomes [*a raison de*] another interpretation or several other interpretations or ways of hearing *logos*, the word or the vocabulary, the sense of *legein, logos*: it really is a question of a sort of war and conflict of forces in which reason wins by force, and along with reason (*ratio, Vernunft*) the rationalism of what will come later, as we shall see, to be inscribed in the concept of *animal rationale* or *zōon logon ekhon*. This will mean not a conflict or a simple opposition, as one often thinks, between force and reason, as between force and right, but a conflict

16. Ibid., p. 94 [p. 130]. [Translator's note: I have modified the translation slightly to remain close to Derrida's own translation into French.]

in which force is on the side of reason, and wins out, a bit like "the reason of the strongest," in another sense and at another level, but concurrently with the discourse of La Fontaine's fable, which maybe finds its fundamental resource here. I am all the less forcing the sense and use and implication of the word *Herrschaft* by translating it as sovereignty or as sovereign domination in this phrase, in that two pages earlier—to which I refer you—speaking of the "logic" that came out of the Platonic school or of a doctrine of thinking become a doctrine of the *logos* in the sense of proposition, speaking also of the rise in power of the logical, of logic, of the logical determination of *logos* in Hegel, Heidegger twice uses the expression "*Machstellung des 'Logischen,'* " and "*Machstellung*" is the positing of force, an expression often used to speak of the state, of the positing of the force of a state, as the expression "*Machtspruch*" signifies decision of force, arbitrary and sovereign decision. Moreover, the French translator, Gilbert Kahn, here translates "*Machtstellung des 'Logischen'* " as "*souveraineté du 'logique'* " ["sovereignty of the 'logical' "].[17]

This doesn't mean that this sovereignty, this hegemony, this superior force of logical reason, has won out over a thinking of the *logos* that, for its part, is innocent, and foreign to all force. We are indeed dealing with a conflict between more than one force. For the *legein* or the *logos* as gathering, as *Sammlung* or *Versammlung*, which Heidegger holds to be more originary than *logos* as reason or logic, is already a deployment of force and violence. Gathering is never, says Heidegger, a simple putting together, a simple accumulation, it is what retains in a mutual belonging (*Zusammengehörigkeit*) without allowing itself to disperse. And in this retention, *logos* already has the violent character of a predominance or, as it is translated [into French], a *perdominance*, a *Durchwalten* of *physis*.[18] *Physis* is that *Gewalt*, that deployment of force, which does not dissolve into the void of an absence of contrasts or contraries (*in eine leere Gegensatzlosigkeit*), but maintains what is thus "*durchwaltet*," traversed, shot through by the deployment of sovereignty, or of forces, in the highest acuity of its tension (its tension itself extreme, one might say sovereign, "*in der höchsten Schärfe seiner Spannung*"). So the *logos* is itself, however one interprets it, as gathering, *Sammlung*, or, later, as logic, reason or understanding—the *logos* is already, always, of the order of power, force, or even violence, of the order of that *Gewalt* that is so

17. Ibid., p. 93. [Translator's note: The English translation has "position of power" for *Machtstellung*.]

18. Ibid., p. 102 [p. 141]. [Translator's note: The English translation has simply "dominance."]

difficult to translate (force, violence, potency, power, authority: often legitimate political power, force of order: *walten* is to reign, to dominate, to command, to exercise a power that is often political: sovereignty, the exercise of
sovereignty, is of the order of *walten* and *Gewalt*).

Still more interesting for us, in this context, is the way Heidegger, in the
same interpretive movement—and the interpretation of the *logos* is also a
sort of exercise of force or violence, of *Gewalt*—[the way Heidegger] situates and interprets the Christian concept of *logos* in the New Testament, the
very concept I was invoking at the beginning when I quoted the opening of
the Gospel of John. "*En arkhē en o logos, In Principium erat verbum*" ["In the
beginning was the Word (*logos*) and the Word (*logos*) was God"]. Prudently,
Heidegger notes that one ought to distinguish here between the Synoptics and the Gospel of John, but he considers that, essentially, at bottom
(*grundsätzlich*), the New Testament *logos* does not mean, as in Heraclitus
for example, the Being of the entity (*das Sein des Seienden*), the gathering of
antagonistic forces (*die Gesammeltheit des Gegenstrebigen*). The *logos* of John
does not signify the Being of the entity or what holds contraries together,
but designates *one* particular entity ("*ein besonderes Seiendes*": Heidegger
emphasizes "*one*"), namely the son of God, in his mediating function between God and man.

This accident of the *logos*, this drift that distances the *logos* from its Greek
originarity is, moreover, a Jewish heritage since, quite rarely for Heidegger,
he judges it necessary, in one sentence, to identify, uncover, or even to denounce, in this representation of the *logos* as mediator, the filiation or influence of what he calls a representation, "that of the Jewish philosophy of
religion" ("*diejenige der jüdischen Religionsphilosophie*") [he doesn't say the
Jewish religion but the Jewish philosophy of religion], here that of Philo
the Jew. Philo, in his philosophy of the creation, Heidegger reminds us, had
indeed attributed to the *logos* the function of *mesitēs*, mediator. This reading of the evangelical *logos* under the influence of Greco-Jewish philosophy,
under the influence of Hellenistic Judaism, basically, is of interest to us for
two reasons as we try to put some order into our *trousseau* of canonical texts.
On the one hand, because in this Christian appropriation of the *logos*, what is
at stake is the performative commandment; *on the other hand*, because what
is at stake is life (life as *zōē*).

How so?

A. *Well, on the one hand, first, then,* in the translation of the Septuagint, in
the translation of what is called the Old Testament, *logos* is the name given
to the word of God as commandment (*Befehl, Gebot*). The "ten commandments" is translated as "*oi deka logoi*." This is, as it is called, the Decalogue.

And *logos* means *kērux*, as Heidegger also recalls, he who proclaims out loud, whence the *kērigma*, the holy proclamation, and *logos* also means *ange-los*, the herald, the messenger who transmits orders and commandments, or the good news of the Gospel. *Logos tou staurou*, the *logos* of the cross, is the word come from the cross. The Gospel of the Cross is Christ himself.

B. *And, on the other hand, second, then,* Christ is the *logos* of redemption (*der Logos der Erlösung*), the *logos* of eternal life, the *logos* of *zōē* (*logos des ewigen Leben, logos zōēs*). Christ in this sense — Heidegger doesn't say so, but I believe I'm authorized to, following his interpretation — not only is a Jew, and not only a Jew, as is well known, by his origins, but is a Jew determined as *logos mesites* on the basis of a Jewish appropriation (Philo) of the Greek *logos*, a zoological Jew, since he is a Jew who unites in his person, as son of God, both *logos* and *zōē*. And he is zoological not only because of the sacrificial lamb, because of the Paschal lamb of the Jews or the mystical lamb that erases the sins of the world. So it is also in this sense that — uniting in one and the same body, or one and the same concept, *logos* and the life of the living, *logos* and *zōē* — a *zoo-logy* or a *logo-zōēy* imposes itself. It will, according to Heidegger, have imposed its authority, even its sovereignty, its hegemonic predominance both over the originary interpretation of the Greek *logos* and over the Aristotelian definition of man as *logon zōon ekhon*, the animal that has the *logos*. As for him, Christ, qua man, not only has the *logos;* he is the *logos*. Incarnate. He incarnates the *logos* that he has.

These statements of Heidegger's, like the *Introduction to Metaphysics,* date from 1935, from courses given in Freiburg. About ten years later, after the war, in 1946, in the *Letter on Humanism*, we find the same view on the subject of the *animal rationale* or the *zōon logon ekhon*, but this time the critique of the biologism — denounced by name (*Biologismus*) — that Heidegger associates with it, doubtless has a political signification (and this is not the first time that Heidegger attacks biologism, which is an at least indirect and virtual critique of something in Nazism); but this indicates, most importantly, that Heidegger, whom one can hardly suspect of lack of interest for the resources and rules of the Greek language, does not place between *bios* and *zōē* the airtight frontier along which Agamben constructs his whole discourse. Before returning to Foucault and Agamben, then finally to Aristotle, let's read a few passages from the *Letter on Humanism,*[19] and let's do so in two stages.

427

19. Martin Heidegger, *Lettre sur l'humanisme,* bilingual ed., trans. and ed. Roger Munier (Paris: Aubier–Éditions Montaigne, 1964); trans. Frank A. Capuzzi and J. Glenn Gray as *Letter on Humanism,* in *Martin Heidegger: Basic Writings,* ed. David F. Krell (New

428   1. *First stage*. Heidegger wants first of all to show that the determination of man as a *rational animal* is insufficiently humanist, as it were, that it misses the humanity of man, what is proper to man. And what thus misses the essence of man is metaphysics.

2. *Second stage*. Heidegger denounces the biologism, the biologistic reduction of this definition of man. And that means that the metaphysics of classical humanism, the metaphysics that is not humanistic enough, is, deep down, the ally or accomplice of biologism and zoologism.

> Metaphysics does not ask about the truth of Being itself. Nor does it therefore ask in what way the essence of man belongs to the truth of Being. Metaphysics has not only failed up to now to ask this question, the question is inaccessible to metaphysics as metaphysics [*Diese Frage ist der Metaphysik als Metaphysic unzugänglich*]. Being is still waiting for the time when it will become thought-provoking [*denkwürdig*: worthy of thought] to man. With regard to the definition of man's essence, however one may determine the *ratio* or the *animal* and the reason of the living being, whether as a "faculty of principles" [*Vermögen der Prinzipien*] or a "faculty of categories" [*Vermögen der Kategorien*], or in some other way, the essence of reason is always and in each case grounded in this: for every apprehending of beings in their Being, Being itself is already illumined and comes to pass in its truth. So too with animal, *zōon,* an interpretation of "life" is already posited which necessarily lies in an interpretation of beings as *zōē* and *physis,* within which what is living appears. Above and beyond everything else, however, it finally remains to ask whether the essence of man [*das Wesen des Menschen*] primordially and most decisively lies in the dimension of *animalitas* at all [*in der Dimension der animalitas*]. Are we really on the right track toward the essence of man as long as we set him off as one living creature among others in contrast to plants, beasts, and God? We can proceed in that way;
429   we can in such fashion locate man within being as one being among others. We will thereby always be able to state something correct about man. But we must be clear on this point, that when we do this we abandon man to the essential realm of *animalitas* [*in den Wesensbereich der animalitas*] even if we do not equate him with beasts but attribute a specific difference to him. In principle we are still thinking of *homo animalis* — even when *anima* [soul] is posited as *animus sive mens* [spirit or mind], and this in turn is later posited as subject, person or spirit [*Geist*]. Such positing is the manner of metaphysics. But then the essence of man is too little heeded and not thought in its origin, the essential provenance that is always the essential future for his-

---

York: Harper and Row, 1977), pp. 193–42. [Translator's note: I have made the occasional very slight modification to the translation to ensure consistency with Derrida's commentary.]

torical mankind. Metaphysics thinks of man on the basis of *animalitas* and does not think in the direction of his *humanitas*.[20]

And here is the passage that concerns the critique of biologism (one can say, without violation, the critique of biopoliticism):

Ek-sistence [*Ek-sistenz*] can be said only of the essence of man, that is, only of the human way "to be." For as far as our experience shows, only man is admitted to the destiny of ek-sistence. Therefore ek-sistence can also never be thought of as a specific kind of living creature among others — granted that man is destined to think the essence of his Being and not merely to give accounts of the nature and history of his constitution and activities. Thus even what we attribute to man as *animalitas* on the basis of the comparison with "beast" is itself grounded in the essence of ek-sistence. The human body is something essentially other than an animal organism [*Der Leib des Menschen ist etwas wesentlich anderes als ein tierischer Organismus*]. Nor is the error of biologism [*Die Verirrung des Biologismus*] overcome by adjoining a soul to the human body, a mind to the soul, and the existential to the mind, and then louder than before singing the praises of the mind — only to let everything relapse into "life-experience," with a warning that thinking by its inflexible concepts disrupts the flow of life and that thought of Being distorts existence [there are many enemies lurking here . . .]. The fact that physiology and physiological chemistry can scientifically investigate man as an organism is no proof that in this "organic" thing, that is, in the body scientifically explained, the essence of man consists. That has as little validity as the notion that the essence of nature has been discovered in atomic energy. It could even be that nature, in the face she turns toward man's technical mastery, is simply concealing her essence. Just as little as the essence of man consists in being an animal organism can this insufficient definition of man's essence be overcome or offset by outfitting man with a immortal soul, the power of reason, or the character of a person. In each instance essence is passed over, and passed over on the basis of the same metaphysical projection.[21]

430

Here, of course, we're not getting into Heidegger's discourse on the animal, on the beast that is *weltarm*: that would require much more time, and I hope to do it next year. Heidegger's propositions that I was concerned to recall today so as to reconstitute a context, with a view to approaching the opening of Aristotle's politics on man the political animal, are propositions that are quoted neither by Foucault (who practically never talks about Heidegger, not even when he introduces his problematic of biopower), nor by

20. Ibid., pp. 53–57 [pp. 203–4].
21. Ibid., pp. 57–61 [pp. 204–5].

Agamben, who, for his part, knows Heidegger well and of course quotes him, but not at all as he should have done in this context, recalling at least Heidegger's two major texts—as well known as they are accessible—on these questions. Even in the last part of *Homo Sacer*, even in the long note in small print that I have already quoted and in which he declares in cavalier fashion that, I quote, "only when situated in the perspective of modern bio-politics does [the relation between Martin Heidegger and Nazism] take on its proper significance (and this is the very thing that both Heidegger's ac-cusers and his defenders fail to do [this is a pure untruth, but no matter])"[22] or again when, as you remember, he is the first to discover that Lévinas was the first to "underline the analogies between this new ontological determi-nation of man [on the basis of the 'hermeneutics of factical life (*faktisches Leben*)'] and certain traits of the philosophy implicit in Hitlerism," well, even there, even if he does quote the *Introduction to Metaphysics*, he does so only in order to bring out the fact that Heidegger's condemnation of a certain circulating image of the philosophy of National Socialism actually attests, I quote, to "the essential proximity" of Heidegger and National So-cialism.[23]

But on all the texts we have just read about the *logos*, about *zōē*, the zoo-logical interpretation of man, about metaphysics and technology and Chris-tianity as prevalent interpretations of *logos* and *zōē*, about the condemna-tion of biologism, absolute silence from Agamben. I'm sure he knows these texts, even if he seems to have omitted them or needed to omit them, as he well knows that he wouldn't have been the first to read them, which no doubt discouraged him from looking at them again more closely.

And yet it goes without saying that when Heidegger *on the one hand* condemns biologism (and clearly modern biologism), and *on the other hand* denounces as metaphysical and insufficiently questioning the zoologism of a definition of man as *zōon logon ekhon* or, a fortiori, as *zōon politikon*, he is going exactly in the direction of this whole supposedly new configuration that Agamben credits Foucault with having inaugurated, even if the same Agamben proposes to "reconsider" Foucault's "formulations" or to "com-plete and correct" his theses.

So that things are clear, I recall two things:

1. That, as always—I shall quote him in a moment—Foucault makes not the slightest allusion to Heidegger;

22. Agamben, *Homo Sacer*, p. 150.
23. Ibid., pp. 164–66.

2. That Agamben, who in these pages does not name Heidegger either, said the following about Foucault, which I quoted a moment ago but I believe needs to be read again: "In Foucault's statement according to which man was, for Aristotle, a 'living animal with the additional capacity for political existence' it is therefore precisely the meaning of this 'additional capacity' that must be understood as problematic."[24]   432

Two pages later, you remember, Agamben goes further than "reconsidering"; he says "corrected and completed":

> The Foucauldian thesis will then have to be corrected or, at least, completed [this is not at all the same thing, as we were saying, but let's pass over this strategy or this rhetoric], in the sense that what characterizes modern politics is not so much the inclusion of *zōē* in the *polis* — which is, in itself, absolutely ancient — nor simply the fact that life as such becomes a principal object of the projections and calculations of State power. Instead the decisive fact is that, together with the process by which the exception everywhere becomes the rule, the realm of bare life — which is originally situated at the margins of the political order — gradually begins to coincide with the political realm, and exclusion and inclusion, outside and inside, *bios* and *zōē*, right and fact, enter into a zone of irreducible indistinction.[25]

The whole difficulty depends on the fact that Agamben wants absolutely to define the specificity of modern politics or biopolitics (which Foucault makes his theme at the end of *The Will to Knowledge* and at least the possibility of which Heidegger, let's say, didn't fail to think), Agamben wants absolutely to define this specificity by putting his money on the concept of "bare life," which he identifies with *zōē*, in opposition to *bios*. It is even this specificity that Foucault, who died too soon, supposedly missed. And already in the expression "biopolitics," to which Agamben would no doubt have preferred "zoopolitics." Agamben writes: "Foucault's death kept him   433 from showing how he would have developed the concept and study of biopolitics" [which Agamben does by adding or exploring developments missed by Foucault]. Agamben continues:

> In any case, however, the entry of *zōē* into the sphere of the *polis* — the politicization of bare life as such — constitutes *the decisive event of modernity* and signals a radical transformation of the political-philosophical categories of classical thought. It is even likely that if politics today seems to be

24. Ibid., p. 7.
25. Ibid., p. 9.

passing through a lasting eclipse, it is because politics has failed to reckon with this *foundational event of modernity*.[26]

I repeat or paraphrase, in Agamben's own words: politics is subject today to a lasting eclipse, he says, but we don't know whether it's politics (the thing, political life, political history) or the discourse on politics; and if politics is today subject to a lasting eclipse (but lasting since when, until when?), it's only "probable," says Agamben, and due to what? Well, to a forgetting. Politics (the political thing or the thinking of politics) has forgotten. What? "The founding event of modernity," namely what founds modern politics and what politics has forgotten. Now what does this founding event consist in? In, I quote again, "the introduction of *zōē*" [audaciously translated as "bare life," and therefore life without qualities, without qualification, the pure and simple fact of living and of not being dead, "life as merely life," as the stubborn people mocked by Heidegger were saying: *"Den Eigensinnigen ist Leben nur Leben"*] — [now what does this founding event consist in? In, and I quote again, "the introduction of *zōē*] into the sphere of the *polis*."

To show this, Agamben is required to demonstrate that the difference between *zōē* and *bios* is absolutely rigorous, already in Aristotle. Can he do this? Before proceeding down this path, I should like to take a precaution. My questions or my reservations here, whether directed toward Foucault or, more precisely here, toward Agamben, don't mean that I have no interest in anything that could be called a specificity in the relations between the living being and politics, in what these authors so calmly call "modernity." New things are certainly happening in this respect today.

As they always are, aren't they?

No, my doubts and my dissatisfactions concern the concepts or the conceptual strategies relied on in order to analyze and characterize these novelties. I don't believe, for example, that the distinction between *bios* and *zōē* is a reliable and effective instrument, sufficiently sharp and, to use Agamben's language, which is not mine here, sufficiently deep to get to the depth of this "[so-called] founding event." Nor that the category of forgetting is sufficiently pertinent here for a more or less competent philologist, capable of seeing the difference between *bios* and *zōē*, to reawaken politics to itself today and make it come out of its oblivion or its sleep. The more so in that said philologist must repeatedly recognize that not only did Aristotle, many centuries ago, talk of *zōon politikon* (and that the "plus": *zōon* + *politikon* is, as we shall see in a moment, a very fragile threshold), but that sometimes,

434

26. Ibid., p. 4.

and I recalled earlier an example to do with God, *zōē* designates a life that is qualified, and not "bare."

Everything is at stake here, since we do have to return to Aristotle's *Politics,* which undeniably defines man as *politikon zōon* — everything is at stake, then, between two often indiscernible ways of interpreting the mode of attribution of *politikon* to *zōon*. Agamben intends to make a distinction between "*politikon*" as an "attribute of the living being as such," and what he calls "the specific difference that determines the genus *zōon*." I'll quote first and we shall see later that not only is this difference between "attribute" and "specific difference" difficult to identify, but that there exists what I shall call a first or third reading that renders all these hypotheses even more fragile.

After having declared in the opening lines of his book:

> The Greeks had no single term to express what we mean by the word "life." They used two terms that, although traceable to a common etymological root [what is more!], are semantically and morphologically distinct: *zōē,* which expressed the simple fact of living common to all living beings (animals, men or gods), and *bios,* which indicated the form or way of living proper to an individual or a group.[27]

435

Having said that, then, then recognized a first exception (i.e. precisely the "*zōē aristē kai aidios*," the noble and eternal life of God, the second exception being none other, basically, than Aristotle's *zōon politikon*, we're getting there), Agamben must also, on the following page, pause before what this time, then, looks like a major exception to the rule he has just stated, namely Aristotle's *politikon zōon*: i.e. a *zōē* that is qualified and not bare.

Here the choice is a tough one: you must *either* demonstrate, which is indeed what Agamben would like to do, that there is a tenable distinction between an attribute and a specific difference (it isn't easy, I think it's even impossible), *or else* admit (which Agamben doesn't want to do at any price, because it would ruin all the originality and supposed priority of what he is saying) that Aristotle already had in view, had already in his own way thought, the possibility that politics, politicity, could, in certain cases, that of man, qualify or even take hold of bare life (*zōē*), and therefore that Aristotle might already have apprehended or formalized, in his own way, what Foucault and Agamben attribute to modern specificity. Which would explain why both of them, Foucault and Agamben, like everyone else, have to quote this bit of Aristotle and get embroiled in reading this enigmatic passage.

27. Ibid., p. 1.

And Agamben begins with an "It is true that": "It is true that in a famous passage . . . ," which looks like a concession, a concession that actually
would ruin everything he is saying: but he will withdraw the concession and
put his money on this subtle and in my view untenable distinction between
"attribute of the living being" and "specific difference that determines the
genus *zōon*," i.e. the same living being. How, I ask you, can you distinguish
436   between "attribute of the living being," and "the specific difference that determines the genus *zōon*,"[28] i.e. the same living being? Agamben writes this
at the moment when he really is compelled to recognize that there is some
non-bare *zōē*, as it were (I am going to read a long passage that diagnoses
both the merits and the insufficiencies of Foucault as well as of Arendt, and
I shall then content myself with two observations):

> It is true that in a famous passage of the same work, Aristotle defines man
> as a *politikon zōon* (*Politics*, 1253a, 4). But here (aside from the fact that in
> Attic Greek the verb *bionai* is practically never used in the present tense),
> "political" is not an <u>attribute</u> of the living being as such, but rather a <u>spe-
> cific difference</u> that determines the genus *zōon*. (Only a little later, after all,
> human politics is distinguished from that of other living beings in that it is
> founded, through a supplement of politicity tied to language, on a commu-
> nity not simply of the pleasant and the painful but of the good and the evil
> and of the just and the unjust.)
>
> Michel Foucault refers to this very definition when, at the end of the
> first volume of *The History of Sexuality,* he summarizes the process by
> which, at the threshold of the modern era, <u>natural life</u> begins to be included
> in the mechanisms and calculations of State power, and politics turns into
> *biopolitics*. "For millennia," he writes, "man remained what he was for Ar-
> istotle: a living animal <u>with the additional capacity</u> for political existence;
> modern man is an animal whose politics calls his existence as a living being
> into question." (*La volonté*, p. 188)[29]
>
> According to Foucault, a society's "<u>threshold</u> of biological modernity"
> is situated at the point at which the species and the individual as a simple
> living body become what is at stake in a society's political strategies. After
> 1977, the courses at the Collège de France start to focus on the passage from
> the "territorial State" to the "state of population" and on the resulting in-
> crease in importance of the nation's health and biological life as a problem

28. Ibid., p. 2.

29. Michel Foucault, *La volonté de savoir* (Paris: Gallimard, 1976), p. 188; trans. Robert Hurley as *The History of Sexuality,* vol. 1: *An Introduction* (New York: Pantheon
Books, 1978), p. 143.

of sovereign power, which is then gradually transformed into a "govern-ment of men."[30] "What follows is a kind of <u>bestialization of man</u> achieved through the most sophisticated political techniques. [This is literally Hei-degger.] For the first time in history, the possibilities of the social sciences are made known, and at once it becomes possible both to protect life and to authorize a holocaust." In particular, the development and triumph of capitalism would not have been possible, from this perspective, without the disciplinary control achieved by the <u>new</u> bio-power, which, through a series of appropriate technologies, so to speak created the "docile bodies" that it needed. [What bothers me is not the idea that there should be a "new bio-power," but that what is "new" *is* bio-power; not the idea that there is some-thing new within bio-power, which I believe, but the idea that bio-power *is* something new . . .]

437

Almost twenty years before *The History of Sexuality* [always·Agamben's concern to know who came first . . .], Hannah Arendt had already ana-lyzed the process that brings *homo laborans* — and with it, biological life as such — gradually to occupy the very center of the political scene of moder-nity. In *The Human Condition,* Arendt attributes the transformation and decadence of the political realm in modern societies to this very primacy of natural life over political action [she was not without having read some Heidegger]. That Foucault was able to begin his study of biopolitics with no reference to Arendt's work (which remains, even today, practically without continuation) bears witness to the difficulties and resistances that thinking had to encounter in this area. And it is most likely these very difficulties that account for the curious fact that Arendt establishes no connection be-tween her research in *The Human Condition* and the penetrating analyses she had previously devoted to totalitarian power (in which a biopolitical perspective is altogether lacking), and that Foucault, in just as striking a fashion, never dwelt on the exemplary places of modern biopolitics: the concentration camp and the structure of the great totalitarian states of the twentieth century [which is, literally, false].[31]

Two really quite simple observations:

1. *First observation.* First of all a logical-type observation. I see no clear or necessary difference in this case between "attribute of the living creature as such," and "specific difference that determines the genus *zōon*." Aristotle might very well have said, and in my opinion certainly did say, that "the at-

438

---

30. [Translator's note:] Michel Foucault, *Dits et écrits,* 4 vols. (Paris: Gallimard, 1994) [reprinted in 2 vols., 2001], 3:719 [2:719].

31. Agamben, *Homo Sacer*, pp. 2–4. Derrida's underlinings.

tribute of the living being as such" (and thus of bare life, as Agamben would say), the attribute of the bare life *of the being called man* is political, and that is his specific difference. The specific difference or the attribute of man's living, in his life as a living being, in his bare life, if you will, is to be political. Foucault's "with the additional capacity" indeed echoes this when he says, seeming to oppose with an "in question" two possibilities that I for my part find to be perfectly reciprocal or reciprocable or complementary: [Re-quote the whole of Agamben's paragraph quoting Foucault] "For millennia man remained what he was for Aristotle: a living animal *with the additional capacity* for political existence; modern man is an animal whose politics calls his existence as a living being into question."[32]

2. *Second observation.* Once again, I am not saying that nothing new is happening "today" (incidentally, when does "today" start, or modernity?). I am not saying that nothing new is happening "today" in these domains: that would be stupid. Too *bête*, if you like. And if Agamben thinks that anybody is ready to say that nothing new is happening in these domains, then he must feel that he is surrounded by a lot of idiots, who are more *bêtes* and more blind than is possible. So I am not saying that there is no "new biopower," I am suggesting that "bio-power" itself is not new. There are incredible novelties in bio-power, but bio-power or zoo-power are not new.

What surprises me most, incidentally, and constantly disconcerts me in Agamben's argumentation and rhetoric, is that he clearly recognizes what I have just said, namely that biopolitics is an arch-ancient thing (even if today it has new means and new structures). It is an arch-ancient thing and bound up with the very idea of sovereignty. But then, if one recognizes this, why all the effort to pretend to wake politics up to something that is supposedly, I quote, "the decisive event of modernity"? In truth, Agamben, giving nothing up, like the unconscious, wants to be twice first, the first to see and announce, and the first to remind: he wants both to be the first to announce an unprecedented and new thing, what he calls this "decisive event of modernity," and also to be the first to recall that in fact it's always been like that, from time immemorial. He is the first to tell us two things in one: it's just happened for the first time, you ain't seen nothing yet, but nor have you seen, I'm telling you for the first time, that it dates from year zero. Listen:

> Although the existence of such a line of thinking seems to be logically implicit in Foucualt's work, it remains a blind spot [poor Foucault! He never had such a cruel admirer . . .] to the eye of the researcher, or rather something like a vanishing point that the different perspectival lines of Fou-

32. Foucault, *La volonté de savoir,* p. 188 [*History of Sexuality,* p. 143].

cault's inquiry (and, more generally, of the entire Western reflection on power) converge toward without reaching.

The present inquiry concerns precisely this hidden point of intersection between the juridico-institutional and the biopolitical models of power. What this work has had to record among its likely conclusions is precisely that the two analyses cannot be separated, and that the inclusion of bare life in the political realm constitutes the original — if concealed — nucleus of sovereign power. *It can even be said that the production of a biopolitical body is the original activity of sovereign power.* In this sense, biopolitics is at least as old as the sovereign exception. Placing biological life at the center of its calculations, the modern State therefore does nothing other than bring to light the secret tie uniting power and bare life, thereby reaffirming the bond (derived from a tenacious correspondence between the modern and the archaic which one encounters in the most diverse spheres) between modern power and the most immemorial of the *arcana imperii*.[33]

Why so much emphasis on the detail of these texts, in this case those of Agamben and Foucault, Agamben with or, more precisely, right up against Foucault, close up to him but paying him the homage of a multiple and pressing objection, Foucault whose theses should be, says Agamben whom I quote again, "reconsidered, corrected and completed"?

If I emphasize them so much, it's because these discourses are highly interesting, first of all; they go to the heart of what matters to us in this seminar: sovereign power, life and death, animality, etc. In Foucault, you should reread closely, among other things (as I did not so long ago, here and elsewhere,[34] I don't want to go back to it now) concerning sovereign power as power of life and death, in [the first volume of] *The History of Sexuality,* the last chapter, entitled "Right of Death and Power over Life."[35] That's where you find the discourse on "the austere monarchy of sex"[36] that I tried to interrogate and interpret in *Resistances* ("To Do Justice to Freud")[37] and

440

---

33. Ibid., p. 6.

34. See among other places the first session (December 8, 1999) of the seminar on the Death Penalty (1999–2000), in which Derrida comments on Foucault's *Discipline and Punish.*

35. Michel Foucault, "Droit de mort et pouvoir sur la vie," in *La volonté de savoir,* pp. 177–81 [*History of Sexuality,* pp. 135–59].

36. Ibid., p. 211 [p. 159].

37. Jacques Derrida, "Être juste avec Freud," in *Résistances — de la psychanalyse* (Paris: Galilée, 1996), pp. 139, 144 n. 1 [trans. Peggy Kamuf, Pascale-Anne, and Michael Naas as "To Do Justice to Freud," in *Resistances of Psychoanalysis* (Stanford: Stanford University Press, 1988), pp. 70–118 (pp. 116–17, 127 n. 21)]. This text first appeared in *Penser la folie: Essais sur Michel Foucault,* Actes du XIe colloque de la Société d'histoire de la

on an "analytic of sexuality" that supposedly followed on from a "symbolics of blood." In passing, Foucault declares that he "could have taken, at a different level, the example of the death penalty."[38] So he does not take it, but explains that, if he had, he would have related the decline of the death penalty to the progress of biopolitics and a power that "gave itself the function of managing life." Supposing that things are this way, and that some decline of the death penalty is principally to be explained by the new advent <of biopolitics> (which Foucault dates to the end of the classical age) (which calls for another discussion with Agamben as to the concept of *threshold*, precisely, of what Agamben, referring to Foucault, calls "the decisive event of modernity" or again the "founding event of modernity," having in mind above all the genocides of the twentieth century, the concentration camps and the Shoah)—[Supposing, I was saying, that things are this way, and that some decline of the death penalty is to be explained principally by the new advent <of biopolitics> (which Foucault dates to the end of the classical age)], we have to wonder what politico-juridical consequence should be drawn, and whether we should regret this decline of the death penalty. But above all—and this is my response to the question I just asked ("Why so much emphasis on the detail of these texts, in this case those of Agamben and Foucault, Agamben with or, more precisely, right up against Foucault . . . ?")—because they are very interesting, these texts, I repeat, and go to the heart of what matters to us here, but above all because the difficulties they encounter, the confusions and contradictions we have just been noting (for example, in the pretension to be the first to discover absolutely new, "decisive and foundational" events, events that at the same time are said to be ageless and in fact "immemorial," etc.), all of those things compel us, and we have to be grateful to them for this, to reconsider, precisely, a way of thinking history, of doing history, of articulating a logic and a rhetoric onto a thinking of history or the event.

psychiatrie et de la psychanalyse (23 novembre 1991) (Paris: Galilée, 1992). In this note, Derrida refers to an unpublished lecture entitled "Au-delà du principe de pouvoir" [Beyond the Power Principle], presented on the occasion of a homage to Foucault organized by Thomas Bishop at New York University in April 1986. The first two pages of this unpublished lecture (typescript "Au-delà du principe du pouvoir," pp. 8–9, Derrida archive at IMEC, Caen) were excerpted and enlarged by Derrida at the end of his homage to Foucault in *Chaque fois unique, la fin du monde*, ed. Pascale-Anne Brault and Michael Naas (Paris: Galilée, 2003), pp. 118–20 [trans. Brault and Naas as *The Work of Mourning* (Chicago: University of Chicago Press, 2003), pp. 88–90].

38. Foucault, *La volonté de savoir*, p. 181 [*History of Sexuality*, p. 137].

To call into question not only the concern to periodize that takes such forms (a modernity about which we don't know when it begins or ends, a classical age the effects of which are still perceptible, an Ancient Greece whose concepts are more alive and surviving than ever, a supposed "decisive event of modernity" or "founding event of modernity" which only reveals the immemorial, etc.) — [to call into question this concern to periodize that takes such forms] is not to reduce the eventness or singularity of the event: on the contrary. Rather, I'm tempted to think that this singularity of the event is all the more irreducible and confusing, as it should be, if we give up that linear history which remains, in spite of all the protests they would no doubt raise against this image, the common temptation of both Foucault and Agamben (the modernity that comes after the classical age, the *epistēmē*s that follow on from each other and render each other obsolete, Agamben who comes after Aristotle, etc.) — if we give up this linear history, the idea of a decisive and founding event (especially if we try to rethink and reevaluate the enduring and aporetic experience of what "decision" means in the logic of sovereign exception), if we give up the alternative of synchronic and diachronic, an alternative that remains presupposed in the texts we have just been reading. To give up the idea of a decisive and founding event is anything but to ignore the eventness that marks and signs, in my view, what happens, precisely without any foundation or decision coming along to make it certain. Which explains, moreover — at least a supplementary sign of what I am putting forward — that the texts from Aristotle's *Politics*, for example, or Bodin, or so many others, and texts that are not always books of philosophy or political science, or even books at all, are to be read, difficult as they may be to decipher, indispensable in all their abyssal stratifications, be they bookish or not, if we want to understand politics and its beyond, and even the bio-powers or zoo-powers of what we call the modernity of "our time."

The fact that there is neither simple diachronic succession nor simple synchronic simultaneity here (or that there is both at once), that there is neither continuity of passage nor interruption or mere caesura, that the motifs of the passage of what passes and comes to pass [*passe et se passe*] in history belong neither to a solid foundation nor to a founding decision, that the passage has no grounding ground and no indivisible line under it, requires us to rethink the very figure of the *threshold* (ground, foundational solidity, limit between inside and outside, inclusion and exclusion, etc.). What the texts we have read call for is at least a greater vigilance as to our irrepressible desire for the threshold, a threshold that *is* a threshold, a single and solid

443   threshold. Perhaps there never is a threshold, any such threshold. Which is perhaps why we remain on it and risk staying on the threshold for ever.

The abyss is not the bottom, the originary ground (*Urgrund*), of course, nor the bottomless depth (*Ungrund*) of some hidden base.

The abyss, if there is an abyss, is that there is *more than one* ground [*sol*], more than one solid, and more than one single threshold [*plus d'un seul seul*].

More than a single single; no more a single single.[39]

That's where we are.

Next time: Aristotle and the Bible (Genesis and Noah), and discussion.

---

39. "Plus d'un seul seul" in the typescript.

March 27, 2002

. . . we spoke about the threshold last time, and we really stayed on the threshold.[2]

I noticed, if you'll allow me to confide in you something about the way I work or let myself get worked on, that in preparation for the first session of this seminar I had begun to develop something on my computer, and then I thought that before reaching that point (I'll tell you what point in a moment), we really would need a protocol, some premises, a detour, and, from week to week, on my computer, these few pages that should have been at the beginning found themselves at the end of each session, and I never got to them, and so I still haven't said what I thought I was going to say as the first sentences of the first session. It was (I'll say a word about it in a moment) a reading of Genesis and the moment of creation, the naming of the first words and then also what it means to commence, command, recommend, recommence, and some questions of syntax and authority at play in such an initiative.

Today, as promised, we are going to devote a good part of the session to discussion. And we will, but if you will permit me, I'd like to introduce that discussion by offering you, not a summary, which would be absurd and impossible, but a few reflections that try to pull together some things

1. This thirteenth session corresponds to the twelfth in the typescript (see "General Introduction to the French Edition" above, n. 4). In this final session of the year, Derrida was expecting to talk about Genesis, as he had announced at the end of the previous session, and the typescript indeed contains a long extract from a lecture devoted to this subject, already published in *L'animal autobiographique*. But because the session was also to be devoted in part to discussion, he organized the first, improvised part differently and did not use this text, merely telling his listeners how to get hold of it (see note 17 below). As with the ninth session, and for the same reasons, we do not here transcribe the discussion but only the improvised talk that preceded it.

2. The very opening words of the session were not recorded.

that have become dispersed and fragmented throughout this year's seminar, these twelve sessions, because I'm aware, as are you, no doubt, that when one improvises a discussion, certain fundamental schemata, certain indispensable outlines, appear more clearly than when one minutely prepares a text to be simply read. So I've chosen, in attempting this quasi-concluding reflection as a kind of premise for the discussion that will follow, to mark, remark, and have you remark with me the fact that at bottom everything we have spoken about came down to problems of translation. Translation in a sense at once fundamental and diverse. Translation, first of all, because between animal and man—what is often called by these names, following distinctions received in an all-powerful and still living, surviving, tradition—people speak of differences in manifestation, in signification, in significance (I've often emphasized this, because it holds true from Descartes to Lacan, inclusive), and they oppose a logic of programmed reaction in the animal to a logic of free and sovereign responsibility in man. And between what is interpreted as reaction and what is interpreted as response, responsibility, or responsible response, what is at stake is, precisely, a translating interpretation—and every interpretation is a translation. It's in our way of translating what are called animal reactions that we believe ourselves able—but this is a risk of translation—to discern or trace a limit between animality and humanity, reactive animality and responsive or responsible humanity. It's a question of translation between languages.

447 There's another dimension to this problematic of translation, and it concerns basically all the words we have used, many words, and in particular the fundamental, guiding words, starting with "animal" or "beast." I entitled this seminar *The Beast and the Sovereign* because, in French, *bête* is not the same thing as "animal," and you will remember the fearsome problems of idiom we had to deal with when we had to distinguish *bête* from *bestialité* and above all from *bêtise,* given that these are not necessarily characteristics of the animal. And you remember too that the word *bêtise*, the French word *bêtise,* came up against impassable limits as to its translation, the word-for-word translation, the translation of the word, the vocable: there is no word in the world that translates the French word *bêtise*. This, I think, we have shown. This means, among other things, that the way that we French or Francophones live, experience, practice, and put to work the word *bête* or the word *bêtise* is each time conditioned by contextual systems such that, even in French, the word *bêtise* is not translatable from French into French: I use the word *bêtise* in one sense in one context, and in another sense, with another connotation, with another performative effect, in another context—in other words, the word *bêtise* is untranslatable from French into

French. It is untranslatable, i.e. it does not have a fixed or univocal meaning or signified that would allow us to say that we are speaking of the same *bê-tise* here and there, about one person or another, one action or another, one language or another. And the fact that the context (what we name with this somewhat facile word "context," i.e. the pragmatic situation) determines in such a constraining fashion each time the meaning of the word *bête* or *bê-tise* — this fact means that between the language spoken by those men and women called French, and animal language, i.e. something commanded by complicated programs or wiring, there is no easily formalizable difference. This doesn't mean that we speak like beasts every time we use the word *bêtise*, but that the privilege of the idiom — which can be the privilege of poetry, which can be the privilege, of course, as is always the case with the idiom, the privilege of the unique event of language that is, for example, termed "poetic" — this doesn't merely mean the poem, it also means a certain contamination by what we attribute to so-called reactive or reactional animality.

So you see that this question of translation is very broadly overdetermining for all the problems we are discussing here. These are of course, as I just pointed out, problems of translation in discursive language, discursive praxis, what we call "human language," but already the circumscription of what is called "human language" becomes problematical for the reasons I have just given. But this is where we are going to encounter another problem of *translatio,* of translation [*de translation, de traduction*], folding back on itself or folding and refolding this first translation: this is that, when we tried to name animality in non-French languages, we encountered words like *bios* and *zōē,* two ways of naming life with all the problems you remember, which we tried to deal with last week in reference to — using as our pretext — Agamben's text: does the animal come under *bios* or *zōē?* etc. And we naturally bounced back, as to language and as to this distinction between *bios* and *zōē,* as to the animal or human living being, onto the fundamental word *logos* — man defined as *zōon logon ekhon,* the animal, the living being possessed of *logos.* What does that mean? It has governed an enormous tradition. The whole tradition we are speaking about has been governed by this definition, the difficulties of which we were seeing last week, depending on whether one accepts or not Agamben's proposed distinction between "essential attribute" and "specific difference," a distinction that I found to be fragile. In any case, *logos* itself, whether one translates it as language, as is often done, as discourse, or as reason or else as calculation, counting (that the word *ratio* will translate: reason as counting, as calculus), the word *logos* itself raised considerable issues when it comes to translation. We got just a small idea of them, an idea at least, by following Heidegger's interpretation (itself a translating interpretation) when, even as he himself is protesting, proposing the deconstruction of the classical definition of man as *zōon logon ekhon,* as *animal rationale,* he invites us to consider the fact that the Greek *logos,* the *legein,* which is all at once saying, gathering, assembling, reading too (*legere* comes from it), had been diverted from its meaning, which (as Heidegger sees it) is what gathers, maintaining opposites, contraries, by force, and all this in an element where we are dealing with the *physis* that can't even be translated as *nature.* Another problem of translation: *physis* is not, for Heidegger, *natura; physis* is everything that grows, *phyein,* what increases and in what increases, in the world or in being as *physis,* the *logos* plays, represents, precisely, a "force," and Heidegger insists on the force (recall words I emphasized last time, such as *Herrschaft* or *Machstellung,* which appeal precisely to a deployment of force), a force of maintaining contraries together — well, that force, the sense of that originary force of the Greek *legein* (in Heraclitus, for example), has supposedly been diverted or occulted or perverted — so many possible interpretations — supposedly forgotten, in any case, for example, when John, John the Evangelist, says that "in the beginning was the *logos,*" identified not with the Being of beings, but with a particular entity, i.e. Christ, the mediator; when John, influenced by Philo the Jew, interpreting precisely *logos* as mediation, as mediator, translates, identifies the *logos* with Christ, and there too Heidegger talks of a *Herrschaft,* a *Machstellung,* i.e. an operation of sovereignty, of a force that comes to win out over another force. So we are dealing here, as to translative interpretation, with a translation that is not merely a peaceful dictionary-based or interlinguistic operation: it is an interpretive translation that brings with it the whole of culture, and which is not separable from historial movements in which all the forces of the world and the age are engaged. It is not a matter of philologists who decided all on their own to translate, to interpret *logos* as Christ, as mediator: it is the whole force of history that is at work to produce this translation. And obviously, just as this translation occults, or forgets, or deforms, or corrupts, or perverts, according to Heidegger, the originary sense of *logos,* so, in the text by Aristotle that carries such authority, Aristotle's *Politics* (I'll come to it in a moment), that defines man as a *zōon,* as a living animal possessed of *logos,* there too the *logos* is no longer the originary *logos,* and this is what will give rise to the entire tradition of rational man, man as rational animal, calculating animal, etc. So you see that what is at stake in translation cannot be limited to the great question that we are dealing with here, "the beast and the sovereign," to the operation of lexicologists or academic semanticians or of literary traductology: it really is the whole of the history of the Western world that is in play in these operations of translation, and thus in the definition of the relations between the beast and the sovereign, since the relations between the beast and the sovereign are also relations between an animal, a *zōon* supposed to be without reason, and a *zōon* supposed to be rational, the sovereign being posited as human, on the divine model, and as a human who naturally has reason, responsibility, etc. And so we are dealing with questions of translation that are absolutely determining, determining and difficult to determine, difficult to circumscribe: there are no limits, no frontiers that can contain these issues of translation.

But before returning to a couple of texts that I wanted to look at quickly with you, so that the year wouldn't end without our having at least looked at Aristotle's text (I had meant to last week but didn't manage it . . .), I wanted to read to you a text I discovered a short while ago and that I regret not knowing when we invited so many wolves into our seminar. I've chosen to read this text, and I shall do so, because, let me recall briefly, you must have noticed that the historical corpus, a particular historical corpus (this was not premeditated on my part, it happened to me during preparation and at the beginning of the year, I didn't think that that was how it was going to be in December) imposed itself on us, on me, a historico-political corpus that to a large extent has been that of a French sequence — and I want to emphasize that we have had a *French* seminar (the sessions devoted to *bêtise,* to bestiality in Lacan and Deleuze, were French problems, the Frenchness of which had to be thought). Well, the historico-political corpus on the question of the sovereign that imposed itself on us and in any case on me was, broadly speaking, that of a sequence that runs from the great age of French royalty, the "Grand Siècle," and a little before, up to the French Revolution, decapitation, the guillotine, the history of Capet, of Louis Capet, and, whether directly or through Celan's "Meridian," it was always the question of the French Revolution that happened to the sovereign, to the absolute sovereign, to absolute monarchy, in France, at the time of the Revolution, that concerned us, necessarily and inevitably. Well, the interesting thing about the text I'm going to read to you is that it deals with the wolf from the point of view of French royalty — we spoke of the Dauphin, the Dauphin and the wolf — and to link it to a concept, or in any case to a word, which is that of translation, *translatio*. It's from a book by Jean-Clet Martin, *Ossuaires: Anatomie du Moyen Âge roman* that I'd like to read to you — like the last day of grade school, just before vacation, when we were children,

451

they would read us stories for a break — I'm going to read you this text on the wolves and the king. It starts on page 163 of *Ossuaires*, in a chapter called "A Political Hagiography":

> Everything happens, as it were, between Reims, Laon, and Soissons. A suspended wing-beat that goes from Louis IV to Louis VI. Here a rare and precious parenthesis opens in which very different forces confront each other but turn indecisive on a line opposing Cluny to the bishoprics, king to lords [remember the opposition in which the word *Dauphin*, also an untranslatably French word, which allies the dolphin to the figure of the crown prince, in a sequence that had to do with the annexation of the Dauphiné],[3] the Peace of God to the state, to the Church, the saints to the popes, all according to a skein of metastable tracks, perpetually in breach, a skein capable of addressing the people, the event-power of the people — 1038, a year of revolt and insurrectional jubilation — popular compositions about which André de Fleury tries to understand how "the mass of unarmed people was able, like armed troops, to sow fear among the warriors and scare them to such an extent that they fled, abandoning their châteaux, before the humble rustic cohorts, as though before the most powerful of kings."[4] How could that have been possible without the intercession of the holy names and their relics, those names that the Capetians in turn were to confront in the form of the legend of Saint Marcoul?
>
> Between Reims and Laon, Laon and Soissons, spreads the forest. There, in this triangle, the legend configures its desert, redistributing the *topoi* of power that it is feudalizing in new relations. In this dark forest prowls a wolf without equal[5] [a wolf that we are adding, then, to our innumerable pack: here's one more . . .]. Enormous [we're only dealing with enormous animals — remember Louis XIV's elephant — next year maybe we'll deal with smaller animals: this year it was the big ones]. An animal. Of course, an animal! But an animal whose name becomes something else [this is the beginning of the translation], by designating a heterogeneous multiplicity, a procedure that with Abelard we thought of as a chimera. It is this shadowy wolf, both animal and symptom, astride [a wolf on horseback!] forests and towns, which he protects by spreading his disease, an animal that King Louis [one of the Louis, one of the many we have talked about] will confront, at the end of the summer of 954, an animal in which the other Louis

⁴⁵² in left margin

---

3. [Translator's note:] The interpolation in square brackets is syntactically incomplete in the French edition.

4. See André de Fleury, *Miracles de saint Benoît*, cited by Georges Duby in *Les trois ordres, ou l'imaginaire du féodalisme* (Paris: Gallimard, 1978), p. 231.

5. This episode of the wolf and the king is recounted by Flodoart. See *Les annales de Flodoart*, ed. Philippe Lauer (Paris: Les Belles Lettres, 1906), p. 138.

will be announced, devined by Arnoul right on his fantastic shadow. This is the same Wolf [with a capital letter now] that will unseat Louis IV and cause the birth of Louis VI, after a chaotic parenthesis in which all possibilities show up, freed from the mesh or the screen of the state.

On the basis of the description by Canon Flodoart, the wolf in question is far from reducible to the mere presence of an animal. It is a translation of a wolf [translation again], the *ethos* on which it branches out defining a set of similarities, a series of variables that he links up again like the stained-glass window in Poitiers, where movements-spaces capable of conserving the greatest distances, of respecting their respective anatomies, are articulated together. Wolf rises up like a shadow, like a wolf, something extending its name toward incommensurable meanings [translation of wolf "extending its name toward incommensurable meanings": the wolf in translation, then, in *translatio*] juxtaposed in a sort of diagram. This name, the name "wolf," unfolds the diagram or the ramified volume according to which a rubric takes shape, a noncategorial rubric, since it bites [a rubric that bites!] into universes of similarity the *topoi* of which are not the same: a set-up that will make possible the configuration of the Capetian dynasty to the detriment of the last Carolingians, whom this name never stops cursing, designating the illness they are suffering [a war between two dynasties, basically].

Cursed by this enormous wolf, which unseats him, King Louis dies of an elephantiasic, elephantine affection—a lupullation that pullulates on the royal genealogy as a contagion called "Lupus Vulgaris." An illness that on the threshold of the XIIIᵉ century will be designated by the simple word "wolf" [so "wolf" is the name of an illness, as we already mentioned]. In short, from the wolf, whose terrifying shadow comes to cross the King's path, is detached a nominal simulacrum [also called a "species" . . .] capable of describing the royal illness, a statement that the becoming of the name disperses according to an *ethos* in which can be distributed similarities that, not belonging to the same *topos*, necessarily bifurcate. Which is why, *horla*[6] [so it's the outlaw, the *horla*, and you recall that the werewolf—we were talking about it in the early sessions—is the *horla*, the outlaw that, like the sovereign, makes the law from a place external to the law that is outside the law, and you remember that in English *loup-garou* [in Rousseau] is translated by "outlaw"], the name escapes, fibers out into similar echoes, caught up in other conditions of space and time. Then there are gatherings of discordances as remote as those that separate from animal tuberculosis the animal, the saint, the landscape whose contour and drunken diagonal it marks.

6. [Translator's note:] This is a reference to Maupassant's famous horror story "Le Horla."

453

Marcwulf, the wolf from the forest, defines a nominal complex, a differently orientable, modulable, plank or Plaint, a *planctus* on which illness diffuses, carrying off the last Carolingians. But this plaint is also the surface on which the people begins to pullulate, of the legend that carves it up and feudalizes it to make a place for the Capetian king. The wolf, the king, the saint will then be incorporated [incorporation of the beast and the sovereign] into a set-up in which each term will express a function that the other feudalizes according to a new function. Feudality is here the index of a multiple-subjection function, an assemblage that the name "Marcwulf" delimits and individualizes much better that the ceremony of the consecration, unable to account for the process of subjectivation capable of inscribing the saint and the king, the king and the wolf into one and the same heterotopic *ethos*.

Marcwulf, the "wolf of the marches" ["march" in the sense of limit, or limen, frontier], the processual wolf, designates this popular chimera that the people constantly celebrates as the machination of its own consistency, an animal sent from the people like the *leitmotiv* of a social crystallography, a motif capable of configuring the forces that traverse it and that relaunch themselves as a multiform, thaumaturgical king [remember the thaumaturgical kings we mentioned when we were reading Marin, and in connection with Kantorowicz's *King's Two Bodies,* preceded by Marc Bloch's book *Les rois thaumaturges*]. A king who, moreover, depends more on the saint and the wolf, to whom he will be like a vassal, than on the foundational consecration conceived of as a sticking point, a blockage of dubbings. There is of course no doubt that the consecration, the ceremony of investiture, succeeded in the end in taking hold of the feudal machine to make it into that state apparatus magnified by Adalbéron, a royalty allied to the pope and to the reformed Church [this is of course a huge story . . . I'm reading fast and you'd need to read the whole book]. But the fact that the confrontation of the feudal machine be abolished in the mesh of power knotted vertically around a centralized state does not prevent that fact that there was a confrontation, a suspension of political singularities, in the passage from the Carolingians to the Capetian dynasty.[7]

I'll finish my quotation here. You can see clearly that it's also about a conflict for sovereignty between two dynasties, with the stake being the affirmation of a state sovereignty on the basis of feudal structures, a war between lords and king. I especially wanted to read you this text, not only because of the wolves and the Capetians and the Carolingians, but also because what's going on here is a translating operation, rhetorical, metonymical, a force that displaces names, and there too, in a sense, it's about *logos*. What I want to

7. Jean-Clet Martin, *Ossuaires: Anatomie du Moyen Âge roman* (Paris: Payot, 1995), pp. 163–65.

say very quickly about *logos* is this: at bottom, what one might call — what I myself have long called — "logocentrism," precisely, which in my usage has always designated a forced hegemony; a forcing, imposing a hegemony, does not only signify the authority of *logos* as speech, as language — that's already an interpretation — but also signifies an operation that is properly, I would say, in quotes, "European," which gathers together biblical traditions (we saw a certain passage from Philo the Jew to John the Evangelist) and then the philosophical tradition: broadly speaking the monotheistic religions, the Abrahamic religions, and philosophy. This logocentrism of the Abrahamic religions and of philosophy signifying not so much that the *logos* was simply the center of everything, but that it was in a situation, precisely, of sovereign hegemony, organizing everything on the basis of its forced translations.

455

So, on that basis, I suggest two things for the twenty minutes or so we have left: first to have a quick look at *logos* in Aristotle's *Politics*, in the famous passage in which Aristotle defines man as *zōon logon ekhon,* and then, if we have time, a word about the Bible, with which I meant to start at the very beginning.

As I was saying very quickly last time, it's the very beginning of book 1 of the *Politics*, that's where it starts, and Aristotle is defining the *polis*, the state as a sort of community (*koinōnia*), which, as a community, is constituted with a view to a certain *good*. The state is a community organized with a view to a good, *agathon*. One might say that this *agathon* is naturally sought, as a good, by every community, even an animal community, but what Aristotle announces from the start is that the state as human community, as human *koinōnia*, is organized with a view to the good as *sovereign* good;[8] this is the standard translation, and of course the word translated as sovereign is, as you'll remember from when we were talking about Bodin, the word that is most often used in Greek to designate sovereignty, *kurios*:

> ... it is obvious that all aim at a certain good and that precisely the sovereign good [*kuriōtatou*, the sovereign good, the supreme good] among all goods is the end of the community that is sovereign [*kuriōtatē*] among all [the community is basically sovereign over all, and so the notion of sovereignty is defined here, from the start, inscribed into the very concept of state, *polis,* and community] and includes all the others: the one called the City or the political community [*e koinōnia e politikē*]. (1252a)[9]

456

8. Aristotle, *Politics,* 1.1252a.

9. [Translator's note:] Although I have consulted and to some extent followed the Jowett translation of Aristotle's *Politics*, in the interests of consistency with Derrida's commentary I have quite often (especially in these opening passages) altered the transla-

Then, in the following paragraph, he will define, precisely, what is called a master or a king, a man of state:

> All those who imagine that a statesman (or magistrate), a king, a head of household, a master of slaves [*despotikon*] are identical, do not express themselves correctly [so he will distinguish between the statesman [*politikon*], the king, the head of household, the slave-master: those who imagine that these are the same thing, are identical, are wrong, are not expressing themselves correctly, do not choose their words well]; indeed they see in each of these only a difference of degree and not of kind: for example, if one exercises authority over a small number, one is a master; if over a greater number, a head of household; if a still greater number, a statesman or a king, as though there were no difference between a large family and a small City [in other words—and this is a tradition that will run up until Schmitt, you must not imagine that the state is simply an enlarged family; so there is a structural difference between a family community and a state community]; as for statesman and king: if a man exercises power alone, he is a king; if on the contrary he exercises it following the norms of political science, being in turn governor and governed, he is a statesman. But this is not true, and what I have to say about it will be obvious to anyone who examines the question following our normal method.¹⁰

There follows a methodological exposé which tries, which claims, to go back *ex arkhēs,* to the beginning (the word *arkhē,* I recall, is the commencement and the commandment): "so it is in examining things develop from their origin [*ex arkhēs*] that here as elsewhere we can come to the best view of them." So let's go back to the origin:

457

> In the first place there must be a union of those who cannot exist without each other; namely, of male and female, that the race may continue (and this is a union which is formed, not of deliberate purpose, but because, in common with other animals and with plants, mankind have a natural desire to leave behind them an image of themselves) [in other words, generation and reproduction is the proper of all living beings, be they plants, animals, or humans], and of natural ruler and subject, that both may be preserved [this is natural, by nature, *phusei*]. For that which can foresee by the exercise of mind is by nature [still *phusei*] intended to be lord and master, and that which can with its body give effect to such foresight is a subject, and by nature a slave; hence master and slave have the same interest. Now nature [always *phusei*] has distinguished between the female and the slave. For she is not niggardly, like the smith who fashions the Delphian knife for many

---

tion (sometimes quite substantially) on the basis of the French translation by Jean Aubonnet (Paris: Les Belles Lettres, 1991), which Derrida is using.

10. Aristotle, *Politics,* 1.1252a 4–23.

uses; she makes each thing for a single use [. . .]. But among barbarians no distinction is made between women and slaves, because there is no natural ruler among them [i.e. neither woman nor slave has what naturally rules]: they are a community of slaves, male and female. Wherefore the poets say, "It is meet that Hellenes should rule over barbarians"; as if they thought that the barbarian and the slave were by nature one.

Out of these two relationships between man and woman, master and slave, the first thing to arise is the family [I'm reading rather fast to come on quicker to the *zōon logon ekhon*], and Hesiod is right when he says, "First house and wife and ox for the plough," for the ox is the poor man's slave. The family is the association established by nature for the supply of men's everyday wants, and the members of it are called by Charondas "companions of the cupboard," and by Epimenides the Cretan, "companions of the manger." But when several families are united, and the association aims at something more than the supply of daily needs, the first society to be formed is the village. And the most natural form of the village appears to be that of a colony from the family, composed of the children and grandchildren, who are said to be suckled "with the same milk." And this is the reason why Hellenic states were originally governed by kings; because the Hellenes were under royal rule before they came together, as the barbarians still are. Every family is ruled by the eldest, and therefore in the colonies of the family the kingly form of government prevailed because they were of the same blood. As Homer says [etc.].[11]

And this is where we come to things that are decisive for us:

The community born of several villages is the City, perfect, now reaching, as it were, the level of complete self-sufficiency [*autarkeia*, independence, then, the fact of commanding oneself, to have its own *arkhē* within itself]: being formed to permit *life* [here, it's *zēn*, the verb for *zōon,* the fact of living], it exists in order to allow one to *live well* [*eu zēn:* so a political community, a city, has as its aim to *live well* (*eu zēn*). And so it's from this truth, as it were, this essence of the *polis* that Aristotle will go on to the definition of man as he who, precisely, has the *logos.*] This is why every city exists naturally [still *phusei*], just like the first communities; it is indeed, their end, and the nature of a thing is its end; because what we call the nature of each thing is what it is when its growth is complete, for example, a man, a horse, or a family. What is more, the final cause and the end is what is best; now to be self-sufficient (*autarkeia*) is both an end and what is best.[12]

That's the ontological definition of sovereignty, namely that it's better — since we're trying to live well (*eu zēn*) — to live in autarchy, i.e. having in

458

11. Ibid., 1252a 27–1252b 22.
12. Ibid., 1252b 27–1253a 4.

ourselves our principle, having in ourselves our commencement and our commandment, is better that the contrary: "the final cause and the end is what is best; now to be self-sufficient (*autarkeia*) is both an end and what is best." From which will follow the definition, which is basically essential and necessary, of sovereignty: the sovereign is one who has his end in himself or is the end of everything.

459   So now, after these premises, here is the fundamental canonical text around which, you recall, the discussions and disagreements begin. You remember Agamben's interpretation that we discussed, Heidegger's interpretation that puts into question this very definition of man as *zōon legon ekhon*, which he says is unworthy of the humanity of man, not only in that it is a "zoological" definition, says Heidegger, not only because one attributes the *logos* to this *zōon*, but because one surreptitiously neglects an interpretation of the *logos* that is itself already contestable according to Heidegger. What is <to be noted> (I say this in parentheses because it is also a place or a field that I had hoped to get into this year, but we didn't have time, and I hope to come back to it next year) is that Heidegger, from this point of view, is both breaking with the tradition, which he wants to deconstruct in his manner, the tradition of a certain metaphysical humanism that defines man as *animal rationale*, a definition he calls "zoological" — so he's claiming to interrupt this great tradition — but, at the same time, it's the same Heidegger who, in many texts (which I'd hoped to read with you this year and will read with you, I hope, next year) denies the animal a very large number of essential features he grants the man, the human *Dasein,* whom he wants to withdraw from the tradition of the *zōon logon ekhon* — i.e., precisely, speech, death, the experience of death as such, the "as such" and especially the opening to the world as such, the opening to the "as such." When he defines the animal, in a famous seminar from 1930[13] that I hope to read with you, as "poor in

460   world [*weltarm*]," whereas man is capable of forming a world and the stone for its part has no world — *weltlos,* the stone and nonliving things, *weltarm,* the animal, *weltbildend,* man who forms a world — the animal poor in world especially because it has no relation to being as such, to the "as such" of the thing (the animal has a relation to the sun, it feels the warmth of the

13. Martin Heidegger, *Die Grundbegriffe der Metaphysik: Welt—Endlichkeit— Eisamkeit,* in *Gesamtausgabe, II Abteilung: Vorlesungen 1923–44,* vol. 29/30, ed. F. W. von Hermann (Frankfurt am Main: Klostermann, 1992); trans. William McNeill and Nicholas Walker as *The Fundamental Concepts of Metaphysics: World, Finitude, Solitude* (Bloomington: Indiana University Press, 2001). See Jacques Derrida, *The Beast and the Sovereign*, vol. 2 (2002–3), forthcoming.

sun or the light of the sun, but has no relation to the sun as such), and this privative definition of the animal does not seem incompatible to him with his contestation of the zoological definition of man, to the contrary, and it's because he wants to accentuate, aggravate, sharpen this limit between the animal and human—the thing we are problematizing here—that, on the one hand, he criticizes, or deconstructs if you prefer, the metaphysical tradition that makes man an *animal rationale* and that, on the other hand, he aggravates the distinction between the animal and the human. And thus (we'll return to this) his critique, if you like, of *zōon logon ekhon*, the *animal rationale*, concerns not only the definition of man in his relation to *logos*, but also the definition of the political: man as political animal is indissociable from the definition of man as having the *logos*, *logon ekhon*.

So here is Aristotle's text:

> From these considerations it is clear that the City is a natural reality and that man is naturally a being destined to live in a City [political animal, *tōn phusei e polis esti, kai oti anthōpos phusei politikon zōon*: is a political animal]; he who is cityless is, by nature and not by chance, a being either degraded or else superior to man [the one who is without a City, who is *apolis*, who is apolitical, is either below or else above man, either an animal or else god: the political is properly human, what in life is properly human: "he who is cityless (*kai o apolis dia phusin kai ou dia tukhēn*, etc.), is, by nature and not by chance, either below or else above man"]: he is like the man Homer reproaches with having "no clan, no law, no hearth"; a man this way by nature is by the same token warlike; he is like an isolated pawn in chess. And so the reason is clear why man is a *political being* more than any others, bees or gregarious animals. As we maintain, indeed, nature does nothing in vain; now alone among animals man has speech [*logon dē monon anthrōpos ekhei tōn zōon*: so, there is an essential link between politicity and the disposition to the *logos*, they are indissociable.] No doubt the sounds of the voice [*phonē*] express pain and pleasure, and so they are found in all animals: their nature allows them only to feel pain and pleasure and to manifest them among themselves [so *phonē* does not suffice to define *logos*].[14]

461

(When I distinguished—a very long time ago—between logocentrism and phonocentrism,[15] it was precisely to mark the fact that logocentrism, by reference to this signifier, this vocable, *logos*, which is proper to the historico-cultural zone I was defining a moment ago (Abrahamic, evangelical reli-

14. Aristotle, *Politics,* 1253a 2–14.

15. See, among other places, Jacques Derrida, *De la grammatologie* (Paris: Minuit, 1967), pp. 21–24; trans. Gayatri Chakravorty Spivak as *Of Grammatology* (Baltimore: Johns Hopkins University Press, 1976), pp. 11–14.

gions, and philosophy), this logocentrism appeared to me to determine this zone or this epoch in human history; but phonocentrism seemed to me, still seems to me, to be universal, in that it defines the authority or hegemony accorded to vocal speech and to phonetic writing in all cultures; which is to say that there is a phonocentrism the signs or symptoms of which can be identified well beyond Europe and even in cultures that practice writing of a nonphonetic type—apparently nonalphabetic, nonphonetic. You know that in Chinese culture, for example, writing is not of the phonetic type although there are phonetic elements in it; nevertheless, there are many signs of a recognized authority of the vocal, which means, in my opinion, that phonocentrism is universal, which logocentrism is not. In any case, the *phonē* named here by Aristotle only concerns the emission of sounds, and this can, indeed, appear in animals without reason, without *logos*: there is *phonē* without *logos*.)

462

> No doubt the sounds of the voice [*phonē*] express pain and pleasure, and so they are found in all animals: their nature allows them only to feel pain and pleasure and to manifest them among themselves. But speech [*logos*], for its part, is made to express the useful and the harmful and consequently the just and the unjust [in other words, there is an essential link between speech (*logos*) and the good (*agathon*), the just and the unjust (*dikaion/adikon*). Animals are incapable of this: they do indeed have *phonē*, but they have neither *logos* nor a relation to the good, to the sovereign good, to the just or the unjust]. This is, indeed, the distinctive character of mankind compared to all the other animals: [*pros talla zōa tois anthrōpois idion*: what is proper (*idion*) to man faced with (or in the eyes of) all the other living beings] he alone perceives good and evil, the just and the unjust [*to monon agathou kai kakou kai dikaiou kai adikou*], and the other values [*kai tēn allōn aisthēsin*]; now it is the common possession of these values that makes family and city.[16]

Which obviously leaves entire the question that we were raising last time, that of knowing whether, in saying this, Aristotle—how should we put it?—was already sensitive, accessible, open or not to what, in a certain French modality, is called "biopolitics." You remember the distinction Agamben was trying to make, which seemed to me untenable, between the definition of the *zōon politikon* as essential attribute or as specific difference. But precisely, what Aristotle says—and this is where this distinction between the two attributions does not work—is that man is that living being who is taken by politics: he is a political living being, and essentially so. In other words, he is zoo-political, that's his essential definition, that's what

16. Aristotle, *Politics,* 1253a 10–18.

is proper to him, *idion*; what is proper to man is politics; what is proper to this living being that man is, is politics, and therefore man is immediately zoo-political, in his very life, and the distinction between bio-politics and zoo-politics doesn't work at all here — moreover, neither Heidegger nor Foucault stays with this distinction, and it's obvious that already in Aristotle there's thinking of what is today called "zoopolitics" or "biopolitics." Which doesn't mean — as I suggested last time and I'm stressing today — which doesn't mean, of course, that Aristotle had already foreseen, thought, understood, analyzed all the figures of today's zoopolitics or biopolitics: it would be absurd to think so. But as for the biopolitical or zoopolitical structure, it's put forward by Aristotle, it's already there, and the debate opens there.

So, a difficult question for me, because we'd really need the time for discussion . . . I'd hoped — but I'll come back to it next year, I can't do it now, it would take too long — to read with you the two narratives from Genesis and then Noah, the Noah episode, but I'm giving up on that now. I had tried, if you'll allow me to refer you to it, to deal with the question in a text that's a fragment of a long, two-day lecture I gave a few years back, a fragment that's included in the volume entitled *L'animal autobiographique*: so there's a text of mine that proposes a reading of the Bible, of Genesis, on the subject of the mastery of man over animal (this is one of the two Genesis narratives), on the one hand, and then, as for Noah, in my little book *The Gift of Death*, there's also a reference to what happens at the moment God repents . . .[17]

That's all. I think it would be improper of me to prevent discussion today, so I'll stop here and hand over to whoever wants to speak.

17. See Derrida, "L'animal que donc je suis (à suivre)" (see session 1 above, n. 20), pp. 265–69; *L'animal que donc je suis,* pp. 33–37 [trans. Wills, pp. 14–18]; and *Donner la mort* (Paris: Galilée, 1999), pp. 187–89 [trans. David Wills as *The Gift of Death,* 2nd ed. (Chicago: University of Chicago Press, 2008), pp. 141–42].

MICHEL LISSE
is a researcher at the Fonds national de la recherche scientifique in
Belgium and professor at the Université catholique de Louvain.

MARIE-LOUISE MALLET
holds the agrégation in philosophy and has been a program director
at the Collège international de philosophie.

GINETTE MICHAUD
is professor in the Département des littératures de langue française at
the Université de Montréal. Editorial work on the French edition
of this volume was supported by a research grant under her direction from
the Conseil de recherches en sciences humaines du Canada.

GEOFFREY BENNINGTON
is Asa G. Candler Professor of Modern French Thought
at Emory University.